Human Security

Theory and Action

ABOUT THE PEACE AND SECURITY
IN THE 21ST CENTURY SERIES

Until recently, security was defined mostly in geopolitical terms with the assumption that it could only be achieved through at least the threat of military force. Today, however, people from backgrounds as diverse as the Pentagon and peace activism think in terms of human or global security, where no one is secure unless everyone is secure in all areas of their lives. This means that nowadays it is impossible to separate issues of war and peace, the environment, sustainability, identity, global health, and the like.

The books in the series aim to make sense of this changing world of peace and security by investigating security issues and peace efforts that involve cooperation at several levels. By looking at how security and peace interrelate at various stages of conflict, these titles explore new ideas for a fast-changing world and seek to reconsider and redefine what peace and security mean in the first decades of the new century.

Multidisciplinary in approach and authorship, the books cover a variety of topics, focusing on the overarching theme that students, scholars, practitioners, and policy makers have to find new models and theories to account for, diagnose, and respond to the difficulties of a more complex world. Authors are established scholars and practitioners in their fields of expertise.

In addition, it is hoped that the series will contribute to bringing together authors and readers in concrete, applied projects, and thus help create, under the sponsorship of Alliance for Peacebuilding (AfP), a community of practice.

The series is sponsored by the Alliance for Peacebuilding, http://www.allianceforpeacebuilding.org/, and edited by Charles Hauss, government liaison.

Human Security

Theory and Action

Second Edition

David Andersen-Rodgers
California State University, Sacramento

Kerry F. Crawford
James Madison University

ROWMAN & LITTLEFIELD
Lanham • Boulder • New York • London

Executive Acquisitions Editor: Michael Kerns
Assistant Acquisitions Editor: Elizabeth Von Buhr
Marketing Manager: Kim Lyons
Sales and Marketing Inquiries: textbooks@rowman.com

Credits and acknowledgments for material borrowed from other sources, and
reproduced with permission, appear on the appropriate pages within the text.

Published by Rowman & Littlefield
An imprint of The Rowman & Littlefield Publishing Group, Inc.
4501 Forbes Boulevard, Suite 200, Lanham, Maryland 20706
www.rowman.com

86-90 Paul Street, London EC2A 4NE

British Library Cataloguing in Publication Information Available

Library of Congress Cataloging-in-Publication Data
Names: Andersen-Rodgers, David, author. | Crawford, Kerry F, author.
Title: Human security : theory and action / David Andersen-Rodgers,
    California State University, Sacramento, Kerry F. Crawford, James
    Madison University.
Description: Second edition. | Lanham : Rowman & Littlefield, [2022] |
    Series: Peace and security in the 21st century | Includes
    bibliographical references and index.
Identifiers: LCCN 2022018122 (print) | LCCN 2022018123 (ebook) | ISBN
    9781538159927 (cloth) | ISBN 9781538159934 (paperback) | ISBN
    9781538159941 (epub)
Subjects: LCSH: Human security. | Human rights.
Classification: LCC JC571 .A535 2022 (print) | LCC JC571 (ebook) | DDC
    323—dc23
LC record available at https://lccn.loc.gov/2022018122
LC ebook record available at https://lccn.loc.gov/2022018123

For our children,

Allan
Lucca
Soren
Emilia
Isabella

Contents

List of Tables, Boxes, and Figures

TABLES

BOXES

FIGURES

Preface

The difficulty of writing a book on complex and current global problems is that neither those problems nor the responses to them are static. You do not have to be an international relations scholar to see how complex problems seem to develop rapidly and shift the realities of high-level decision makers and ordinary people alike. To offer just two examples: the time between our sending the first draft of this edition out for review and receiving those reviews back saw the Omicron variant of SARS-CoV-2 overtake the world, sickening millions of people in weeks. As we sent the final revisions to the publisher, Russia was amassing its army on Ukraine's border, and shortly thereafter the full-scale invasion began and much of the West responded immediately with sanctions. More broadly, the changes that unfolded in our world between the publication of the book's first edition and this second edition are too numerous to list here. Writing about security means writing about a constantly changing state of affairs; the opportunity to write a second edition transforms what could have become a historical relic into a living document.

This edition follows the same structure as the first edition but with a few important changes. The book's first two chapters now provide a more comprehensive theoretical discussion of human security and the role that security perspectives play in supporting or challenging human security practice. This includes a more detailed discussion of durable security and its linkages to norms and institutions. We have moved the discussion of security perspectives to chapter 1 and refined the description of each perspective. The second edition discusses nativist, statist (which we called "nationalist" in the first edition but revised to "statist" to avoid conflation with resurgent nationalist movements), and cosmopolitan security perspectives, along with a fourth perspective, new to this edition: the federalist perspective. Discussion of this perspective adds essential recognition of the role of international law and organizations, as well as cooperation among states, in securing human rights, lessening vulnerability, and creating opportunities to thrive. In the second edition, we have made the policy environment illustrated through the "three boxes" model a consistent feature throughout the book. Rather than introducing this tool at the end of the book, readers will now encounter it in chapter 3, and subsequent chapters discuss how the model applies to the topics and cases addressed. We found it helpful to introduce this model much earlier than the final week of our respective courses and are confident that it will help readers draw more concrete connections between human security theory and practice as they navigate the book. The security perspectives and "three boxes" model give students, instructors, security practitioners, and other readers new conceptual lenses through which to view security threats, security providers, and challenges in the policy-making process.

In the first edition, we did not incorporate adequate discussion of race and racial and ethnic inequality. The past several years have seen increased efforts to work toward (and accompanying retaliation against) racial justice and equity in the United States and around the world. In an effort to apply human security theory to these contemporary movements, we have included a more deliberate focus on race and racial inequality, with new sections on policing and security-sector reform in chapter 7 and racial inequality in chapter 4.

As in the first edition, the book's key features help individual readers and course instructors alike think deeply about and discuss human security theory and practice. The case-based chapters help readers connect human security concepts (theory) to real-world applications (practice). The "Think about It" boxes provide instructors with ready-made writing assignments or group-discussion prompts; for the independent reader, they offer prompts to consider or to discuss with reading groups.

Our core goal for the book remains unchanged: we hope that all readers will find the concepts discussed here to be useful lenses to viewing and understanding human security theory and practice. Human security is well suited to addressing the world's complex threats; the key is ensuring that policies and actions account for context and recognize the experiences and voices of those they aim to protect and empower.

Acknowledgments

We gratefully acknowledge support from the International Studies Association James N. Rosenau Postdoctoral Fellowship program, the Mr. and Mrs. F. Claiborne Johnston Jr. Endowment Junior Faculty Grant Program of James Madison University, and the Sacramento State Research and Creative Activity Faculty Awards Program.

The manuscript benefited from the guidance of numerous colleagues and anonymous reviewers. We wish to thank Jessica Adolino, Rebecca Anastasi, Marie-Claire Antoine, Kelly Bauer, Chris Blake, Chip Hauss, Patrick James, Michael Kerns, Mary Malley, Dhara Snowden, Katelyn Turner, and the staff at Rowman & Littlefield.

Our students at James Madison University and California State University, Sacramento, helped us realize the need for a book like this one, and they deserve our thanks. They inspired and challenged us and, through their questions and discussions, encouraged the changes we have made in this second edition. We are heartened by the growing interest in human security among university students.

Last here but first always, we thank our families for their support and patience, especially Elizabeth Andersen-Rodgers and Tyler Belling. Our children give us reason to hope for and work toward a more equitable and just world.

List of Abbreviations

African Union (AU)
Amnesty International (AI)
Armed Forces Revolutionary Council (AFRC)
Association of Southeast Asian Nations (ASEAN)
Biological Weapons Convention of 1972 (BWC)
Black, Indigenous, Person of Color (BIPOC)
Black, Asian, and minority ethnic (BAME)
Cities Climate Leadership Group (C40)
carbon dioxide (CO_2)
Center for Civilians in Conflict (CIVIC)
Centers for Disease Control and Prevention (CDC)
Central African Republic (CAR)
Chemical Weapons Convention of 1993 (CWC)
Chinese Communist Party (CCP)
chlorofluorocarbons (CFCs)
Civil Defense Force (CDF)
Commission on the Status of Women (CSW)
Convention on the Elimination of All Forms of Discrimination against Women (CEDAW)
Cooperation Council for the Arab States of the Gulf (Gulf Cooperation Council; GCC)
Defense of Marriage Act (DOMA)
demobilization, disarmament, and reintegration (DDR)
Democratic Republic of the Congo (DRC)
Don't Ask, Don't Tell policy (DADT)
Economic and Social Council (ECOSOC)
European Union (EU)

Famine Early Warning Systems Network (FEWS NET)
Federal Emergency Management Agency (FEMA)
Food and Agriculture Organization (FAO)
Food and Drug Administration (FDA)
Force Intervention Brigade (FIB)
GLBTQ Legal Advocates & Defenders (GLAD)
Global Gender Gap Index (GGGI)
Gender Inequality Index (GII)
gross domestic product (GDP)
Group of Seven (G7)
Group of Twenty (G20)
High Ambition Coalition (HAC)
Human Development Index (HDI)
Human Rights Watch (HRW)
Human Security Unit (HSU)
hydrochlorofluorocarbons (HCFCs)
hydrofluorocarbons (HFCs)
Independent Commission on Policing (ICP)
Inter-Agency Working Group on Human Security (IAWGHS)
Interagency Standing Committee (ISAC)
intergovernmental organizations (IGOs)
Intergovernmental Panel on Climate Change (IPCC)
internally displaced persons (IDPs)
International Commission on Intervention and State Sovereignty (ICISS)
International Committee of the Red Cross (ICRC)
International Covenant on Civil and Political Rights (ICCPR)
International Covenant on Economic, Social and Cultural Rights (ICESCR)
International Criminal Court (ICC)
International Fund for Agricultural Development (IFAD)
international nongovernmental organizations (INGOs)
International Organization for Migration (IOM)
international organizations (IOs)
international relations (IR)
International Rescue Committee (IRC)
lesbian, gay, bisexual, transgender, and queer/questioning (LGBTQ)
Local Committees for Supply and Production (CLAP)
mutually assured destruction (MAD)
Mano River Women's Peace Network (MARWOPNET)
Médecins Sans Frontières (also Doctors without Borders; MSF)
Millennium Development Goals (MDGs)
multinational corporations (MNCs)
National Patriotic Front of Liberia (NPLF)

nationally determined contributions (NDCs)
nongovernmental organizations (NGOs)
North Atlantic Treaty Organization (NATO)
Office for the Coordination of Humanitarian Affairs (OCHA)
Open Working Group (OWG)
Organization of American States (OAS)
Organisation for Economic Co-operation and Development (OECD)
Peace Accord Matrix (PAM)
Peace Research Institute Oslo (PRIO)
Peacebuilding Commission (PBC)
personal protective equipment (PPE)
Police Service of Northern Ireland (PSNI)
Protection of Civilians (POC)
Provisional Irish Republican Army (IRA)
Responsibility to Protect (R2P)
Revolutionary Armed Forces of Colombia (FARC)
Revolutionary United Front (RUF)
Royal Ulster Constabulary (RUC)
security-sector reform (SSR)
Supplemental Nutrition Assistance Program (SNAP)
Sustainable Development Goals (SDGs)
transnational advocacy networks (TANs)
truth and reconciliation commissions (TRCs)
twenty-first session of the Conference of Parties (COP 21)
Ulster Defence Association (UDA)
United Nations (UN)
United Nations Action against Sexual Violence in Conflict (UN Action)
United Nations Children's Fund (UNICEF)
United Nations Commission on the Status of Women (CSW)
United Nations Department of Peacekeeping Operations (UNDPKO)
United Nations Development Programme (UNDP)
United Nations Economic and Social Commission for Western Asia
    (ESCWA)
United Nations Economic and Social Council (ECOSOC)
United Nations Emergency Force I (UNEF I)
United Nations Framework Convention on Climate Change (UNFCCC)
United Nations High Commissioner for Refugees (UNHCR)
United Nations Military Observer Group in India and Pakistan (UNMOGIP)
United Nations Mission for Ebola Emergency Response (UNMEER)
United Nations Mission in East Timor (UNAMET)
United Nations Mission in Sierra Leone (UNAMSIL)
United Nations Mission in South Sudan (UNMISS)

United Nations Mission of Support in East Timor (UNMISET)
United Nations Multidimensional Integrated Stabilization Mission in the Central African Republic (MINUSCA)
United Nations Office on Drugs and Crime (UNODC)
United Nations Organization Stabilization Mission in the Democratic Republic of the Congo (MONUSCO)
United Nations Stabilization Mission in Haiti (MINUSTAH)
United Nations Transition Assistance Group (UNTAG)
United Nations Transitional Administration in East Timor (UNTAET)
United Nations Truce Supervision Organization (UNTSO)
United Nations Trust Fund for Human Security (UNTFHS)
United States Agency for International Development (USAID)
United States Department of Agriculture (USDA)
Universal Declaration of Human Rights (UDHR)
Uppsala Conflict Data Program (UCDP)
Women, Peace, and Security (WPS)
World Food Programme (WFP)
World Health Organization (WHO)

Section I

INTRODUCTION TO HUMAN SECURITY

Chapter 1

Human Security—A New Security?

Learning Objectives

This chapter will enable readers to

1. recall and discuss essential characteristics of human security
2. identify differences between national, global, and human security
3. identify the various actors tasked with the provision of national, global, and human security
4. and identify and describe the concept of a human security norm and its implications.

This book is about *human security*, the idea that people, and the protection of human life and dignity, should be the central focus of security policy and practice. This, to be sure, is not on its surface a controversial statement. A large body of international humanitarian law and legal discourse condemns the arbitrary and indiscriminate killing of civilians and noncombatants. Yet within the prism of security studies, the idea that the protection of human life, broadly speaking, should take precedence over the protection of other referent objects such as the state, a kinship group, or the international system of states is problematic. This becomes even more complex when the concept of security is widened to include other formulations of security, such as economic security, environmental security, or cultural security. By engaging the theoretical underpinnings of human security and what human security would look like in practice, particularly in the construction of functional norms and institutions that prioritize human dignity, we can improve security outcomes overall. Therefore, to better understand what human security means in practice, we first ask what we mean by security more broadly.

Table 1.1. Security Approaches and Purposes

Security Approach	Purpose of Security Provision
National security	To protect the state from external threats and internal instability
Global security	To protect the stability of the system of states
Human security	To protect individuals and their communities from threats to their well-being and physical security

In its most basic form, *security* is protection from harm. The field of security studies, traditionally a part of the broader discipline of international relations, has mostly been concerned with two forms of security: national and global. **National security** focuses on the protection of the individual state from external harm and internal challengers or instability, whereas **global security** focuses on the protection of the stability of the system of states or international order (see table 1.1). How states have sought to maintain their security has, at times, led to severe harm to the human populations that live within them. The internment of Japanese-Americans in the United States during World War II, for one, exemplifies how a national response to an external threat can lead to hardship and insecurity for individuals and communities within the state. After the attack by Japan on the US naval base at Pearl Harbor in December 1941, more than one hundred thousand individuals of Japanese heritage—a majority of whom were US citizens—living near the Pacific coast were forcibly relocated to camps in interior states out of fear that they might pose a national security risk if their allegiance were to Japan. This forced displacement not only violated their dignity, it also had long-term effects on mental health and economic well-being (Chin 2005; Nagata, Kim, and Nguyen 2015). Meanwhile, no corresponding action was taken toward US citizens of German heritage, reflecting the racist underpinnings of the policy.

Security, therefore, does not always have the same implications for individuals, states, or the global system as a whole, and there are different approaches to achieving security as well as diverging understandings of who ought to provide security and for whom security ought to be provided. Building on both theoretical concepts and historical examples, this book explores a third approach to security that seeks to ensure and prioritize the protection of individuals and communities from harm: *human security*.

RESPONSIBILITY FOR SECURITY

The overarching theme of this book is the question of where responsibility for security provision lies and the norms and institutions that facilitate that provision. We examine the shift in responsibility for security from states alone to the combination of states and exogenous (outside) actors; such actors may include humanitarian agencies, nongovernmental organizations, foreign states, transnational social movements, and international organizations. We use the term **security provision** to convey the general practice of preventing or mitigating harm or of providing assistance and resources in response to situations of insecurity at the individual, state, or international levels.

Traditional understandings of security follow a basic security narrative: a threat, either real or imagined, to an identified referent object (such as individuals, the state, the planet) require protection from a specified actor (Wibben 2016). Often it is assumed within these narratives that the state is the primary guarantor of protection and stability. A **state** is a centralized political entity that holds territory, has a stable population, exercises legal authority over its population, and is recognized by other states in the world. This formulation of the state stems from the notion of the **social contract**, or the agreement between individuals and a government that the latter will provide for the common security in exchange for the allegiance of its people. This trade-off has also meant that the state "claims the monopoly of the legitimate use of physical force within a given territory" (Weber 1946, 78). Therefore, when we discuss state security or national security, we tend to focus on the security and stability of the political entity of the state and its territorial integrity; a secure state is typically understood as able to defend its borders, protect its population from outside threats, manage internal challenges and instability, and continue its political and economic functions. A state that is secure, according to traditional understandings of security, fulfills its social contract with its population by providing for the protection and stability of its territory and people from external threats.

Beyond external threats, people and communities may also face insecurity because of their own state's policies or national insecurity. Sometimes the state does not provide security but instead directly undermines the security of its own people. Myanmar's attacks on Rohingya Muslims offer one such example. The Rohingya ethnic minority living in the northern part of Myanmar, formerly Burma, have always been denied citizenship and experienced other forms of discrimination by the predominately Buddhist state. In 2017, following a series of attacks by Arakan Rohingya Salvation Army (ARSA) militants against numerous police posts, the state responded by deploying troops to Rohingya villages, burning homes and killing civilians. Médecins Sans Frontières estimates that over 6,700 people were killed and hundreds of thousands more fled across the border into Bangladesh (Médecins Sans Frontières 2018).

Ethnic cleansing and genocide are extremes among a number of challenges that a national government may pose to human security. Other challenges include unequal access to rights and services for people on the basis of sex or race, economic policies that exacerbate poverty, and poor health services. Some threats to human security are not intentional but result from a state's lack of capacity or ability to provide the services, rights, and stability that are essential to protecting individuals from harm. For instance, a state with a large amount of territory but a limited ability to enforce laws or maintain security throughout that territory may find itself unable to prevent or control the rise of militias or nonstate armed groups that seek to gain territory or resources. Violence against civilians caused by such nonstate armed groups is not a direct result of intentional harm by the state but, rather, is related to the state's lack of capacity to provide for the security of the population.

Furthermore, modern security problems may be **globalized** and beyond the ability of any one state to address. The interconnected world in which we live allows people from all over the globe to exchange goods, services, and ideas; it also allows security threats to cross borders quickly and easily. Challenges to public health—pandemics, drug-resistant illnesses, rising costs of vital medications—do not respect territorial borders. Similarly, environmental threats—rising global temperatures, sea level rise, drought, devastating hurricanes or typhoons—have the potential to have an impact on all states. Many of the threats affecting human security, including the daily lives of individuals, also threaten national security, yet these are problems that states must work together to address.

Yet when a state is unable to provide security, whether from external, internal, or globalized threats, should responsibility shift to other actors? Can outside organizations or other states provide the security a state is unable or unwilling to provide? **Collective security organizations**, like the North Atlantic Treaty Organization (NATO) or the United Nations (UN), are one type of exogenous or outside actor tasked with the provision of security. These organizations, made up of nation-states, seek to cooperate to protect all of their members from harm. **Humanitarian organizations**, such as Médecins Sans Frontières (or Doctors without Borders, MSF) or the International Committee of the Red Cross (ICRC), seek to protect individuals from harm, regardless of political affiliation, ethnic or racial identity, or any other characteristic. These nonstate actors are unaffiliated with state governments and provide aid in response to natural disasters, war and armed conflict, and public health crises. States may also seek to provide assistance to other states or people or groups within those other states. A state may engage in **humanitarian intervention**, or the use of force within another state to protect people from harm when another government's policies and instability cause destruction and insecurity. States may also offer **humanitarian assistance**, provision of aid and support without the use of force, in response to natural disasters, famine, or public health crises in another state. In today's world, outside organizations and states have the potential to become involved in security issues and problems far from their geographical bases.

The complexity of today's world with threats to people's security coming from myriad multifaceted and interconnected sources requires us to think thoughtfully about our policy approaches. Traditional notions of security—those that focus on the sovereign state as the primary guarantor of security for its people—are unable to account fully for the shifting responsibility for security provision and the new types of protectors and protection that we can see in the world today. Amid rising nationalist and populist sentiments within some wealthy Western states, threats posed by transnational terrorism, efforts to foster collaborative responses to problems like climate change and global hunger, and other complex problems in our interconnected and globalized world, security studies and policy making require nuanced, careful analysis of competing and complementary security approaches and perspectives on security provision. The **human security approach**, with its focus on prioritizing human life, provides a framework for overcoming many of the obstacles these complex problems pose. However, human security is not one-size-fits-all and requires practitioners to carefully consider the consequences, both intended and unintended, of their actions. Therefore we aim to foster careful and nuanced thinking through an examination of human security practice.

HUMAN SECURITY AND THE RECONCEPTUALIZATION OF SECURITY

The ending of the Cold War rivalry between the United States and the Soviet Union generated new discussions about how security should be conceptualized in a world recently freed from bilateral rivalry between nuclear armed states. The United Nations Development Programme's (UNDP) 1994 Human Development Report issued the first comprehensive and direct definition of human security. The report observed that the concept of security had for too long focused entirely on conflicts between states and the threats to their borders, while individual people have always understood security to mean stability in their daily lives and the safety of their surroundings. Within the context of this conceptual divide between what makes the state secure and the types of security that individual human beings wish for themselves and their communities, the Human Development Report identified **human security** as a twofold concept: first, "safety from the constant threats of hunger, disease, crime and repression"; and, second, "protection from sudden and hurtful disruptions in the pattern of our daily lives—whether in our homes, in our jobs, in our communities, or in our environment" (United Nations Development Programme 1994, 3).

Human security, then, exists when individuals and communities are safe from both chronic, long-term threats to their well-being and from more sudden threats to their physical safety. In its broadest sense, human security is not just about protection from *physical* harm but about stability, well-being, freedom, and the capacity of individuals to thrive. Individuals, therefore, should be able to live their lives free from war and physical violence, as well as from systemic deprivation, adversity, inequity, and human rights violations. Because of this dual focus on imminent and chronic threats to safety and well-being, those who seek to ensure human security for all people address not only wars and national security crises but also societal norms and institutions, as well as global factors, that contribute to day-to-day insecurity and systematic harm for people and their communities. Put simply, if people feel that their basic needs are being met today and will continue to be met for the foreseeable future, thus empowering them to live full lives with dignity, these people can be said to have human security. Thus a key component of human security is the creation of functional norms and institutions that help people achieve these empowered lives.

That said, there is an important caveat to this point: Oftentimes obtaining safety and well-being can come, intentionally or not, at the expense of another's safety and well-being. This reality poses an important question that should be kept in mind throughout this text: *Can human security exist for one person or community if obtaining that security undermines, even if indirectly, the human security of others?*

The UNDP's 1994 Human Development Report engages this problem when it outlines four fundamental characteristics of human security encompassing universality as well as interdependence:

1. "Human security is a *universal* concern"; it affects all people in all areas of the world.
2. "The components of human security are *interdependent*"; if one population is suffering from chronic hunger, war, or air pollution, the effects of that insecurity extend globally in some way, whether directly or indirectly.
3. "Human security is *easier to ensure through early prevention* than later intervention"; for example, it is easier and cheaper to prevent malaria transmission through the use of mosquito-repelling bed nets than to treat a malaria patient with medications or to respond to a large outbreak of malaria.
4. "Human security is *people-centered*"; it focuses on the daily lives of individuals and their communities, their overall well-being, and their potential to live a free and healthy life (United Nations Development Programme 1994, 22–23, italics added).

Human security is often said to be divided between two core ideas: *freedom from fear* and *freedom from want*. These notions stem from the 1994 Human Development Report, with deeper roots in the Universal Declaration of Human Rights and US president Franklin Delano Roosevelt's "Four Freedoms" speech (given on January 6, 1941), and they form the backbone of the concept of human security. (See chapter 8 for additional discussion.)

It should be immediately apparent that human security can suffer from definitional ambiguity. This has been one of the core criticisms of the term in general, particularly within the academic field of security studies. Roland Paris, for instance, argues that the term is not merely vague and overly expansive but also that its main backers have worked to keep it that way; thus the term loses its analytical usefulness through ambiguity (Paris 2001). Barry Buzan offers a similar critique but also highlights some of the dangers of idealizing security as an end goal. "Securitizing" human rights is a core component of the human security framework, but Buzan fears that this moves it away from the normal politics by which human rights can be more effectively addressed and sustained (Buzan 2004). That said, it should be noted that *security* in and of itself has been criticized as an ambiguous concept (Baldwin 1997; Wolfers 1952).

Past efforts over time to create measurable variables for human security have gained little traction and been short-lived. Gary King and Christopher Murray (2001, 585), for instance, made an early attempt at quantifying the "number of future life years spent outside a state of 'generalized poverty.'" Because the term was first widely introduced within the Human Development Report, efforts to operationalize, or to measure, human security have frequently been linked to some aspect of development. In fact, its introduction closely corresponded with the creation of UNDP's Human Development Index (HDI), which seeks to measure development based on life expectancy, education, and income. Human security, however, is not simply a synonym for development, and others have tried to develop measures that reflect its multifaceted meaning.

One approach is to distinguish between direct and structural violence and demonstrate how different human security challenges arise under different conditions (Christie 1997). *Direct violence* concerns immediate physical threats to one's life, such as armed conflict or state violence; *structural violence*, on the other hand, is violence caused by the organization of social, political, and economic structures (Galtung 1969). Both have implications for human security and match closely with the *freedom from fear/freedom from want* dichotomy. For instance, a woman who experiences sexual violence at the hands of armed actors is experiencing direct violence, whereas a woman living in a place with social and economic structures that discriminate based on gender in such a way that her life expectancy is lower than a man's is experiencing structural violence. Different approaches are required to address these different forms of insecurity.

Some argue that the difficulty in finding a coherent means for operationalizing human security hinders efforts to develop what can be described as coherent human security practice. The basic premise of this argument is that human security should be understood as a dependent variable that is either increased or decreased overall by specific actions. The difficulty, however, is that, once a specific measure has been identified, human security practice may begin prioritizing measurable outcomes over less-quantifiable factors that may in fact have greater impact on overall security. In addition, an outcome for one community may not be appropriate in another community. Therefore, it is key to see human security practice as context-specific and strongly contingent on the needs and inputs of the communities impacted by those policies. Human security, therefore, is perhaps better understood as set of practices centered on an ethical framework. In that sense, human security's place in international relations fits most comfortably within constructivism's focus on ideas and norms and critical theory's focus on emancipation (Christie 2010; Newman 2016, 2010; MacFarlane and Khong 2006; Wibben 2016).

As human security is concerned with the protection of the *individual* from harm, we should consider what constitutes *harm*. During violent conflict, it is not just those doing the fighting who are at risk of death or injury. Modern warfare increasingly targets noncombatant populations. Ethnic cleansing and genocide, conflict-related sexual violence, the recruitment of child soldiers, and the use of indiscriminate weapons such as land mines are all profound threats to human security in armed conflict. Terrorism—the deliberate targeting of civilians by nonstate actors—also violates principles of human security. Additionally, individual security can be threatened by more than guns, bombs, and direct physical attack; environmental degradation, insufficient access to food, or lack of appropriate health infrastructures, both in and outside of armed conflict, pose real challenges to human security. When we discuss protection, the responsibility for providing protection and fostering human security, and the justification for protection, we refer to the broad sense of protection as the absence of physical threats, the provision of basic needs, and the foundation for empowerment.

Furthermore, where the responsibility to protect and empower individuals lies and the methods by which those goals are implemented are highly contested. Thus the study of human security encompasses a range of problematic issues that require examining both the governance of human populations and the underlying politics that inform that governance. In the two decades since it was first articulated, human security has become a core aim of the policies of some states as well as intergovernmental and nongovernmental organizations (IGOs and NGOs). The foreign policy initiatives of Canada and Japan in particular illustrate how states may take different approaches to promoting human security. Canada has focused on freedom from fear, prioritizing protection from imminent physical harm. Japanese foreign policy has emphasized freedom from want, focusing on development and protection of an adequate standard of living (more on this in chapter 2; Commission on Human Security 2003, iv; Hanlon and Christie 2016, 4–9).

Today, however, the term *human security* is less likely to be found in states' foreign policy initiatives. Canada, for instance, dropped the term entirely when Conservative Party member Stephen Harper served as prime minister (2006–2015). Additionally, many early state-led cooperative efforts to promote human security, such as the Human Security Network, have largely faded away (Martin and Owen 2010). By the end of the 2000s, the use of *human security* as a term that defined the United Nations' engagement with the world was largely relegated to smaller, less ambitious projects. While this does not diminish the importance of human security as a core area of inquiry, it means that the aspirational approach of the 1990s and early 2000s is less useful in understanding it. That said, with increased episodes of armed conflict, the COVID-19 pandemic, and worsening effects of climate change, there has been a resurgence of interest in human security around the world. UN secretary-general António Guterres is once again referencing human security in his speeches (previous secretaries-general had shied away from its use), and high-level meetings on human security are once again taking place between states.

Regardless of whether the term *human security* is part of official discourse, the promotion of human security norms has been a consistent component of international politics for the past three decades. A wide acceptance of the relevance and importance of freedom from fear and freedom from want, coupled with specific actions tasked to specific actors, creates a human security norm. A **norm**, generally speaking, is a commonly accepted belief or idea that provides standards for behavior (Finnemore and Sikkink 1998). According to Michelle Jurkovich (2020b), for something to be a norm it must possess three elements: (1) a moral dimension or a sense of "oughtness," (2) a specific expected action that would realize the norm, and (3) a specific actor who is expected to carry out the norm. For a **human security norm** to exist there would need to be a consensus among a significant group of states and international organizations that individuals and communities are entitled to protection from harm and that specific, identifiable actors (including foreign states or organizations) are tasked with the responsibility of guaranteeing that protection. As we will explore throughout this volume, these three requirements are not always clearly met.

It is not enough, then, to simply claim that human populations should be protected from harm; this in and of itself is not generally a contested point. How that protection occurs, what constitutes protection (simply safeguarding against direct physical threats, defending human rights and dignity, or some combination thereof), and the extent of responsibility allotted to various actors, however, are. For example, many conflicts result in the large-scale displacement of human populations. When this occurs governments, nongovernmental organizations, and international organizations all must consider whether and how to respond. The refugee flows resulting from the civil war in Syria, for example, led to vastly different responses from the states into which the refugees moved, ranging from attempts to close borders (as Hungary did) to relative openness (as in the case of Germany). Contrast this to the nearly universal acceptance that European states showed to Ukrainian nationals fleeing Russia's military invasion of their territory in 2022.

How, then, do these decisions get made? Why are some human security issues addressed while others seem to be routinely ignored?

Understanding Security Approaches

We can begin to answer these questions by thinking about how individuals, states, and the global system of states justify protection toward themselves and others. Protection for oneself in its most basic form can be understood in terms of **self-interest**. In most circumstances an individual, state, or even the global system as a whole will see the perpetuation of its own survival as its primary goal. Yet individuals, states, and the global system also pursue policies aimed at protecting others even without the existence of a norm promoting human security. The state has an incentive to protect individuals living within its borders, as the stability that protection provides should contribute to its long-term survival. Nevertheless, protection by the state is not absolute, and under certain circumstances the state may consider some individuals expendable—for instance, opponents to the political regime that controls the state. The state also has an incentive to protect the global system or international order of states, particularly if it considers the current status quo beneficial. This logic extends to the global system's interests in preserving the state (see table 1.2).

If we work through each cell—or box—within table 1.2, we can see how self-interest will guide individuals, states, and the global system to offer forms of protection to themselves and the level both immediately above or below them, even without a consensus around the importance of human security and the protection of the individual. Individuals, for example, can protect the state through such acts as military service, paying taxes, and pledging fidelity when they consider the preservation of the state to be beneficial to them. While a state may be able to coerce this type of protective behavior

Table 1.2. Justifications for Security Provision without a Human Security Norm

		Who Provides Security?		
		Individual	*State*	*System*
For Whom Is Security Provided?	Individual	Self-interest	Preservation of state, but individual may be expendable	Only if protection of individual can be linked to maintenance of system
	State	If status quo favors individual	Self-interest	Preservation of system, but an individual state may be expendable
	System	Only if protection of system is linked to security of individual	If status quo favors state	Self-interest

from the individual in the short term, taking measures to create a cohesive national identity can, in the long term, be a more effective strategy. The state, then, is motivated to provide protection to individuals in such a way that garners loyalty. Of course, without an embedded human security norm the state also may be motivated to eliminate those individuals who don't adhere to its form of national identity.

What is perhaps less obvious is why the global system or international order would overly concern itself with protecting the individual. Under assumptions of self-interest, a global system whose primary interest is self-preservation should not be overly concerned with the protection of individuals if the integrity of the states that make up that system is not in jeopardy. However, as we will discuss in chapter 2, much of the work being conducted by the institutional structure initially designed to preserve the global system—namely, the United Nations—is focused on human security issues.

The United Nations High Commissioner for Refugees (UNHCR) is one international agency working to establish human security for specific populations—individuals displaced by armed conflict or humanitarian crises. UNHCR is tasked with directly assisting refugees and displaced populations and coordinating other organizations and agencies seeking to provide assistance and resolve issues that contribute to displacement. UNHCR is not a state entity but, rather, an international agency within the United Nations system. Efforts toward human rights promotion, peacekeeping, protections for displaced populations, poverty reduction, and sustainable development goals epitomize the type of human security work being pursued by global and regional organizations.

What effects does the development of a human security norm have on the relationships between the system, the state, and the individual? For one, we should expect to see a stronger linkage between the global and the individual. Instead of a self-interested system with a purpose of maintaining the global status quo alone, we will see the international system organize itself to protect the security of individuals as well. It will do so by creating organizations and rules that reflect its growing acceptance of human security as a priority. Individuals, on the other hand, will see the value of engaging global actors when advocating for their security. **Transnational advocacy networks**—individuals and organizations connected through their pursuit of a common goal—emerge and engage with international institutions and states to create change. The international coalition that came together in the 1990s and successfully banned antipersonnel land mines through the Ottawa Treaty is one example of a transnational advocacy network of organizations and individuals working to improve human security by reducing the use of indiscriminate weapons. The closure of the gap between the global and the individual puts pressure on the state to adopt policies that also reflect the prioritization of human security.

Thus we should expect to see three changes in behavior as a human security norm becomes more clearly articulated and accepted by individuals, their states, and the broader global system. The process should follow what is understood as the *norm-development cycle* (Finnemore and Sikkink 1998). First, individuals will adopt and promote the discourse of human security more broadly when advocating for their rights. They will emphasize the importance of their well-being and the protection of their fundamental rights, perhaps even directly challenging the prioritization of state security concerns. Second, states will enact domestic policies that reflect human security discourse and, at least in principle, support global organizing around human security norms. Even if states do not abandon their narrow concern for political stability, they will begin to speak about the rights and protection of individuals and communities at home and abroad. Human security advocates, of course, would argue that safeguarding people's rights is the most efficient way to guarantee political stability in the long run. Third, international organizations will work to create a global bureaucracy that promotes human security norms and will identify the actors responsible for upholding those norms. Organizations, such as the United Nations, will begin to discuss the security and rights of individuals and groups, especially in times of crisis and threats against human rights; beyond discussion, these organizations may themselves take action—such as ordering economic sanctions or deploying a peacekeeping operation—or call on states to take action in response to human security threats. These changes reflect a shifting understanding of responsibility for the provision of security.

Table 1.3 illustrates the shifts in justification for protection when a human security norm guides individual-, state-, and system-level behavior and beliefs. It should be clear that today's global system is not one that has universally accepted a human security norm. Nor do we claim that the presence of said norm is the sole factor informing when and how security is provided. States continue to be driven by their national interests and are reluctant to intervene in other states when mass atrocities are committed. The armed conflicts and humanitarian crises in Rwanda, Darfur, and Syria all provide examples of states' reluctance to protect against humanitarian crises. Even for those individuals, states, and organizations that deliberately try to incorporate a human security norm, justifications for providing security will still reflect

Table 1.3. Justifications for Security Provision Incorporating a Human Security Norm

		Who Provides Security?		
		Individual	*State*	*System*
For Whom Is Security Provided?	Individual	Self-interest	Preservation of state, but individual may be expendable *or* Protection of individual because it is the right thing to do *or* Protection of individual because it is politically costly to harm individual	Protection of individual because it is the right thing to do *or* Protection of individual because it is politically costly to permit harm to individual
	State	If status quo favors individual	Self-interest *or* Protection of state in the interest of protecting population	Protection of state in the interest of protecting population
	System	If status quo favors individual	If status quo favors state *or* Protection of system in the interest of protecting state population *or* Protection of system in the interest of protecting global population	Self-interest *or* Protection of system in the interest of protecting population

a range of motivations; the presence of and compliance with a norm will not necessarily snuff out self-interest. For example, states may commit their armed forces through unilateral (single state) or multilateral (cooperation of multiple states) action in a humanitarian crisis, but each state's motivation may be different and will range from a purely humanitarian goal to save as many lives as possible to a more strategic approach related to resources, national interests, or political alliances tied up in the conflict. For this reason, table 1.3 still includes the self-interested justifications for security provision seen in table 1.2; even if human security matters to some or many international actors, there will still be reasons for individuals, states, and the international system to act on the basis of self-interest, and we will still see occasions on which human security is not a priority.

Individuals, states, and even the system still wish to survive, but in a world full of individuals, states, and organizations guided by a human security norm, the ways in which these actors seek to promote their survival and protect others will look different from a world without a human security norm. Further, individuals, states, and organizations may comply with a norm not because they believe in its appropriateness and value but because *others* do and to violate a norm held by others in the global system would be politically—and sometimes economically—costly.

There are also strategic reasons for states and global security actors to pursue a human security approach. Providing for basic needs, eliminating scarcity and discrimination or oppression, protecting communities from violence, and helping individuals realize opportunities are not exclusively a normative endeavor; success in these areas can be key to ensuring the state's political and economic stability, stabilizing a region after armed conflict, or countering transnational threats like terrorism and violent extremism.

Today numerous individuals, states, intergovernmental organizations, and nongovernmental organizations are motivated by a human security norm that prioritizes the security of individuals, but the norm is not accepted by all international actors and is not the only factor motivating these policies. Given these mixed motivations, it can be difficult to determine when a norm is compelling behavior or when a behavior that would be pursued regardless uses the language of the norm as a kind of justification. One reason why it remains difficult to clearly observe the norm's impact is that, although human security, state security, and global security can be at odds, there are significant points of overlap and complementarity among them; in other words, the three security approaches are often synchronous.

We will continue to explore these points, as well as the ways in which human, state, and global security are at odds, throughout the book.

BOX 1.1. THINK ABOUT IT . . . HOW DO WE KNOW *SECURITY* WHEN WE SEE IT?

1. What does security look like in our daily lives?

Consider the people, objects, or routines that make you feel safe and secure in your daily life. Working through these questions will give you a sense of what security means to you, personally:

a. When you picture the word *security*, what comes to mind in your own daily life?
b. Who or what (institutions, individuals, objects) provides for your security?
c. Who or what has the potential to threaten your security?

2. What does security look like from your national government's perspective?

Now imagine that you are in charge of national security—the safety and protection of your homeland. Working through these questions will help you envision what national security is:

a. What comes to mind when you picture a secure state?
b. Who or what provides for the security of the state?
c. Who or what has the potential to threaten the state's security?

3. What does security look like from a global perspective?

Picture a world that is safe and secure for all people, in all states and nations. Working through these questions will prompt you to think about what global security looks like:

a. What comes to mind when you picture a secure world?
b. Who or what should provide for global security?
c. Who or what has the potential to threaten global security?

PERSPECTIVES ON SECURITY

For the diverse array of security providers to work together to achieve common goals, there must be some degree of mutual trust and an absence of global disruptions or instability. Assumptions about what constitutes security, who or what provides it or ought to provide it, and who or what threatens it are inherent in any approach to security. When we consider security provision, especially human security provision, we must consider the ways individuals seek to maintain or improve their own security. To date, this consideration is missing from much of the research on and discussion of human security.

International relations (IR) literature in the realist paradigm characterizes states as self-interested actors. We know that individuals are similarly preoccupied with their safety and well-being. If the individual is at the center of security in the human security approach, then it is a useful exercise to consider the competing perspectives through which individuals assess their own security and how best to achieve it. To an individual, security generally involves a combination of economic, physical, and cultural aspects, and each person makes conscious or subconscious decisions every day in pursuit of their security. Pursuing one's own security does not necessarily guarantee an interest in pursuing or providing security for others; in fact, it can be easy to view security gains for others as security threats to oneself. Just as realist IR posits that states pursuing their self-interest will inevitably end up in situations of insecurity and less-than-ideal outcomes in a world made up of similarly self-interested states, individuals may also perceive security to be a win-lose (or zero-sum, in the language of realist IR) situation in which security for oneself necessarily comes at the expense of security for others. It is for this reason that guaranteeing one's individual security does not necessarily constitute human security practice.

The human security approach developed out of recognition of human rights as universal and human development as essential. As the concept of human security developed, so too did the expectation that the state and international community (especially the United Nations) would promote and protect human rights and pursue human development. Yet it is not clear that recognition of universal human rights and the importance of human development or the expectation that states and international organizations will provide these are accepted without question. Individual security perspectives come about through a confluence of experiences, norms, interests, and beliefs, all of which vary across communities, even within the same state or region. In short, individuals may not see security provision that is conceived as a global, top-down endeavor as the best way to guarantee their own security, and the conflict between individual perspectives on security and approaches to security can lead to flawed policy initiatives (see Autesserre 2014 for research on the effects of this incompatibility).

Security perspectives are formed around two basic elements: one's perspective on the state's role in providing security for oneself or one's community, and one's perspective on the universality of rights extending beyond one's kinship group. Using these two parameters, we can group individual security perspectives into four broad categories: statist, nativist, federalist, and cosmopolitan (see table 1.4).

The **statist perspective on security** sees the state as the primary provider of security but rejects or deemphasizes the universality of rights. This perspective tracks closely with the traditional or state security and global security approaches. According to this perspective, the state is the primary provider of security, and the individual expects to receive protection from the state, as established by the notion of the social contract. While holders of this security perspective might see the guarantee of their own rights as an important component of their relationship with the state, the guarantee of rights for others outside their own sovereign territory is inconsequential.

The **nativist perspective on security** places the primary security provider closer to home. This perspective does not see the state as central to protecting their physical security, and neither does it see rights as universal; but those holding this perspective likely adhere to localized cultural norms. To this group, security is best provided by a group or groups below the level of the state, including sectarian, ethnic, religious, racial, or other identity groups. Because the state is not seen as the primary guarantor of security in this perspective, in response to situations of real or perceived insecurity, individuals may come to rely on, support, or participate in nonstate armed groups, such as militias, insurgent factions, or terrorist organizations. It should be noted that not all nativist security measures entail armament. In Colombia, for example,

Table 1.4.   Security Perspectives and Their Implications

Security Perspective	Implications
Nativist	Security is best provided by one's own local kinship group. Rights are determined by the kinship group.
Statist	Security is best provided by the state for the citizens of that state. Rights are determined by the state.
Federalist	Security is best provided by the state but follows a universal set of norms regarding rights.
Cosmopolitan	Security is best provided through the acceptance of a universal set of norms and a broad sense of obligation to others. Rights are universal, but the identity, nationality, and lived experience of different communities are retained.

the Indigenous communities have organized the Indigenous Guards, armed only with specially decorated staffs, to protect their communities and traditional lands from both state and violent nonstate actors (Jackson 2007). The nativist perspective may be held more frequently in a state incapable of or unwilling to provide protection for all segments of the population, meaning the state has failed in its responsibility to provide security. It may also be present when the state *is* able and willing to provide security for its population but segments of the population instead associate effective security provision with their own identity group rather than with the broader state. The nativist perspective is similarly suspect of global policy efforts to provide security.

The **federalist perspective on security** sees the state as the central provider of security but also sees that responsibility couched within a framework of international law that supports universal rights broadly. International norms around rights are key, but the enforcement of such norms should happen within the framework of a system of sovereign nation-states, and there is leniency regarding how said rights are protected in any given nation-state. The federalist perspective on security is often reflected in liberal institutional approaches to international relations and broadly informs support for intergovernmental organizations such as the United Nations.

The **cosmopolitan perspective on security** links our security with those of other communities. It does not necessarily see the state as central in the provision of physical security but holds that rights should be universally accepted while maintaining cultural and community identities. The cosmopolitan perspective, therefore, leads individuals to see their security as closely aligned with the security of others around the world, regardless of differences in identity, nationality, and lived experiences (Appiah 2019). Individuals who see the world from a cosmopolitan viewpoint see global cooperation and agreements as necessary components of overall security but emphasize the importance of local and state participation in shared efforts. The cosmopolitan perspective envisions security policies and initiatives as functioning best when they are created through inclusive processes that incorporate diverse insights and experiences from different sectors of society. While the state may play a role in this process, the cosmopolitan perspective is suspicious of the state's ability and motivation to wage violence against its citizens. Civil society organizations are most likely to adhere to this perspective, which tracks most closely (but not completely) with the human security approach.

The four different perspectives on security and security provision have the potential to affect the implementation of human security policy on both sides of the security provision nexus: the population in need of assistance will have a perspective on the most logical or capable security provider, and the entity tasked with security provision will also have a perspective on how to perform that role. To examine how perspectives come into play in global human security provision, we can take the example of the statist perspective on assistance. If a statist perspective is the dominant security perspective, then there may be pressure on that state to limit the resources directed to communities that are perceived as different, foreign, or incompatible with the constituencies of the state. This attitude is driven by the idea that the state's essential role is to provide security and protect the rights of its own population over others. This can be further amplified if there are strong elements of the nativist perspective in the population as well. Consider the responses to the Syrian refugee crisis among segments of the population within the United States and in some European states. Some constituencies within these states—states that have a history of resettling refugees—have pushed back against the notion that their communities have an obligation to provide for and take in refugees who practice a different religion, come from a different culture, and speak a different language.

Similarly, a nativist perspective within a population in need of assistance would lead to acceptance of assistance from states or groups with a shared identity but less so from those perceived as different, foreign, or incompatible with the needs and identity of the local population. Consider efforts by NGOs, UN entities, or foreign states to promote gender equality and women's rights in culturally conservative states; these efforts may meet with resistance if they are perceived by constituencies within the local population as attempts to impose so-called Western values (see chapter 10 for further discussion). If individuals' unique perspectives on security are not taken into account when states, IGOs, NGOs, and other security providers determine their response to a given situation of insecurity, there is an underlying risk of failure—or at least inefficiency.

We revisit these four security perspectives throughout the book in order to examine potential obstacles to the human security approach. These competing views on security provision do not doom human security to failure, but practitioners, policy makers, and researchers would do well to be mindful of these perspectives and invite dialogue and frame human security initiatives in a way that engages and reconciles rather than ignores and exacerbates the potential obstacles arising from competing perspectives.

WHY HUMAN SECURITY?

Human security has been a key framework for thinking about how to approach an array of complex policy problems for over thirty years. As we will explore in this volume, the norms around human security have been an important part of how we make sense of the world around us and the range of possible responses to complex problems. The actions of states, international organizations, and substate actors can all be viewed through a human security lens. The critical evaluation of these actions can result in policy better constructed to enhance human dignity and life. Human security–focused policy making, however, does not have a single approach, and neither do we attempt to propose one here. As will become clear, human security practice is contextual and requires input from various stakeholders, especially those whom the policies and actions aim to protect or empower. We hope that readers of this book can use these ideas to think more deeply about how we address a wide array of complex policy problems facing the world today.

PLAN OF THE BOOK

Building on the concepts presented in this chapter, the first section of this volume proceeds by examining the historical foundations of human security. Chapter 2 explores how the idea of human security evolved. Why did human security as we understand it today emerge in the 1990s? The focus in this chapter is on the three aspects that created a global political environment conducive to the emergence of human security: the changing nature of war, the expanded role of the United Nations, and greater recognition of human rights within the international community. The chapter discusses the shifting justification for and conduct of war, the discussion of human development in the United Nations, and the origin of contemporary human rights discourse after World War II and the reinvigoration of human rights protection in the 1990s. The chapter concludes by discussing what is meant by the term *human security approach* and then introduces the differences between protection in war (human security in armed conflict) and durable human security (long-term or "peacetime" human security).

Chapter 3 discusses the implementation of human security concepts by introducing the range of actors involved in the provision of human security. This chapter serves as a reference point for proceeding chapters and offers an overview of the human security landscape. A vignette exploring the evolution of the UN's Millennium Development Goals and Sustainable Development Goals considers the expanded range of relevant actors in human security provision.

Chapter 4 expands on the foundational concepts of human rights and freedoms presented in chapter 2 and traces the roots of modern human rights. Human security depends in large part on the recognition and protection of human rights, and this chapter discusses the connection between the development of international human rights discourse and the pursuit of human security. The concept of protecting human rights for historically excluded groups is introduced, with a particular focus on LGBTQ+ rights and racial and ethnic inequality.

The book's second section discusses human security in armed conflict and war. Here we discuss the protection of individuals from direct physical harm or the threat thereof. Armed conflict triggers some of the most urgent physical, social, political, and psychological threats to short- and long-term well-being.

Chapter 5 draws on arguments about responsibility from this first chapter to discuss how human security–based justifications for intervention have been used since the end of the Cold War. It highlights how acute conflict creates high levels of human security threats. This chapter includes a section on just war theory and the emergence of Responsibility to Protect (R2P). Also highlighted are some of the key concerns that an overreliance on militarized interventions creates regarding questions of human security and the role of outside interveners and local actors. Here we consider the first international intervention authorized with an explicit R2P mandate, the NATO-led intervention in Libya in 2011, and compare it to nonintervention in the Syrian conflict.

Chapter 6 examines how human security issues are (or are not) addressed during peace processes, with a focus on the various actors that participate in these processes. It discusses comprehensive peace accords and the evidence suggesting that accords including a broader range of human security–focused issues have greater likelihood of durable success. This chapter explores women's involvement in peace negotiations in Liberia to demonstrate the effectiveness of inclusive peace processes.

Chapter 7 looks at human security through the frame of peacebuilding—or rebuilding society after intrastate or interstate armed conflict. Peacebuilding encompasses the scope of efforts to transition a society from war to peace, including rule of law provisions, infrastructure, social services, combatant demobilization, economy, and politics. Using UN peacekeeping efforts as a central illustration of how the international community cooperates in peacebuilding efforts in vastly different contexts, the chapter explores both short- and long-term initiatives. Additionally, the chapter examines the ways human security is realized through transitional justice mechanisms—including postconflict tribunals, truth and reconciliation commissions, and special courts. With this, we then examine broader concepts of retributive and restorative justice and how they relate back to the human security approach. The chapter examines policing reforms in Northern Ireland after the signing of the Belfast Agreement.

In addition to considering the impact of armed conflict on human security and the ways in which security needs change in war, we also discuss what we call **durable human security**. Durable human security includes the dimensions of security not necessarily related to armed conflict—though they may certainly exist in wartime—that threaten the daily lives and livelihoods of individuals and communities through dysfunctional norms or institutions that create the conditions for harm. Durable human security incorporates the concepts of freedom from want and freedom from fear, as both are essential for the realization of long-term, sustainable human security. When states are unable to provide the ingredients for durable human security—such as effective public health institutions, adequate food supply, protection from widespread poverty and inequality, environmental protection and stability, gender equality, and human rights—both individuals and the state will face insecurity and instability. Here we consider these issues of durable human security, and from multiple perspectives, when looking at the broader picture of what security means and how individuals and communities can live without fear. Chapter 8 bridges sections II and III with a discussion of the transition from the concept of human security in armed conflict to the notion of durable or "peacetime" human security. Chapter 8 also incorporates a discussion of economic insecurity as a durable human security challenge in armed conflict and in times of relative peace.

Chapter 9 looks at the impact of public health crises on human, national, and global security. Public health crises present acute threats to the individual and community but also trigger a broader effect on state stability and economic growth if the threat is widespread. Illustrating the key differences between chronic and sudden individual health problems and health *security* threats, the chapter revisits the notion of a threshold for human security concerns and discusses the threat posed by and responses to the COVID-19 pandemic.

Chapter 10 provides an overview of the ways in which gender equality, or a lack thereof, can impact both human and national security. Through an introduction of the Gender Inequality Index (GII) and the Global Gender Gap Index (GGGI), the chapter illustrates the multifaceted nature of gender equality and the impact of gender discrimination on many dimensions of social, political, and economic life. The chapter identifies the links between gender inequality and decreased human security and state and global instability. Highlighted here are the progress of and obstacles facing gender equality efforts developed from within and outside of the state in Afghanistan and Sweden.

Chapter 11 examines climate change and the role of environmental instability in shaping human, national, and global security. The chapter introduces the scientific evidence for climate change and general predictions of its effects before turning to international efforts and failures to address the widespread challenge. The efforts of youth climate activists to convince states of the urgency of climate change are examined.

Chapter 12 discusses the roots and effects of hunger, malnutrition and undernutrition, and dysfunctional distribution of resources. We revisit the impacts of climate change introduced in chapter 11 to underscore the widespread and chronic nature of food insecurity and the need for international cooperation to address its causes and effects. Food insecurity in the United States and famine in South Sudan offer a glimpse into the problem of food security in both wealthy and fragile states.

The fourth and final section of the book applies the concepts presented in previous sections to security policy and practice. Chapter 13 returns to the three views of security to synthesize the concepts and challenges presented in the preceding chapters. The discussion presents the requirements for effective and durable human security and aims to promote critical thinking and analysis by highlighting the advantages of and challenges to utilizing the human security approach to respond to twenty-first-century security challenges. The chapter highlights the examples of violent extremism and transitional justice, examining the potential contributions a human security response could offer. The discussion is designed to prime the reader to consider the promise of and obstacles facing human security practice.

DISCUSSION QUESTIONS

1. Human security is often described as encompassing freedom from fear and freedom from want. In what ways are the terms *want* and *fear* useful for thinking about policy priorities? In what ways do the terms' subjectivity hinder policy priorities?
2. Do efforts to promote national security threaten or undermine efforts to provide human security?
3. How might efforts to improve national security enhance the security of individuals?
4. In what ways might efforts to provide human security threaten or undermine efforts to promote national security? Conversely, how might efforts to provide human security increase national security? Are there any agencies, organizations, or institutions that provide for national security *and* human security?
5. What is a human security norm, and how does it impact the behavior of (a) individuals, (b) states, and (c) the global system?
6. In what ways does a globalized world impact human security?
7. Thinking of the four security perspectives, in what ways can someone with each perspective help or hinder human security? If a security perspective is hindering human security practice, are there practical mechanisms to address it?

Chapter 2

Historical Foundations of Human Security

Learning Objectives

This chapter will enable readers to

1. identify the three central characteristics of the political context for the emergence of human security
2. identify the foundational principles for human security, including human rights and human development
3. compare and contrast human security in war and durable human security
4. and identify and discuss the motivations and characteristics of a human security approach.

THE POLITICAL CONTEXT FOR A NEW SECURITY

The fall of the Berlin Wall in November 1989 and the subsequent ending of the Cold War brought hope to many for a more peaceful world, free of superpower rivalry. That hope, however, was soon muted by the breakup of Yugoslavia, Iraq's invasion of Kuwait, and civil wars in Rwanda, Liberia, Somalia, the Democratic Republic of Congo, and elsewhere. While for years the number of **intrastate wars**, wars being fought within states rather than between states, had been rising, images of the starving and maimed being shown on people's television sets around the world, coupled with increased activism by civil society groups, put more pressure on governments and international organizations to develop policies that emphasized the physical and legal protection of humans. With the rapidly changing structure of the international system as a backdrop, earnest discussion within the

UN and among state policy makers, as well as within academia, began to engage whether security should be reimagined to fit these new global realities. Three key international political developments provided a supportive environment for these discussions: (1) a shift in the character of war, (2) an expanded role for the UN after the end of the Cold War, and (3) an increased recognition of human rights.

This chapter explores each of these developments in turn before turning to a discussion of the human security approach.

The Changing Character of War

The romanticized notion of war being fought between trained soldiers on a battlefield removed from civilian populations has never matched the historic reality. Ancient texts expose such myths of war; in his *History of the Peloponnesian War* (431–404 BC), for example, Thucydides writes of Athenians killing all Melian men of military age and enslaving their women and children prior to colonizing their territory. In the twentieth century the introduction of strategic bombing, nuclear weapons, and the rise of identity-based conflicts delineated even further the distinction between military and civilian targets (Bellamy 2012). While we can measure whether wars are becoming more or less frequent or more or less violent, there have also been changes in how we think about war as either a justified or unjustified human activity. Thus the changing nature of war should be understood not simply as a metric but as a phenomenon that profoundly impacts human life.

Prior to the disbandment of the Soviet Union (1991), global politics for years had been deeply embedded within a framework of superpower rivalries and ideational differences. During the Cold War most states were aligned in some capacity with either the United States or the Soviet Union. In fact, the influence of the superpower rivalry on global politics was so dominant that the group of states choosing to not align themselves with one side or the other still highlighted this dynamic by referring to themselves as the Non-Aligned Movement. The ending of the Cold War, therefore, caused a major jolt to the international system as states had to adapt their foreign policies away from their former superpower patrons.

This had different impacts on different regions. In Latin America the elimination of ideological rivalries helped bring an end to civil wars in El Salvador and Guatemala (although Colombia's civil war continued for more than twenty-five additional years). It also helped usher in a wave of democratization to many formerly authoritarian regimes as the United States intervened less frequently in domestic affairs in the region once it became less fearful that leftist parties would align with the Soviet Union.

Many states in Africa and the former Soviet states, on the other hand, saw a number of civil wars either begin or intensify. Several states with weakened authoritarian leaders saw a subsequent rise in ethnopolitical conflict as competing identity groups challenged their rule and battled for greater control of the state. Thus in the aftermath of the Cold War there was a substantial shift from ideational conflicts to identity-based conflicts (Gurr 2000; Kaldor 2005). One consequence of this shift was that in many of these conflicts, parties were not divided by their ideological beliefs (i.e., communism versus capitalism) but by their ethnic or religious identities. Thus we began to observe more deliberate targeting of civilians based primarily on their ethnic or religious identity, as was seen in Rwanda, the former Yugoslavia, and Darfur.

While the ending of the Cold War certainly reduced the risk of global nuclear annihilation, it is not readily obvious whether as a result the world became more or less violent. The total number of intrastate or interstate conflicts has fluctuated, but according to the Uppsala Conflict Data Program (UCDP), from 2011 onward these have been at a historical high, with 2020 having the highest number of recorded armed conflicts since 1945, with fifty-six active armed conflicts (Pettersson et al. 2021). UCDP classifies an *armed conflict* as any conflict (interstate, intrastate, or internationalized intrastate) that records twenty-five or more fatalities in a single calendar year.

Another way to gauge the intensity of conflict for any given period is by calculating the total number of **battle deaths**. Battle deaths are fatalities that occur due to combat in two-sided conflict in which at least one of the belligerents is a state. During the Cold War, three conflicts saw over one million battle deaths: the Vietnam War (1955–1975; 2,097,705), the Korean War (1950–1953; 1,254,811), and the Chinese Civil War (1946–1949; 1,200,000). In addition, the Iran–Iraq War (1980–1988) had 644,500 battle deaths, and the Afghan Civil War (1978–2002) had 562,995 battle deaths (Lacina and Gleditsch 2005, 154). In contrast, no conflict since the end of the Cold War has reached these totals of people killed in conflict. Syria, which has the highest total number of battle deaths recorded during the period, experienced 392,000 deaths between 2011 and 2021 (Pettersson et al. 2021, 816).

Battle deaths, however, are distinct from **one-sided violence**, which is violence perpetrated against noncombatants without fear of reciprocation. The 1994 Rwandan genocide, for instance, is considered one-sided violence, as are executions or firing on nonviolent protesters (Lacina and Gleditsch 2005). In addition, many deaths during wartime are caused by **indirect violence**, or the harm caused to civilians due to the collateral consequences of war, such as decreased access to food, clean water, or health care.

The Democratic Republic of the Congo (DRC) provides a stark example of the difference between battle deaths and indirect violence. While accurately counting war deaths is methodologically tricky (Spagat et al. 2009), according to the Peace Research Institute Oslo's (PRIO) battle deaths data set, the best estimate of the number of battle deaths in the DRC between 1996 and 2008 is 151,618. However, a mortality study conducted by the Human Security Report estimates that during that same period there were likely 863,000 and upward of 2.4 million excess deaths in the general population (Human Security Center, Human Security Report Project, Simon Fraser University 2011, 131). These excess deaths were due to the decreased access civilians had to food, clean water, and health care services as an indirect consequence of war. Needless to say, only examining one aspect of war obscures how deeply it affects a broader swath of the population.

The conflicts of the 1990s brought increased visibility to a number of trends in the conduct of war—such as ethnic cleansing, the use of sexual violence as a weapon of war, and forced displacement—which lent greater urgency to a new human security discourse (Kaldor 2005). This corresponded with greater activism on a global scale to bring attention to the suffering of people during warfare. The International Campaign to Ban Landmines, discussed further in the final section of this chapter, drew focus on how an indiscriminate weapon, the land mine, could cause suffering to the greater population long after a peace accord was signed. The creation of criminal tribunals for the former Yugoslavia (1993) and Rwanda (1994) as well as the subsequent creation of the International Criminal Court (ICC) in 1998, each tasked to try individuals for war crimes and crimes against humanity, was the result of long-standing efforts by global activists to bring force to the principle of civilian immunity during war. This activism, and other actions like it, helped transform the discourse around war, brought renewed attention to its devastating consequences to civilian populations, and created mechanisms to punish those responsible for the greatest atrocities.

The terrorist attacks directed against the United States by al Qaeda operatives on September 11, 2001, emphasized a second type of security problem. **Terrorism** is the use of violence by nonstate actors toward nonmilitary targets and noncombatant populations; the ultimate goal is to send a message to the state in which the terrorist organization is based, to the population of that state, or to foreign states and populations. While terrorism as a form of violence and political communication was not new, the magnitude of those attacks, as well as al Qaeda's emphasis on targeting US symbolic centers of power, was new. The aftermath of the attacks on September 11, 2001, presented several challenges for the human security agenda. One that began to emerge within the context of ethnopolitical conflict but took on new significance with the rise of transnational terrorism was the accountability of nonstate actors to instruments of international law and the question of who has the authority to respond to nonstate actors residing within the territory of another sovereign state.

Did September 11 and the US-led response represent a setback to the human security agenda? In many ways the initial response to September 11 mirrored a traditional state-centric security response. The United States and its NATO coalition first overthrew the Afghan government, which at the time was led by the Taliban, rather than targeting al Qaeda directly. The Battle of Tora Bora (al Qaeda's suspected hideout) did not occur until after the Taliban government had been deposed—two months after the initial invasion. The overthrow of the Taliban regime and the insertion of a pro-Western government in its place then gave NATO the authority to operate freely throughout Afghanistan.

Almost twenty years after the terrorist attack, the United States withdrew its forces from Afghanistan, leading to an almost immediate collapse of the US-supported Afghan government to the Taliban insurgency. The Taliban quickly formed a new government and, despite promises to the contrary, re-implemented restrictions on several rights—particularly the rights of girls and women. While the ascension of the Taliban did lead to a subsequent decrease in militarized violent conflict in most parts of the country, many other threats to human security remained, and new ones have emerged—including a collapsing economy in the face of a severe drought (Baloch 2021). The intervention in Afghanistan (and the subsequent intervention in Iraq) led to many core human security questions, including the responsibilities of intervening states to protect vulnerable populations, the role of the United Nations in authorizing military interventions, determining whether human security goals can be properly met through the foreign policies of a hegemonic power, and ascertaining how international bodies and legal mechanisms can be applied to nonstate actors.

Questions of governance highlight another key set of events that defines this era—namely, the ongoing struggle between prodemocracy movements and autocratic governments throughout the world, including in many former Soviet states, the Middle East, and Asia. For instance, the Arab Spring, which began in Tunisia in December 2010 when a Tunisian street vendor, Mohamed Bouazizi, set himself on fire to protest the widespread joblessness and lack of opportunities faced by many young people. In response, a series of social protests erupted throughout the Arab world—in Tunisia, Egypt, Syria, Libya, Yemen, Bahrain, and other Arab states—in which governments were called on to reform themselves toward greater openness and political participation.

States responded in multiple ways to the protests. Some led to moderate reforms. In Egypt, authoritarian leader Hosni Mubarak was overthrown. In Libya a UN-authorized international coalition helped lead to the overthrow of Muammar Gaddafi. However, in both cases the ousting of the authoritarian leader did not lead to improved human security. In fact, one could make a strong argument that in the aftermath of these protests important aspects of human security have weakened (Kuperman 2013). The most glaring example is the Arab Spring protests in Syria, which led to what has become one of the most violent and destructive post–Cold War conflicts and triggered the greatest refugee crisis since World War II. The violence, instability, and lack of effective rule of law contributed to the increased influence of violent nonstate actors such as the so-called Islamic State and motivated new interventions by multiple states, including the United States and Russia.

Despite these outcomes, prodemocracy activists in the Arab world have continued to advocate for greater political rights. In Sudan protesters adjusted their tactics and in 2019 successfully ousted longtime dictator Omar al-Bashir. Also in 2019 protests in Algeria known as the "Revolution of Smiles" helped oust long-term president Abdelaziz Bouteflika. As with earlier Arab Spring movements, however, the difficulty remains in postrevolutionary governance, as multiple factions, including the armed forces, vie for political power within these new governments. In October 2021 Sudan's efforts to democratize suffered a severe setback when Prime Minister Abdalla Hamdok was removed via military coup. Even in Tunisia, where the Arab Spring began and which was seen as the most successful nation participant in the Arab Spring, progress has backslid; President Kais Saied dissolved parliament and dismissed the prime minister in July 2021, causing many to fear that Tunisia was returning to one-man rule.

The Arab Spring protests and the subsequent violent conflicts arising from them highlight a number of questions about our current understanding of human security, particularly as it relates to the responsibility that a state has to protect its own citizens and the responsibilities of others when the state fails to do so. Social movement challenges to states are not just relegated to authoritarian regimes. Protests in the United States and throughout the world regarding policing and its complicity in violently targeting Blacks and other minority groups further underscore the complicated balance between the construction of state security forces nominally designed to enforce laws meant to improve public safety, and their actual use, especially in cases where their monopoly on violence disproportionally targets different out-groups. Beyond policing, wide-scale social protests in Colombia during the summer of 2021 and in Chile from 2019 onward have addressed a wide range of social policy issues, ranging from taxation to hikes in public transportation fares.

Wars of conquest, while rare, remain a looming threat to state, global, and human security. Russia's invasion of Ukraine on February 24, 2022, for example, demonstrates how quickly wars between states can undermine all three forms of security. Not only was Ukraine's sovereignty violated, but global security was threatened when Russian president Vladimir Putin put Russia's nuclear forces on alert and threatened devastating consequences to any country that came to Ukraine's aid; this challenged the idea that nuclear powers are sufficiently constrained by the international legal order meant to sustain a stable system of sovereign states. The devastating consequences for human security have been even more profound. Immediately, millions of Ukrainians were displaced from their homes as Russia's military displayed a willingness to target civilian population centers. Credible evidence shows that Russian forces have engaged in looting, sexual violence, summary executions, and indiscriminate targeting of civilian populations—actions which violate international humanitarian law (Human Rights Watch 2022). Furthermore, the human security consequences of war do not just impact those in the war zone. At the time of writing, the disruption to the grain typically produced in Ukraine is profoundly affecting global food prices and hunger, particularly in Africa and Asia, and global energy costs have greatly increased as the world has sanctioned Russia's oil and gas sectors.

What these examples demonstrate is that we should not equate state security with human security, as one does not guarantee the other. At times, efforts by states to improve their own security have had devastating consequences for their own citizens. However, the void that is left when the state weakens or disappears also has dramatic consequences for human security. This problematic balancing act that the state performs between providing or denying human security will be a continual theme of this volume.

The United Nations' New Role

The emergence of human security–related efforts is linked not only to the apparent need for a different view of security—as made clear by the horrific intrastate wars and transnational advocacy efforts to monitor human rights abuses and violence against civilians in the 1990s—but also to the recognition of the potential for a more significant role for a global institution founded to establish global peace and security. Founded in 1945 as a collective body of sovereign states with a core purpose of providing the institutional mechanisms that would lessen the likelihood for future interstate conflict, the United Nations was often hampered by Cold War power politics and the veto-wielding powers of the United States and the Soviet Union. The end of the Cold War and the UN's role in authorizing the US-led response to Iraq's invasion of Kuwait in 1990 brought hope in many quarters that the UN could play a more direct part in resolving conflict.

In his report to the Security Council in June 1992, Secretary-General Boutros Boutros-Ghali mapped out a new, more influential role for a post–Cold War UN. "An Agenda for Peace" highlighted the need and opportunities to make UN efforts toward preventive diplomacy, peacekeeping, and mediation more efficient and effective. Each of these related efforts is focused on preventing and resolving armed conflict through peaceful means, and each envisions more active involvement on the part of the UN. In the context of the UN's role in the maintenance of international peace and security, the secretary-general cited the responsibility of all elements of the organization and its members to work toward achieving human security (Boutros-Ghali 1992). The reference to this new approach to security makes sense, given the report's focus on maintaining peace in a world that had very recently been dominated by a decades-long conflict between two superpower states whose principal focus was ensuring the survival of their political influence. In short, the human security norm began to take shape as the once-taken-for-granted centrality of superpower states and their influence started to wane.

However, the expanded vision presented in "An Agenda for Peace" was quickly challenged by conflicts in Somalia, the former Yugoslavia, and Rwanda, each of which saw human deprivation on such a large scale that they overwhelmed the UN's capacities to act effectively. Indecisiveness, member states' unwillingness to commit resources, regional and global politics, and rivalries all plagued the UN responses.

These early failures should not overshadow the successes that a more active United Nations has had. For instance, when UN peacekeeping forces are present in the tenuous postconflict period, the situation is more likely to remain peaceful (Fortna 2008). UNHCR has helped many postconflict states successfully manage their displaced populations and assisted refugees in the early stages of the resettlement process (Adelman 2001). UN system-wide efforts to improve the representation of women within peacekeeping forces, state governments, and UN agencies have led to modest but meaningful advances in more equitable and gender-sensitive policy and postconflict reconstruction efforts (Karim and Beardsley 2017; Crawford, Lebovic, and Macdonald 2015; Verveer and Dayal 2018).

While "An Agenda for Peace" focused on what are typically seen as traditional security concerns—the prevention, resolution, and management of violent conflict—the Human Development Report focused on an alternative understanding of development. As we noted in chapter 1, the 1994 Human Development Report offered the first comprehensive definition of *human security* as safety from both chronic threats and sudden interruptions to the daily lives of individuals. **Human development** is an approach to international development that seeks to improve the well-being and capabilities of individuals and communities rather than focusing solely on the wealth and growth of the economy in which those individuals live. Whereas traditional economic development approaches aim to expand the economy, a human development approach aims to enrich people's lives by focusing state resources toward improving health, access to education, job-skills development, and other goals that secure the well-being of individuals. Given the opportunity to live a longer and healthier life, pursue a quality education, and obtain the skills necessary to engage in rewarding employment, an individual will contribute substantially to their home state's economic, political, and social stability. The ripple effects of a life full of rewarding opportunities and over-all well-being extend throughout the individual's family—especially to children—and social network. In theory, successful human development will lead to a more stable economy and economic growth by empowering individuals, helping them improve their skills and abilities, and giving them a wider array of choices and opportunities to improve their livelihoods.

One way to measure human development is through the **Human Development Index (HDI)**, created by economist Mahbub ul Haq in 1990 and used in the UNDP's Human Development Reports. HDI is a measure of growth that attempts to account for human capabilities and opportunities and, therefore, takes into account indicators that measure a population's health and life expectancy, access to education, and standard of living. Human development offers a more holistic view of economic growth and development and provides a basis for the "freedom from want" aspect of human security.

Early optimism for a more robust UN gave way to the complexities of international politics. While there had been more cooperation between the veto-wielding powers of the UN Security Council, that cooperation has been severely strained, particularly as China and Russia have increasingly objected to the Security Council's Western powers (the United States, France, and the United Kingdom) pushing for greater United Nations involvement in a number of high-profile conflicts. Additionally, several scandals involving UN peacekeeping forces—most notably the cholera outbreak in Haiti and a litany of sexual assault and exploitation charges against UN peacekeeping personnel—have weakened the UN's legitimacy in the populations it purports to serve.

Another challenge facing the United Nations has been to coordinate between different actors working on interconnected issues, specifically those in humanitarian, development, and peacebuilding sectors. Often underdevelopment, humanitarian crises, and violent conflict go hand in hand. But trying to bridge these gaps while avoiding overlapping policies has been an ongoing struggle between different humanitarian agencies and NGOs also working on these issues. At the 2016 World Humanitarian Summit, and in the face of a global refugee crisis, agreement was reached between states and major humanitarian and development organizations to create more integrative and holistic ways to coordinate efforts, with a greater focus placed on empowering and supporting local actors. Later, in 2017, UN secretary-general António Guterres added a third sector to the humanitarian/development nexus—

peacebuilding (Barakat and Milton 2020). While these efforts between the United Nations and its partners are designed to address many of the past shortcomings of development, humanitarian, and peacebuilding efforts, many hurdles remain, including the difficulty of implementation (Howe 2019). Because these three dimensions are heavily linked to the broader human security agenda, how their difficulties are solved have important implications for the future of human security practice.

Nevertheless, these early efforts to define the parameters of what is broadly understood as human security has had a major influence on how the international community thinks about and frames policy. By identifying sets of measures—such as found in the HDI, as well as the more ambitious Sustainable Development Goals (SDGs) and Millennium Development Goals (MDGs)—states and activists have been able to speak a common language regarding policy goals. Despite its flaws, the United Nations remains the sole global intergovernmental organization in which these debates can regularly occur.

Increased Recognition of Human Rights

A third factor contributing to the introduction and promotion of a human security norm unfolded in tandem with the UN's increased role in global affairs: nongovernmental organizations (NGOs), transnational advocacy networks (TANs), and other nonstate actors increased their advocacy on behalf of human rights and the victims and survivors of human rights violations. **Human rights** are the rights to which all human beings are entitled simply by virtue of being human—regardless of their nationality, sex, ethnicity, race, religion, language, state or territory of residence, or any other factor or status. Such rights are universal (meaning all humans everywhere are entitled to them) and inalienable (meaning no one can deprive another person of their rights except through the due process of law). Examples of human rights include liberty, life, equality before the law, access to education, and freedom to practice or not practice a religion. Human rights are, by their very nature, focused on the individual; protection of human rights requires protection of individuals and their freedoms. Increased prioritization and monitoring of human rights by NGOs and TANs called attention to the many threats confronting individuals and communities, whether posed by the government, nonstate actors like armed groups and militias, or more globalized challenges like environmental instability. After the Cold War ended, advocates pressured states and the United Nations to uphold the human rights commitments they had already made.

Activism on behalf of human rights became more common in the 1990s, but the concept of human rights has a much longer history, which we will discuss in chapter 4. The **Universal Declaration of Human Rights (UDHR)**, adopted by the UN General Assembly on December 10, 1948, documents much of what we understand about human rights today and lists specific human rights. (See box 4.1 in chapter 4 for the list of rights enumerated in the UDHR.) Early discussion of human rights—as articulated by ancient Greek and Roman philosophers and legal systems, medieval religious texts and doctrine, and political philosophers and popular revolutions of the eighteenth century—preceded the UN declaration by centuries. The UDHR became a landmark text, however, because it was the first international statement of human rights. Drafted and adopted after World War II, the UDHR was a response to the atrocities and violations of individual security and rights that occurred in all states affected by the war. The international agreement formed a basis for the understanding and protection of fundamental freedoms and human rights. Just as human rights issues were far from the top of the list of global priorities during earlier times of colonial expansion, economic depression, and world wars, the potential outbreak of war among superpower states stifled much discussion of human rights after the UDHR's adoption in 1948.

In spite of its historical importance, the UDHR does not have the legally binding force of a treaty in its own right, but the UN General Assembly adopted two succeeding agreements in 1966 to complete the **International Bill of Human Rights**. Intense debate over the scope and form of the International Bill of Human Rights demonstrates the impact of national security and ideological concerns on human rights issues. **The International Covenant on Economic, Social and Cultural Rights (ICESCR)** and the **International Covenant on Civil and Political Rights (ICCPR)** (both signed in 1966 and entered into force in 1976) have the legally binding force of treaties; states that signed the covenants are obligated to uphold the rules and procedures agreed upon in the documents.

While human rights are universal and inalienable in theory, states are aware of their unique abilities to protect certain rights more than others and of their inability or unwillingness to guarantee some rights. The Soviet Union based its political ideology on providing for the economic and social stability of its people, so rights to education, employment, and leisure time fit naturally with the state's goals and vision. The United States, on the other hand, advocated freedoms of religion, speech, and assembly, freedoms that resemble those enumerated in the US Constitution. Many states, of course, signed on to and ratified both covenants, but that there are two covenants when the original intention was to create and implement *one* legally binding agreement on human rights demonstrates the power of state interests in regulating human rights. Although the Cold War–era superpowers contributed to the division of human rights into two separate covenants, newly decolonized states—notably Jamaica—were the moral force behind the negotiations that brought the human rights frameworks into being in the 1960s and 1970s (Jensen 2016).

As the UN gained more influence in the 1990s and intrastate wars featured grave human rights abuses, NGOs and TANs pushed states and international organizations to uphold their human rights commitments. At the close of the twentieth century, states were not the only significant players in international politics; instead, they often felt real pressure from NGOs and TANs and at the UN. Although the documents in the International Bill of Human Rights had been adopted decades prior, the collective efforts of NGOs and TANs in the 1990s to monitor human rights abuses in intrastate wars, to secure the rights of women, children, and minority groups, and to question the central focus on the security and well-being of the state led to renewed international recognition of human rights.

The international campaign to recognize and protect women's rights as human rights is one example of a human rights cause that became successful in the 1990s because of the persistence of NGOs and individual advocates. Efforts and advocacy during the UN Decade for Women (1975–1985) produced the **Convention on the Elimination of All Forms of Discrimination against Women (CEDAW)**, a legally binding international agreement adopted in 1979 that outlines efforts to protect women from gender-based discrimination, such as unequal pay and lack of property rights. The UN formed the Commission on the Status of Women, which then organized UN World Conferences on Women in Mexico (1975), Copenhagen (1980), Nairobi (1985), and Beijing (1995). The international movement to secure women's rights strengthened through these conferences because NGOs and advocates had a common forum in which to share ideas and strategies, solicit the support of state governments, and publicly shame governments or groups that violated women's human rights.

The Beijing Platform for Action, adopted in 1995, recognized the need for urgent action in response to various forms of gender-based inequality related to poverty, education, health, violence, war, the economy, political participation, and the environment, among other concerns (United Nations Women 1995). The realization that violence against women occurred on a massive scale in the bloody intrastate wars in the former Yugoslavia and Rwanda gave the movement further momentum and solidified international legal recognition of sexual violence as a human rights violation and a war crime. Legal and political acknowledgment and protection of women's rights as human rights came about through the increased influence of the UN, NGOs, and advocacy networks in a time of international political upheaval surrounding the breakup of the Soviet Union and graphic internationally broadcast news coverage of horrific intrastate wars. Discussion of human security was thus a natural complement to the expanding recognition of human rights.

DEBATING SECURITY

The effects of these transformations were also reflected in debates within the academic literature on security. The field of security studies largely originated from a desire to understand the causes of war and how the introduction of nuclear weapons into an international system of had states changed strategic calculations (Walt 1991). Scholars began focusing on models of rational interdependent decision-making, particularly examining issues of threat, counterthreat, power balances, material capabilities, and misperception (Jervis 2017; Fearon 1995; Bueno de Mesquita and Lalman 2008; Keohane and Nye Jr. 1973; Barnett and Duvall 2005). This strategic approach, they found, had tended to be state-centric, relying on a logic that sometimes led to perverse outcomes—mutual assured destruction, or MAD, being most prominent. Strategic approaches to the field of security studies were increasingly scrutinized both on moral and logical grounds, and competing approaches quickly proliferated into a number of branches both widening and deepening our understanding of security (Buzan and Hansen 2009).

Early challenges to the strategic approach to security came from the field of peace studies, which focuses on the reduction of armed conflict, with a strong emphasis on arms control and disarmament. Peace studies challenged the inevitably tragic assumptions built into strategic security approaches, proposing both institutional and strategic mechanisms for reducing the likelihood for armed conflict (Bull 1968). Ideational or constructivist approaches also questioned the rationalist assumptions of strategic security studies by examining how ideas, norms, beliefs, identities, and other less tangible factors helped us better understand why and how conflict would emerge (McSweeney 1999). Others, such as the Copenhagen School, asked what exactly *security* constitutes. In a complex, interdependent world, myriad issues could rise to the level of a "security threat." Thus Copenhagen School scholars highlighted processes of *securitization*, in which influential advocates elevate issues from normal politics to security threats in the hopes of securing higher priority and resources and being shielded from the constraints of democratic debate (Buzan, Waever, and de Wilde 1998). One could convincingly argue that the UNDP's 1994 Human Development Report uses the term *human security* so as to securitize development issues to elevate their status on the post–Cold War policy agenda.

Another crucial reformulation of security studies began questioning how the field was traditionally and primarily centered on the most powerful actors while excluding everyone else and also how many of the field's core assumptions perpetuated existing power structures. Critical security studies, for instance, seeks to understand power structures with the purpose of discovering ways to transform them to a more just and emancipated world (Cox 1981). Oliver Richmond and Jason Frank's (2009) work, for instance, examines how UN peacekeeping's one-size-fits-all assumptions about postconflict state building can lead to poor postconflict governance that perpetuates existing power structures, doing little to create a better world for those who have suffered most during the conflict. Critical examination of the institutional approaches used by international actors, and many of the destructive consequences these practices produce, helps open the door for more just postconflict institution building, often with a focus on local practices (Fontan 2012; Autesserre 2021).

Who is seen by and who is ignored by the security lens, so to speak, has been a key question raised by both feminist and postcolonial security studies scholars. Feminist security scholars shed light on the ways the masculine has been prioritized in determining what constitutes a security problem (Hansen 2000). Accounts of war focus on men as combatants and obscure both women's agency (as combatants or as agents of peacebuilding) and men's vulnerability (as civilians or targets) (Sjoberg 2014; MacKenzie 2015). Similarly, postcolonial or "decolonized" security studies seek to expose the deeply entrenched hierarchical legacies left by colonialism and consider how that legacy shaped and continues to manifest itself in the organizational structure of the international system. Colonialism has resulted in a legacy of exclusion of peoples and issues not traditionally considered acceptable topics of security studies (Adamson 2020). Race structures and influences global politics but has been marginalized in the study of international relations (Zvobgo and Loken 2020). When we consider who and what are included and excluded from notions, discussions, and implementations of security, we should take into account the identities of the scholars and practitioners who are influencing the academic field and the state, nonstate, and global institutions engaged in security practice.

All of these debates challenge the historically narrow focus of the field of security studies and argue that security is better understood by not just examining the powerful but by also examining the vulnerable and those groups traditionally excluded from security paradigms. We argue that the human security concept serves as a bridge between these different approaches while also providing practitioners with an ethical framework for evaluating competing policies.

BOX 2.1. THINK ABOUT IT . . .
WHAT MOTIVATES INTERNATIONAL
ACTORS TO CHOOSE HUMAN SECURITY?

Different international actors (states, international organizations, NGOs, and individuals) may have different motivations for advocating or opposing a human security norm or for calling for a human security or traditional state security approach to a specific problem. Consider each of the situations listed here. Research each situation to identify the goals of the listed action.

Consider the context for the development of human security discussed in this chapter as well as the motivations for action introduced in chapter 1—self-interest, protection of the individual, protection of states, and protection of the global system—and any other factors that you think may explain each situation. Given the global political context and the identity of each intervening state or organization, does each situation appear to be motivated by a human security approach, a state security approach, a global security approach, or some combination of these approaches? Does each situation uphold or challenge the human security norm?

1. NATO-led, UN-authorized intervention in Libya in 2011
2. Multistate intervention in Syria beginning in 2014
3. The UN and global response (or nonresponse) to the Rohingya crisis in Myanmar between 2010 and 2019
4. Operations against Daesh/ISIS in Iraq between 2015 and 2018
5. The Brazilian and international responses to the Amazon wildfires of 2019

HUMAN SECURITY: A REIMAGINED SECURITY

We approach our discussion of human security from a *practices* lens—the set of "competent performances" conducted on a day-to-day basis concerning a specific issue area (Adler and Pouliot 2011). Human security as a practice is rooted in these critical challenges to traditional security studies. Human security requires that we shift our lens toward those who have too often been ignored in policy making and seek to develop mechanisms by which their needs can be better served. When international actors—including states, international organizations (IOs), NGOs, TANs, other nonstate actors, and individuals—adopt a **human security approach**, they seek to ensure the protection of individuals and communities from harm and create a stable and equitable society that allows them to thrive. This is done through meaningful institutional transformation to implement human security norms both immediately and over the long-term.

Institutional transformation can happen on the global, state, and local levels. We contend and seek to demonstrate through our exploration of the range of human security concerns presented in this book that the human security approach is necessary for twenty-first-century policy makers, security providers, and researchers. We do not argue that state security or global security is irrelevant in the modern era; on the contrary, the often-synchronous nature of the three approaches suggests that each offers important insights into security threats, effective solutions, and responsibility for security provision.

A human security approach places the individual at the center of the political, humanitarian, development, military, or human rights effort. This reorientation of security practice is not easy, but it is conceivable. For instance, the transnational effort to ban antipersonnel land mines, led by the International Campaign to Ban Landmines, demanded that states focus on the security of individuals even at the expense of cost-effective defensive security tactics. Antipersonnel land mines can relatively cheaply slow or stop an adversary's advance by making terrain too dangerous to cross. However, land mines do not have mechanisms that allow them to distinguish between combatants and civilians, and they can lie dormant for an indeterminate amount of time, causing injury and death among civilian populations during and long after active armed conflict. By condemning the use of a traditional weapon for the indiscriminate harm it poses during and after war, advocates made clear that they prioritized human security over military strategy, and they asked states and the UN to do the same. The risk to noncombatants far outweighed the utility of land mines. The fact that a majority of states in the international system signed and ratified the resulting Ottawa Treaty demonstrates that, given sufficient advocacy and awareness of the human costs at stake, states can be persuaded to place the security of individuals and communities ahead of traditional security interests.

Some states have worked to promote human security goals through support for various forms of humanitarian assistance and peacebuilding activities in war-torn states. Some middle-power states, such as Japan, Norway, and Canada, have explicitly integrated human security goals into their foreign policy agendas. For Japan, these efforts have largely focused on freedom-from-want issues, pursuing human development goals through economic assistance. Canada, on the other hand, has focused its efforts on freedom-from-fear issues, with a specific emphasis on public safety, protection of civilians, conflict prevention, governance and accountability, and peace support operations.

Development agencies of various states often provide grants for governments and nongovernmental organizations to incorporate human security approaches into their activities. Conversely, other branches within the same government pursuing a different set of goals can sometimes contradict these efforts. Policy confusion caused by the coimplementation of competing approaches can undermine a state's ability to achieve any of its goals, so coordination is essential.

The prioritization of human security by any given state will largely be contingent on who controls the government. Both Japan and Canada's human security agendas faltered with the elections of governments more circumspect of human security goals—although the 2015 election of Prime Minister Justin Trudeau has placed some human security concerns back onto Canada's foreign policy agenda (Smith and Ajadi 2020). The 2016 election of Donald Trump in the United States led to a reversal of many US policies that had fit within a human security framework, particularly those concerning refugees. Starting in 2021 the new Biden administration began restoring some of those priorities but that September relied on Trump's executive orders on asylum to deny asylum-seeking Haitians entry to the United States. Thus in a system where states are the sole meaningful actors it is unlikely that the human security approach would be engaged in any meaningful way over the long term without being subordinated to various interpretations of the state's national or global security goals.

Still, adopting a human security approach does not necessarily mean that international actors will abandon self-interest and a traditional security approach altogether; a human security approach may be adopted to resolve one situation while a traditional national security approach will guide other efforts. Consider, for example, the US humanitarian relief effort in response to the 2004 Indian Ocean earthquake and tsunami: the administration of George W. Bush pledged $35 million in aid and sent additional direct naval humanitarian assistance to the states affected by the natural disaster (Weisman 2004). At the same time, the United States was embroiled in national debates over immigration, post-9/11 security concerns, and its military operations in Iraq and Afghanistan, each of which involved a strong focus on the preservation of national (traditional) security. The United States did not give up its national security interests to pursue a human security approach in response to the earthquake and tsunami, but by the same token human security efforts were not completely eclipsed during a time of intense national focus on traditional security concerns.

Human Security in Armed Conflict and Durable Human Security

A human security approach can apply to situations involving armed conflict as well as to longer-term "peacetime" concerns. We call these *human security in armed conflict* and *durable human security*, in keeping with the Human Development Report's consideration that true human security establishes protection from both sudden and chronic threats. In January 2001 the UN established the Commission on Human Security, and in May 2003 the commission's co-chairs, Sadako Ogata and Amartya Sen, released *Human Security Now*, a report clarifying the facets of human security and steps the international community should take to ensure freedom from want and freedom from fear for all people (Commission on Human Security 2003, iv). The report defines *human security* as the protection of "the vital core of all human lives in ways that enhance human freedoms and human fulfillment" (Commission on Human Security 2003, 4). This human security approach entails the protection of freedoms, protection from severe and chronic threats, and empowerment through support for individual strengths and goals. The report does not, however, provide a specific list of protections and capabilities that constitute human security.

Paragraph 143 of United Nations General Assembly Resolution 60/1 (otherwise known as the 2005 World Summit Outcome document) articulates a similarly broad view of human security: "We stress the right of people to live in freedom and dignity, free from poverty and despair. We recognize that all individuals, in particular vulnerable people, are entitled to freedom from fear and freedom from want, with an equal opportunity to enjoy all their rights and fully develop their human potential. To this end, we commit ourselves to discussing and defining the notion of human security in the General Assembly" (United Nations General Assembly 2005, 31). We adopt this broad view of human security and seek to refine it through discussion of responsibility for security provision and the connection between insecurity and harmful norms or flawed or failed institutions.

What one person in one society considers vital or important to achieving human security differs from what someone else in another context might consider essential to that aim. A human security approach works best when it is dynamic, adapting to the political, social, economic, environmental, and other constraints and opportunities in a particular situation. Although devising universally applicable policies and programs is thus difficult—or nearly impossible—using a true human security approach ensures that all efforts seeking to protect and empower the individual share a common fundamental characteristic: placement of the individual's safety, dignity, and opportunities at the center of any effort.

Armed conflict requires a different set of protections and considerations for individuals than does peacetime, given the immediate physical and existential risks associated with active hostilities. Human insecurity in armed conflict results from the breakdown of positive norms and functional institutions, eroding or eliminating the protections and rights that individuals and their communities may have enjoyed in peacetime (or worsening the situation of groups already insecure or marginalized prior to conflict). A human security approach to conflict-related threats may involve the following general protections, as well as others unique to the context of the conflict:

- provision of medical care to all parties and the protection of medical staff
- protection, basic necessities, and shelter for individuals and groups displaced by the fighting
- international or regional assistance with the protection of civilians from hostilities (humanitarian intervention)
- international or regional assistance with mediation and peace negotiations
- reconstruction of infrastructure and services after the conflict
- and transitional justice processes and mechanisms to restore order and peace and to prevent the outbreak of violence in the future.

Put more simply, a human security approach to armed conflict seeks to treat the wounded and dying, protect innocent bystanders from physical harm, and help move from conflict to peaceful normalcy and good governance as efficiently and effectively as possible. Section II addresses these protections and processes in detail.

Durable human security deals with longer-term—or chronic—threats and seeks to establish stable societies that equally respect the rights and freedoms of all individuals and groups. A durable human security approach, like human security in armed conflict, prioritizes the individual and group while working toward the ultimate goal of creating stability in states, regions, and the global system. A lack of durable human security is the result of harmful societal norms—including systematic discrimination and inequality—and institutions that lack the capacity or mandate to protect all individuals. When norms and institutions prioritize some individuals and communities and place others at a disadvantage, durable human security is threatened. Still, it is important to remember that for an issue to rise to the level of a human *security* concern, the problem should be systematic or widespread, arising from some flaw in overall governance.

Threats to durable human security may include:

- poverty and income inequality
- health crises (crucially, but not limited to, the outbreak of contagious diseases)
- gender, racial, ethnic, or social inequality and discrimination against people on the basis of their sex, gender, sexual orientation, race, ethnicity, nationality, religion, or other facets of their identity
- climate change
- and food insecurity (including famine, malnutrition, and undernutrition).

Although threats to durable human security may not kill an individual immediately—as an attack in a war zone might—in the long run they can devastate individuals, families, society, the state, and the global system. Durable human security seeks to make life better for everyone, with the ultimate effect of making states more stable and peaceful.

Section III discusses the major threats to durable human security and efforts to mitigate them; specifically, chapter 8 examines the connections between human security in armed conflict and durable human security. These security threats are not simply normative or moral concerns; they can have a long-term effect on states' domestic stability and foreign policy successes. A shrewd policy maker will see the strategic value in bolstering human security.

The Human Security Approach and Its Challenges

New norms and approaches to solving the world's problems are shaped by the global political context of the time, and human security is no exception. The concept of human security was introduced during a time of global upheaval: the changing character of war from interstate to predominantly intrastate conflicts, the expanded role and increased legitimacy of the UN, and greater global consideration of human rights laid the foundation for a new approach to security. Although the emergence of a human security norm and the application of a human security approach in practice does not signal states' abandonment of their self-interests, efforts have been made by states, the UN, organizations, and advocacy networks to place individuals at the center of policies, aid programs, and armed interventions.

The human security approach to security is not a cure-all for the world's problems, of course, and remains the subject of much debate. One common critique is that, in attempting to account for a wide range of security threats, the human security approach becomes unwieldy; if a concept includes everything, it means nothing (Paris 2001). Furthermore—and quite troubling from a practical policy-making and humanitarian perspective—if the concept of human security expands beyond the context of armed conflict and what we call *durable human security threats* are met with militarized policy solutions, then the discussion of human security could risk inviting more armed interventions to counteract civil- and human rights problems (Grayson 2003; Liotta 2002; MacFarlane and Khong 2006). Ultimately, this could leave people at greater risk for harm. On the other hand, traditional security-focused entities, like state armed forces and foreign policy agencies, are already beginning to incorporate ideas central to human security into their strategies and operations (Reveron and Mahoney-Norris 2011). Adding to the discussion, some scholars insist that recognizing the importance of freedom from want—or durable human security—is essential to ensuring overall human security and perhaps even addressing the root causes of conflict (Hanlon and Christie 2016).

The debate over human security—and especially over the kinds of threats and challenges that should be considered human security threats—is still unfolding. We take the broad view of human security, including both insecurity in armed conflict and threats to well-being in times of relative peace. By examining the ways in which various issues and threats can become human security issues and how they in turn affect national and global security, we aim to foster critical thinking about the notion of security in general as well as improved understanding of the utility of the concept of human security more specifically.

DISCUSSION QUESTIONS

1. Would the human security norm have emerged without the increase in intrastate wars?
2. What are the advantages and disadvantages of an expanded role for the UN in implementing human security policies?
3. How does a human development approach differ from a traditional development approach?
4. How do your human rights shape your daily life?
5. Durable human security deals with longer-term, or chronic, threats. What are the most pressing threats to durable human security in your community?
6. The concept of human security, as we understand it today, took shape in the 1990s and early 2000s, as discussed throughout this chapter. Given what you now know about human security and the context in which the human security norm emerged, consider each of the following time periods and identify the barriers to human security in each context:

   a. the interwar period, 1918–1939
   b. and the Cold War, 1947–1991.

Chapter 3

Human Security Actors

Learning Objectives

This chapter will enable readers to

1. identify types and examples of actors who contribute to the provision of human security
2. identify types and examples of actors who degrade human security
3. understand conditions in which human security policy gets implemented
4. and recognize and discuss the Millennium Development Goals (MDGs), Sustainable Development Goals (SDGs), and their role in fostering human security.

Up to this point we have discussed the political and historical context in which human security developed as a normative challenge to traditional understandings of security. The articulation of any norm, however, does not have much significance until it is reflected in practice; this refers to specifically designated actors and actions that implement the expected behavior associated with that norm. Thus human security needs to be understood in the context of those actors with the capabilities to implement the human security approach. This chapter therefore offers readers an overview of the types of actors that provide or degrade human security. Furthermore this chapter explores the implementation of the human security approach by key actors, the obstacles and threats to human security posed by certain types of actors, and the mechanisms by which human security policy can be implemented.

In comparison with national and global security, the range of actors and mechanisms involved in the provision of human security is wider and more diverse. The diversity of actors and mechanisms through which human security can be established makes this approach to security less concrete and more complex than the other two security approaches. The wide range of actors and mechanisms, however, serves to bring previously silenced voices into the discussion of individual needs and wants if discussions surrounding new initiatives and policies are sufficiently inclusive.

That said, we should not ignore those actors who degrade human security, whether as a direct strategy or an unintended consequence of their actions. The range of actors contributing to insecurity contains many similarities when we look at the different approaches to security, but, as with a consideration of human security providers, the range of actors that may pose human security threats expands beyond those that would normally be considered threats to state or global security and stability.

Human security is neither completely independent of nor seamlessly integrated into national or global security. To achieve human security, states must be secure, and the international system should be stable. We contend that this statement is also true in reverse: that state and global security benefit from the realization of human security and that stability at the individual level flows up to the national and international levels. The question of how best to provide human security, however, is a difficult one to answer. There are competing perspectives on security, the responsibility for providing it, and who should benefit from security provision.

SECURITY PROVIDERS

The focus or purpose of security provision differs depending on what is meant to be protected. The most common way to think about security is the protection of the state through its national security apparatus; it is this approach that receives the vast majority of material outlays. In 2020 the total world military expenditure was just under $2 trillion (SIPRI 2021). Because of the dominance of state security approaches, both global security and human security approaches have been heavily reliant on the same actors to engage in multiple forms of security. The three approaches to security, then, involve different actors tasked with responsibility for security provision and prioritize different beneficiaries of security efforts. This section briefly discusses the types of actors that provide for national and global security before introducing the broad range of actors involved in human security provision. (See table 3.1 for a list of types of security providers.)

Table 3.1. Security Approaches, Goals, and Providers

Security Approach	Purpose of Security Provision	Main Security Providers
National Security	To protect the state from external threats and internal instability	State armed forces State intelligence agencies Local- and state-level law-enforcement agencies State border-protection agencies Foreign service and diplomatic corps Multilateral collective security agreements and alliances
Global Security	To protect the stability of the system of states	Stable states Strong states in favor of the status quo Intergovernmental organizations (IGOs) Regional blocs and organizations International law, treaties, and agreements *Multilateral collective security agreements* Multilateral military and peacekeeping mechanisms
Human Security	To protect individuals and their communities from threats to their well-being and physical security	*Stable states* *State armed forces* *State intelligence agencies* *Local- and state-level law-enforcement agencies* *State border-protection agencies* *Foreign service and diplomatic corps* *Multilateral collective security agreements* *Multilateral military and peacekeeping mechanisms* *Strong states in favor of the status quo* *Intergovernmental organizations (IGOs)* *Regional blocs and organizations* *International law, treaties, and agreements* Nongovernmental organizations (NGOs)—international NGOs and local NGOs Social movements and advocacy networks Civil society Local community organizations Individuals

National Security Providers

Providers of state or national security are united in their shared goal of keeping the state protected from external threats and internal instability. Since the purpose of national security is to ensure that the state is safe from external threats and internal challenges to the government's stability, efforts to keep the state secure focus squarely on maintaining the state's borders and ability to govern its territory. This prioritization means that the state will pursue policies aimed at keeping in check its external and internal challengers—whether real or imagined. Thus national security is pursued primarily through the state's armed forces, as well as security-focused agencies.

The state's armed forces serve the dual function of deterring or responding to external threats—threats of harm from other states or nonstate actors—and maintaining internal order if the state's stability is threatened by violent challengers from within the state, such as insurgents or revolutionary movements. Intelligence and law enforcement agencies can detect and respond to potential threats from within and outside the state. Border protection agencies serve the function of maintaining control of the flow of people and goods at the state's territorial borders. Beyond military and police security providers, a state's foreign service agencies and diplomatic corps help manage the state's position in the world, maintain its alliances, protect its interests, and project its values. During crises, a state's diplomatic corps often works to reach an optimal outcome without having to resort to military force. Similarly, collective security agreements, alliances, and multilateral organizations help states band together with allies and other states with similar goals to strengthen their capacity to respond to external threats—perhaps from an adversary with superior military capability—and provide reassurance of assistance if a conflict or crisis should arise.

A secure state can benefit individuals and communities. Without an explicit focus on a human security norm, however, the human security benefits of state security provision are by-products or externalities, not the direct objectives, of national security providers. Furthermore, the human and national security approaches can be in conflict, especially in times of crisis when the state responds to perceived or actual threats by restricting human and civil rights or targeting specific communities within the domestic population or foreign populations. In states where human rights are routinely disregarded and where the population has little recourse to address grievances with the state, achieving human security in its broad sense is difficult, if not impossible. As chapters 2 and 4 discuss, human rights are central to human security, and any attempt by the state to secure itself through human rights restrictions—even temporary restrictive measures—places the national security approach at odds with the human security approach.

Global Security Providers

The global security approach is a logical extension of the national or state security approach, but its emphasis is on the stability of the state-based international system. In a world characterized by interdependent states and complex, borderless threats like transnational terrorism, cyberattacks, and climate change, it is difficult for states to consider their security interests and threats in isolation from the wider world. Global security's central focus is on maintaining international order, containing crises and armed conflicts so that they do not threaten overall peace and stability, and maintaining a relatively stable balance of power among states.

Many of the security providers that contribute to state security also contribute to global security, because the existence of stable states ensures the overall stability of the international system. Stable states are states that have achieved national or state security and are not threatened by major crises like widespread famine, insurgency or armed conflict, epidemic disease, or economic collapse. Along with state stability, global security is well protected when the most powerful states in the system are generally in favor of the status quo. If great powers perceive that their state security and interests are well served by the **international order**—the political, economic, and normative arrangements in the international system—and have no pressing interest in changing the structure of global politics, then they will work to maintain international order and stability—or they will simply abstain from not threatening it. If, however, at least one great power views the international order as unbeneficial to their interests, or if a state or group of states pursues aggressive or expansionist policies that threaten that order, then global security will decrease. It is important to note here that the way in which the post–World War II international order was established is not universally perceived as the most just and equitable way to organize the world, especially given that postcolonial states did not consent to this approach to order.

Security providers within the global security approach, then, are the states and organizations or arrangements meant to promote and protect stability in the international system. In addition to stable states, the types of actors that provide global security include regional blocs, **intergovernmental organizations (IGOs)**, international law and agreements, multilateral collective security arrangements, and multilateral military and peacekeeping mechanisms. **Regional blocs** or groupings—including the European Union (EU), Association of Southeast Asian Nations (ASEAN), the African Union (AU), the Cooperation Council for the Arab States of the Gulf (or the Gulf Cooperation Council, GCC) and the Organization of American States (OAS)—are formal institutions that reduce barriers to economic and political cooperation. These arrangements promote regional stability, and in turn global stability, by facilitating discussions, transparency, interdependence, and the development of shared norms among states. IGOs similarly provide member states with forums for discussion and resource sharing, avenues for communication and transparency about goals and planned policies or military actions, and mechanisms for socialization and development of new norms. IGOs may be global in nature (as in the case of the United Nations and its agencies), or membership may be limited to states with similar political, economic, or military interests and identities (as with the Organisation for Economic Co-operation and Development [OECD], the Group of 7 [G7], or the Group of 20 [G20]).

Multilateral collective security agreements or organizations function as both coordination and socialization forums—not unlike IGOs or regional blocs—and as a means of deterring external attacks on member states. Collective security agreements, like NATO, are based on member states' commitment to defend one another, to respond to any attack on any member state as an attack on all member states. By pledging to share military resources, the weaker states gain protection from the stronger members and the stronger members expand their influence and capacity. Assuming the deterrent effect of collective security works as intended, and member states themselves comply with international norms and laws prohibiting aggression, these arrangements promote global stability by decreasing the likelihood of armed conflict. Multilateral military and peacekeeping operations seek to protect global security by responding to situations that threaten to upset regional or international stability or violate accepted international norms. Multilateral military and peacekeeping mechanisms involve the collaboration of many states with a shared goal of restoring peace in a conflict-affected region with the larger goal of maintaining international stability. These operations are usually authorized by, and work under the supervision of, the UN, although some involve coordination between the UN and NATO. (See chapters 5, 6, and 7 for in-depth discussion of humanitarian intervention, peacekeeping, and peacebuilding.)

Finally, international law, treaties, and agreements foster global security by placing limitations on what states can and cannot do without fear of repercussion from other states or IGOs. International law includes prohibitions on aggression or expansion (states cannot legally start wars without just cause, for revenge, or to acquire more territory or resources), certain types of weapons (antipersonnel land mines and chemical weapons are considered unacceptable), and human rights violations, among other things. These accepted rules promote global stability by providing states with reasonable expectations about other states' behavior and incentives for complying with the international community's expectations.

Overall, global security and stability require a careful balance of diplomacy, resource sharing, transparency, and cooperation. In the post–World

War II international order, much of this work has been done through the UN and member states' interactions in UN forums. The key to global security and the focus of security providers is to protect the international system from the kinds of shocks that result from widespread crises and armed conflict.

Human Security Providers

The question of who provides human security is at the heart of this book. As table 3.1 demonstrates (above), the same actors that provide state and global security are also the ones most often called on to provide human security—and they often do. When the actors discussed in the previous two sections either reorient their strategies and operations to account for human security threats and needs, or when human security is supported as a result of the provision of state or global security, then we can consider these actors to be human security providers as well.

It is important to revisit the importance of the state in the provision of human security once again, as the stable state—at least within the construct of the current international system—is *the* actor without which human security cannot be achieved. As noted previously, one of the state's primary functions is to protect against external threats and internal instability. The state security approach seeks to maintain the state's ability to govern its territory and to survive as a political entity. This continued stability and protection from external harm creates a situation that can be conducive to human security, provided the state does not infringe upon human rights and the security of individuals and communities in its pursuit of national security. In providing for the common defense and establishing and maintaining institutions and norms that make the state secure *and* recognize the rights, freedoms, and needs of individual people, the state forms the foundation for human security.

UN General Assembly Resolution 66/290 (2012, 2) makes the role of the state explicit: "Human security does not replace State security"; indeed, "governments retain the primary role and responsibility for ensuring the survival, livelihood and dignity of their citizens." When it not only provides the common defense of the population from threats and instability but also establishes social safety nets to protect against threats to durable human security and maintains institutions and norms that foster equal opportunities and fulfillment of human and civil rights, the state is the most important provider of human security. It can also be the most formidable threat to human security, as we discuss later in this chapter.

Alongside—or in the absence of—the state as security provider, several other types of actors contribute to human security. An international order that is stable but in which millions of people suffer from extreme food insecurity, poverty, and marginalization may be acceptable from a national or global security perspective but unacceptable from a human security perspective. When the national and global security providers discussed previously ignore these conditions, others step in to either address them directly or to put pressure on those providers to do so themselves. In the remainder of this section, we turn to these other human security providers whose work does not always immediately register in considerations of state and global security.

Chapters 1 and 2 explored the United Nations' role at the epicenter of the development of human security as a concept. Through the 1994 Human Development Report and continued discussions of the importance of recognizing the roles and needs of individuals and specific groups in peace, security, and development, the UN became a key incubator of the concept of human security (MacFarlane and Khong 2006). IGOs like the UN provide states with a framework for coordination and communication that promotes global stability and, for many states, national security; its role in the conceptual development of human security and implementation of programs that promote human security make the UN a key human security provider as well. This is particularly notable when we look at the many agencies and units within the UN system that are tasked with human security–related missions.

The UN Trust Fund for Human Security (UNTFHS) finances UN programs that address human security issues in armed conflict and relative peacetime; in supporting initiatives to rebuild conflict-affected regions, reduce extreme poverty, and provide assistance after natural disasters strike (to name only three of the many efforts), UNTFHS takes a broad view of human security—one that is consistent with the UN's focus on both freedom from fear and freedom from want. The Human Security Unit (HSU), which manages the UNTFHS, was established in May 2004 and works with regional IGOs, nongovernmental organizations, academics, and civil society to develop tools and programs that implement human security. The HSU, crucially, takes General Assembly and Security Council resolutions and translates them into programs around the world.

To coordinate the human security efforts of diverse UN entities and outside experts, the HSU supports the Inter-Agency Working Group on Human Security (IAWGHS), which began meeting in October 2014. The IAWGHS helped the HSU develop a Framework for Cooperation to ensure system-wide application of the human security approach. Released in September 2015, the framework ties the human security approach to the central mission of the UN, envisions a more comprehensive approach to human security, and lays out a shared understanding of human security based on General Assembly Resolution 66/290. The Framework for Cooperation notes that "the human security approach can contribute to and strengthen the work of the United Nations system," underscoring the complementary nature of the three approaches to security and the importance of human security for the realization of broader global political objectives (United Nations Human Security Unit 2015, 5). For example, in 2021 UNTFHS worked closely with the Arab League, the International Organization for Migration (IOM), and the United Nations Economic and Social Commission for Western Asia (ESCWA) to study how human security approaches could be used to help conflict-affected countries in the Arab region attain Sustainable Development Goals (SDGs).

After years of languishing at the UN level, recent global crises stemming from conflict-induced migration and the COVID-19 pandemic have refocused attention at the UN on the human security approach. In June 2021 the Group of Friends of Human Security was relaunched in an effort to better implement human security–focused policies that address a wide array of human security challenges. Their initial meeting included sixty-three member states as well as a keynote address from Secretary-General António Guterres. This is notable, as past secretaries-general have gone out of their way to avoid using the term *human security* in their official discourse (Martin and Owen 2010).

Outside of the HSU but within the UN system, agencies such as UNDP, the Office for the Coordination of Humanitarian Affairs (OCHA), the Office of the UN High Commissioner for Refugees (UNHCR), the World Food Programme (WFP), the Food and Agriculture Organization (FAO), UN Action against Sexual Violence in Conflict (UN Action), UN Women, UN Department of Peacekeeping Operations (UNDPKO), and the World Health Organization (WHO) are several of the agencies and units within the UN system that undertake work relevant to the human security approach. Each of these offices and agencies is focused on a specific set of issues related to the UN's more general mission of maintaining international peace and security.

For example, as we will discuss in greater depth in chapter 6, several recent UN peacekeeping operations have been assigned specific civilian protection mandates, placing UNDPKO in a position to consider human security in conflict zones. The WHO, as we will discuss in chapter 9, helps states coordinate their responses to communicable disease outbreaks and other threats to individual health and well-being, positioning WHO's work within the human security approach. Separately, each agency or unit possesses a wealth of information on its set of issues and maintains networks of contacts within and outside of the UN system. When entities with a connection to human security combine their capabilities in crosscutting efforts, they have the potential to implement comprehensive programs and provide effective tools to respond to the complex security issues that arise today.

Nongovernmental organizations are another group of important human security actors. NGOs are organizations that focus on a particular issue or set of issues and operate independently of states and IGOs. These organizations usually function on a not-for-profit basis and depend on support from donors, which may include individuals, corporations, other organizations, states (often through funds designated for foreign aid or domestic social programs), and IGOs. The International Committee of the Red Cross (ICRC) is a prominent NGO with a long history of providing humanitarian assistance in armed conflicts and natural disasters and maintaining political neutrality.

Médecins Sans Frontières (MSF) too sends medical personnel to conflict zones, areas suffering from humanitarian crises, and regions affected by natural disaster to provide medical care; but MSF is also known for its activist stance and history of speaking out against injustice. For example, in May 2017 the head of MSF Italy criticized G7 leaders for framing the displacement crisis as a national security issue rather than a humanitarian one (Médecins Sans Frontières 2017). In 2015 MSF also condemned Ukrainian separatists in Luhans'k who refused MSF permission to access the region. The organization has also loudly condemned those who have targeted and bombed medical facilities.

Human Rights Watch (HRW) and Amnesty International (AI) monitor human rights violations and spread global awareness of systematic abuses and grave insecurity to generate political, economic, and social pressure for change. Some NGOs focus on particular groups of people, like Save the Children (focused on children's well-being and security) or Promundo (focused on improving gender justice and equality through engagement with men and boys). NGOs often work in tandem with other NGOs, IGOs, states, international financial institutions, corporations, and civil society to achieve common goals and reach larger populations.

Local participation in human security initiatives is especially important, given in-country NGOs' and local civil society groups' familiarity with the security needs, cultural considerations, political situation, and other factors relevant to human security provision. Providing human security should not necessarily happen from the top (international level) down, as it is easy to envision when we consider the central role of the UN in human security discussions. Instead, the human security approach should involve collaboration between security providers at all levels, engaging the insights and preferences of the individuals whose security is at stake. Research on peacebuilding has demonstrated that local populations are skeptical of outside actors' efforts to impose values or institutions, especially when they find their concerns have not been taken into account. This type of security initiative without collaboration can lead to flawed or failed programs and sustained insecurity (Autesserre 2014). Human security efforts function most efficiently and effectively when local stakeholders have a voice in decision-making and program implementation; individuals and communities must perceive efforts as legitimate for human security initiatives to work, and local groups know what will resonate and work best in their communities.

When different types of human security providers, ranging from the local to international levels, work together with a focus on a specific issue and a shared goal, they form a transnational advocacy network (see chapter 1). TANs may include actors at all levels of the international system, including locally and internationally focused NGOs, IGOs, sympathetic states, businesses and other donors, influential individuals (e.g., celebrities, former heads of state, Nobel laureates, or currently serving policy makers), and civil society groups (e.g., campus organizations, professional associations, or clubs). Networks amplify the concerns of local NGOs or civil society groups working to change situations of insecurity or to stop human rights violations; by connecting local actors with international resources, visibility, and the political leverage of IGOs and states, TANs place pressure on the state or other actor responsible for creating the problem or threat (Keck and Sikkink 1998). By connecting multiple human security providers around a single issue or set of connected issues, TANs enable organizations, states, and other entities to share expertise and resources, ideally providing a more comprehensive and effective response to a human security problem.

Advocacy networks have formed around a multitude of issues, including (but not limited to) environmental protection and sustainability, the nonproliferation and limitations on certain types of weapons, women's rights, the rights of children in war, Indigenous persons' rights, and global hunger. Not all issues or cases will generate a response from a relevant transnational advocacy network. NGOs must be mindful of their limited resources, ability to assist in a given situation or crisis, and donors' preferences (Carpenter 2007). When the most reputable and influential NGOs consider an issue or particular case deserving of attention, other NGOs and human security providers in the TAN will follow suit; these NGOs are considered the "gatekeepers" of transnational advocacy (Carpenter 2011).

IGOs are constrained by their member states' politics and preferences and the global political environment, although IGOs likewise tend to develop their own bureaucracies and practices and can place constraints on their member states (Barnett and Finnemore 2004). The UN's limited ability to respond to human rights violations during the Cold War is a prime example of the limitations imposed on IGOs by powerful member states and the structure of the international system.

Another factor that determines the global response to a particular problem is public attention (or lack thereof): public outcry can be fickle, limited to certain areas of the world, and short-lived. Public attention can shape states' willingness to address an issue, donors' interest in an issue, and NGOs' capacity (especially in terms of funding) to respond to an issue. Public recognition of a problem is also shaped by the actions of states, NGOs, and IGOs and the extent to which those actors consider an issue to be a problem, leading to a virtuous circle or vicious cycle of recognition or nonrecognition. TANs gain momentum when global public opinion supports action, and public recognition is similarly bolstered by the actions of TANs.

Human security exists when individuals and communities are safe from threats to their physical security and long-term well-being through the support of durable norms and institutions. In evaluating the need for collaboration among human security actors, the HSU's Framework for Cooperation notes "there is growing acknowledgement that most of today's development or humanitarian challenges are the confluence of multiple factors that are interconnected and mutually reinforcing, and as such require greater integration of activities across the United Nations system" (United Nations Human Security Unit 2015, 3–4). We can apply this call for action and integration to the broader range of human security providers, both within and outside of the UN system. The human security approach has the potential to make security practice more inclusive, to spread out the burden of security provision across multiple types of actors, and to bring new ideas and experiences to the table for more effective and comprehensive policy making in response to complex twenty-first-century threats.

This type of security provision requires effective governance at the level of the state, effective state institutions, and social norms conducive to the realization of freedom from fear and freedom from want. While the focus of human security is the individual—and, by extension, the community—the primary onus to provide this security remains with the state. Where the state is unable or unwilling to fulfill this responsibility, the wide range of human security actors discussed here work to fill in gaps in capacity or persuade the state to change. Human security cannot exist where human rights are routinely violated, where the state is fragile or failing, where systematic discrimination and inequality (of any form) are tolerated or promoted by the state's institutions and norms, where opportunities for self-sufficiency and well-being are few or limited to particular social groups, or where the threat of violence is pervasive. It requires all relevant actors to operate as if a human security norm exists and matters, factoring in the effects of policy decisions and security provision on individuals and communities.

That said, many communities, having experienced years of neglect or direct persecution by the state, are wary of any state efforts to expand its capacity regardless of the stated purpose. Given the current structure of the international system, a stable state is a necessary but not a sufficient condition for achieving human security. The key challenge—or opportunity—is to promote communication and collaboration among human security providers with the communities they purport to serve and to expand the discussion of security needs and provision to all relevant stakeholders.

RESPONDING TO THREATS TO HUMAN SECURITY

Many of the key providers of state and global security also function as human security providers. By that same token, the actors and phenomena that degrade state and global security also threaten human security; human security is jeopardized when the state is fragile, failing, embroiled in armed conflict, or otherwise seriously threatened. The actors and phenomena that challenge state and global security affect human security differently or more immediately, although the overall effect of decreased state or global security is similar in the long run. For example, nonstate armed groups may extract resources from communities, exploit or abuse civilians in armed conflict, or target individuals in terrorist attacks. These actors ultimately seek to destabilize the state, but they do so through direct harm to individuals and communities. Like the people and groups that constitute threats, the phenomena that challenge state and global security can also affect human security first; this point is clearest when considering pandemic disease (the effects of which devastate individuals, families, and communities before jeopardizing the security of the state or international community), climate change (see chapters 11 and 12 for discussions of famine and climate refugees, respectively), and financial crises (in which individuals stand to lose their jobs, homes, and self-sufficiency). Precisely because human security may be affected before state and global security are challenged, the human security approach accounts for a wider range of threats to security. This approach requires that practitioners, policy makers, and researchers widen their understanding of what constitutes a security threat; the linkages between human, state, and global security—as explored in sections II and III—justify the conceptual complexity.

It is important to note here that some of the key providers of state and global security may also have the effect of degrading human security. Even though human, state, and global security can be synchronous much of the time, there are clear points of conflict between the approaches. We can look at cases of ethnic cleansing and genocide—in Germany and occupied territories before and during World War II, in Bosnia and Kosovo in the 1990s, in Rwanda in 1994, and in Sudan and South Sudan in the 2000s—to see how a state can quickly turn its means of protection (military, law enforcement, intelligence agencies, and even communications infrastructure) against segments of its population. Genocidal campaigns begin with the language of threats, in which a group is cast as the enemy, an other, and a threat to the state or to other groups within the state. Violence by the state can also be directed against political opponents. The purges of perceived political enemies by Stalin in the Soviet Union and Mao in China left millions of people dead or in prison. Military dictatorships throughout the world have been responsible for disappearances, extrajudicial killings, torture, and politically motivated arrests. These examples are, of course, cases of extreme human insecurity.

We can also look at more common threats to human security that exist within the context of relatively secure states and a stable international system. Food insecurity is one such example; episodic or chronic food insecurity can affect individuals and communities within wealthy, developed states as well as in fragile states. Food insecurity can result from policy failures that create the conditions for famine, from strategic starvation in which belligerents withhold food supplies from a population, or from insufficient social safety nets (see chapter 12 for a full discussion of food security). If the state's institutions and social norms are insufficient to protect individuals from—or directly create threats to—their physical safety and well-being, then human and state security are in conflict. Similarly, if the state lacks the capacity to provide for the physical safety and well-being of its population (including access to vital services, fulfillment of human rights, and enjoyment of equal opportunities), human security is threatened.

The actors and phenomena that threaten human, state, and global security share a common theme: they degrade governance, destabilize institutions, and challenge norms. To achieve human security it is necessary (but, as discussed previously, insufficient) to maintain state and global security. There is a great deal of overlap between the approaches, and accounting for the common threats to each type of security helps to determine the most effective policies and approaches to achieving overall security. Understanding the points of conflict and confluence helps practitioners, policy makers, and researchers craft more effective security initiatives.

This conclusion leads to another question: *What do efforts to improve human security and overcome threats look like in practice?* The next section provides a framework to think through how a milieu of actors with varying visions for a secure world approach policy challenges. We conclude the chapter by exploring the global effort to achieve human development and reduce poverty and associated threats. The Millennium Development Goals and Sustainable Development Goals are two related global initiatives that have brought states, IGOs, NGOs, and communities together to create the conditions for improved well-being.

BOX 3.1. THINK ABOUT IT . . . GLOBAL-LOCAL PARTNERSHIPS AND PERSPECTIVES ON SECURITY

In 2016 the office of the UN High Commissioner for Refugees observed that every minute in 2015 an average of twenty-four people had to flee their homes. By the end of 2015, 65.3 million persons or refugees had been internally displaced, well surpassing the UNHCR's previous all-time high of sixty million displaced, tallied after World War II (Edwards 2016; Zampano, Moloney, and Juan 2015.) (See chapter 5 for additional discussion of internally displaced persons and refugees.) Record displacement calls for vastly increased security provision and humanitarian assistance.

A look at just one arrival point in Europe, the island of Lesbos in Greece, shows the wide range of actors—from individuals through UN agencies—involved in providing assistance to refugees. Between September and November 2015 alone, UNHCR had set up 226 Refugee Housing Units and distributed 77,000 nonfood items through a presence of dozens of UN staff members (United Nations High Commissioner for Refugees 2015). Prominent NGOs like Médecins Sans Frontières and the International Rescue Committee (IRC) provided medical, psychological, and other humanitarian assistance to refugees arriving on the island from war-torn states.

One January 2016 report in *The Guardian* newspaper questioned whether there were too many NGOs operating in Lesbos, with a count of eighty-one organizations at the time. Residents and public officials on the Greek isle expressed both appreciation for the outpouring of help and concern about the lack of coordination between some organizations and local government (Nianias 2016). Individuals too have stepped in to provide assistance on the island by offering translation services, meals, shelter, boats, and other supplies (Gaglias 2016). A diverse set of security providers with different skills, resources, and perspectives has the potential to improve the response to any humanitarian crisis, especially a large-scale crisis like record forced displacement. Still, careful coordination and clear communication among these actors are keys to improving outcomes for the vulnerable.

By August 2016, the number of refugees arriving in Greece decreased with a politically controversial deal made between the European Union and Turkey, which forced refugees arriving in Greece to be returned to Turkey in exchange for the resettlement in Europe of Syrians who had sought asylum in Turkey. The one-for-one deal left refugees in a state of uncertainty amid the new restrictions and diminished global attention to the plight of refugees on Lesbos and other Greek islands and along European migration routes. Tourism in Lesbos also decreased in the wake of the refugee crisis, causing concern about the local economy and threatening the livelihoods of Greek nationals, thus creating another dimension of insecurity (Alderman 2016).

Search the Web for discussion of the refugee crisis in Greece in 2015 and 2016. Pay particular attention in your search to security providers assisting refugees and the responses from different communities in Greece. The United Nations High Commissioner for Refugees (UNCHR), the BBC, *Foreign Policy*, and Amnesty International are just a few of the international agencies, NGOs, news services, and magazines that covered the crisis and offer continued access to coverage of the crisis. The UNHCR is a key source of information on displacement more broadly. In addition, search the Web for public opinion on the 2015–2016 refugee crisis, collected and maintained by think tanks and fact tanks like Pew Research, along with information on public attitudes toward ongoing issues of displacement and migration.

After you have gathered resources to deepen your understanding of the 2015–2016 refugee crisis in Greece, answer the following questions:

1. What are the advantages of the involvement of a diverse set of security providers in a situation like the arrival of hundreds of thousands of refugees on Lesbos? What are the disadvantages of the diversity of security providers?
2. Are there ways in which individuals, NGOs, local governments, national governments, and intergovernmental organizations (like the UN) can better coordinate to ensure more comprehensive security provision for refugees? How might efforts improve?
3. How do differing national public opinions regarding refugees affect the viability of a local, national, or global effort to provide human security?
4. According to the statist security perspective, which actor or actors are responsible for providing security to refugees? How might a statist security perspective have viewed the effect on the local economy in Lesbos?

THE THREE POLICY BOXES:
PROBLEM, POLICY, AND OUTCOME

At this point it is helpful to examine how these actors interject themselves into the policy processes that promote human security. Different actors have different motivations for adopting or rejecting a human security approach. We propose that motivations are at least partly driven by two factors: (1) one's understanding of how the world is and (2) one's desires for how the world should be. To illustrate this, we use three boxes to help visualize how decisions about policy approaches are contingent on how these two frames are interpreted and negotiated between multiple actors (see figure 3.1).

Key to developing any policy is trying to understand the world in which that policy will be implemented—or Box 1, Perception of the Problem. The problem is that each of us is motivated by underlying sets of biases and worldviews that may or may not entirely reflect reality. These worldviews are simplified into a set of heuristics that enable us to better process the complex world that we live in. At the same time, others that share the policy world with us have other biases and worldviews that could contradict our own. Because of the inherent interdependent nature of policy making, even if one actor holds a perfect understanding of reality, they may still not find policy success if other relevant stakeholders hold a fundamentally different worldview. How policy makers perceive and construct the environment they will be operating in affects the types of policy choices that will be made. Incorrect assumptions about the world can lead to perverse and counterproductive policy choices.

For example, in many introductory international relations courses, students are introduced to the Prisoner's Dilemma—a very basic game theory problem designed to demonstrate the complexities of interdependent decision-making in which, under certain very specific conditions, players may be incentivized to make choices that lead to suboptimal outcomes. The dilemma is set up this way: Two incarcerated prisoners are isolated from one another and pressured to inform on each other. If one prisoner informs on the other but the other refuses to speak, the informer will be set free but the one who remains silent

Figure 3.1. The Three Policy Boxes

will serve three years. If they betray each other, they each serve two years. If they both remain silent, they both serve one year (on a lesser charge). The solution is that they both betray each other (defect), because this will result in the better outcome for each individually, regardless of what the other chooses to do. This solution is, of course, a suboptimal outcome, since they would have only served one year and thus been collectively better off if they had both stayed silent (cooperated). The risk of staying silent while the other defects is—at least according to its mathematical solution—too great a risk.

Unfortunately, the Prisoner's Dilemma is too often understood as not simply an easily solvable game for students being introduced to game theory but as the actual state of the world. Believing that the world works as a Prisoner's Dilemma has obvious ramifications, foremost an inclination to defect—an artificial conclusion derived entirely from how the Prisoner's Dilemma is taught. However, if a situation is, in fact, not a Prisoner's Dilemma, then the inclination to defect would lead to suboptimal outcomes.

The second part of the framework involves each actor's aspirations for how the world should be (Box 3, Ideal Outcomes). Policy making is concerned with outcomes, and so a clear articulation of desired outcomes is key. Desired outcomes may be highly aspirational and abstract in their details (i.e., world peace) or very specific (i.e., reducing the number of people living in poverty by half). Just as perceptions of the world vary, so do the many different desired outcomes vary from the myriad actors trying to insert their voices into the policy process. Finding acceptable common ground between actors with fundamentally different visions of an ideal world is the crux of the policy world.

In addition, each actor—particularly state actors—may hold several self-contradicting desired outcomes within different policy arenas. This may be especially pronounced when one more abstract aspiration competes with an aspiration that has more immediate and tangibly felt effects. For instance, a state may hope that human security is achieved but may also want cheap consumer goods for its citizens that can only be achieved through exploitative labor practices that are practiced in other states. In such a case, it is common to see policies aimed at the abstract aspiration—in this case, human security—become subordinate to the more tangible aspiration—cheap consumer goods.

Box 2, Policy Options, is where actors take their understanding of their world as it is and negotiate the actions that will hopefully lead to their desired outcome. It is in this space that interdependent actors negotiate over policy. Many advocates of human security occupy this space to pressure states, IGOs, multinational corporations (MNCs), and other powerful actors to adopt policies that bring the world closer to their ideal vision. Policy action is also guided by principle, meaning that certain actors will refuse on principle to adopt policies that would require them to act in a way that violates their behavioral values. If an ideal outcome is only attainable by nonideal means, then it is unlikely that that action will be adopted. In fact, at least in the short run, it may lead to a reconceptualization of the problem in the first place. For instance, if addressing global climate change means higher amounts of government regulation of industry, some policy makers may find it more useful to deny that climate change exists than to adopt policies that violate a principled belief in minimal government regulation.

As we evaluate the human security approach throughout this book, we will revisit these three boxes to explore how and why action on human security can be thwarted. It also helps us better understand why actors that profess a human security ideal might not be able to successfully implement policies that reach that ideal. This process is engaged during the creation of Millennium Development Goals (MDGs) and Sustainable Development Goals (SDGs), which we explore in the next section.

EXPLORING GLOBAL COLLABORATION AND EVOLVING GOALS: THE MDGs AND SDGs

As we discussed in chapter 2, global politics shifted significantly with the changing nature of war, the UN's expanded role in international affairs, and increased recognition of human rights after the end of the Cold War. In the aftermath, with the unevenness of global development so evident, conditions were conducive to pursuing global governance related to development, human rights, and protection of marginalized or underrepresented individuals and communities. One such governance effort involved setting long-term development goals with a focus on human rights and needs. In 2000 the **Millennium Development Goals (MDGs)**—eight global human development goals with a target date of 2015—focused UN member states' and international organizations' efforts on fostering development through attention to hunger, health, gender inequality, education, and other durable human security issues. Table 3.2 enumerates the eight MDGs, which gained the support of 191 UN member states and 22 international organizations.

The MDGs arose from broader considerations of the UN's role in the twenty-first century and how UN agencies and member states might go about fulfilling the UN's central mission of maintaining peace and security in the world. In August 2000, the "Report of the Panel on United Nations Peace Operations"—otherwise known as the Brahimi report—disclosed the shortcomings of and challenges facing UN-led peace operations and suggested improvements. Specifically highlighted were the UN's critical failures to respond to genocide in Rwanda and the massacre of civilians in Srebrenica in the 1990s. The Brahimi report called for stronger commitments from mem-

Table 3.2. The MDGs and SDGs, side by side

Millennium Development Goals, 2000–2015	Sustainable Development Goals, 2015–2030
MDG 1: Eradicate extreme poverty and hunger.	SDG 1: End poverty in all its forms, everywhere.
MDG 2: Achieve universal primary education.	SDG 2: End hunger, achieve food security, and improved nutrition and promote sustainable agriculture.
MDG 3: Promote gender equality and empower women.	SDG 3: Ensure healthy lives and promote well-being for all at all ages.
MDG 4: Reduce child mortality.	SDG 4: Ensure inclusive and equitable quality education and promote lifelong learning opportunities for all.
MDG 5: Improve maternal health.	
MDG 6: Combat HIV/AIDS, malaria, and other diseases.	SDG 5: Achieve gender equality and empower all women and girls.
MDG 7: Ensure environmental sustainability.	SDG 6: Ensure availability and sustainable management of water and sanitation for all.
MDG 8: Create global partnerships for development.	SDG 7: Ensure access to affordable, reliable, sustainable, and modern energy for all.
	SDG 8: Promote sustained, inclusive, and sustainable economic growth, full and productive employment, and decent work for all.
	SDG 9: Build resilient infrastructure, promote inclusive and sustainable industrialization, and foster innovation.
	SDG 10: Reduce inequality within and among countries.
	SDG 11: Make cities and human settlements inclusive, safe, resilient, and sustainable.
	SDG 12: Ensure sustainable consumption and production patterns.
	SDG 13: Take urgent action to combat climate change and its impacts.
	SDG 14: Conserve and sustainably use the oceans, seas, and marine resources for sustainable development.
	SDG 15: Protect, restore, and promote sustainable use of terrestrial ecosystems, sustainably manage forests, combat desertification, halt and reverse land degradation, and halt biodiversity loss.
	SDG 16: Promote peaceful and inclusive societies for sustainable development, provide access to justice for all, and build effective, accountable, and inclusive institutions at all levels.
	SDG 17: Strengthen the means of implementation, and revitalize the Global Partnership for Sustainable Development.

Sources: United Nations, n.d.; United Nations Department of Economic and Social Affairs, n.d.(a).

ber states and UN-level institutional changes to support effective conflict prevention and peacebuilding, improved efforts to build up and reform local police organizations, inclusion of human rights specialists in peacebuilding, enhanced financial support and rapid-deployment capabilities, and clear, feasible mandates for peace operations (United Nations General Assembly, Security Council, 2000). The high-level review of UN peace operations focused in the aftermath of two shocking failures on how the UN and member states might improve their efforts to protect individuals and communities from imminent threats to their physical security—ensuring freedom from fear.

One month later, UN agencies and member states began exploring improvements to global economic development, with the objective of improving the well-being of the world's poor. From September 6 to 8, most of the world's leaders gathered at UN headquarters in New York City for the Millennium Summit. The resulting Millennium Declaration called for the world's states to observe international human rights law and international humanitarian law and foster sustainable development. The declaration's eight chapters focus on key issue areas that would become the MDGs: values and principles; peace, security, and disarmament; development and poverty eradication; protecting our common environment; human rights, democracy, and good governance; protecting the vulnerable; meeting the special needs of Africa; and strengthening the United Nations (United Nations General Assembly 2000).

Drawing from this broader institutional context, the MDGs quantified goals with clear targets and an explicit time frame for their achievement. The structure and content of the MDGs reflect the perspectives of the individuals who drafted the goals, the interests of donor states and organizations, and the global political context of the year 2000. A small group of experts drafted the list in the basement of UN headquarters—a process casual enough that MDG 7, ensuring environmental sustainability, had accidentally been left out until Mark Malloch-Brown, then head of the UN Development Programme, happened to walk past the head of the UN Environment Programme and was suddenly struck by the omission (Tran 2012).

Years later, reflecting on the comparison between the MDG drafting process and the process that would later lead to the SDGs, Lord Malloch-Brown said his small team had to juggle the interests and priorities of various global constituencies. As a result the final list of MDGs reflects the human rights approach of the Development Programme's Human Development Report, the market-oriented development approach of the World Bank, and the target-focused approach of donors from the OECD. The listed goals also had to please multiple donor states and organizations, as well as the full UN membership, requiring the drafters to use language and establish goals and targets that would appease competing views on what constitutes development and how far the enforcement of certain rights should go (MDG 3, addressing gender equality, for example, met some opposition from more conservative states). In seeking universal acceptance of the goals from member states, drafters of both the MDGs and the SDGs had to leave establishment of democratic and accountable government institutions out of the lists of goals (Tran 2012).

The MDGs were written and accepted in 2000, in a time of relative optimism less than a decade after the end of the Cold War, and before the global political context would shift abruptly just one year later after the September 11 attacks. Then Western donor states would begin to focus their foreign policy efforts on combating transnational terrorism in an effort led by the United States and its Global War on Terror.

In the years since the list of Millennium Development Goals was drafted, laudable achievements have been made, including a 40 percent drop in HIV/ AIDS infections since 2000, a more than 50 percent reduction in both the number of children out of school and child mortality (measured against 1990 levels), and more than one billion fewer people living in extreme poverty (measured against 1990 levels) (United Nations Development Programme 2015). Still, progress made in realizing the MDGs by 2015 was uneven, with some goals meeting more success than others and some states achieving greater gains than others; critics note that the metrics used to assess progress are of questionable reliability (Jurkovich 2016; United Nations Millennium Development Goal Gap Task Force 2015; Sandbu 2015).

The broad range of durable human security concerns addressed by the MDGs had been drafted by a small group of people with little input from those most affected by the problems at issue. The path to the Sustainable Development Goals, in contrast, speaks to the evolution of global efforts to improve human security by expanding access to the negotiating table and working to ensure that global governance efforts recognize the diverse contexts and needs of the world's population.

The **Sustainable Development Goals (SDGs)**—also known as the Global Goals—were developed from the framework of the MDGs and from analysis of the progress still to be made when the MDGs' target date passed in 2015: There are still hungry people in the world. Children are still out of school. Efforts to improve the sustainability of natural resources and energy sources have fallen short. The SDGs consist of seventeen goals (with 169 targets across all of the goals) that pick up where the MDGs left off and run through an end date of 2030 (United Nations Department of Economic and Social Affairs, n.d.[a]).

The more inclusive drafting process for the SDGs began shortly before the Rio+20 conference in June 2012, twenty years after the initial United Nations Conference on Environment and Development in Rio de Janeiro (see chapter 11 for the connection between the earlier Rio Earth Summit and broader efforts to address climate change). The outcome document of the 2012 conference, *The Future We Want*, establishes central themes to be addressed by the SDGs and calls for a coordinated process leading to achieving goals that are aspirational, easily communicated, and feasible, taking varying state and local capacities and resources into consideration. Unlike in the process leading to the drafting of the MDGs, sustainability was central to the creation of the SDGs from the start. States renewed their "commitment to sustainable development and to ensuring the promotion of an economically, socially and environmentally sustainable future for our planet and for present and future generations" (United Nations Conference on Sustainable Development 2012, 1).

The conference outcome document called for an Open Working Group (OWG) to draft the goals and their targets. This thirty-seat group was established by the UN General Assembly in January 2013 and included more than thirty states, as groups of states shared seats (United Nations General Assembly 2013). In July 2012, just before the formation of the OWG, UN secretary-general Ban Ki-moon established a High-Level Panel of Eminent Persons on the Post 2015 Development Agenda to consider the UN's development role moving forward from the establishment of the MDGs. The panel was tasked with holding inclusive discussions on the post-2015 agenda that would integrate insights from civil society groups, individuals in the private sector, UN personnel, and academics in addition to the state representatives on the panel. The panel's final recommendations resulted from discussion with academics, regional organizations, more than 500 civil society groups, and 250 heads of corporations. These recommendations centered on continuing the work started by the MDGs, especially with a core focus on ending extreme poverty, but called for more emphasis on the devastating (and development-inhibiting) role played by armed conflict and violence and the potential for climate change to hamper the UN's development agenda if left unaddressed (High-Level Panel of Eminent Persons on the Post-2015 Development Agenda 2013).

The SDGs provide a framework for collaboration among a wide array of actors involved in global human security efforts. The more inclusive drafting process for the SDGs led to a greater number of goals with more nuanced targets. It is important to note as well that the SDGs are all interdependent, and success or failure in one will help or hinder the others. For example, SDG 4 calls for "inclusive and equitable quality education," SDG 8 seeks to "promote sustained, inclusive, and sustainable economic growth," and SDG 10 aims to "reduce inequality within and among countries" (United Nations Department of Economic and Social Affairs, n.d.[a]). Each of these three goals shares an explicit focus on reducing inequality and barriers to opportunity, and efforts to reach one of the goals will advance progress toward the others: Education itself is a powerful equalizer. Inclusive economic growth and reduced social inequality improve access to quality education. Improved equality within the state and more broadly within the international community increases both sustainable development and access to quality education.

The creation, implementation, and limitations of the MDGs and SDGs speak to the need for global collaboration to achieve human security. While the two sets of goals are cast in the language of development, the conditions created by the achievement of the goals would advance the protection of individuals from threats to their physical security and well-being in both the immediate and long terms.

The MDGs and SDGs originated at the international level, largely from within the UN architecture, and require a cosmopolitan view of security provision and governance that emphasizes the shared burden of all people, communities, states, and organizations to band together to solve the world's problems. Nevertheless, fostering local- and state-level involvement or buy-in with global-development goals can help skeptical constituencies see the merit in the effort. To the extent that the SDGs appeal to, involve, and improve the capacity of local communities and states struggling in our interconnected world, the case can be made that the goals and targets strengthen local and national security and serve related interests.

CONCLUSION

Human security is neither completely independent of nor seamlessly integrated into the state and global security approaches. As we have explored in this chapter, many of the actors that create security or insecurity in one approach also have an impact on the others. For this reason, we maintain the assumption throughout the book that the three approaches to security are synchronous in some cases and conflictual in others.

To achieve human security, the world needs secure states with functional institutions and social norms that promote the core values central to human security (namely, human rights), while also promoting inclusive dialogue to account for and navigate competing security perspectives. To achieve human security, the world also needs a relatively stable international system in which far-reaching threats are absent and states act in concert with one another. But this state of affairs cannot come at the expense of communities and cultures whose traditions and modes of governance fall outside of the Western models in which that system was built.

There is not one perfect formula for ensuring human security, and we do not seek to propose one in this book. Likewise, we could not address every kind of security provider and threat in this chapter and throughout the book; no single volume can account for all the world's heroes or problems. We hope instead that the discussions here help readers think about who or what provides and threatens security in every sense of the word and then apply the concepts learned here to the myriad security challenges facing the world today.

DISCUSSION QUESTIONS

1. Think about a human security issue that you have heard or read about before (e.g., refugee resettlement, famine, civilian protection in armed conflict, or systematic racial discrimination). Who are the main contributors to this problem? Who are the central actors working to solve this problem and create human security? Do the different actors work together, or is the effort disjointed?
2. Is there a policy problem that you can identify in which competing sides greatly differ on their understanding of the issue? In what ways do they understand the problem differently, and what do you think causes these disparate worldviews? How have these differences impacted policy on this problem?
3. The SDGs are significantly more complex and comprehensive than the MDGs, largely as a result of the more inclusive drafting process that led to the SDGs. How might the longer list of goals and targets affect global progress toward achievement of the goals?
4. What are the potential effects of political polarization on human, national, and global security? What efforts, if any, might be undertaken to foster collaboration?

Chapter 4

Human Rights and Human Security

Learning Objectives

This chapter will enable readers to

1. identify the historical and philosophical origins of human rights
2. examine the role of human rights in establishing human security
3. identify and discuss the role of states and nonstate actors in securing human rights
4. and apply the concept of universal rights to the accounts of advocacy on behalf of LGBTQ+ rights and of racial and ethnic discrimination in the United States and China.

Human security and human rights are closely intertwined but conceptually distinct. Human rights are universal, fundamental, and inalienable; this means they are the most basic rights, which apply to all people without regard to any aspect of their identity and cannot be withheld or taken away, except through the due process of law. Discussion of human rights, or more generally of the protections and freedoms to which people are entitled, predates the discussion of human security by thousands of years, but the continued violation of the rights of individuals and communities around the world led NGOs, TANs, and the UN to redouble their efforts to secure them at the close of the twentieth century.

The dual emphases on the sanctity of the individual and the relationship between the individual and the state at the heart of human rights scholarship, advocacy, and policy discussions highlight a strong link between human rights concepts and the formation of human security theory and practice. By providing, protecting, respecting, and fulfilling human rights, states and the international community lay the groundwork for the individual's ability to thrive (Younis 2004; Jurkovich 2020a, 27–28). Where human rights are violated, there is no human security; in other words, a state that violates the human rights of its population or of particular groups therein violates the basic tenets of human security, even if that state is otherwise stable and secure from a state security perspective.

Similarly, conditions of extreme insecurity and vulnerability prevent the enjoyment of human rights. The Commission on Human Security articulated the complementarity of human rights and human security in *Human Security Now*. By creating and enabling the conditions that make it possible for states to protect, respect, and fulfill human rights and for individuals to enjoy their human rights, human security strengthens human rights. In his contribution to the report, Amartya Sen says that "human security can make a significant contribution" to human rights theory and practice "by identifying the importance of freedom from basic insecurities—new and old" (Commission on Human Security 2003, 2, 9).

From the strategic perspective of the state, securing human rights ensures peace and stability within the domestic population—contentedness does not lead to unrest—and enhances or maintains the state's reputation within the international community through compliance with human rights law and norms. From the global perspective, observance of human rights indicates compliance with the norms of the international community, which is desirable not only from a normative perspective but also from a global security perspective, since stable states are less likely to engage in armed conflict. In this chapter we explore the concept of human rights and its roots, as well as the connection between human rights fulfillment and the establishment of human security.

THE ROOTS OF HUMAN RIGHTS

Like human security, the concept of human rights stems from the notion of a common humanity and the inherent dignity of human life. As we discussed in chapters 1 and 2, the development of human security as a concept and a practice is due in part to renewed advocacy around human rights after the end of the Cold War. It is helpful, then, to understand how the concept of human rights developed over centuries.

At the center of human rights is the recognition of a moral authority higher than that of the political order. Human rights are protected under national and international law, although the reality is that the protection varies, depending on the state or the international community's willingness or ability to step in and enforce human rights laws. At times it is the state itself that violates the human rights of some portion or of its entire population. An extreme example of this is the genocide perpetrated by Adolf Hitler and the Nazi forces in Germany and other European states from 1933 to 1945: the Nazi regime and its armed forces deprived millions of individuals of their access to employment, freedom of movement, access to education, freedom to marry, freedom to have and raise children, and, ultimately, the right to life. Indeed, the profound humanitarian tragedies of the Holocaust and in World War II more broadly inspired much of the content of the Universal Declaration of Human Rights (or the UDHR, introduced in chapter 2 and presented here in box 4.1) three years after the war's end. Human rights, then, form the conceptual roots of human security: human rights are articulated, recognized, and enforced to protect the individual and to ensure that all people may live with dignity.

Long before anyone spoke directly of *human security*, the conventional wisdom was that every individual is entitled to basic rights and freedoms, first among them the right to life. The concept of human rights existed even before the international community documented a consensus around them in the UDHR. Historically, concepts related to human rights evolved from religious and philosophical understandings of a morality or authority beyond the person or people with power in a society. This sense of a universal set of principles is at the center of what ancient Greek philosophers called natural law. **Natural law** refers to a foundational (or basic), unchanging morality that serves as a guide to human behavior at all times in all places. A common or natural sense of right and wrong prohibits most people from taking the life of another person except in extreme circumstances; this common inhibition is suggestive of natural law. Stoic philosophers also referred to **natural rights**, or privileges to which all rational human beings are entitled (Cranston 1962, 4; Donnelly 1982). Human rights articulated in the twentieth century are rooted in the principles of natural law and natural rights.

Eastern and Western religious and secular traditions have typically shared consensus on the basic rights to which human beings are entitled; these include life, justice, and dignity. Interestingly, in addition to the core belief that human life is sacred and to be protected, core texts and philosophers observe the importance of order and the state. For example, the Christian gospels permit obedience to earthly kings (or states), noting that Christians may participate in war if the state deems a war necessary, even though the gospels send a more broadly pacifist message and the Ten Commandments of Judeo-Christian faiths explicitly forbid killing.

Natural Rights

From the foundation of natural law, seventeenth-century philosophers derived the concept of natural rights, which closely resemble human rights. Prominent thinkers in the Age of Reason and the Age of Enlightenment invoked natural law to challenge the notion of the **divine right of kings**, which held that rulers are not subject to human authority but to divine—or absolute—authority. This notion prohibited people from challenging a ruler's legitimacy or right to govern. Natural law, with its emphasis on *human* morality and basic individual rights, provided a foundation from which philosophers articulated a set of rights common to all people, which cannot be disregarded or abridged by rulers.

Natural rights are closely tied to what would later be called human rights and refer to those rights and freedoms to which all individuals are entitled by virtue of being human. John Locke, Jean-Jacques Rousseau, Thomas Hobbes, Immanuel Kant, Thomas Paine, and John Rawls, among other philosophers, envisioned a world in which individuals are free and equal, the state is limited in its scope and reach, and the state and its citizens are tied together willingly through the social contract (Boucher and Kelly 1994; Rawls 1971). The consensual nature of the agreement between citizen and state lays the foundation for the expectation that the state will respect and protect certain individual rights. One of the most basic natural rights is to liberty: individuals are free to do as they wish in pursuit of their own fulfillment. Natural rights give individuals their freedom, agency, and independence; natural law is the set of common principles that place limitations on individuals, but these principles are presumably innate rather than decreed by a government or ruler. Although they are often *also* written into law, natural rights and natural law should guide human behavior even in the absence of legal constraint.

Writing at the time of the English Revolution of 1688, Locke, asserted that individuals have the natural rights of life, liberty, and property (Cranston 1962, 1–3; Donnelly 1982). At the time, this was a revolutionary idea. On December 16, 1689, the Parliament of England passed the Bill of Rights, which placed limits on the monarchy's powers and established the rights and authority of Parliament and of individuals (Cranston 1983, 1). By emphasizing the individual's rights and needs and by constraining the monarchy (at least to some extent), the Bill of Rights reflected the concepts of natural rights and natural law.

Of course, not all philosophers and certainly not all political actors of the day were supportive of the idea of natural rights. Jeremy Bentham, David Hume, and Edmund Burke were three prominent thinkers who opposed the notion that natural rights are somehow innate, or that they exist outside of human-authored law. Bentham saw "natural rights" and the declarations arising from them as governments' attempts to resist real change by making lofty rhetorical statements; individual rights should instead come through the creation of laws, he believed (Cranston 1983, 4). Hume and Burke, who rarely agreed with Bentham on philosophical matters, were similarly wary, seeing the potential for "natural rights" rhetoric to justify uprisings and revolutions

(Cranston 1983, 4). Indeed, both the American and French Revolutions (starting in 1775 and 1789, respectively) would soon be justified on the basis of securing individual rights and freedoms—at least for some people.

The American Declaration of Independence, adopted on July 4, 1776, contends that all people (at the time, men alone were explicitly named, and enslaved men were not included) are born equal and are entitled to the natural rights of "life, liberty, and the pursuit of happiness" (Second Continental Congress 1776). The US Constitution (ratified in 1788), and especially the Bill of Rights (introduced in 1789), further specify the rights of individuals relative to the state, including the rights to freedom of speech, assembly, and religion, the right to keep and bear arms, freedom from arbitrary search and seizure, and the right to a speedy and public jury trial, among other rights. The French Declaration of the Rights of Man and Citizen, passed in the National Constituent Assembly in August 1789, echoes the rights enumerated by the Americans, stating that individuals (again, only men at the time) are born free and have equal rights and that the state's purpose is to provide, protect, and observe the natural rights to liberty, property, security, and resistance to oppression. Because individuals had lived for so long under monarchical rulers who failed to grant, protect, or observe individual rights, there was immense popular support for revolutions within Colonial America and France (Cranston 1983, 2). The three documents—the Declaration of Independence, the US Constitution, and the Declaration of the Rights of Man and Citizen—reflect philosophical discussions of natural rights *and* strengthened the foundation for future discussion of human rights (Commission on Human Security 2003, 9).

The philosophical and historical roots to our understanding of human rights underscore the idea that some form of universal humanity binds all people together and that each person is entitled to certain rights and protections simply on the basis of being human. What this looks like in practice, however, has varied widely over time and across countries.

HUMAN RIGHTS AND THE PROTECTION OF A COMMON HUMANITY

At the root of any discussion of human rights is the interest in preserving common humanity by protecting the security, freedom, and well-being of individuals. All human rights are linked by the common premise that the individual possesses inherent dignity deserving of protection, so much so that when the human rights of one person are violated, the common thread of humanity frays. Some rights require that governments take action or actively provide something, while other rights require that the government refrain from taking an action harmful to or constraining an individual. In this section we examine international efforts to preserve the sanctity of the individual.

So many terrible things happened on such a large scale in the first half of the twentieth century that the newly formed UN General Assembly adopted the first common declaration of human rights, the **Universal Declaration of Human Rights**. In international law, **declarations** do not formally possess the binding force of law; but as states adhere to their provisions over time, they take on law-like influence. Adopted on December 10, 1948, the UDHR represents the cornerstone of global discussions of human rights since it was the first and most comprehensive international document enumerating human rights (see box 4.1).

From the late 1800s through the mid-1900s, the focus of international conventions and agreements had been on protecting humanity in warfare (expressed in international humanitarian law). Although the UDHR list rights that should be preserved even during the extreme duress and acute insecurity of warfare, the rights enumerated within the declaration are intended to be preserved and protected every day, all over the world.

All member states of the UN are expected (but, again, not legally obligated) to comply with the UDHR; they are encouraged to provide and protect the listed rights. The UDHR underpins all **international human rights law** after World War II, and it was intended to be a minimal list of the most basic human rights. While the UDHR was drafted long before the concept of human security took shape, its articles lay out a framework for the state's responsibility to respect and protect the most basic rights of its population. Still, at the time of its adoption, the rights listed in the UDHR were not uniformly accepted by states; rather, considerable debate ensued about which rights are the most fundamental, with particular emphasis placed on the obligations of states and citizens (Jurkovich 2020a, 25–29).

The UDHR was never intended to be the final word on human rights; in fact, its principles have carried over into conventions and treaties that *are* legally binding. In 1966 the UN General Assembly adopted two legally binding covenants on human rights—the International Covenant on Civil and Political Rights (ICCPR) and the International Covenant on Economic, Social and Cultural Rights (ICESCR)—both introduced in chapter 2. Unlike declarations, international *covenants* are written legal agreements that states sign, ratify, and enforce. International **covenants**, **conventions**, and **treaties** are all formal agreements between states; they are legally binding on those states that ratify them (United Nations 1969). The ICCPR enshrines the rights that most closely resemble those articulated by the American Declaration of Independence, the US Constitution, and the French Declaration of the Rights of Man and Citizen. The ICESCR focuses on rights that require states to take action to provide social and economic protections.

BOX 4.1. HUMAN RIGHTS IN THE UNIVERSAL DECLARATION OF HUMAN RIGHTS

1. All human beings are born free and equal in dignity and rights.
2. All human beings are entitled to the rights and freedoms in the UDHR, and no right or freedom may be denied on the basis of individual identity or place of residence.
3. All human beings have the right to life, liberty, and security of their person.
4. No human being may be enslaved.
5. No human being may be tortured or subjected to cruel or inhuman punishment.
6. All human beings have the right to recognition as a person before the law.
7. All human beings should be free from discrimination and are entitled to equal protection under the law.
8. All human beings have a right to legal recourse if their rights are violated.
9. No human being may be arbitrarily arrested, detained, or exiled.
10. All human beings are entitled to a fair, public, and impartial trial if criminal charges are brought against them.
11. All human beings charged with a crime have the right to be presumed innocent until proven guilty according to the law; no human being may be charged with committing a crime if no crime was committed.
12. All human beings are entitled to their privacy and protection from interference in their privacy, family, home, correspondence, and reputation.
13. All human beings have the right to freedom of movement and residence within their state; all human beings have the right to leave any state and to return to their home state.
14. All human beings have the right to seek asylum in other states.
15. All human beings have the right to a nationality, and no human being may be denied the right to change nationalities.
16. All human beings have the freedom to marry and form a family without discrimination; no human being may be forced into marriage; marriage is entitled to protection by the state.
17. All human beings have the right to own property; no human being may be arbitrarily deprived of their property.
18. All human beings have the right to freedom of thought, conscience, and religion.

19. All human beings have the right to freedom of opinion and expression.
20. All human beings have the right to freedom of peaceful assembly and association; no human being may be forced to join an association.
21. All human beings have the right to participate in their home state's government; all human beings have the right to equal access to public services in their home state; the will of the people should be the basis of the government's authority.
22. All human beings have the right to social security and the realization of their economic, social, and cultural rights.
23. All human beings have the right to work, to choose their employment, and to enjoy fair working conditions; all human beings have the right to equal pay for equal work; all human beings who work have the right to compensation and—if necessary—social protection; all human beings have the right to join unions.
24. All human beings have the right to rest and leisure time.
25. All human beings have the right to a standard of living that ensures health and well-being for themselves and their family; motherhood and childhood are entitled to special protections, and all children are entitled to the same protection.
26. All human beings have the right to an education; education should promote respect for human rights, tolerance, understanding, and global friendship; all parents have the right to choose the kind of education their children receive.
27. All human beings have the right to participate in the cultural life of their community; all human beings have the right to protection of their intellectual property.
28. All human beings are entitled to a global order that protects the rights in the UDHR.
29. All human beings have duties to the community that supports their rights; all human beings are subject to limitations of their rights only with regard to respect for the rights of others; no rights or freedoms may be exercised in ways contrary to the principles and purpose of the United Nations.
30. None of the rights enumerated by the UDHR may be interpreted as implying the right of any state, group, or person to do anything intended to destroy the rights and freedoms set forth by the UDHR.

Source: This text paraphrases the Articles of the UDHR (United Nations General Assembly 1948). The full text is available through the United Nations UDHR web page, at http://www.un.org/en/universal-declaration-human-rights/.

Both covenants were drafted, negotiated, and adopted during the Cold War period, when tensions between the United States and the Soviet Union were high and new states had been formed through decolonization. The division between the ICCPR and ICESCR reflects the interests and priorities of the states that championed each covenant; interests, priorities, and conceptions of the role of the state in providing for human rights diverged sufficiently to make a single covenant politically untenable. Indeed, human rights had been a politically fraught issue throughout the early twentieth century because the notion of inherent dignity fundamentally conflicted with the way powerful states had configured the political world. Human rights advocacy by states in the Global South, with issues of racial and religious discrimination at the heart of the effort, drove the negotiations that ultimately led to the creation of these legally binding covenants on human rights; the international community, dominated by Western interests, had lacked the political will to do so in prior decades (Jensen 2016).

Together the UDHR, ICCPR, and ICESCR comprise the International Bill of Human Rights. This framework places the responsibility for providing, protecting, and preserving human rights in the hands of states. By signing and ratifying the ICCPR and ICESCR, states agree to respect human rights and provide or abstain from violating them. States, then, are at the center of discussions of human rights and human security.

Further, with the end of the Cold War and the increased presence and strength of NGOs, nonstate actors gained the ability to monitor and report on progress toward human rights fulfillment as well as human rights violations. The UN and its agencies, including the General Assembly, Human Rights Council, and High Commissioner for Human Rights, also have varying capabilities to comment on and act in response to human rights violations. When these organizations and agencies comment on human rights violations, they tend to focus on the state, or at least on the state's inability to protect rights when a nonstate actor is violating them (as in the case of a state that lacks the capacity to stop abuse by nonstate armed groups within its borders or a state that lacks the legal framework and investigative capabilities to address oppression of or violence against particular groups of people). While states are not the only entities responsible for monitoring and contributing to the preservation of human rights, states are at the center of discussions of human rights precisely because of the assumption that the primary function of the state is preserving the security and rights of its people.

Even when a state has not ratified a legally binding convention, covenant, or treaty, the terms of an international agreement can still apply to that state over time through the evolution of international customs—or customary law. **Customs** (or **customary law**) derive from states' adherence to specific practices over time, such that they begin to take on the force of law (United Nations

1969). Some actions, atrocities, and rights violations are not explicitly governed by formal legal agreements but are instead forbidden by powerful international norms. Peremptory norms (or *jus cogens*) are norms with the binding force of law; the process through which a norm attains this status is not fully defined in scholarship or international law, but among these powerful norms are bans on slavery, genocide, and international aggression (Bassiouni 1996). Both customs and peremptory norms exist outside of formal legal agreements, though some international legal frameworks (including the International Bill of Human Rights) restate both customs and peremptory norms.

Conceptualizations of Human Rights

We can view human rights through three different but related distinctions. First, we can understand human rights in terms of civil and political rights or economic, social, and cultural rights. Or we might also look at certain rights as belonging to one of several generations of human rights. Finally, a third distinction is between positive and negative rights. We can even discuss human rights in some combination of these three distinctions.

Civil and political rights are most easily understood as the human rights that allow individuals to participate fully in society—including and especially in political processes—without fear of discrimination or harm. Civil and political rights protect individuals from state repression, discrimination, and overreach, and rights such as freedom of assembly, speech, and religion, as well as security of person and property, bring to mind the natural rights advocated by the philosophers and political revolutions in the seventeenth and eighteenth centuries. Much of what we discuss today pertaining to civil and political rights is built on the foundation of natural rights; indeed, these rights are visible in the US Declaration of Independence, the US Bill of Rights, and the French Declaration of the Rights of Man and Citizen. The UDHR, of course, also establishes these rights as universal human rights.

Economic, social, and cultural rights are likewise laid out in the UDHR. These rights further clarify human rights, establishing that the state and its agencies must provide certain services and resources as needed to enable individuals to thrive. Such rights include the rights to food, housing, and education.

There is no overt distinction between civil and political rights and economic, social, and cultural rights in the UDHR. The ideological divisions of the Cold War and the differing conceptions of the role of the state in fulfilling rights spurred the distinction: Western capitalist economies aligned with the United States prioritized civil and political rights, whereas centrally planned economies aligned with the Soviet Union promoted economic, social, and cultural rights (United Nations Office of the High Commissioner for Human Rights 2008a, 9).

During his tenure as secretary-general of the International Institute of Human Rights, Karel Vasak discussed human rights in generational categories (Domaradzki, Khvostova, and Pupovac 2019). **First-generation rights** are chiefly civil and political rights, the earliest human rights discussed by philosophers and political actors. These rights establish the basis for a more participatory and less discriminatory society in which individuals do not need to fear state-perpetrated interference or harm. **Second-generation rights** apply the notion of human rights to the vision of a more egalitarian society in which individuals' basic needs (food, shelter, education, and employment) are met and they are able and empowered to participate in society to the fullest extent (Brander et al. 2020). Both first- and second-generation rights are enumerated in the UDHR, and the UDHR itself does not distinguish between them, but the ICCPR and ICESCR are divided along these lines, with the former containing first-generation rights and the latter focusing on second-generation rights.

Third-generation rights encompass a wider range of rights specific to groups of people, identities, and even the environment. Although human rights are universal in theory, in reality certain groups are routinely denied their human rights (or even their full humanity), and the establishment of third-generation rights seeks to remedy this. Two examples of international agreements establishing third-generation rights, or peoples' rights, are the Declaration on the Rights of Indigenous Peoples (adopted by the UN General Assembly in 2007) and the Convention on the Rights of the Child (which was adopted by the UN General Assembly in 1989 and entered into force in 1990). Third-generation rights include the right to cultural heritage, minority rights, children's rights, women's rights, and environmental rights, among others. Not all human rights agreements, statements, or documents are legally binding: the Declaration on the Rights of Indigenous Peoples is a General Assembly resolution and as such is nonbinding; the Convention on the Rights of the Child is a treaty and is therefore binding on states that have signed and ratified it.

Positive rights, a term also used by Secretary-General Vasak, requires that someone (usually the government, but possibly also an agency, institution, or fellow human) *do something* to take action to provide that right if necessary. Examples of positive human rights include the rights to food, education, shelter, and health care, all of which are generally considered economic, social, and cultural rights. Each of the aforementioned rights requires someone to provide food, public schools, adequate shelter, and health services if an individual cannot access those resources on their own. Civil and political rights can also be positive rights; one such example is the right to legal representation for those who must stand trial but cannot afford a lawyer or counselor.

Negative rights, on the other hand, require that someone abstain from a specific action; in order to enjoy these rights the government, other entities or institutions, or people must not affect an individual's choices, freedoms, beliefs, or actions. Most often negative rights are civil and political rights, including freedom of speech and religion (no one should stop an individual from speaking their mind or practicing—or not practicing—a religion), security of person and property (no one should take an action that harms a person or their home or possessions), the right to life, and the right to remain free from torture. Negative rights loosely correspond with first-generation rights, while positive rights are more closely aligned with second- and third-generation rights.

There is some disagreement over the usefulness of these distinctions between human rights, especially regarding the three generations of rights and the categorization of rights as positive or negative. One such critique, made by Maurice Cranston is that since second- and third-generation rights usually require resources that may not always be available, they cannot be true human rights (Cranston 1967); if some rights cannot reasonably be protected and enjoyed by all, he reasons, then the fabric of all universal human rights begins to fray. Still, employing alternative conceptualizations helps us envision how the discussion of human rights has evolved over centuries and how the prioritization of certain human rights will vary by state, community, and individual identity.

BOX 4.2. THINK ABOUT IT . . . HOW WELL DO YOU KNOW YOUR HUMAN RIGHTS?

If you'd had to list your human rights before reading this chapter and reviewing the UDHR, could you have done it? Which rights would you have included in your list?

If you could have listed only a few of your human rights, why did you choose those?

Where and when did you first learn about your human rights?

What are the potential consequences of *not* knowing your human rights?

What can be done to improve global awareness of human rights?

Which human rights does the government of your state (country) seem to respect most?

Are there any human rights that are not adequately protected in your state? If so, has there been any advocacy or policy effort to change this?

After you have considered these questions, discuss them with a family member, roommate, community member, or classmate. Are their responses similar to yours? If so, why? If their responses are very different from yours, what do you think explains those differences?

RESTORING HUMAN RIGHTS THAT HAVE BEEN DENIED

Recognition and enforcement of human rights change over time as norms, beliefs, identities, and laws evolve. Historically excluded populations and identities have not enjoyed the same degree of protection of their human rights. The enumeration of third-generation human rights is part of an attempt to remedy the historical denial of rights to particular groups and communities. Just as the notion of human security was introduced and has gained greater acceptance because of the historical and political context of the 1990s and 2000s, efforts to protect human rights and respond to systematic denials of human rights can take root in a hospitable political, social, and/or cultural climate.

We can look at changes in human rights through two different lenses: claims to human rights made by a group of people who share a particular identity, and recognition of a particular act or set of norms and institutions as a violation of human rights. To explore changes in human rights, we briefly look at the push for **lesbian, gay, bisexual, transgender, and queer/questioning (LGBTQ+)** rights in the United States and movements addressing racial inequality in the United States and ethnic inequality in China.

The LGBTQ+ Rights Movement

For much of the twentieth century in the United States, if you did not conform to the established norms of gender and sexuality you could be barred from working for the government, serving in the military, or even gathering at bars. Homosexuality was considered a mental illness, a perversion, and—in the eyes of the government in 1950—a security risk (United States Senate 1950); from January 1, 1947, to August 1, 1950, 1,700 applications for federal jobs were rejected on the basis of homosexuality or "other sex perversion" (Davidson 2012). Employees were subject to intrusive investigations into their private lives. The US military's Don't Ask, Don't Tell (DADT) policy affecting LGBTQ+ military personnel, in effect from February 1994 until its repeal in September 2011, prohibited discrimination and harassment of LGBTQ+ personnel or applicants as well as investigations into the sexuality of personnel or applicants; in this respect it loosened prior federal restrictions on employment. Yet DADT also barred openly LGBTQ+ persons from serving in the military, citing a negative effect on morale and unit cohesion. In 2016, five years after the repeal of DADT, the US military continued to grapple with the integration of transgender service members. Rights violations were not (and are not) limited to employment discrimination but extended to the right to marry and the right to be secure in one's person.

The federal Defense of Marriage Act (DOMA) of 1996 defined marriage as a union between a man and a woman and allowed states to refuse to recognize same-sex marriages granted in other states; this effectively blocked same-sex couples from federal employee benefits, Social Security benefits, bankruptcy benefits, tax returns, immigration processes, and adoption of children. In 2013, in *United States v. Windsor*, the Supreme Court ruled that DOMA violated the Due Process Clause of the Fifth Amendment and thus was unconstitutional. Still, same-sex marriage was prohibited in many states until the Supreme Court's decision in *Obergefell v. Hodges* on June 26, 2015, which established that marriage is a fundamental right to which same-sex couples are entitled under the Fifth and Fourteenth Amendments.

Attention was drawn to the lack of anti-hate-crime laws and legal protections for LGBTQ+ individuals across the United States in the wake of the 1998 murder of Matthew Shepard, a gay student at the University of Wyoming, and by the film and play *The Laramie Project*, which told his story. On October 28, 2009, the Matthew Shepard and James Byrd, Jr., Hate Crimes Prevention Act became law, and through it the federal anti-hate-crime protections expanded to cover the prohibition of violence motivated by an individual's gender, sexuality, or perceived gender or sexuality.

Behind each legal advance was a persistent advocacy effort to secure LGBTQ+ civil and human rights. Organizations and advocacy efforts such as the Human Rights Campaign, the It Gets Better Project, PFLAG, and GLBTQ Legal Advocates & Defenders (GLAD) continue to work for a more inclusive society in the United States through legal advances, public discourse and education, and social support. Certainly legal advances do not end all discrimination and violence against LGBTQ+ persons, as tragically evidenced by the mass shooting at the Pulse nightclub in Orlando, Florida, on June 26, 2016, and by the 2016–2017 legal battle of the Gloucester County, Virginia, school board over a transgender student's access to restrooms. In 2021, school boards across the United States faced protests—at times violent—from community members as they took up consideration of policies that would allow students to use the restroom or locker room of the gender with which they identify, a measure aimed at decreasing discrimination against transgender youth that was vehemently contested by social and religious conservatives. Defining and protecting the rights of a specific group of people can be contentious, especially when perceptions about the group's shared identity polarize the population.

Similar movements working to secure LGBTQ+ civil and human rights are gaining momentum throughout the world, facing many of the same cultural and legal obstacles that activists in the United States have faced. The movements have found more success in the Americas and Western Europe, while in much of Africa, Eastern Europe, the Middle East, and Asia, states have been more reluctant to formally recognize and expand LGBTQ+ rights. The LGBTQ+ rights movement demonstrates that the emergence of a new human rights norm does not guarantee its universal acceptance or legal protection; rather, broad recognition of new rights takes time and considerable effort by advocates.

Racial and Ethnic Violence: A Look at the United States and China

Facets of identity have differing degrees of salience in different societies. As societal norms create divisions among people based on race, ethnicity, nationality, religion, gender, or other identities, the potential for systemic inequality, discrimination, and violence arises. Minority groups are particularly vulnerable to denial of human rights and the resulting lack of human security.

Racial Injustice in the United States

Race is a salient identity in the United States, and systemic racism has made it difficult for Americans who are Black, Indigenous, or People of Color (**BIPOC**) to access the same opportunities and resources as White Americans. **Systemic racism** (or *structural racism*) involves the perpetuation of racial inequality and White supremacy through the institutions, norms, and interactions that shape both government and daily life; because of systemic racism, BIPOC face inequality in access to employment, education, housing, health care, political participation, and justice, among other vital resources and opportunities. We focus here on a brief account of how systemic racism has affected Black Americans and the fulfillment of their human rights.

The Southern United States powered much of its economy through the labor of enslaved people until the mid-1860s. The issue of slavery had been a point of contention between the Northern and Southern states since before the forming of the republic, but the fight flared into violence upon the secession of most slaveholding states from the Union and with the subsequent civil war waged to forcibly reunite them. While the Emancipation Proclamation legally freeing all slaves was issued by President Lincoln on January 1, 1863, its effects were not instant, and people enslaved in Texas did not even learn of their freedom until federal troops arrived with the news in June 1865, a full two and a half years later (Pruitt-Young 2021). For hundreds of years people enslaved in the United States and their descendants had been unable to possess property, earn wages, build intergenerational wealth, and enjoy basic human rights; the effects of that long-running, systematic denial of rights persist even today.

The legal recognition of their freedom did not create equality, and US power holders who decried the legislation set to work to create barriers to education, employment, property ownership, and political participation, institutionalizing discrimination through legal frameworks that segregated people by race and perpetuated White supremacy long after the last shot had been fired in the American Civil War. The Jim Crow laws enacted in the Southern states are perhaps the best-known formal legal framework codifying discrimination, but informal norms and practices also maintained racial segregation through much of the United States.

A series of decisions by the US Supreme Court (including *Brown v. Board of Education* in 1954, *Heart of Atlanta Motel, Inc. v. United States* in 1964, and *Loving v. Virginia* in 1967) and Congress (the Civil Rights Act of 1964 and the Voting Rights Act of 1965) began to formally dismantle legal obstacles to equality, all against the backdrop of the grassroots civil rights movement that was calling for an end to racial discrimination across the country. As civil rights icons like Martin Luther King Jr., John Lewis, W. E. B. Du Bois, and Ruby Bridges woke the United States up to the realities of racism and formal racial discrimination, the nation took important steps toward realizing "equality for all," a right long enshrined in its founding documents.

But of course systemic racism did not end with the civil rights movement of the 1950s and 1960s. Beginning in the 2010s, racial justice advocates began particularly decrying the racial discrimination and bias that leads to disproportionate numbers of Black people being killed by law enforcement. The advocacy group Black Lives Matter formed in 2013 after George Zimmerman was acquitted of the murder of Trayvon Martin; the group gained strength and national recognition through social media advocacy and mass demonstrations after the deaths of Michael Brown (2014), Eric Garner (2014), and George Floyd (2020) at the hands of police (Black Lives Matter, n.d.).

Awareness of systemic racism increased as the COVID-19 pandemic reached the United States in the early months of 2020 and Black and Latinx Americans were disproportionately affected through a confluence of factors like inequitable access to quality health care, temporary or permanent job loss, and heightened risk of disease exposure through employment in frontline or essential positions (in chapter 9 we discuss the COVID-19 pandemic as a syndemic of interrelated social, health, and economic effects). In the midst of the pandemic, protests against police brutality and unequal treatment in the justice system grew stronger, leading some to describe the era as a revival of the civil rights movement or a new civil rights movement altogether (Fayyad 2020).

The new civil rights movement does not simply ask people not to be racist (or to passively accept the notion of equality); instead, it demands that people become antiracist and actively challenge and work to transform racist policies and institutions so that all people may fully enjoy their human rights and equality (Kendi 2019). To do this work requires, first, recognition of the harms perpetrated by dysfunctional norms and institutions that have maintained racial inequality in the United States and, second, efforts to right past wrongs and build more equitable institutions.

The Repression of the Uyghur People in China

The Uyghur population is a predominantly Muslim, Turkic-speaking ethnic group living in Xinjiang, a region in northwest China. Since 2017 over one million Uyghurs have been forcibly held in detention or reeducation camps, but governmental efforts to repress the people extend back to 2001, when Islamophobia reached a fever pitch in much of the world after the terrorist attacks of September 11 (Abbas 2020; Roberts 2020). The Chinese Communist Party (CCP) considers Islam and other religions to be a threat to the state and a potential trigger for separatist movements; the crackdown on Uyghur Muslims has unfolded alongside broader efforts to counter extremism and increase surveillance within the state (Maizland 2021).

Through the 1990s and 2000s, people in Xinjiang had begun mobilizing in anti-Han (the dominant ethnicity in China) and separatist demonstrations. In 2009 a protest against Han migration and economic and cultural inequality in Urumqi, Xinjiang's capital, led to rioting and the death of two hundred people (BBC News 2021b; Maizland 2021). In the years after the riot, the Chinese state increased surveillance and security measures (including the installation of ubiquitous cameras, use of facial-recognition technology, and increased police presence) in an effort to deter what the CCP considers to be separatism and extremism.

Mass detention of Uyghur Muslims and ethnic Kazakhs and Uzbeks in Xinjiang reportedly began in 2017, scaling up from reeducation efforts that likely began in 2014, though the Chinese government denies allegations of mass detention and does not publicly release information about what it calls its "vocational training sites" (Maizland 2021). Most Uyghur detainees have not committed any crimes, and human rights advocates allege that they have been detained because they are observant Muslims living in a region claimed by China (Maizland 2021; Abbas 2020). Human rights advocates have condemned the detention and forced labor of Uyghurs, calling on major consumer brands that manufacture their goods in China to examine the labor practices used in their production facilities (UN News 2021a). The United States, Canada, the Netherlands, and human rights advocates have accused China of committing genocide, due to the forced separation of children from their parents, mass detentions, attempts to suppress cultural and religious expression and traditions, and reports of torture, forced sterilizations, and mass rapes in detention camps (BBC News 2021b; Associated Press 2020; Human Rights Watch 2021).

The systematic human rights violations in Xinjiang highlight the effects of ethnic discrimination on both human rights and human security. The failure of other states and of global governance institutions to take meaningful action to address the abuses against the Uyghur people in China demonstrates the potential for state strength and political and economic interests to threaten and undermine international human rights law and norms.

Which Rights?

Asserting the rights of a particular group or contending that a tradition, practice, or action is a human rights violation demands normative change, disrupts long-held ideas, and requires that human dignity be prioritized over both the status quo and state power. The rights themselves are not actually new; instead, the shifting dialogue creates recognition of long-standing denial of particular groups' fundamental rights. It is often in human rights advocacy that we can see where, how, and to what extent human security conflicts with state security.

Because many human rights initiatives face daunting challenges before they are accepted as global norms, it can be difficult to sort out competing perspectives. When discussing differing views on human rights, scholars and public decision makers sometimes point to the concept of **cultural relativism**, the understanding that an individual's morals, values, and beliefs are rooted in their culture, meaning that one culture's norms will differ from another's. This concept presents a counterpoint to the argument that human rights are universal, as it creates gray areas wherein one can argue that in some contexts and certain regions, championing the rights of women, religious minorities, or LGBTQ+ people challenges tradition, identity, and culture. From the point of view of human security, what matters most is that the individual remain safe from threats and free from obstacles to empowerment.

In theory the human security approach aligns with the notion of universal human rights. In practice the best way to establish the individual's security and foster empowerment will vary by individual, community, state, or region, and so policy prescriptions and initiatives are best created with attention to the specific cultural, political, economic, and social context in mind and the empowerment and support of local, grassroots advocates and organizations (Harris-Short 2003). Cultural competency and local participation are crucial aspects of any successful human rights movement.

HUMAN RIGHTS AND HUMAN SECURITY

Human rights and human security are mutually reinforcing. Conversely, the erosion of human rights erodes human security, and vice versa. The prominence of human rights in much of political philosophy and international political discourse emphasizes the importance of the individual. At the heart of human security are the individual human and the communities formed by individuals who share some facet of their identity.

In sections I and II we discuss the concept and emergence of human security and the interplay between human security and armed conflict. During conflict, human rights are severely strained. Human rights advocates have worked to more clearly define not only what rights people have during warfare but also how violations of those rights should be punished. These efforts have focused both on the responsibility of the state to protect the rights of its citizens and on the responsibility of the international community to stop mass human rights violations.

The United Nations Trust Fund for Human Security recognizes that peace, human rights, and development are critically linked not only in crises, conflicts, and times of instability but also during times of relative peace (United Nations Trust Fund for Human Security 2016, 6). In section III we explore the concept of "durable" human security, which relates to long-term or chronic security issues stemming from the norms and institutions within a society. When durable human security exists, individuals and groups enjoy their human rights and freedoms, they thrive in their societies, and their states are politically and economically stable. Individuals whose human rights are protected and guaranteed can work together toward long-term peace and stability because they do not live in fear that their personal security, ability to adhere to their beliefs, stability of their employment or access to education, or freedom from discrimination will suddenly be denied.

The international legal framework that protects human rights (the International Bill of Human Rights and other treaties, conventions, and declarations) establishes a foundation for durable human security and lays the groundwork for the protection of individuals from chronic harms and for the provision of the basic needs that allow individuals to thrive. The international framework for human rights establishes the state as central to the preservation of human rights—and ultimately of human security. Recall that international treaties and conventions are binding legal agreements *between states*. States, then, take on the responsibility of ensuring that their citizens enjoy their rights and freedoms.

Of course, states do not always comply fully with their international legal obligations and agreements. When a state fails to provide for the human rights and human security of its population, nonstate actors like NGOs, civil society networks, and international organizations like the UN act as monitors and report on the state's actions. Nonstate actors play an important role in ensuring that the human rights and human security needs of individuals and groups are met. By publicly agreeing to respect human rights, states make themselves accountable and invite this form of scrutiny both from

other states and from nonstate actors. When states fail to meet their obligations to their people, it is not always due to malicious intentions. Sometimes
states do not have the capacity to enforce domestic or international law
(including the provision of human rights) within their own territory. With
the rise of NGOs, actors other than the state government can become service providers, monitors and defenders of human rights, and advocates in
partnership with or opposition to states.

DISCUSSION QUESTIONS

1. For what reasons might states sign on to legally binding human rights
   treaties?
2. What common themes are visible across early human rights documents
   (US and French declarations), the UDHR, and more recent agreements or
   advocacy campaigns?
3. How do human rights violations against a given group affect their human
   security and that of the broader population?
4. How useful is the distinction between generations of rights? What about
   the distinction between civil/political and economic/social/cultural
   rights? Are the dual concepts of positive and negative rights helpful?
   Why or why not?
5. Should cultural or social differences determine the extent to which human
   rights may be enforced?
6. Is human security an essential condition for the enjoyment of human
   rights? Why or why not?

Section II

ARMED CONFLICT AND HUMAN SECURITY

Chapter 5

From Nonintervention to the Responsibility to Protect

Learning Objectives

This chapter will enable readers to

1. understand the relationship between sovereignty and the principle of non-intervention
2. describe the scope and type of conflict in the international system today
3. examine the ways that international humanitarian law has evolved to better account for civilian protection
4. and understand the norms leading to the responsibility to protect (R2P), criticisms of R2P, and how it has been applied.

The human security approach can be practiced at the local, state, or international level, but most policy discourse on human security has focused on how states can integrate human security norms into foreign policy or how intergovernmental organizations can promote those norms globally. Human security in practice, therefore, must contend with a core construct of the international system: the **sovereignty** of states. **Sovereignty**, in its simplest form, is the idea that a state has legal jurisdiction over its own territory and that other states are not to interfere in each other's internal affairs. This includes, in its strictest form, the right of the state to create laws and to determine how those laws are enforced, including the parameters by which force can be used against its citizens. It is presumed that those governing structures would be built upon the values of that state. Within a system of sovereign states, the norm of **sovereign equality** says that all states are legally equal. The strict interpretation of sovereignty implies a **principle of nonintervention** by states or other outside actors into the domestic affairs of other states, up to and including using force to stop a state from violating the human rights of its own citizens.

As we will see in this chapter, however, this strict interpretation of sovereignty neither matches reality nor conforms to modern legal understandings of the term. This chapter begins by exploring the concept of sovereignty and its implications for how security is practiced. We then turn to the evolving norms of protection and the development of the Responsibility to Protect (R2P) doctrine. The chapter's vignette introduces the multilateral intervention in Libya, the first explicit R2P mission, and compares it to the nonintervention in Syria before offering concluding thoughts.

SOVEREIGNTY AND THE
PRINCIPLE OF NONINTERVENTION

The modern-day origins of sovereignty evolved from principles articulated in the Treaty of Westphalia of 1648, which ended the Thirty Years' War. In this original articulation, sovereignty was based on the notion that monarchs are equals and have the right to rule over their subjects as they please, particularly in terms of determining the religion to be practiced within the state. Of course the idea that a single individual has absolute authority over their subjects has been challenged by calls for **self-determination** and for government that adheres to the consent of the governed. **Self-determination** is the right of the citizens of a territory to choose for themselves what type of political system they are to live under and the ensuing expectation that the government is tasked with the protection of their rights. As we discussed in chapter 4, the American and French Revolutions and the political systems that arose from them were direct challenges to monarchal rule, driven by the principle of self-determination. Later the dismantling of the European imperial international order after World War II was also driven by the principle of self-determination. Today the principle of sovereignty is the underlying legal mechanism that governs the international political system. How security is provided, and to whom, must be considered under this framework.

The state, however, is a highly contested space. Multiple factions within a state can make competing claims over who ultimately has the right to exercise control of the state. These challenges are rooted in debates on national identity and who constitutes a "true" citizen and are reflected in the four security perspectives introduced in chapter 1. States, therefore, face ongoing internal challenges to their domestic political institutions. To illustrate this, think about your own community: Would you say there is universal agreement on how the state should operate and who should rule? Who controls the state and the types of institutions the state supports has implications for every person living in it. How are these disagreements resolved?

In a state with functioning democratic forms of government, those challenges would ideally happen through the formation of political parties that compete through electoral politics—although it should be noted that democracies can also experience large amounts of social protest by groups feeling that key issues are not being adequately addressed within the current governing structure. In more authoritarian systems of government, challenges come through riskier forms of engagement, as citizens in these types of states typically have fewer political rights and the state, when challenged, faces fewer limitations on the use of oppressive security tactics. The socioeconomic makeup of the state can also have implications for political contestation. Scholarship has shown that states with large economic and political disparities between ethnopolitical groups are more likely to experience political violence. For example, prior to descending into civil war in the early 1990s, the former state of Yugoslavia had large economic and political disparities between its various ethnic groups (Cederman, Weidmann, and Gleditsch 2011).

The ongoing contestation of the state has consequences for human security. An ethnically divided state, for example, could spell disaster for a minority group that does not have adequate security or legal protections. A state that does not adequately provide for the basic needs of its citizens creates the conditions in which human security is most likely to be threatened. A strict interpretation of sovereignty, however, leaves a dismal outlook for how such threats to human security could and should be addressed. Under strict interpretations of sovereignty, people that find their personal security threatened by the actions (or lack of action) of the state they live in would only be able to rely on their own or domestic sources for recourse. In many cases, this would mean that there are few options available—except, perhaps, to flee, engage in risky social protest, or take up arms.

The historical record shows quite clearly that, despite an international system of sovereign states constructed on the principle of nonintervention, states have found numerous justifications to engage in intervention, whether on national, global, or human security grounds. Therefore a key legal concern of international politics is determining when intervention by an outside power into the affairs of another state is justified (if ever).

The human security approach requires that we think deeply about the juxtaposition between protecting human life and the fundamentally problematic nature of interventionist policies. This raises several important questions that are at the crux of the human security approach: Can a state, under the guise of sovereignty, rightfully carry out actions against its own citizenry that, if carried out by a foreign or occupying power, would be considered violations of international humanitarian law? If the answer is no, then what instruments are available to prevent those actions from happening and to punish those responsible once they do happen? The other side of this question is the consideration of what rights or obligations others have to intervene in a state when that state is unable or unwilling to protect its citizens from widespread harm to its population—whether harm in the form of war, natural disaster, or famine. Furthermore, what responsibility do outside actors have for the unintended consequences and failures that often accompany interventionist policies? It is under these parameters that the complex challenges to the principle of nonintervention emerge.

Why Nonintervention?

While *sovereignty* implies a principle of nonintervention, intervention by states into the affairs of others has been a permanent feature of international affairs. States have a key interest in how other states behave. Thus a state's foreign policy is largely focused on how to influence other states to align their behavior more closely with the state's own interests—or at least to reduce the harm that other states' interests might cause for the state. While much of this will be pursued through diplomatic persuasion, intervention occurs when a state uses more forceful efforts to compel changes in other states' behavior. Intervention can take on many forms, military intervention being the strongest and most visible approach; however, intervention can include economic and diplomatic tools as well.

Because the international system is said to be **anarchic**, meaning there is no overarching authority capable of punishing rule violators, states are seen to be on their own when it comes to guaranteeing their security. Such a **self-help system** means that war, if not common, is expected, as each state sees military force and other aggressive tactics as legitimate means for pursuing their own interests and compelling others to change their behavior. This world order, coupled with technological advances in weaponry, led to disastrous results in the first half of the twentieth century. The catalysts for both World War I and World War II were rooted in attempts by predatory states to expand their borders and increase their global power. Global institution building following both world wars (the League of Nations following World War I and the United Nations following World War II) was founded on a desire to resolve the instability seen to be the result of a purely self-help system. Both the League of Nations and the United Nations were attempts to create a **collective security system**, in which predatory behavior by one state would elicit a collective response by all international actors (Hathaway and Shapiro 2018).

The weakness of the League of Nations was laid bare by the onset of World War II. The creation of the United Nations following World War II, therefore, tried to address those weaknesses while also creating the mechanisms to better respond to the human suffering that occurred during that war, including the Holocaust, the deliberate targeting of civilian populations, and the mass displacement of persons. This happened in three ways: (1) the UN reaffirmed the principle of sovereignty but couched it within the principle of self-determination, (2) it defined rules regarding the conduct of war between states, and (3) it articulated a set of universal human rights for all peoples, regardless of national origin.

The principle of nonintervention is embedded within the United Nations Charter. According to Article 51 of the UN Charter, a state may take military action of its own accord only in self-defense. In other instances the UN Security Council is tasked with overseeing matters that pose threats to international peace and security. Resolutions by the UN Security Council must pass with a majority of voting members and without a veto from any of the **permanent five members** (or P5; China, France, Russia, the United Kingdom, and the United States). One of the pressing questions facing the UN Security Council asks what constitutes a threat to international peace and security. Should internal conflicts fall into this category—thus becoming a legitimate concern of the Security Council? The answer over time has become a clear yes, but this position evolved slowly, in part due to the rapidly changing transformation of the international system.

After World War II, the world saw a steady dismantling of the European colonial system. When the UN Charter was signed in 1945, there were only forty-nine sovereign states in the world, with large portions of Africa and Asia under colonial rule by European powers. Today 195 states are officially recognized as independent and sovereign. The transition from a global system once dominated by colonialism to one of independent sovereign states opened the possibility for wide-scale conflict if newly independent states looked to shape their borders to include traditionally held territory and kinsfolk. To try to avoid this outcome, the UN system recognized newly independent states based on the boundaries that had been drawn by the former colonial powers, not adhering to any ethnic or religious divisions that might exist within those borders. This may have reduced the amount of potential interstate conflict, but it also increased the number of intrastate conflicts as different ethnic, religious, and ideological groups competed, often violently, for control of the newly formed state (Cederman and Vogt 2017). The Cold War rivalry between the United States and the Soviet Union often exacerbated these conflicts, as each power sought to support and arm those groups that professed allegiance with their own political ideologies. After the Cold War, these ideological divisions, subsided for the most part, only to expose the ethnic or religious fissures that had often been at the heart of the earlier conflict (Marks 2004).

The form of violence that accompanied the rise of identity-based conflicts—ethnic cleansings, forced displacement, wartime sexual violence, genocide—have led to a global reconceptualization of sovereignty and the responsibility that states and intergovernmental organizations have to stop these atrocities. These debates, however, should not ignore the colonial legacies of today's international system and the lasting ramifications of that history (Acharya 2022). As we have seen, the way borders were drawn as the great powers lost their colonial territories meant that the formerly imposed colonial systems, which frequently favored one identity group over others, remained a fixture of the newly formed states and generated a source of future conflict (Wucherpfennig, Hunziker, and Cederman 2016). In addition, when these new states falter, the great powers are often quick to impose what could be described as neocolonial solutions onto the faltering state—whether structural adjustment programs or a prioritization of military assistance to the state's security forces. These approaches often reinforce the elites already in power and further marginalize disenfranchised people.

Thinking about the four security perspectives introduced in chapter 1, it is clear that post–World War II policy making has been driven by those holding either a statist or federalist security perspective. These two perspectives emphasize a strong state that is ultimately responsible for its own security, with the federalist perspective allowing for more coordination between states within the framework of intergovernmental organizations. The emphasis on the militarized state as the system's core unit and the tremendous number of resources the state can potentially extract for those that control it creates the conditions for violent contestation of the state. While both the nativist and the cosmopolitan security perspectives challenge the primacy of the state as security provider, any discussion of human security during acute violent conflict needs to consider these complicated legacies. Therefore the means by which these changes have taken place are constrained by these institutional realities (which we will discuss further in chapter 6).

Human Insecurity in Acute Conflict

Human security is most immediately threatened during **acute conflict**. While conflict is a constant feature of interpersonal and intergroup interaction, acute conflict has a substantial probability of violence (Sharp 1998). It is difficult to capture within a text the experience of living through war. All civilians face greater risks of violence during conflict. However, different people's experiences differ from conflict to conflict and even within the same armed conflict. A rural farmer, for instance, will likely face fundamentally different threats to their security than a poor urban dweller. During conflict, women, men, and children all experience a variety of threats (see chapter 10 on gender equality). Boys and men, for instance, are more likely to be pressed into military service or to be killed by enemy forces (Carpenter 2003; Sjoberg 2014). Women and girls are frequently targeted for indentured servitude or sexual violence and exploitation.

There are also structural changes during wartime that threaten people's security. War destroys economies, health care systems, and agriculture and poisons water supplies. These conditions can greatly affect the mortality rates of people living in conflict-affected areas, as they are not able to access the basic necessities for sustaining life. The loss of life due to these indirect factors is sometimes referred to as **structural violence**. In fact, the immediate and long-term damage to a state or locality's infrastructure and services is often a greater cause of human mortality than direct violence.

The roots of conflict are complex and multifaceted and cannot be adequately addressed in this volume (see Mason and Mitchell 2016). Nevertheless, understanding the type of conflict matters if we want to understand how human security is affected. For example, a revolutionary group trying to impose their ideology onto the state might try to limit civilian casualties, as that could undermine its support among the greater population, which the group will need to rule effectively (Weinstein 2006). At the same time, however, those civilians may see certain human rights severely restricted by the revolutionary ideology. Identity-driven conflicts, on the other hand, are motivated by exclusionary ideas and, therefore, may be more likely to involve forced displacement, ethnic cleansing, or genocide, as groups try to re-create the state around their own ethnic or religious identity.

Gathering statistics on harm to civilians during conflict is difficult. Access to combat zones is often limited, and armed actors rarely collect data on how their own actions harm the civilian population (although they will certainly highlight how their opponents' actions do). International organizations like the United Nations High Commissioner for Refugees (UNHCR), for example, track the number of global refugees, and NGOs such as the Internal Displacement Monitoring Center gather data on the number of internally displaced persons. NGOs also play an important role in providing information on civilian casualties in conflict. Humanitarian agencies, such as Médecins Sans Frontières or the International Committee of the Red Cross (see chapter 3), often see firsthand the ways in which combatants target civilians. Other NGOs have worked to develop methods for systematically collecting data on civilian harm. The Center for Civilians in Conflict (CIVIC), for example, has found that during conflict civilians are often left to their own, often ad hoc, survival strategies. The collection of these data have greatly helped researchers and policy makers better understand the effects of conflict on civilian populations.

Events in Syria since 2011 have demonstrated that a single conflict can rapidly devastate those living in a war zone and can have broader ramifications well beyond its borders. The brutality of the conflict in Syria contributed to the highest total number of battle deaths since the end of the Cold War (Pettersson et al. 2021). In addition, this single armed conflict has led to the displacement of over thirteen million people, with 6.6 million refugees and 6.7 million internally displaced persons, according to UNHCR—contributing to the highest global number of displaced persons since World War II (United Nations Refugee Agency, n.d.). The recent surge of violent conflict around the world reminds us that downward trends in violence are reversible under the right conditions and that we have transitioned into an era in which the norms and structures that sustained a previous peace have eroded.

Mary Kaldor (2007, 3) defines wars following the end of the Cold War as *new wars*—that is, wars that are fought "in the context of the disintegration of states" rather than state-building exercises, which she characterizes as *old wars*. That said, it should be noted that the structural dynamics of these wars were not, in fact, new (Kalyvas 2001). According to Kaldor, "old wars" were fought in accordance with certain rules codified under the Geneva and Hague Conventions. These rules governed conduct regarding civilian casualties and prisoners of war. However, the rules were primarily concerned with the conduct of states engaged in military action against other states, particularly while occupying foreign territory. It was not always clear how those rules would apply to the conduct of violent nonstate actors or state responses against those actors. This legal ambiguity has contributed to the free reign that those fighting these wars have had with respect to their treatment of civilian populations. It has also raised questions about who has the responsibility to protect people from harm and what mechanisms should exist for redressing atrocities committed against civilian populations.

EVOLVING NORMS OF PROTECTION

The argument that civilians should be protected during warfare is not new, but how they should be protected and who is responsible for that protection remain difficult questions to answer. Norms of **civilian protection** have evolved over time. One important consideration is that the changing nature of both the international system and warfare has implications for how we think about these questions.

Limiting the Brutality of War: Just War Theory and International Humanitarian Law

Just war theory, rooted in the teachings of Saint Augustine, Saint Thomas Aquinas, and later theologians, provides a framework articulating when, how, and why governments may engage in warfare (it is helpful to note here that the modern state system was not yet in existence when Augustine and Aquinas wrote about war). **Just wars**—wars fought with good intentions for one's own state or on behalf of others—are permissible according to Judeo-Christian texts and philosophy. The Quran similarly condones war for a just cause, chiefly in defense of Islam, and places restrictions on combat that protect women, children, and the elderly. Islamic philosophers also believed that leaders had divine authority, albeit with limited power, and tasked individuals with obedience to the state as long as the state did not demand disobedience to God.

In each tradition there is an apparent tension between the sanctity of life and the necessity of state-imposed order, a trade-off that persists when wars and human rights violations occur today. Just war theory acknowledges that violence is an inevitable aspect of the human condition and does not seek to ban war but, rather, to "harness" it to achieve good ends (Hoffmann 1981, 47). At its core, just war theory recognizes that while war and violence should be avoided when possible, there are circumstances in which war is an appropriate means to restore justice. Wars may be appropriate when they adhere to the constraints outlined in the three pillars of just war theory: ***jus ad bellum***, ***jus in bello***, and (the newest pillar) ***jus post bellum***. The first limits the causes for which war is justifiable (e.g., in self-defense or in defense of civilians persecuted by their government). The second outlines expectations for moral behavior in warfare that minimizes harm to those fighting in wars as well as noncombatants (e.g., injured or surrendering combatants and civilians do not pose a threat and are entitled to special protections). The third pillar has taken shape in recent years and places the responsibility for reconstruction and reestablishment of a just order after the end of armed conflict on the parties to the conflict, especially the victor.

The principles of just war theory have endured over the 1,600-odd years since Augustine wrote about them and are embodied in the treaties and conventions that comprise international humanitarian law, the rules of warfare developed in the nineteenth and twentieth centuries. **International humanitarian law** places limitations on the use of force by states and the conduct of combatants acting on behalf of states. The will to compose and comply with laws of war arose in response to recognition of the horrors individuals experienced in armed conflict. The **Geneva Conventions** resulted from a series of meetings between states between 1864 and 1949; these international treaties outline rights and protections related to combatants, prisoners of war, and civilians caught up in armed conflict. The International Committee of the Red Cross was cofounded in 1863 by Henry Dunant, a businessman who became an international humanitarian relief advocate after witnessing the mass casualties and lack of medical treatment in Italy at the Battle of

Solferino in 1859. The ICRC played a central role in establishing a legal framework for humanitarian assistance and protection of human life in wartime through the Geneva Conventions.

The **First Geneva Convention (1864)** pertains to the welfare of wounded combatants and establishes a right to medical care and protection for International Committee of the Red Cross members working in war zones. The **Second Geneva Convention (1906)** applies to sailors in armed forces, expanding the protections of the First Geneva Convention to war at sea. The **Third Geneva Convention (1929)** establishes protections for prisoners of war. The **Fourth Geneva Convention (1949)** outlines the rights of and protections for civilians in armed conflict but retains its focus on conflict between states and conduct involving the other party's population and not one's own. Colonial powers used this distinction to justify repressive responses to liberation movements within their colonial holdings as those populations, according to the colonial powers' logic, were part of their territory (Elkins 2022). The Geneva Conventions were not the only attempts to regulate the conduct of warring parties. The **Hague Convention of 1899** was a multilateral treaty that proposed a framework for conflict prevention through mediation, protocols for declarations of war, and rules for humane treatment of prisoners.

Another set of treaties has focused on restricting the types of weapons that can legally be used in warfare, focusing on those with more indiscriminate properties, such as land mines or biological, chemical, and nuclear weapons. The **Hague Convention of 1907**, for instance, outlawed the use of poison gas and aerial bombing (from balloons, since airplanes had yet to appear on the battlefield). The **Biological Weapons Convention (BWC) of 1972** bans the development, production, stockpiling, and use of biological weapons, and the **Chemical Weapons Convention (CWC) of 1993** similarly bans chemical weapons. The **Treaty on the Prohibition of Nuclear Weapons of 2017** takes the same approach and gained enough parties to enter into force in January 2021. Unlike the BWC and the CWC, however, none of the states who possess nuclear weapons have joined the treaty. States have shown to be much more capable of reaching consensus on prohibiting weapons of mass destruction. The antipersonnel mine treaty is one of the few treaties that seeks to eliminate an entire class of conventional weaponry.

International treaties and agreements seeking to keep warfare within certain moral boundaries embody the concepts of just war theory and hold states accountable for their actions. The changing scope and nature of warfare in the twenty-first century calls into question the extent to which agreements devised by and for states apply to today's armed conflicts and the nonstate parties to those conflicts. While the deliberate targeting of another state's civilians or injured combatants in war is clearly understood as a violation of international law, it has been less clear how the same legal principles apply if the action was carried out by a state against its own citizens or by nonstate combatants in insurgencies, civil wars, or actions against multilateral interventions.

Common article 3 of the Geneva Convention of 1949 says that civilian protections extend to "noninternational armed conflict," so in principle international humanitarian law regarding the protection of civilians applies to intrastate conflict as well, with all sides held responsible for not directly targeting civilians, avoiding indiscriminate attacks, and conducting military operations in such a way as to limit civilian casualties. This ambiguity has been further rectified through several international agreements and treaties that address violence against civilians by their own state. These include the human rights treaties previously discussed in chapter 4, as well as the Genocide Convention (1948), the Refugee Convention (1951), and the Guiding Principles on Internal Displacement (2001).

One key problem of this body of law is that there is not a consistent and standard mechanism for enforcement—meaning violators have routinely avoided consequences for their actions. This has been partly addressed through the Rome Statute of the International Criminal Court (1998), a legal framework that holds individuals criminally accountable for the ordering or carrying out of atrocities against their own civilians (which we will discuss in chapter 7).

The United Nations and Civilian Protection

The most pressing human security threat during conflict is direct or indirect violence against civilian populations. According to international humanitarian law, civilians are a protected class during conflict, and intentionally targeting them constitutes a war crime. Yet during the Cold War the debate at the UN on civilian protection during intrastate conflict was limited to basic (and severely contested) questions on human rights and refugee issues (MacFarlane and Khong 2006). As we discussed in chapter 2, a string of atrocities following the end of the Cold War—including the dissolution of Somalia, the genocide in Rwanda, and the massacre at Srebrenica—brought greater attention to the threats faced by civilians during conflict. Beginning in the mid-1990s, the United Nations began to adopt a series of resolutions, protocols, and guiding principles drafted to protect civilians during armed conflict. This included efforts to develop a set of principles for states to follow regarding internally displaced populations and the creation of judicial instruments capable of trying and punishing individuals who commit war crimes. The actual implementation of these norms, however, has been applied unevenly.

The United Nations Security Council is the body specifically tasked with the "primary responsibility for the maintenance of international peace and security" (United Nations 1945, Article 24.1). Therefore, the most direct way that the United Nations has engaged human security issues during ongoing conflicts has been through Security Council resolutions. These resolutions use a wide range of tools to address human security concerns during conflict, including diplomatic engagement, such as offering good offices (i.e., using the prestige of the UN to help facilitate negotiations between groups in conflict), fact-finding missions, mediation, and civilian monitoring; the deployment of military force; the levying of sanctions; and the condemnation of one or more parties engaged in the conflict (Beardsley, Cunningham, and White 2017). However, because the Security Council is made up of individual nation-states, the security issues that it chooses to engage are limited to those not threatening one of the veto-wielding states' self-identified national security interests. This dynamic was particularly present during the Cold War, when the United States and the Soviet Union continually vetoed or threatened to veto Security Council resolutions endangering either of their interests, but it still remains a challenge today.

Russia's invasion of Ukraine in February 2022 further demonstrated this challenge but also highlighted mechanisms through which a unified international community can respond to unprovoked acts of aggression. When action by the United Nations Security Council was blocked by Russia's veto, the General Assembly voted overwhelmingly to condemn the invasion. This condemnation has been accompanied by a series of punitive and targeted sanctions against Russia as well as its removal from numerous international bodies, including the UN Human Rights Council. Whether these actions will in the long run have the effect of fully restoring Ukraine's sovereignty remains to be seen; but they do signal to possible future aggressors that conquest does not pay.

After the Cold War, there was renewed emphasis on creating a more effective UN system. Part of this derived from a desire to resolve the record-high number of intrastate conflicts taking place at that time. These efforts largely came from the UN's Office of the Secretary-General, beginning with the publication of "An Agenda for Peace" in 1992, but were also supported by an unusual degree of Security Council consensus on greater international engagement in ongoing crises. This included the authorization of a number of new peacekeeping operations that increasingly included civilian protection mandates (discussed in more detail in chapter 7). The early optimism, however, faded with the harsh realities of intervention; the UN was criticized either for acting only after mass atrocities had already happened, as was the case in Rwanda, or for being impotent in the face of an ongoing atrocity, as was the case during the massacre at Srebrenica. Because the UN relies on member states to supply military personnel to conduct its missions, a rapid response to crises is often logistically impossible, and the organization imposes strict and extremely cautious rules of engagement once forces are on the ground.

To counter these issues, both the Security Council and the secretary-general's office began to codify the obligations states have toward civilian populations during conflict. In September 1999, Secretary-General Kofi Annan issued on behalf of the UN Security Council a report on the protection of civilians (United Nations Security Council 1999a). In that report, Annan offered recommendations for how the UN and its member states could better address civilian protection issues. These recommendations included encouraging states to ratify and implement international instruments designed to protect civilians and to punish war crimes, specifically supporting the creation of the International Criminal Court. Further, Annan urged states to follow new protocols regarding the rights and treatment of internally displaced populations as well as the treatment of humanitarians working in combat zones. This report was followed by a series of Security Council resolutions that further emphasized civilian protection during conflict.

Since the 1999 report, how civilian protection concerns are integrated into Security Council resolutions has become increasingly institutionalized. In 2007, Secretary-General Ban Ki-moon issued a new report on the protection of civilians that called for the creation of "a dedicated, expert-level working group to facilitate the systematic and sustained consideration and analysis of protection concerns" (United Nations Security Council 2007). The informal group of experts formed upon this recommendation meets regularly to help craft language on civilian protection issues being addressed in Security Council resolutions. The recommendations are based on the evaluation of a conflict in six areas: (1) the conduct of hostilities and its impact on civilians, (2) violations and abuses of human rights, (3) humanitarian access, (4) protection issues related to displacement, (5) gender-based protection concerns, including sexual violence, and (6) protection concerns related to children.

Additionally, the Commission on Human Rights and, since 2006, the Human Rights Council, as well as the High Commissioner for Human Rights (established in 1993), have been tasked by the Security Council with investigating and reporting on human rights violations all over the world, with the purpose of better informing the Security Council on human rights violations when they are crafting resolutions. These efforts have resulted in more specific tasks related to civilian protection concerns within UN Security Council resolutions themselves.

Due to the voting rules of the Security Council, resolutions do not provide a consistent response to violations of humanitarian law. Many long-lasting conflicts are immune from Security Council resolutions due to the national security interests of one or more of the veto-wielding P5 members. For instance, a resolution was unable to pass regarding Kosovo in 1994 due to

Russia's objection (which is what eventually led to the unauthorized NATO response). Israel's occupation of the Palestinian territories is essentially immune from Security Council interference due to the relationship between the United States and Israel. Any resolution on the conflict in Syria was largely watered down or rejected due to Russian support for the Assad regime. China, while often abstaining rather than vetoing, has continued to raise objections to resolutions that it sees as violating the principle of sovereignty and since 2007 has often sided with Russia in vetoing resolutions that call for increased UN intervention. France, on the other hand, has pledged to not veto any resolution that directly responds to a humanitarian crisis.

To overcome the power politics of the Security Council, the UN General Assembly, made up of all member states, has used its voting powers to create an expansive bureaucracy designed to help the UN respond to humanitarian crises around the world. Some of the earliest votes taken by the General Assembly concerned the rights of refugees, which eventually led to the Refugee Convention in 1951 and the creation of the UNHCR in 1950, which now provides support for displaced persons in conflicts around the world. As discussed in chapter 3, other UN agencies that have been tasked with providing assistance to people experiencing humanitarian crises include UNICEF and the World Food Programme.

The end of the Cold War created an environment that led to institutional changes within the UN in an effort to engage conflicts as they occur. These changes created a host of new agencies and reorganizations to already-existing ones. While the Security Council is the body of the UN that is tasked with overseeing peace and security issues, numerous other agencies are engaged in tasks that facilitate various peace processes. These agencies have been given the institutional capacity to carry out the Security Council's resolutions when asked to but are also able to engage in various activities even without an explicit mandate.

Of major concern for UN agencies is determining when to become involved in a crisis and how to avoid multiple agencies overlapping with each other and with the NGOs also working in the area. The impetus for these changes started with General Assembly Resolution 46/182 in 1991, which called for strengthening UN capacity to respond to complex humanitarian emergencies. While the resolution was primarily meant to respond to natural disasters, over time its framework has been used to provide mechanisms to mitigate humanitarian disasters caused by warfare. The resolution created two new tools for response: the Emergency Relief Coordinator, who serves as a focal point for the multiple agencies tasked with overseeing humanitarian emergencies, and the Interagency Standing Committee (ISAC), which includes all humanitarian partners, from those working within the UN to various relief funds to the Red Cross Movement to NGOs working in the field. ISAC works to ensure interagency and partner coordination during emergencies. In 1998, additional reforms to improve this interagency coordination during conflict were enacted, including the creation of the United Nations Office for the Coordination of Humanitarian Affairs, tasked with overseeing these processes and evaluating when humanitarian crises—both human-made and natural—were likely to emerge. At the 2016 World Humanitarian Summit, further efforts were made to improve coordination between the development, humanitarian, and peacebuilding sectors both within the United Nations and among its local and global NGO partners (Barakat and Milton 2020).

Has this attention to civilian protection at the UN level made any difference? Certainly the United Nations and its partners have been able to provide services that relieve immediate suffering. The UNHCR in particular has effectively provided both short- and long-term shelter for displaced populations. In addition, the UNHCR has helped states register displaced populations and develop mechanisms for resolving displacement. That said, a series of international crises beginning in the 2010s has been particularly brutal toward civilians, severely straining the UN's abilities to effectively prevent atrocity. At least in the foreseeable future, the UN (and regional organizations such as the African Union) will continue to face challenges as a human security actor due to lack of available resources and constraints imposed by its member states.

In the next section, we discuss the responsibility to protect (R2P) as an attempt to develop a more universal framework for responding to mass atrocities.

HUMANITARIAN INTERVENTION AND THE RESPONSIBILITY TO PROTECT

Conflicts driven by ethnic, tribal, or religious divisions have renewed discussion of how to protect individuals, particularly noncombatants, during conflict. Starvation and the disintegration of the state in Somalia, ethnic cleansing during the breakup of Yugoslavia, and the genocide in Rwanda, among other atrocities, forced the international community to consider what, if anything, should be done in response to similar crises. As we discussed in the previous section, much of the existing international legal framework dealing with civilian protection was focused not on intrastate conflicts but on cases in which a state was in a conflict with another state. Thus the bulk of international humanitarian law concerning the protection of civilians focused on outside parties or occupying powers and was ambiguous regarding how civilians are to be treated by their own state.

However, with conflicts now more likely to happen within states, a growing network of global activists, both within governments and the NGO community, have begun to draw attention to the security threats people face in conflict. These activists put pressure on their governments, the United Nations, and various regional organizations to develop better response mechanisms to humanitarian crises. Consequently, the international community has begun to work toward creating a stronger set of mechanisms to respond to these crises, particularly when mass atrocities have occurred. This has led to efforts to create a more precise legal framework, embedded within multilateral institutions, that determines when the use of force to intervene in the affairs of other states can be justified (Finnemore 1996). These efforts have led to a more activist UN, particularly within the Office of the Secretary-General and at the Security Council, which saw the instability and human suffering caused by these conflicts as threats to international peace and security.

The translation of civilian protection concerns into policy, however, has followed a disjointed and controversial path. While there is little vocal opposition to the idea that noncombatants should not be deliberately targeted during intrastate warfare, how to prevent it is not always clear. Consider efforts to protect **internally displaced persons (IDPs)**, people who are displaced from their homes due to conflict or natural disasters but do not cross an international border. **Refugees**, people who are displaced from their homes and do cross an international border, are granted legal rights under the 1951 Convention relating to the Status of Refugees. This disparity between the legal protections offered to two groups facing similar circumstances led a global group of activists and officials within the United Nations to create a set of guiding principles for the treatment of internally displaced populations, based on existing international law.

Francis Deng, appointed the UN's first Special Rapporteur on the Human Rights of Internally Displaced Persons, coined the term **sovereignty as responsibility**—the obligation of a sovereign state to protect the human rights of its citizens. A state, then, is obligated to prevent displacement of persons from occurring in the first place, to protect the rights of the displaced when displacement does occur, and then to find an acceptable durable solution to the displacement (Cohen 2012; Andersen-Rodgers 2019).

All of this, however, is complicated by the fact that states are often the actors responsible for atrocities against their own civilian populations. This, coupled with norms of nonintervention, prevents any type of serious international response. United Nations peacekeeping was originally conceived as a mechanism by which the international community could serve as neutral observers between armed actors, but only after a cease-fire or peace accord had been agreed upon. The peacekeeping forces, therefore, would be in the country with the state's consent and could be asked to leave at any time. Consequently, the principle of nonintervention meant that the international community would be required to stand by while mass atrocities were knowingly taking place.

It is under these circumstances that justifications for humanitarian intervention have been made. **Humanitarian interventions** are military interventions, ideally under the auspices of a UN Security Council resolution, with the intended purpose of relieving the ongoing human suffering of people living in conflict zones or areas affected by natural disasters. The term *intervention* implies that the effort happens without the consent of one or more parties to the conflict or violence, thus presenting a challenge to the sovereign norms that have governed the international system.

Prior to the end of the Cold War, humanitarian interventions were essentially nonexistent, largely due to the structural limitations imposed by the Security Council veto and the presence of both the United States and the Soviet Union on the council. While there are cases in which an intervention did relieve human suffering—such as Vietnam's intervention in Cambodia in 1979, which effectively stopped the ongoing genocide—the primary purpose of these interventions was to advance the intervening state's foreign policy goals, and the relief of human suffering was more or less an unintended or secondary consequence. After the Cold War ended, international actions justified on humanitarian grounds became more common. Western powers in particular became much more willing to frame interventions in the language of humanitarianism. While Operation Desert Storm in 1991 was not justified on humanitarian grounds, but rather to respond to Iraq's invasion of Kuwait, the establishment of a no-fly zone in Northern and Southern Iraq to protect Kurd and Shiite populations at the close of the war *was* justified on such grounds (Zieliński 2021). Later, the 1999 NATO intervention in Kosovo was justified entirely on humanitarian grounds, although without Security Council approval.

BOX 5.1. THINK ABOUT IT . . .
RESPONSIBILITY TO PROTECT (R2P)
VERSUS PROTECTION OF CIVILIANS (POC)

This chapter examines the emergence of *Responsibility to Protect* (R2P) as a norm aimed at protecting civilians against the most egregious war crimes and human rights violations. The following chapters use a different term: **protection of civilians** (POC). What is the fundamental difference between the two? Both concepts emerged in the international discourse at about the same time in response to mass atrocities committed during the mid-1990s. The UN Security Council first passed a resolution on POC in 1999 (Resolution 1265), and *The Responsibility to Protect: The Report of the International Commission on Intervention and State Sovereignty* was drafted at the end of September 2001.

Both are rooted in the same goal: protecting civilians from harm from violent conflict.

Not without controversy, R2P was unanimously agreed to at the 2005 World Summit. According to the summit's Outcome Document, R2P represents an agreement that states will be "prepared to take collective action" when a state "manifestly fail[s] to protect its citizens from genocide, war crimes, ethnic cleansing, and crimes against humanity" (United Nations General Assembly 2005). According to R2P, that action must be authorized by the UN Security Council, and force is to be used only as a last resort. But as we will see, how to apply R2P in practice is riddled with challenges and controversy.

The notion of POC, on the other hand, grew from the increasing pressure on UN peacekeeping missions to be better prepared to protect civilians. POC is deeply grounded within international humanitarian law. That said, there are varied interpretations of what exactly POC means—from the protection norms found in the Geneva Conventions to the narrower goal of physically protecting civilians from harm during an ongoing peacekeeping operation. Thus, while R2P has by many accounts fallen out of recent favor, POC language is now a key component of international discourse. Protecting civilians has become an operational requirement for peacekeeping. In 2017 ten missions that had explicit mandates to protect civilians. Nevertheless, protection mandates often use confusing language and can suffer from promising more than what can reasonably be delivered, leaving UN peacekeepers confused as to how far any given mandate extends. In some cases, peacekeepers themselves have been the perpetrators, through sexual exploitation and abuse of the very populations they are supposed to be protecting.

Consider the following questions:

1. Who has the responsibility to protect civilians during conflict?
2. Should the same principles that inform the collective security system of the United Nations be extended to apply to the protection of human populations in other states?
3. What do you think about the increased use of civilian-protection mandates in peacekeeping operations? What are the practical implications for peacekeeping operations that have such a mandate?
4. Does the failure to implement civilian-protection mandates damage UN credibility or limit its ability to broker or maintain peace?

Humanitarian arguments as justification for military intervention persists, even where the humanitarian aims are dubious at best. Despite its deliberate targeting of civilian populations throughout the conflict, Saudi Arabia, for example, justified its intervention in Yemen on the basis of its "responsibility" to "protect the people of Yemen" (Royal Embassy of Saudi Arabia Information Office 2015). This is one of the key criticisms of humanitarian interventions: it is unclear what actions by a state against its citizens should justify an intervention. Therefore, critics have argued, much of the stated need for intervention reflects powerful states' national interests rather than a just and systematic response to relieving human suffering. States born of former colonies have expressed concerns about humanitarian intervention, which has typically been accompanied by military force and the imposition of Western institutional structures, a veiled form of neocolonialism. Proponents of creating a robust civilian protection regime have recognized these criticisms and sought to create a clearer and more just set of criteria for responding to mass atrocities. The primary effort through which this has happened has been the development of the **Responsibility to Protect** (R2P) doctrine.

When Serbian forces began conducting a campaign of ethnic cleansing in Kosovo in 1998, hopes for an international militarized response with the backing of a UN Security Council resolution were dashed when Russia and China promised to veto any such resolution. When NATO intervened anyway, they violated Article 2(4) of the UN Charter, which prohibits the use of force without Security Council authorization. This led Secretary-General Kofi Annan to begin a process to more clearly address the issues related to humanitarian interventions. In his 1999 opening address to the General Assembly, Annan argued that the international community had to find a balanced solution between the principle of nonintervention and a state's obligation to protect the rights of its citizens. He further argued that the UN has a role in helping states fulfill their obligations to their citizens and that any principle of intervention needed to be "fairly and consistently applied." Thus starting in 1999 the United Nations began to systematically formalize a set of strategies to protect civilians in armed conflict (United Nations Security Council 1999a).

Canada took up Annan's challenge and in 2000 established the International Commission on Intervention and State Sovereignty (ICISS). In December of 2001, the commission released *Responsibility to Protect*, a report arguing that states are obligated to protect their citizens from what are known as the four crimes: genocide, war crimes, ethnic cleansing, and crimes against humanity (see table 5.1). When the state is either unwilling or unable to provide these protections, the responsibility to act falls to the international community (Bellamy 2011).

Table 5.1. The Four Crimes: Genocide, War Crimes, Ethnic Cleansing, and Crimes against Humanity

Crime	Definition
Genocide	Acts meant to destroy, in whole or in part, a national, ethnic, racial, or religious group
War Crimes	The "serious violations of the laws and customs applicable in international armed conflict"
Ethnic Cleansing	The planned, deliberate removal from a specific territory, persons of a particular ethnic group, by force or intimidation, in order to render the area ethnically homogenous
Crimes against Humanity	Acts such as murder, extermination, enslavement, deportation or forcible transfer of population, torture, rape, enforced disappearance of persons, apartheid, or similar inhumane acts committed in a widespread or systematic attack against a civilian population

Sources: International Criminal Court 2011, articles 6, 7, and 8; United Nations Security Council 1994, 33.

R2P is constructed around three pillars: *Pillar one* is the state's responsibility to protect its own citizens from genocide, war crimes, ethnic cleansing, and crimes against humanity. According to the secretary-general's report on implementing R2P, states can work toward fulfilling these obligations by becoming parties to the already-existing human rights treaties that obligate signatories to protect the rights of their citizens. In addition, states should integrate the principles of human rights and international humanitarian law into their domestic legal systems. This commitment to protecting citizens' rights would, presumably, lessen the chance that internal conflict in a state would escalate to the point that any of the four crimes would be committed. *Pillar two* is the responsibility of the international community to help states fulfill their responsibility to protect. Much of the activity supported by pillar two is part of norm promotion. The international community would encourage states to fulfill their pillar one commitments and provide technical assistance when requested. *Pillar three* is the international community's responsibility to take action, with Security Council authorization, when a state refuses or is unable to fulfill its responsibility to protect its citizens from one or more of the four crimes. Thus, while R2P challenges a strict norm of nonintervention, it also limits what states can justify as a reason to intervene.

According to Gareth Evans, co-chair of ICISS, R2P was innovative in four ways: First, it reframed the debate, moving from the right to intervene to the responsibilities that each state has to protect its own citizens and citizens in other states from mass atrocity crimes. Second, R2P expanded the range of actors beyond those that had the military capabilities to project force abroad. By focusing on the responsibility for each state to protect its own citizens (pillar one) and then moving to how outside states can assist others in reaching that obligation (pillar two), R2P became an ongoing commitment based primarily on prevention activities. Third, R2P broadened the range of responses beyond military intervention. According to R2P, military intervention is seen as a means of last resort, and pillar three activities include any number of coercive activities, such as sanctions or international criminal prosecutions, that do not include the use of force. Fourth, R2P sought to clarify when pillar three uses of force would be justified. This included Security Council authorization as well as the creation of a set of benchmarks that needed to be met in order for force to be legitimate. These benchmarks included seriousness of the harm being threatened, the motivation of the proposed military action, whether peaceful alternatives existed, the proportionality of the response, and whether more good than harm would result from the intervention (Evans 2010).

The merits of R2P were debated at the 2005 World Summit and again in 2009 at the United Nations General Assembly. These debates demonstrated that there was an agreement between almost all states on a number of key points, including prevention as a key component of R2P, that R2P was not a new legal principle but grounded in already-established international law, that it could only be invoked to prevent or stop one of the four crimes, and that there was a need for political will in order for R2P to be successfully implemented (Hehir 2012). While there were (and still are) critics of the doctrine, particularly around the use of pillar three, R2P was unanimously adopted at the 2005 World Summit.

Even so, R2P remains controversial, even among its supporters. Those who saw R2P as a welcome tool for the prevention of mass atrocities fear that there are a number of weaknesses in the doctrine that could prevent its effective implementation. For one, the structural conditions under which force must be justified (i.e., through the authorization of the UN Security Council) remains in place, meaning that international action remains coupled to great power politics and the national interests of Security Council members. The secretary-general's report pleaded with Security Council members to not use their veto when a clear case has been made that one of the four crimes is being committed. As seen in the response to Syria's civil war, such moral restraint is difficult when one or more Security Council members see vital national interests at stake. This problem is coupled with the fact that there is no single agency within the UN system that has the mandate to determine authoritatively and independently whether and when one of the four crimes is being committed. Furthermore, the UN's lack of a rapid-reaction force specifically trained in responding to the four crimes means that forces must be put together on an ad hoc basis. This means that the mission is limited to the contributing states' capabilities, willingness to commit specific types of personnel (i.e., air power versus ground troops), and response time. Such problems run the risk of delegitimizing the principle of R2P when the international community is unable to respond or responds poorly. This problem is exacerbated by the fact that it has never been decidedly resolved whether unilateral action by a state is permissible if the UN Security Council fails to act.

Critics suggest that R2P operates as an extension of past colonial structures and power dynamics in which the Global North continues to impose its institutions and values onto the Global South. Interveners, it is argued, are rarely satisfied with simply preventing or stopping atrocities from occurring. If a state is willing to commit one of the four crimes once, what is to stop it from doing so again short of replacing the government entirely? This ambiguity helps interveners justify much more involved interventions wherein efforts are made to force the targeted states to adopt democratic and neoliberal forms of governance. Thus R2P cannot be decoupled from old power dynamics associated with colonial rule (Mallavarapu 2015). It is important to note that this line of criticism does not say that states should be able to commit any of the four crimes; rather, it points out that the historical power structures embedded in R2P perpetuate unequal power relationships between states and thus lack universal legitimacy.

In addition, R2P has been criticized for its continued reliance on the use of military force, even as a last resort. Numerous risks are associated with use of force, including the risk of accidentally targeting the same civilians the intervention was meant to protect. This risk is exacerbated when the intervening force relies on air power or when its ground troops are not adequately trained to distinguish between those they are protecting and those they are protecting against. There is also the possibility that armed intervention resulting in the toppling of the target state's government will lead to a power vacuum, which creates the problem of other violent groups forming in order to capture the new state, further endangering the lives of civilians. The question of timing is also important. Can force be used only when one of the four crimes has already been committed, or can it be used preemptively if it has been determined that one of the crimes is imminent? If force is used preemptively to prevent an atrocity but the state later falls into chaos, then it will be difficult to determine whether or not the decision to intervene was sound. While the framers of R2P provide guidelines for addressing these concerns, based on the logic of just war theory, in practice the determination of whether or not to use force and how to deal with the outcomes of that decision are never straightforward.

Most importantly, advocates for human security at the United Nations have worked to decouple the idea of human security from R2P. Recall that General Assembly Resolution 66/290 (discussed in chapter 3) states that "human security is distinct from the responsibility to protect and its implementation" and "does not entail the threat or the use of force or coercive measures." Instead, as the resolution states, "governments retain the primary role and responsibility for ensuring the survival, livelihood ,and dignity of their citizens" (United Nations General Assembly 12b). It is important to not conflate overall human security and the specific doctrine of R2P. R2P is one avenue through which security providers have sought to ensure protection of civilians, but it does not constitute the whole of human security.

How has R2P worked in practice? The UN Human Rights Council has been particularly eager to invoke R2P in their resolutions. Between 2008 and 2016 the Human Rights Council promoted R2P principles in twenty resolutions, particularly in response to the conflict in Syria (Global Centre for the Responsibility to Protect 2019). According to Secretary-General Ban Ki-moon in his 2009 report on R2P, "the world is less likely to look the other way than in the last century" thanks to R2P (United Nations General Assembly 2009). R2P was implicitly invoked after the 2008 Kenyan presidential elections in which opposition leader Raila Odinga claimed that President Mwai Kibaki had stolen the election. The subsequent violence resulted in the deaths of 800 people and displacement of 260,000 people. While Secretary-General Kofi Annan did not use the language of R2P when negotiating with Kenyan leadership to end the crisis, its availability as a tool could be invoked by the Security Council, influencing the negotiations. In addition, multiple governments began calling on Kenya to stop the bloodshed and threatened sanctions if it was unwilling to do so. Similar implicit invocations of R2P were made in Cote d'Ivoire and Guinea. All of these examples demonstrate the important flexibility that pillars one and two of R2P provide the Security Council when they are considering how to respond to mass-atrocity events (Welsh 2021). The case of Libya, however, did trigger a pillar three response.

LIBYA AND THE RESPONSIBILITY TO PROTECT

The 2011 UN-backed intervention in Libya marked the first and only time the doctrine of R2P was explicitly invoked within a UN Security Council resolution to justify military response. Like other states in North Africa and the Middle East during the Arab Spring, Libya saw uprisings against its longtime authoritarian leader, Colonel Mu'ammar Gaddafi. The government response was violent. In March 2011, Gaddafi's forces surrounded the opposition outpost city of Benghazi and, many thought, looked poised to carry out a massacre—an act that, if committed, would clearly constitute a crime against humanity. Many, including Libya's deputy permanent representative to the United Nations, Ibrahim O. Dabbashi, called on the international community to do something to prevent further violence. The Security Council passed two resolutions, both with the purpose of protecting Libya's civilian population. The first, Resolution 1970, passed unanimously and called for financial sanctions, an arms embargo, and a referral to the International Criminal Court. The second, Resolution 1973, passed on March 17, 2011 (but with abstentions from China, Russia, Brazil, Germany, and India), authorized member states to "take all necessary measures . . . to protect civilians and civilian populated areas in Libya" (United Nations Security Council 2011).

Following Security Council Resolution 1973, a coalition of NATO forces led by France, the United Kingdom, and the United States conducted an air assault on Gaddafi's forces and centers of power, quickly weakening the regime. However, as the campaign progressed, concerns arose, particularly from Secretary-General Ban Ki-moon, that the nature of the intervention with its heavy reliance on air support prevented adequate monitoring of civilian protection and wasn't stopping Gaddafi from targeting civilians.

One complication of the Libya intervention was the fact that there also existed an armed rebellion against the Gaddafi regime. Rebels, who had looked on the verge of defeat, were able to regroup and retake territory once the NATO intervention had begun. The fighting continued for several months, with NATO forces regularly backing rebel advances. In August 2011, rebel forces overthrew Gaddafi's regime. Since that time, Libya has struggled to consolidate a government as rival factions have fought to seize power, effectively splitting the country in two between the UN-backed government in Tripoli and a rival government in the east. The decade since the intervention has been one of violent conflict between a complex array of militias, armed forces, rival governing institutions, and foreign powers. The ensuing fighting resulted in thousands of more deaths and evidence of possible war crimes (Malsin 2021). A UN-brokered cease-fire and peace agreement in 2020 raised hopes for peace, but numerous obstacles remain.

The UN-approved military intervention was initially heralded by some as a successful application of the R2P doctrine: Libya had deliberately targeted civilians in its response to antiregime protesters and then appeared poised to carry out an indiscriminate attack on a populated urban area. The Arab Spring protests in Libya had initially been nonviolent, but after Gaddafi's violent crackdown, they morphed into armed rebellion among some parts of the opposition. This raises a critical question: *Does the presence of an armed challenger change how a state may use its armed forces?* Security Council Resolution 1973 was unclear on what was ultimately required to protect civilians and whether that extended to providing military support for an ongoing armed rebellion. Prior to the adoption of the resolution, US president Barack Obama had said that in order for the crisis to be resolved, Gaddafi had to step down. So it was no surprise when the NATO mission pursued that goal. But what does this mean for similar interventions? It is not hard to make the logical step that in order to protect civilians in the long run, governments that have committed or shown willingness to commit one of the four crimes in the past should ultimately be replaced. This opens the door to increased justifications under the guise of R2P for the use of force to not just protect a vulnerable civilian population but also overthrow norm-violating governments (Kuperman 2013).

Another issue related to the question of sovereignty concerns the role that international actors have in the postconflict state. Following the overthrow of Gaddafi, the transitional government in Libya did not want the presence of a large UN mission. Because such missions can operate only with the consent of the recognized government, postconflict Libya had to rely largely on its own limited resources and weak state institutions to restore order—a task that proved difficult. Libya's opposition forces were not united, and the nation, with its deep tribal divisions, quickly deteriorated into ongoing contestation for control of the state.

Juxtapose this to the events that were taking place simultaneously in Syria. When large Arab Spring–inspired protests began in March 2011, the Syrian government responded by deploying its armed forces, killing hundreds of protesters. The violent government response led to further protests, which spread rapidly throughout the country. As the crisis escalated, and with President Bashar al-Assad continuing to use repressive tactics against the Syrian population, members of the UN Security Council once again grappled with whether or not to invoke R2P. This time, however, there was no consensus on a plan of action. As these debates took place in New York, events in Libya cast a shadow on the proceedings, as Russia and China, who had abstained on Security Council Resolution 1973, vetoed a series of resolutions on Syria even as events there devolved into a massive humanitarian disaster. The crisis escalated into a violent conflict between multiple factions, with military interventions by numerous outside powers, including Russia in support of the Assad government and the United States in support of the Free Syrian Army and Kurds.

The Syria case highlights several difficulties of putting R2P into practice, particularly where pillar three is concerned. For one, the intricacies of geopolitics still matter, even in the face of mass atrocities. Whereas Qaddafi had no supporters on the UN Security Council, Assad's friendly relationship with veto-wielding Russia prevented passage of any resolutions condemning his actions. Thus, clearly any possible action by the Security Council can be blocked when atrocities are being conducted by those with allies among the five veto-wielding states—not to mention those cases in which one of these states is the one committing the atrocity. This undermines the universality of the principle. However, the difficulties in securing the peace in Libya made many question the overall effectiveness of military intervention as a means for atrocity prevention in general. Regardless of intention, military intervention is never a straightforward act. While an intervention may be able to stop an ongoing or imminent atrocity, the postintervention order will always be wrought with political competition, complex institution building, and other barriers to peace. That said, it is impossible to determine how things may be different if another policy path had been chosen.

In the aftermath of the Libyan intervention and the Syrian nonintervention, criticism for R2P has only grown, with some arguing that its influence has waned, particularly in relation to pillar three consensus (Hehir 2016). However, there is evidence that normative principles of R2P have continued to be central to international debate while becoming increasingly institutionalized at the UN (Doyle 2016); further, the influence of R2P continues to be seen in global efforts to protect human populations, such as in the drafting of the Arms Trade Treaty (Henderson 2017). The Human Rights Council in particular has framed their work in relation to R2P's first and second pillars, emphasizing government responsibility to protect its citizens from mass atrocity crimes.

Additionally, we continue to see increased calls for the protection of civilians without explicit reference to R2P. According to one study, R2P language has actually increased since the Libyan intervention (Gifkins 2016). A large coalition of states continue to support and strengthen R2P as a principal tool for future prevention of the four crimes. In May 2021 the UN General Assembly passed A/RES/75/277, which calls on the secretary-general to provide an annual report to the General Assembly on the responsibility to protect, further institutionalizing the norm within the UN structure (United Nations General Assembly 2021).

CONCLUSION

This chapter introduces key concerns related to the question of intervention as a possible response to human security concerns. Violent conflict represents the most immediate threat to human security. Nevertheless, as the Libya case demonstrates, military responses, while possibly able to prevent immediate atrocities, do not necessarily lead to long-term, durable structural changes that improve human security over time. In addition, the use of military force always comes with the risk of escalating the violence and creating additional human security threats. It is also clear that military intervention for entirely humanitarian reasons is rarely disconnected from competing national security goals. The world does not possess a neutral force disconnected from the broader national security concerns of other states that can intervene to respond to mass atrocities, and it would be naive to think that human security justifications would be sufficient to trump a state's national security goals. Responsibility to Protect was meant to address just this problem, but the possible and proper applications of this intervention philosophy, too, are limited. Even when the international community is faced with a moral responsibility to act, policy options that have little chance of success should be avoided. The challenge, then, is to discover solutions to human security threats that are realistic within a global framework that continues to privilege sovereignty over normative concerns.

DISCUSSION QUESTIONS

1. Do the principles of *jus ad bellum, jus in bello,* and *jus post bellum* offer important guidelines and limitations in twenty-first-century armed conflict? Why or why not?
2. What are the obstacles to effective human security provision arising from the principle of nonintervention? What benefits or threats to national or state security arise from the principle of nonintervention? What is the effect of observance of the nonintervention principle on global security?
3. What are the political and structural limitations facing action within each of the R2P pillars?
4. Consider a current humanitarian crisis or armed conflict. Does any aspect of that crisis or conflict fit within the notion of the four crimes?

Chapter 6

Human Security in Peace Processes

Learning Objectives

This chapter will enable readers to

1. understand the complex process by which conflicts turn into peaceful settlements
2. consider how a human security lens during peace processes differs from a global security or national security lens
3. delineate between the multiple actors engaged in peace processes and think critically about their competing interests
4. and understand changing norms regarding inclusivity during peace processes.

Violent conflict poses the most immediate threat to human security. As discussed in previous chapters, the effects of violent conflict extend well beyond the individuals directly engaged in the fighting and can have devastating long-term consequences. Beyond the threat to life and personal security, these long-term effects range from displacement, post-traumatic stress disorder, and other physical and mental health consequences. Conflict can shatter economies and livelihoods for generations.

This chapter focuses on how various groups address human security issues during the peace processes meant to resolve an ongoing conflict. While human security threats are present in interstate conflict, we mainly focus on intrastate conflict in this book. The reason for this is twofold. First, since the end of World War II intrastate conflict has been the dominant form of violent conflict. Second, because intrastate conflict is intricately connected to the governance and stability of the state, there will be both chronic and systemic human security threats that accompany a state's breakdown during conflict.

The long-term prospects for durable human security following a conflict are rooted in the nature of the **peace processes** that lead to the conflict's termination. **Peace processes** cover the wide range of activities intended to bring about a cessation of an ongoing violent conflict. These may include informal dialogue between parties, mediation by outside actors, formal negotiations, cease-fires, and, ultimately, peace treaties. Peace processes also include the participation of a wide range of actors, from those who directly participate in and perpetuate the violence to the numerous nonviolent actors that make up civil society, and from foreign governments to international and regional organizations.

There are two ways that human security needs are addressed during peace processes. The first way is by addressing any problems currently threatening human security, independent of any other conflict resolution processes, including immediate humanitarian assistance and protection of vulnerable populations. The second way is through any final agreement that terminates the conflict. Because peace processes tend to favor the interests of those that were most responsible for the violence, the needs of many of the most vulnerable populations are often ignored. Global activists and the United Nations have worked to address this gap by advocating for the rights and protection of noncombatant civilians during conflict. These efforts have resulted in some instances of greater participation by civil society actors in peace negotiations.

During conflict, the question of responsibility for human security becomes strained. During these periods, the state is often unable or unwilling to provide basic security for its citizens and may, in fact, be the one that poses the greatest threat. In El Salvador, for example, the UN-established Truth Commission determined that during the state's twelve-year civil war, government forces had been responsible for 85 percent of reported human rights violations (Commission on the Truth for El Salvador 1993).

During conflict, tensions arise over who has the responsibility and authority to allocate humanitarian aid, protect vulnerable populations, and resolve the conflict itself. Some of these issues are exacerbated by the nature of today's conflicts. Many are communal in nature, meaning that the core contradiction between fighting parties are driven by issues linked to identity. Identity politics are understood as "political ideology, organization, and action that openly represents the interests of designated groups based on 'essential' characteristics, such as ethnic origin or religion, and whose legitimacy lies in the support of important segments of such groups" (Eriksen 2001, 42).

As discussed in chapter 1, when populations within a state consider themselves to belong to distinct identity-based subgroups, individuals may adopt a nativist perspective on security and rely on those subgroups for protection, which can create further cleavages in an already-difficult ongoing conflict. Because most outside actors engaging in conflict resolution prioritize federalist, state, or cosmopolitan security perspectives, incongruities can arise between interveners and these subgroups. In addition, international actors intervening in a conflict, even those with supposedly good intentions, can unwittingly contribute to these divisions. For instance, a group perceiving that humanitarian aid or other forms of assistance from international actors have been distributed unjustly or have given a rival group an advantage, the group may grow to mistrust the intervening actor. This mistrust could result in the aggrieved groups working to undermine the humanitarian work. Such fracturing between groups makes the question of placing ultimate responsibility for security provision more difficult to resolve.

The need to independently address immediate human security concerns during conflict and in peace processes has become a key goal for many international humanitarian actors. How institutions are designed and how different strategies are prioritized and pursued by international, state, and local actors are important factors in how human security needs are addressed during conflict. However, the international system of states has not been particularly well suited to address these needs effectively or consistently. As *Human Security Now* argues, "the existing international security system is not designed to prevent and deal effectively with the new types of security threats. New multilateral strategies are required that focus on shared responsibility to protect people" (Commission on Human Security 2003, 23).

As we will further explore in this chapter, ongoing efforts by the international community are being made to address these gaps. Yet despite attempts to bolster global institutions that have been designed to respond to these crises, these bodies remain weak and under constant challenge. These weaknesses are further amplified by recent backlashes to this global institutional framework. Therefore, when discussing peace processes, it is important to consider the ways in which these activities happen, both within and outside official policy processes.

Furthermore, violent conflict often corresponds with the institutional breakdown of the state. Therefore a peace process will work toward constituting a new ordering of those state institutions. How that state is constituted postconflict has obvious ramifications for the likelihood of future conflict and consequently long-term human security. Perceptions of bias toward one group or another within newly formed political structures can threaten a fragile peace. Typically the state institutions that remain strongest during conflict are those most closely linked to its security sector, which in many cases was a leading source of human insecurity. How the security sector is constituted after the end of armed conflict will be highly contested and have ramifications for postconflict peace and justice. Therefore several questions should be considered when evaluating any given peace process through a human security lens: How will the new state reduce violence against its citizens? How will human rights be protected, and what methods of redress will exist when those rights are violated? How will the postconflict economy be constructed? Will inequalities, which may have been the source of the conflict, be adequately addressed? These questions don't have obvious answers, and different actors will come to different conclusions about the most appropriate outcomes.

This chapter, therefore, seeks to unravel the processes by which wars end and determine how different types of war-termination efforts affect prospects for both durable and short-term human security, with a specific focus on the actors working to address immediate human security needs and the creation of comprehensive peace accords. We will explore how multiple actors are involved in these processes and how they advocate (or fail to advocate) for human security approaches. Importantly, peace processes occur concurrently with violence, and sometimes parties will simultaneously attempt to engage in both negotiation and violence. This duality often makes peace processes appear complicated, contradictory, and hypocritical. While it is easy to become cynical, recognizing the inherent messiness of these processes helps us develop a more realistic understanding of how they work. To demonstrate this complexity—and to show how creative and purposeful engagement by activists during wartime can bring about peaceful transformations—this chapter briefly examines the Liberian civil war peace accord and the role of Mass Action for Peace.

ALL WARS MUST END?

Is it true that all wars must end? More importantly, what do those endings look like? Who are the so-called winners and losers? How does the way the conflict ends impact the human security needs of the populations affected? In general, conflicts can end in four ways: (1) a **one-sided victory**, in which one side is victorious over the other(s), (2) a formal **cease-fire**, in which all sides agree to stop committing violence but with no formal peace accord, although there might be some type of conflict-regulation mechanisms put into place, (3) a formal **peace accord**, in which all or most sides involved in the conflict agree to some form of postconflict governance, or (4) the conflict has no clear resolution, meaning the fighting stops or continues at very low levels of activity without any process to govern that cessation (Kreutz 2010). A one-sided victory is most likely to occur in the first few years of an intrastate war. After ten years, however, it is very rare for one side to have a decisive victory (Brandt et al. 2008).

According to data from the Uppsala Conflict Data Program's (UCDP) Conflict Termination data set, only a small percentage of intrastate conflicts, in fact, end in a formal peace accord. Between 1990 and 2005, 18.4 percent of intrastate conflicts ended in a peace agreement, and 19.7 percent ended in a cease-fire. Only 13.6 percent of conflicts during this period ended in one side's victory. The plurality of conflicts, 48.3 percent, end with no clear resolution (Kreutz 2010, 246). There is one important caveat when interpreting these data: the UCDP data set looks at the termination of *armed conflict*, defined as violent events between two or more groups, of which one is a government, with just twenty-five or more battle deaths. It is not surprising, therefore, that many low-casualty conflicts do not result in a formal peace process, as they never hit a threshold beyond which parties would be motivated to engage in complicated formal negotiations. That also means that the roots of many conflicts remain unresolved, despite a cessation to ongoing violence.

Unsurprisingly, the study of conflict termination has been largely concerned with the bargaining processes that occur between the various groups engaged in the violence. These studies generally consider the groups to be rational, in that they have a relatively fixed set of preferences and political goals that they are pursuing through violent means. If we explain the onset of war using the Clausewitzian dictum, that "war is merely the continuation of policy by other means," then it follows that peace processes are simply one "other means" for how those same armed actors resolve the disputes that initially led to war. Thus these conflict-termination models explain peace processes as negotiated bargains between a limited number of self-interested actors. The conflict terminates once the actors reach an outcome that is mutually acceptable among those at the negotiating table.

A common way to think about war termination is by presenting conflict as a linear progression that moves along an escalation/de-escalation continuum. This simplification helps us better understand many of the discrete events happening throughout the process—and the various points at which warring parties might be compelled to seek a resolution. One common example is Michael Lund's (1996) "curve of conflict," which maps the course of a conflict along two dimensions:. The first dimension is the intensity of the conflict, which ranges from *durable peace* to *war*, and the second dimension is the duration of the conflict, which is measured in stages. The stage and intensity of the conflict at a given point will determine which type of management techniques will or should be engaged. In the Lund model, prior to a conflict's escalation into violence, various prevention techniques, such as routine and preventive diplomacy, would be employed with the intention of de-escalating the situation. Once violence breaks out, however, a new set of tools (i.e., crisis diplomacy, peacemaking, and peace enforcement) would be needed to manage the crisis, limit the violence, and bring parties toward resolution. Once the violent stage of the conflict has ended, tools focused on postconflict peacebuilding and reconciliation would be employed. Similar models have been developed by Johan Galtung (1996) and by Oliver Ramsbotham, Tom Woodhouse, and Hugh Miall (2016).

Escalation/de-escalation models, while useful in their basic framework, have several limitations that we should keep in mind—particularly when applying them to human security questions. First, rarely do conflicts follow such simple trajectories. Violence can be unpredictable, manifesting itself at multiple stages and at various levels of intensity. Therefore it is not always clear at any given time what stage a conflict has reached and consequently what the most effective conflict management approaches would be. Second, placing conflict along a continuum can create the impression that only a narrow selection of conflict management tools can be used at any particular stage. As we will discuss throughout this chapter, a wide range of activities by a variety of actors constitutes a peace process—particularly those activities engaging a human security approach—and these can occur during all stages of a conflict. A third issue is that these models are often elite-focused and ignore the multiple "nonelite" actors engaged in peace processes at all stages of conflict. This begins with the usage of the term *conflict management*, which implies the presence of at least one single actor who has both the authority and power to "manage" multiple violent actors. The assumption that such an actor exists is problematic, as the United Nations, the United States, Russia, and many other of the world's most powerful actors have repeatedly learned. In addition, the elite focus that has dominated security studies in the past underexamines the many nonviolent and grassroots actors engaged in peace activities who are making significant contributions to the nature of a peace process.

From a methodological standpoint, limiting our explanations to a few key variables or actors is important when trying to explain complex phenomena. But what happens when our explanations for war initiation, escalation, and termination include only a small subset of the actors that experience armed conflict? The human security approach challenges us to think beyond these actors and consider the broader impacts of these processes.

FROM CEASE-FIRES TO COMPREHENSIVE PEACE ACCORDS: INTEGRATING HUMAN SECURITY INTO CONFLICT TERMINATION

When neither side in a violent conflict can achieve a military victory, the parties must reach some mutual agreement between themselves on the conditions for conflict termination. Coming to such an agreement, however, can be challenging. Many conflicts can last decades, with neither side ever gaining a clear advantage. Parties with a history of conflict may find it difficult to commit to an agreement if they believe the other side might renege at some point in the future. Even if an agreement is reached, all sides might have a future incentive to reignite the conflict if they believe violence could give them a better deal that what was previously negotiated.

Cease-fires, or agreements between fighting parties to stop using violence or otherwise mobilizing their forces against each other, are often seen as the first step toward reaching peace. Cease-fires usually do not involve much else beyond a non-use-of-force agreement. They can be used to provide the space for humanitarian actors to deliver aid or to start building trust between enemies with the hope that more formal peace negotiations will follow. Belligerents, however, may also use the space provided by cease-fires to replenish their arms or to gain other advantages against the opposition. When new windows of opportunity open, parties may take advantage of their better strategic position and reinitiate hostilities. Thus cease-fires are often violated and rarely bring lasting peace.

These problems mean that peace negotiations often focus on lessening the incentives for violent actors to go back on their commitments. It is for this reason that in **comprehensive peace accords**—agreements in which all the major parties in the conflict are involved in the negotiation process—negotiations go beyond basic issues of postconflict governance to also address the substantive issues that fueled the conflict (Joshi and Darby 2013), focusing on provisions that directly affect the fighting parties. Comprehensive peace accords are typically centered on agreements over policy and military reform, political reform and shared governance, and development issues.

The assumption that peace is best achieved by focusing on the interests of the armed actors has meant that human security concerns are often excluded from agreements or are only referenced in the most general terms. This has led to one of the core critiques of peace processes—that the overarching focus on elites means that those who did not participate in the violence but nevertheless suffered throughout the conflict are ignored and continue to suffer deprivation long after the fighting has stopped (Strasheim 2019). This raises the question of whether or not a peace process that overwhelmingly rewards the violent actors and does not adequately address victims' needs can be seen as a just peace.

Research suggests that when peace processes involve a greater segment of civil society—consequently, also the actors most engaged with addressing human security concerns—they are more likely to be successful than those accords narrowly focusing on the interests of the armed actors (Paffenholz 2014; Wanis-St. John and Kew 2008). An examination of peace agreements shows that the more mechanisms contained within an agreement, the more likely the peace process is to succeed, and a wider set of provisions within the agreement better integrates the complex interdependence between military, economic, and societal aspects of a postconflict state (Badran 2014). Other research has shown that the inclusion of women contributes to the likelihood of an accord's success (Caprioli, Nielsen, and Hudson 2010; Nakaya 2003).

There is a logic to these findings: when a deal is struck only between those capable of using violence, there are few incentives to stop them if they believe at some later date they can get a better deal by reinitiating hostilities; however, when more segments of society are brought into the peace process, more people have buy-in to the long-term success of the accord, meaning more people are working to ensure a sustainable peace. This creates broader pressure on combatants to follow through on their commitments. While this does not guarantee that an armed actor will not try to take up arms at some future date, the interconnectedness of these more-comprehensive peace accords makes reinitiating violence more difficult. Additionally, a comprehensive peace agreement is much more deeply rooted in the society's rule of law and becomes part of its constitutional legal framework. This creates mechanisms for future grievances to be more readily addressed through normal judicial processes.

One way to visualize the extent to which human security–focused provisions are included in comprehensive peace accords is by examining data from the University of Notre Dame's Peace Accord Matrix (PAM) (Joshi, Quinn, and Regan 2015). PAM is a data set that consists of thirty-four peace accords negotiated between 1989 and 2012. As is evident in figure 6.1, most accords

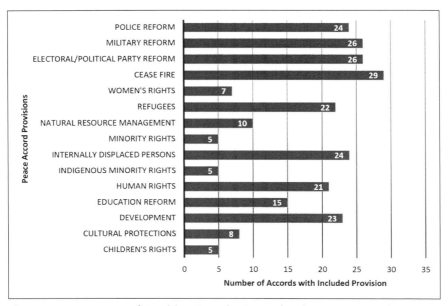

Figure 6.1. Frequency of Provision Types in Comprehensive Peace Accords. *Source:* Kroc Institute for International Peace Studies, n.d. Also see Joshi, Quinn, and Regan 2015.

contain provisions for cease-fires, police and military reforms, economic development, and electoral reforms. Provisions that specifically address issues such as women's rights, children's rights, and cultural protections are far less likely to be included in an agreement. For instance, only seven of thirty-four accords catalogued in PAM had provisions specifically addressing women's rights. Human security issues most likely to be included in agreements are those that address human rights in general and refugee/IDP issues. While evidence points to the importance of addressing broader human security issues within peace accords, they still often take a secondary position in official peace processes.

Nevertheless, several ongoing initiatives are promoting more-inclusive human security concerns within both the negotiation process and the final agreement. Security Council Resolution 1325 (United Nations Security Council 2000), for instance, encourages more participation by women in peace processes (see chapter 10 for more discussion of Resolution 1325). There has also been increased pressure to include local civil society actors in the negotiation process. In the Colombian peace process, for example, victims were given the opportunity to testify before the negotiators, part of an effort by mediators to make victims' rights a central component of the agreement. That said, the inclusion of human security issues in a peace accord does not necessarily guarantee that those issues will be addressed during implementation. Research on the inclusion of IDP provisions in peace accords, for instance, shows that many of the promises made toward displaced populations often go unfulfilled, even as the peace holds (Andersen-Rodgers 2015).

Ultimately, a peace accord serves as a marker between a period of violent conflict and a period of potential peace. As ongoing conflict represents the time during which human security threats are most severe, the simple act of stopping conflict may greatly reduce the threat. Still, it is not enough to simply stop the violence between competing forces. Political violence can easily transition into criminal violence if ex-combatants are unable to transition into a new role. In addition, populations feeling that a peace accord did not adequately address their grievances or that the accord lacks sufficient justice mechanisms for those who committed violent acts against them may choose to restart the conflict. Thus the content of the peace accord matters. But, as we will examine here (and in chapter 7), how provisions in an accord are actually implemented will significantly impact the level of human security that people will experience.

HUMAN SECURITY DURING CONFLICT: PROTECTION, ASSISTANCE, AND ADVOCACY

During times of conflict, human security threats are at their most extreme. This is when human security actors engage in three main activities: protection, assistance, and advocacy. As discussed in chapter 5, protection involves not only shielding noncombatants physical harm but also guarding their basic human rights. In addition to basic protection activities, human security actors may engage in assistance activities, including the provision of immediate humanitarian aid to vulnerable populations. During conflict the capability to providing protection and assistance, and the onus to do so, can become extremely complex as multiple actors seek to pursue their competing missions and interests (to get an idea of this complexity, consider the long list of security providers introduced in chapter 3; then consider that the long list there is just a small sample of the world's security providers). The third area that human security actors engage in is broad-based advocacy, as they attempt to create a normative discourse that pushes human security concerns into formal policy-making apparatuses. This section discusses this complex and interdependent web of actors and their efforts to provide protection and assistance to vulnerable populations as well as advocate for their needs.

Ending violent conflicts is a complicated process and involves actors from many different sectors (i.e., the state, violent nonstate actors, civil society), each with competing demands and visions of what a postconflict society should look like. Different actors engage with a conflict in different ways—some actively participating in the violence, others remaining nonviolent throughout the conflict. Some may not directly commit violence but instead give support to violent actors. Because violence can have a polarizing effect on people, shaping perceptions between groups for generations, long-term mistrust of the other sides' intentions and motivations often emerges. As peace processes unfold, these histories will remain important as different groups evaluate how their grievances are being recognized and addressed through those mechanisms.

How each groups' interests are addressed or not addressed during a peace process has ramifications for long-lasting peace and the creation of durable human security. John Paul Lederach (1997) describes three levels of actors involved in peacebuilding processes. Level 1 actors—and the ones we are most likely to hear and read about in the news—are the military, political, and religious elites. These groups were most likely directing and engaging in the violence to begin with, and therefore they are the ones who are most likely to be involved in high-level negotiations to end the conflict and to be responsible for managing any cease-fire agreement. Lederach's important insight is that, in order to build long-lasting peace, not just those who engage in the violence must be involved in peace processes.

Level 2 actors, therefore, include respected members of different ethnic and religious groups, academics and intellectuals, and heads of higher-profile NGOs. Level 3 actors are made up of grassroots leadership that could include local leaders, leaders of Indigenous NGOs, community developers, local health officials, and refugee camp leaders (Lederach 1997). While many will be excluded from the formal peace process, each of these entities brings its own agenda and influence to these processes, shaping the outcome in ways that may or may not contribute to improved human security. In addition to these domestic actors, intergovernmental organizations such as the United Nations, international NGOs, and other states will often become involved in these processes.

As we examine how different actors contribute or don't contribute to human security practices, it is important to keep in mind that not all actors in a conflict or peace negotiation behave in stereotypical ways or uniformly across cases. Each actor makes strategic decisions based on their specific needs, which are informed by their perceptions of the conflict and who is ultimately responsible for their security. Thus a military elite is not necessarily opposed to engaging in human security activities; the person may, in fact, be a strong advocate for a cosmopolitan security perspective. And neither does it mean that a leader of a grassroots movement is engaging in activities that are always beneficial for peace. We should also keep in mind that few if any of these actors have the unilateral capability to bring about an end to the conflict or to protect human security. Instead these processes rely on cooperation and compromise between many actors.

While many of the basic mechanisms that society has in place to protect individuals are highly strained during violent conflict, there also exists simultaneously a wide range of activities by a variety of actors meant to create the conditions for peace and to protect human security. These activities happen on two levels: the *bottom-up*, which includes the engagement of domestic actors, including the conflict parties and local civil society, and the *top-down*, which involves international engagement by other states, intergovernmental organizations such as the UN, and international nongovernmental organizations (INGOs) (see figure 6.2).

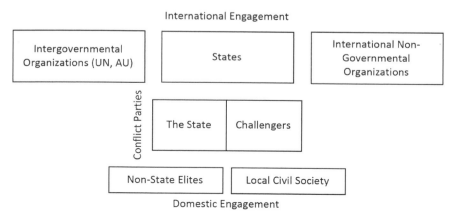

Figure 6.2. Human Security Actors during Conflict

Each of these actors will face different limitations and advantages when engaging with others. The nature of the international system, though, gives distinct advantage to states, as they have institutional advantages (i.e., membership in intergovernmental organizations, a diplomatic corps, legitimacy in the use of force, etc.) unavailable to most nonstate actors. Next, we briefly discuss each of these actors. It is important to recognize that the scope of this chapter does not allow us to engage all the ways in which these groups involve themselves with peace processes, and some actors, such as elite economic interests, are not addressed. Instead, our focus is on the means by which they engage in human security practice.

Domestic Engagement

Often the first area in which human security issues are engaged is on the domestic level. Domestic actors can act both as threats to and guarantors of human security. This section provides an overview of the actors involved in bottom-up activities related to peace processes.

Conflict Parties

The first set of actors to be considered typically consist of the state and the state's various challengers as conflict parties. According to Lederach's framework, these would be considered level 1 actors. During conflict these actors control the physical means to perpetuate widespread violence against civilian populations. States in particular have both the military capacity and the organizational capability to conduct war crimes, ethnic cleansing campaigns, crimes against humanity, and genocide. For example, it was the Bosnian Serb army that carried out the slaughter of eight thousand Muslim men and boys in Srebrenica. This level of atrocity is not limited to state actors, as violent nonstate groups, such as the so-called Islamic State, have also carried out comparably atrocious attacks against civilian populations.

While armed actors, whether state or nonstate combatants, are generally those who are most responsible for the breakdown of human security during conflict, they can also simultaneously serve as human security providers. The mass violation of a population's human security can create severe difficulties with both current and future governance, which conflict actors do care about, especially if they wish to assume control of the state. However, the provision of human security by these actors is typically uneven and limited narrowly toward those groups they consider most aligned with their interests. Populations the armed actors do not consider essential in their ability to govern will be most threatened (Weinstein 2006).

Both the state and its challengers can be pressured to pursue human security policy, even during high levels of violent conflict. This pressure can result in limiting the types of force used and is considered legitimate military targets. This pressure can come from multiple sources, including international actors and local civil society. Ultimately, postconflict stability will require these actors to adopt, at least to some degree, a human security approach toward those populations to which they are linked. Thus conflict actors must weigh the benefits of using violence to pursue their political goals against their long-term goals of effectively governing.

Local Civil Society Activism

While **civil society** is a very broad term, it loosely describes the sphere of voluntary action that is distinct from the state and economic spheres. Civil society can include religious institutions, humanitarian and charity organizations, advocacy networks, and other social groups. Oftentimes civil society advocates are the loudest supporters of addressing a community's human security needs during conflict. For instance, civil society activism can create community space for those affected by conflict. In the Democratic Republic of the Congo, domestic civil society actors—perhaps best known among them Dr. Denis Mukwege and the staff of Panzi Hospital—worked together with transnational advocacy networks to care for and bring attention to the needs of hundreds of thousands of survivors of conflict-related sexual violence (Crawford 2017).

Civil society contributes to what Roger Mac Ginty refers to as everyday peace, or "the practices and norms deployed by individuals and groups in deeply divided societies to avoid and minimize conflict . . . at both the inter- and intra-group levels" (Mac Ginty 2014, 553). In this way civil society may be able to provide space for members from different communities to interact normally. Of course, civil society does not always represent a unified voice, and security providers can even work against each other. In Colombia, for example, different sectors of civil society staked diametrically opposed positions on the October 2016 plebiscite over the acceptance of the peace deal between the Colombian government and the Revolutionary Armed Forces of Colombia (FARC) (Beltrán and Creely 2018). Those who opposed the terms of the peace treaty narrowly defeated those who supported it. After renegotiating the treaty, President Juan Manuel Santos did not present it for a vote the second time around.

Increasingly, local civil society actors are seen as positive contributors to peace processes as well as important monitors of postconflict agreements (Pinaud 2021). A 2011 report by the United Nations Peacebuilding Support

---

BOX 6.1. THINK ABOUT IT . . .
CIVIL SOCIETY DURING CONFLICT

Local civil society actors play an important role both inside and outside of conflict. During the conflict they can be the difference between a community surviving or not. Think about a conflict that is currently ongoing, and look for information about a local civil society group that works in that country. If you can, find statements and reports from the civil society group itself to help answer the questions below.

1. What is the local civil society group, and what is its key mission?
2. How does it pursue its mission within the context of the ongoing conflict? What are the main strategies it uses to achieve its goals?
3. What led to the group's formation? Did this group exist prior to the conflict, or did it form as a response to the violence?
4. How does this group interact with other actors in the conflict? Does it use any specific strategies to help keep it safe from violent actors? Describe these interactions and strategies.
5. Can you think of advantages that this group might have that international actors working to resolve the conflict do not have? What advice would you give an international actor about working with this group?

Office states that civil society has "a crucial role in peacebuilding through legitimizing processes and projects, mediating among state, society, and international community, communicating local-level perspectives and priorities to decision makers, and implementing concrete peacebuilding and development programmes" (United Nations Peacebuilding Support Office 2011, 3). That said, some have critiqued the extent to which civil societies' concerns are addressed during these processes. One concern is that the voices donors and other elite actors listen to are the ones that most closely conform to already-stated elite interests, and some local civil society organizations will, in fact, tailor their positions to attract international aid. Consequently, these critics argue, civil society can end up amplifying elite views rather than acting as a countervoice to it (Mac Ginty and Richmond 2013).

Civil society actors are aware of the potential physical threats they face during conflict and often will engage in **strategic nonviolence**. According to Maria Stephan and Erica Chenoweth, "nonviolent resistance is a civilian-based method used to wage conflict through social, psychological, economic, and political means without the threat or use of violence" (2008,

9). These strategies are used to bring attention to issues facing sectors of civil society. The use of nonviolent resistance, even during periods of violent conflict, can have important strategic advantages over violent methods. First, violently targeting nonviolent movements may have higher costs than targeting violent actors. Therefore a dedication to nonviolent strategies may give those actors more freedom of movement than violent actors have. Second, members of a regime, including civil servants, security forces, and the judiciary, are more likely to shift their allegiance toward nonviolent groups than toward violent groups. Third, the international community is more likely to denounce acts of violence against nonviolent groups than against violent groups (Stephan and Chenoweth 2008; also see Dudouet 2021). That said, challenging violent actors remains risky, particularly in the midst of a conflict. An accusation that a nonviolent movement is aligned with one group over another may be enough to persuade the state to use violent tactics against the nonviolent group. In Syria, for example, President Assad continually equated nonviolent protesters with violent forces, thereby justifying to his supporters his violent response to their opposition.

The intensity and type of violence being perpetrated will also affect how civil society actors are able to act during conflict. Domestic human rights organizations may not be able to exist safely under intensely authoritarian regimes. In such situations the most effective civil society actors may be those that come from long-standing institutions, such as churches, mosques, or other religious organizations. However, such organizations may be restricted on what or for whom they are able or willing to advocate. In addition, conflict itself can generate new civil society actors. Women, for example, may be able to move around combat zones more easily than men in some ways, as they are traditionally viewed as innocent civilians. This has allowed women to become some of the strongest advocates for peace during wartime. In Argentina, for example, a group of women whose children had been disappeared by the military regime during the Dirty War (1976–1983) began gathering in Buenos Aires's Plaza de Mayo in April 1977. Their status as grieving mothers and grandmothers made it difficult for the regime to target and intimidate them or frame their protest as a threat to the state, and the protest brought international attention to the human rights abuses being carried out by the Argentine government. But despite the important role they can serve as advocates, women mostly remain outside the formal negotiating process. UN Security Council Resolution 1325 seeks to change this, but implementation has been slow.

It is also important to note those cases of what Jacques Semelin refers to as "civic action that is taken outside the framework of society" (2011, 2). Organizations that openly challenge the policies of one of the violent actors risk retribution—those who work to rescue potential victims of genocide being one such example. The White Helmets in Syria, ordinary individuals who work together to rescue civilians after airstrikes and bombings, have been persistently accused of harboring "terrorist sympathies" or worse by supporters of the Assad regime. While atrocities are being committed, any action that could be seen as potentially protecting a targeted group could also make the protector a potential target, stifling open civil society.

In many cases, these choices to protect others are made by individuals acting without the backing of a broader organization. In these extreme circumstances, the scope of what one person can do is limited in the face of failing institutions and lack of external assistance and often requires a significant conflict-terminating event to stop ongoing mass atrocities. For instance, Jews continued to be murdered up until the days just prior to the Nazis' surrender to Allied forces during World War II, and the Rwandan genocide was not fully stopped until the Rwandan Patriotic Front's victory in July 1994 (Semelin 2011, 6).

While civil society can play a key role in promoting and providing human security, it is important to recognize the limits of their capabilities. During violent conflict, their resources are often stretched thin, as they have not been constituted to respond to crises, and once violence has started resources can become increasingly scarce. In addition, civil society advocates must always determine the risks of challenging violent actors. While research on organized nonviolent resistance shows that it can be an effective tool, it is not always successful. Individual activists must consider the very real attenuated risks, which, then, essentially creates a collective action problem among civil society activists.

If we think about the role of activism in relation to the three policy boxes discussed in chapter 3—Perception of the Problem, Policy Options, and Ideal Outcome—we can see that violent conflict places strains in all three spaces of the policy process. The societal polarization that accompanies conflict complicates agreement on both the nature of the problem and the ideal outcome. Because one segment of society has chosen to use violence, there is less room for peaceful, deliberative dialogue between all parties. Civil society therefore plays a key role in helping reshape the problem and helping frame an alternative future while opening avenues for dialogue. Action taken in the Liberian civil war by members of civil society illustrates the strengths of and constraints on domestic security providers and advocates, as we will see in the next section.

Liberia and Mass Action for Peace

The important contribution that civil society can make during conflict was highlighted by the actions of a group of women during the brutal civil war between the government of Liberia and Charles Taylor's National Patriotic

Front of Liberia (NPLF) that began in 1989 and culminated in the 2003 Accra Peace Agreement. That conflict led to large-scale displacement, the destruction of Liberia's economy, and devastating violence against the civilian population. Activism on the part of women's organizations throughout the conflict put pressure on the warring parties and the international mediators to bring an end to the conflict.

The effort, known as "Mass Action for Peace," may have appeared to the combatants as spontaneous but was in actuality a well-organized and strategic campaign that brought different Liberian women's groups from many different sectors of Liberian society together, particularly the Muslim and Christian communities. Its key leader, Leymah Gbowee (who later received a Nobel Peace Prize for her efforts), organized women to gather in visible and public places dressed in white T-shirts bearing the organization's logo and wearing white hair ties, while holding signs declaring the message, "THE WOMEN OF LIBERIA WANT PEACE! NOW!" (Gbowee 2011). This organized visibility helped bring greater attention to the devastating effects of the war on noncombatants and eventually led to a meeting with President Taylor where they could formally present their demands.

While the group gained attention both in Liberia and internationally, these activists were not invited to be part of the formal negotiations. Not to be deterred, they traveled to Accra, Ghana, and held demonstrations outside the building where the negotiations were taking place, even blockading negotiators into the room until combatants took their duty toward crafting a comprehensive peace accord seriously. Partly due to strong pressure from these women, the 2003 Accra Peace Agreement went beyond the simple division of spoils between the armed belligerents and addressed many issues critical to human security. The agreement ended Liberia's civil war and included provisions that dealt largely with the rehabilitation of children, women, the elderly, and disabled persons. The peace accord called for the postconflict government to design programs specifically for these groups as well as for child combatants. One of the key questions with a peace accord is implementation and the institutions that will be responsible for it. The Accra Peace Agreement addresses implementation at the domestic level but also calls on various UN and regional agencies for assistance, including the UN Special Representative of the Secretary-General for Children in Armed Conflict, United Nations Children's Fund (UNICEF), and the African Committee of Experts on the Rights and Welfare of the Child. Notably, the elections that followed the signing of the Accra Peace Agreement resulted in Africa's first elected woman head of state, Ellen Johnson Sirleaf.

These efforts were not solely confined to women activists in Liberia, as more women in the region began to organize, creating the transnational Mano River Women's Peace Network (MARWOPNET)—an organization made up of women from Liberia, Sierra Leone, and Guinea. Formed in 2000, MAR-WOPNET has worked to promote peace within each of their countries and for the region as a whole (Ndongo 2020). In 2001 it began a process to get leaders from these war-torn countries to begin talking with each other. After meeting with the network's respective leaders from each country, presidents Charles Taylor of Liberia, Lansana Conté of Guinea, and Tejan Kabbah of Sierra Leone met at a three-day summit in Rabat, Morocco, in March 2002. This summit helped jump-start many of the discussions that would later lead to formal peace accords in Liberia, as well as in Sierra Leone. During the negotiations, MARWOPNET played an important role as an intermediary between the warring factions (Alarakhia 2000).

It is important to not overstate the importance of these networks in conflict termination. The literature shows that, yes, the broad participation of civil society and the addressing of civil society concerns within peace agreements improve the likelihood for success, but conflict actors must still be willing to cease their violent contestations of power. Charles Taylor had to step down from power in order for the conflict to come to an end, and it took a combination of domestic civil society action, sustained regional and international pressure, and acceptable peace-agreement provisions to accomplish this.

International Engagement

Multiple types of external actors engage during civil wars, including states (often pursuing their own national security interests), transnational advocacy networks, and international and regional organizations. These external engagements can impact the conflict both negatively and positively and have ramifications for how human security needs are met. It is at the international level that we observe the constant competition between the three different security approaches—national, global, and human—as different actors prioritize different forms of security.

States and Human Security during Peace Processes

A large part of international engagement into ongoing intrastate conflicts happens through states' varying foreign policies in support of one side or the other, all in pursuit of their own national security interests. States, particularly great powers, care greatly about the outcome of intrastate conflicts, as a new government might have ramifications for the state's alliances and long-term security interests. This type of **proxy war** was fought during the Cold War when the United States and the Soviet Union frequently chose sides in foreign conflicts based on whether a belligerent accepted or rejected Marxist ideologies.

This type of support, however, has continued outside the confines of the Cold War, as seen in Iran's support of the Houthi insurgency in Yemen and Russia's support of the Assad regime in Syria. This kind of support does not necessarily reflect complete agreement with the goals of the foreign group but can sometimes be driven by a desire to weaken another state that supports the foreign group's opposition. This type of engagement can have long-term negative ramifications for human security, since conflicts that experience external intervention in support of one side or another tend to last longer than conflicts without this type of intervention (Cunningham 2010). However, international engagement in the form of third-party guarantees in a peace agreement has also been shown to aid successful resolution of civil wars (Walter 2002). Thus states often play an important role in the negotiation of final peace accords.

More rarely, a state may intervene in a foreign conflict solely to provide humanitarian assistance to a threatened population. While this type of aid would usually come through the auspices of the United Nations, in some instances intervention may happen unilaterally or through a regional organization, as happened in Kosovo in 1999. Justifications for such intervention are myriad, including internalization of the general human security norm or the principles of R2P; internalization of strong norms specifically prohibiting the type of violence or weapons used (e.g., genocide or the use of chemical weapons); religious, ethnic, or other identification with the group targeted for violence; or domestic public pressure on the intervening state to take humanitarian action.

Some states have become vocal advocates of the human security approach and pressure other states to shape their policies in ways that improve human security. This has resulted in many states, particularly middle powers, formally banding together to work on mechanisms for strengthening the global human security architecture. For example, a number of states (including Austria, Brazil, Canada, France, Germany, Norway, the United Kingdom, and Uruguay, among others) have organized a Group of Friends of the Protection of Civilians, which has continued to pressure states to adhere to international humanitarian law and to condemn attacks on civilians and humanitarian workers.

The United Nations System as Human Security Actor

States face a number of constraints on how they can even implement a human security agenda if they so choose. The principle of sovereignty, as discussed in the previous chapter, means that unilateral interventions, even to enforce a widely accepted global norm, are suspect. It is for this reason that state advocates for human security have turned to the United Nations to advance this agenda. Thus the United Nations has become a key actor in encouraging conflict parties to engage human security issues during peace processes.

As discussed in previous chapters, the initial conceptualization of the United Nations was to maintain global security. Initially, it was thought that the task of maintaining peace and security should happen *between* states. Over time, however, the increased prevalence of intrastate wars expanded what the UN saw to be within its mandate to address peace and security issues. This has included a growing engagement with issues related to the protection of civilians during conflict and greater insistence that human security issues be addressed in peace accords overseen by a UN peace-keeping operation. We see this engagement on two levels. First is greater attention by the UN Security Council and the secretary-general to human security threats that intrastate conflicts generate. Second is the creation by the General Assembly of multiple UN agencies tasked with addressing systemic human security threats both in and out of conflict. Because the United Nations is made up of its member states, its main task is engaging with governments, and its institutional design is structured to facilitate that task. As discussed in chapter 5, however, principles of sovereignty limit what the United Nations can do within the territory of a state. These limits block the extent to which the UN as an international institution can successfully engage a human security approach.

International Nongovernmental Organizations

The final type of actor engaged in human security practice during conflict is the international nongovernmental organization. Transnational organizations engage in activities that promote key norms for political behavior. NGOs at the international level have been an important voice in human security discourse in global politics and voice essential concerns that may otherwise be missed between the formal and informal policy processes. There are thousands of international NGOs throughout the world, and they operate in a number of different ways, carrying out various types of activities. As discussed in chapter 3, human rights organizations like Human Rights Watch and Amnesty International, for example, work to document violations of international humanitarian law by conflict actors. Groups such as Médecins Sans Frontières and the International Committee of the Red Cross play a role in providing medical and other lifesaving services to civilians and injured combatants. In the face of inaction by European states, NGOs have been key actors in helping save the lives of refugees and migrants fleeing Libya by crossing the Mediterranean in overcrowded and dangerously inadequate vessels (Amnesty International 2017). Organizations such as Peace Brigades International put observers into conflict zones whose presence helps protect local human rights defenders. International NGOs play a key role in pressuring states and inter-governmental organizations to live up to obligations to protect the lives and rights of those affected by conflict.

A key role for international NGOs has been to help amplify local groups' voices so that they are heard and recognized by more powerful local and global actors (Keck and Sikkink 1998). NGOs are frequently based in Western states and are led by individuals who have access to their government's foreign policy decision makers and to high-level officials within the United Nations. This access can sometimes help bring attention, and in many cases protection, to groups working on human security–related issues in combat zones. This phenomenon, which Margaret Keck and Kathryn Sikkink call *the boomerang effect*, helps open space for local civil society to better engage the political process. However, for this to be effective, the international NGO has to be aware of the local advocates and their activities on the ground and have actual influence with the governments or IGOs they are trying to pressure. Again, the context of these interactions will be an important factor in their overall success.

CONCLUSION

The resolution of conflict is complex. Human security demands that conflict resolution not only focus on the elimination of direct violence but also account for how any resolution process affects different populations. This raises two key questions: *Is human security necessary to end a conflict, and does an insistence on a human security approach in conflict resolution diminish the chances of ending the violence?* Of course, the answers are not clear-cut, and, as the previous discussion highlights, people from all groups in conflict will do what they can to best pursue their interests. Who is heard and how different groups' interests are integrated into a peace process will impact the nature of the postconflict peace.

This chapter has broadly examined a number of areas related to human security during conflict and during the peace processes meant to bring those conflicts to an end. Since the end of the Cold War, concern has grown that warfare now disproportionally harms civilian populations. States are increasingly worried that the internal instability caused by these conflicts threatens both their national security and the overall security of the global system. This has led many to advocate for policy approaches that emphasize a deeper engagement with human security. One of the primary ways that this is happening is through greater recognition within peace processes of the different types of actors that experience conflict. By broadening our scope beyond the conflict actors, we see a much more complex mosaic of interests, grievances, and needs. Activists on both the domestic and international levels have worked to highlight these issues and to promote an international legal framework that addresses the rights of civilians during conflict. Of course we cannot ignore that many of those mechanisms are severely strained as the world faces increased threats to civilian protection, manifested most visibly in the ongoing displacement crisis.

The next chapter examines these issues more closely as it looks at how human security concerns are addressed after conflict through peacebuilding and transitional justice.

DISCUSSION QUESTIONS

1. Thinking about the many people and groups that are engaged in conflict, how might each be motivated or not motivated to address human security issues?
2. Scholars, policy makers, and practitioners are placing greater emphasis on the role civil society can play to help bring about long-term peace. How does civil society contribute to successful peace accords? Can you think of any ways in which the participation of civil society actors could undermine peace?
3. Does peace require human rights?
4. What are the main obstacles to civilian protection? Are there ways to realistically address these obstacles?

Chapter 7

Human Security and Peacebuilding

Learning Objectives

This chapter will enable readers to

1. understand the residual effects of conflict in postconflict societies
2. define the difference between *peacebuilding* and *state building*
3. understand the evolution of UN multidimensional peacekeeping operations
4. consider how different priorities in peacebuilding address human security issues differently
5. and understand what is meant by the term *transitional justice* and the different mechanisms that have been used to try to achieve postconflict justice.

The process of moving from war to a condition of sustained peace is called **peacebuilding** and involves a wide range of efforts, actions, and policies that fit within the human security approach. In 1992 "An Agenda for Peace" defined *peacebuilding* as "action to identify and support structures which will tend to strengthen and solidify peace to avoid relapse to conflict" (Boutros-Ghali 1992, 11). Since then, the international community's understanding of peacebuilding has evolved to encompass a range of activities aimed at rebuilding the political, economic, and social structures of postconflict societies. These activities can include demobilization, disarmament, and reintegration (DDR) of combat troops; security-sector reform; reforming political and judicial structures; establishing the rule of law; and the promotion of just socioeconomic development.

This chapter moves from the period of acute violent conflict and examines the processes that accompany postconflict peacebuilding and justice issues.

How postconflict societies should be constituted has been an ongoing question of international politics. Because conflicts themselves are likely fought over this very question, the answer to this problem is never without contention, and different actors will prioritize different security goals over others. Therefore, we start by examining the question of which threats to human security persist even after violent conflict has ended. This is followed by a discussion of two terms that are typically used to describe postconflict activity—*state building* and *peacebuilding*—and how human security approaches have been integrated into these activities. The chapter ends with an examination of the evolution of UN peacekeeping operations and efforts to create mechanisms better equipped to address justice for victims of atrocities.

In chapter 6 we examined how different types of actors address human security issues during ongoing conflicts. Because war creates threats to human security that are usually sudden and overtly violent, the human security approach in armed conflict is often directed toward immediate protection needs. In this chapter we will continue to explore these issues, but we will shift our temporal frame to the postconflict period. It is important to consider that (1) many of the activities aimed at guaranteeing human security during conflict closely match the types of activities aimed at guaranteeing human security after conflict (Zelizer and Oliphant 2013) and (2) postconflict periods are rarely violence-free and, in fact, are very likely to see a recurrence in violent conflict (Quinn, Mason, and Gurses 2007; Autesserre 2009). Another important contextual point to keep in mind is that civil wars can last for multiple decades (although most average between seven and twelve years), meaning that when peace is achieved, there are many who have known nothing but what it is to live in a state suffering from ongoing violence. There are several key ideas to keep in mind when establishing any human security approach: the human consequences of living through armed conflict, how that experience shapes a person's understanding of the world around them, and what peace actually means for that person (Firchow and Mac Ginty 2017).

SECURITY THREATS AFTER CONFLICT

Human populations continue to face insecurities after violent conflict stops and stable state structures have been put in place. While some of those threats include direct violence from crime or from armed actors not yet fully demobilized, many more are systematic, long-term threats associated with weak institutional performance that, if not addressed, can affect generations. For a population to be healthy, it must have access to health services, which are often severely damaged during civil wars. Hazem Adam Ghobarah, Paul Huth, and Bruce Russett (2003), for example, demonstrate that civil wars have long-term negative consequences for public health after the fighting has stopped. Using data from the World Health Organization, the authors show that the breakdown of health services due to conflict results in higher ongoing instances of infectious diseases, including tuberculosis and malaria. If health services are not reconstructed following the termination of conflict, civilian populations continue to face long-term, systemic threats to their health.

Beyond the breakdown in health services, long-term consequences from conflict may be seen in the education systems and funding for education, which are often destroyed during civil wars (Lai and Thyne 2007). This means children—especially girls—are less likely to attend or complete school, which damages their long-term economic prospects (Shemyakina 2011). It can be years before solutions can be found to accommodate populations displaced by violent conflict—if resolution is possible at all (Smit 2012). In addition, combatants who are reintegrated into postconflict society will not only suffer from psychological distress but also often lack the schooling and training necessary to find skilled employment (Blattman and Annan 2010). This lack of opportunity may push some toward criminal endeavors.

Conflict can also affect the types of economic activity that people are able to engage in when the violence stops; it is not always the case that, postconflict, people can return to the jobs they held before the disruption or even to the profession for which they've been trained. For example, the use of land mines during conflict can render agricultural land unusable until the mines have been cleared, affecting those who work in the fields or with the harvest and limiting the amount of food that can be grown. If not adequately addressed during the postconflict phase, disruptions to education and to job security and other issues arising as a result of the conflict will have generational consequences. Postconflict human security efforts, therefore, constitute essential activities designed specifically to prioritize the mitigation of ongoing human misery suffered because of the violence.

STATE BUILDING, PEACEBUILDING, AND THE HUMAN SECURITY APPROACH

National and global security approaches have tended to prioritize state stability and economic recovery during postconflict peacebuilding. As we've discussed in previous chapters, these approaches see conflict as best managed through the creation of a system of stable sovereign states. Overall, the argument goes, state stability decreases the types of breakdowns that can trigger transboundary conflict, which for both national and global security approaches is a core priority. Therefore, central to these two approaches is a narrow focus on **state building**—which generally consists of reconstituting a core set of state institutions, a market economy, and basic rule of law provision (Richmond and Franks 2009).

Definitions of *peace* are often framed within this narrow state-centric focus. For example, the annual Global Peace Index, published by the Institute for Economics & Peace, lists eight "pillars" of positive peace: a well-functioning government, equitable distribution of resources, free flow of information, good relations with neighbors, high levels of human capital, acceptance of the rights of others, low levels of corruption, and a sound business environment. These eight pillars are heavily predicated on a very specific model of Westphalian sovereignty, which prioritizes the nation-state.

One driving argument for the emphasis on state building is that postconflict development requires a more stable environment for economic activity to resume. Some research has shown that a combination of foreign aid and good governance by the postconflict state leads to positive economic growth (Kang and Meernik 2005). However, uncertainty in the form of spoilers or even future elections, therefore, inhibits the financial investment that is central to reconstituting the state (Flores and Nooruddin 2009). Thus the ongoing questions, *What should be prioritized, and when?*

Peacebuilding, unlike state building, goes beyond the reconstitution of the state and attempts to create institutional frameworks and processes that address the roots of the conflict and establish processes for reconciliation with the intention of lessening the likelihood of conflict recurrence. Thus peacebuilding focuses on questions of reconciliation and coexistence. This may include the establishment of truth commissions and the promotion of forgiveness between victims and perpetrators. As with state building, peacebuilding in practice has been closely linked with the strengthening of state institutions. These processes are often nonlinear, dynamic, and messy, requiring ongoing reconceptualization (Paffenholz 2021).

By explicitly recognizing that long-term human insecurities persist after conflict has ended, the human security approach challenges both the national security and global security approaches to look beyond what policies are institutionally sufficient to stop ongoing violence and to instead establishing how the newly constituted state actually serves its population. Because the outbreak of civil war is often connected to the underperformance of a country's government, it has become a global priority to focus postconflict peacebuilding activities on developing the mechanisms that address the most pressing human needs. Thus there has been an ongoing shift to see postconflict peacebuilding in the light of how governance structures function for their citizens, rather than simply evaluating whether or not those structures can prevent future violent conflict.

What priority postconflict peacebuilding should give to different types of human security issues, however, is an ongoing debate. It is important that we distinguish between those policies that address a human security threat or problem but do not necessarily employ a human security *approach* and those policies that are designed to directly engage individuals' insecurities. While a strong state may be less likely to be violently challenged—and, thus, is presumably at lower risk for the recurrence of civil war—a postconflict peace that only focuses on preventing violence (**negative peace**) and does not adequately provide social welfare, establish rights, and create postconflict justice mechanisms (**positive peace**) can still exist within a miserable environment and, ultimately, undermine prospects for durable human security.

When a state addresses postconflict stability issues in general, human security issues have not by default necessarily been addressed as well. Postconflict activities are identified by many different names, and it isn't always clear which activities fall under which label or whether using a human security approach changes the fundamental nature of postconflict policies. This has led some to ask whether human security is simply "new wine for old bottles" (Hanlon and Christie 2016, 142). The breakdown of states puts tremendous strain on the international system. This may explain why both states and the global system as a whole are incentivized to assist countries emerging from violent conflict. However, what form that assistance takes and which policies get prioritized over others depends on the overall security perspectives of the actors crafting the policy and the normative pressures they may face.

Both the statist and the federalist security perspectives tend to prioritize activities addressing any immediate threat perceived to impact the long-term survival of the state. Hence a greater emphasis on state-building projects emphasizing stability, such as building up law enforcement and military institutions as well as focusing more closely on political reform. While state building may have a residual effect on overall human security, it is not clear that the effects will always be positive. In practice, this means that statist and federalist perspectives address human insecurity only to the extent that doing so assists in the reconstitution of the state.

Introducing the concept of human security, therefore, has helped practitioners better evaluate postconflict activities with humans as the referent. While state building and peacebuilding may help reduce certain threats, their bias toward certain forms of institution building may insulate them from effectively addressing the residual human security needs of certain vulnerable populations after conflict. Therefore we should ask ourselves whether the institutional focus of state building and peacebuilding is sufficient to capture what Ryerson Christie (2008) refers to as the larger *ethos* of human security. This is, in essence, the ongoing human security dilemma: whether the traditional approach to peace operations (typically conducted under the auspices of the UN), with its focus on building institutional capacity, is sufficient for addressing deeper-seated human security needs.

UN PEACE OPERATIONS

The United Nations serves as the main global institution tasked with assisting postconflict states through **peacekeeping** and peace building activities. Regional organizations, such as the African Union, also play key roles in peacekeeping, but often in partnership with a UN mandate. Peacekeeping missions are authorized through UN Security Council resolutions and are understood as the postconflict "deployment of international personnel to help maintain peace and security" (Fortna 2008, 5). Peacekeeping, however, was not a component of the United Nation as originally conceived but, rather, began to evolve as member states saw a greater need for engagement in postconflict peace. In their original conceptualization, UN peacekeepers would begin a mission only once a cease-fire or peace accord had been signed and only with the consent of the warring parties. The idea was that peacekeepers would serve as a neutral observer between the previously warring factions and would only use force in self-defense. Human security norms, however, have not been a consistent component of peacekeeping mandates.

The first UN mission to deploy military forces explicitly with a "peacekeeping" purpose was the United Nations Emergency Force I (UNEF I) in 1956, which oversaw the withdrawal of British, French, and Israeli forces from the Sinai Peninsula and established a buffer zone between Israel and Egypt. (*Note:* Two earlier UN missions—the United Nations Truce Supervision Organization (UNTSO) of 1948 and the United Nations Military Observer Group in India and Pakistan (UNMOGIP) of 1949, both ongoing— have retrospectively been termed peacekeeping operations.)

UN peacekeeping missions initially adhered to a strict global security framework and first required consent from the sovereign authority of the territory before beginning their work. The **multidimensional peacekeeping** missions that have dominated post–Cold War peacekeeping look drastically different. Multidimensional peacekeeping missions seek to rebuild the state institutions that were destroyed during a civil conflict. The shift to these types of peacekeeping missions began in 1989 when the UN Transition Assistance Group (UNTAG) was sent to Namibia to aid in its decolonization from South Africa. The range of responsibilities encompassed in this operation were much wider than those of previous operations and included a mandate to plan and supervise elections, to oversee military disarmament and civilian policing, and to assist in refugee return. (*Note:* The idea that UN missions should include a full spectrum of responses better designed to address the specific context of the conflict has led to greater use of the term *peace operations* to replace *peacekeeping* and *peacebuilding*.) Since then, mandates for UN peace operations have more often reflected the multidimensional aspects of UNTAG than the simple monitoring mission of UNEF I.

Today multidimensional peacekeeping has been institutionalized through a series of reorganizations and bureaucratic reforms. In 1992 the United Nations established the Department of Peacekeeping Operations to manage and report on ongoing peacekeeping missions. In 2000 the Brahimi Report (United Nations General Assembly, Security Council, 2000) provided the basis for many additional reforms, recommending that the United Nations develop permanent capacities to engage in comprehensive peacebuilding activities. Subsequently the UN has taken a series of steps to better integrate all the different actors engaging in postconflict peacebuilding. For instance, in 2005 the United Nations established the Peacebuilding Commission (PBC) in an attempt to better coordinate postconflict peacebuilding activities among various UN agencies, donors, national governments, and international financial institutions. This shift toward multidimensional, comprehensive peace operations integrating UN agencies, national governments, and various non-state actors has continued. In 2015 and 2017 both the General Assembly and the Security Council approved joint resolutions that embrace a broader range of peacebuilding activities (United Nations General Assembly 2015; United Nations General Assembly, Security Council, 2017).

The United Nations has conducted multidimensional peace operations in many locations, including in El Salvador, Guatemala, Cambodia, East Timor, Tajikistan, and Democratic Republic of the Congo (DRC). These operations were comprehensive and designed to develop the institutions that would bring stability and presumably peace to each country. The series of UN operations in East Timor, for instance, included within their mandates multiple provisions meant to stabilize the newly independent state, including UN oversight of elections, management of the state's core administrative structures and the creation of its civil and social services, the provision of law enforcement and public-security personnel, and assistance maintaining the internal and external security of the country. Three successive peacekeeping missions have been undertaken in East Timor: The United Nations Mission in East Timor (UNAMET), in response to violence erupting after the proindependence vote in 1999, was quickly followed by the United Nations Transitional Administration in East Timor (UNTAET), which oversaw the transition to independence from Indonesia. And this was followed by the United Nations Mission of Support in East Timor (UN-MISET), which oversaw the postindependence period up to 2005. While many aspects of these missions have been considered successful, they have been criticized for giving too much of their attention to elite concerns and applying "cookie-cutter" models based on Western ideals of good governance and market economies, leaving many of the most vulnerable out of the decision-making processes (Richmond and Franks 2009).

Overall, scholarship on the effectiveness of UN peacekeeping has generally shown a positive effect. These UN missions are associated with a higher likelihood that postwar peace will last (Fortna 2008) and with an overall improvement in civilian protection when adequately deployed (Hultman, Kathman, and Shannon 2013). In addition, peacekeeping missions have also been shown to prevent the spread of armed conflict into neighboring states (Beardsley 2011). Additionally, UN peacekeeping operations have undergone significant changes as the organization has "learned" how to carry out its activities. According to Lise Morjé Howard (2008), the United Nations' ability to gather information in the field has enabled the institution to better understand the problems extant in the postconflict environment where work is being done. This means that over the decades the United Nations has learned to better coordinate between agencies and partners on the ground and better integrate its operations within postconflict settings, meaning that now work with relevant parties and policy development can be done from the field operations rather than from UN headquarters.

Important shifts in UN peace operations include the timing of new operations entering the field, the increased scope of the operation mandates, and the longevity of the missions even after the initial cease-fire or peace accord has broken down. "An Agenda for Peace" suggested that the United Nations could use peace enforcement to more actively prevent armed actors from carrying out violence. Unlike traditional peacekeeping and peacebuilding, **peace enforcement** puts a UN force on the ground without the full consent from all armed actors. While the idea of a permanent rapid-reaction force at the United Nations has been entertained since its founding, various institutional and political realities have prevented its creation. As discussed in previous chapters, the Rwandan genocide and the Srebrenica massacre put pressure on the UN to better address atrocities before they happen. Consequently, the UN Security Council started to state explicitly that the mandate of a peace operation should include protection of civilians. The first mandate to do so was Security Council Resolution 1270, which in 1999 established the United Nations Mission in Sierra Leone (UNAMSIL) to oversee the implementation of the recently signed Lomé Peace Agreement. The resolution invokes Chapter VII of the UN Charter to justify granting UN personnel the authority "to afford protection to civilians under imminent threat of physical violence" (United Nations Security Council 1999b). Since then, the protection of civilians has taken a more central role within UN mandates.

This growing call for civilian protection has meant that peacekeepers are more likely to stay in the field if a cease-fire or peace accord deteriorates. The United Nations Multidimensional Integrated Stabilization Mission in the Central African Republic (MINUSCA), for instance, prioritizes the protection of civilians and the promotion and protection of human rights. Only after stating these aims does the mandate call for what would be considered more-traditional peacekeeping and peacebuilding activities, such as security-sector reform (SSR) and DDR. Thus, when the cease-fire that initially justified the mission began to unravel, UN forces remained in the country. Consequently, MINUSCA personnel have been the target of ongoing violence from militias and other actors. Additionally, the situation in the Central African Republic (CAR) shows a deployment force's limited ability to carry out its mandate successfully: even after the introduction of UN forces, multiple attacks on civilian populations were perpetuated in CAR, along with tens of thousands of new displacements. Similar dynamics occurred in South Sudan.

One rapid-reaction force authorized by the Security Council has been experimentally deployed to stop an immediate threat to civilians. When in November 2012 the United Nations Organization Stabilization Mission in the Democratic Republic of the Congo (MONUSCO) was unable to prevent the M23 guerrilla group from forcibly taking the capital city of North Kivu province, Goma, the UNSC authorized a first-of-its-kind Force Intervention Brigade (FIB), authorized to carry out "targeted offensive operations," which was then instrumental in defeating M23 and retaking the city (United Nations Security Council 2013). That said, the FIB did not achieve much beyond its defeat of M23, and the particularities of the mission do not necessarily lend itself to replication as a model for future stabilization missions (Tull 2018).

UN use of force in protection of civilians has always been a complicated mandate to fulfill. One 2014 UN evaluation of its peacekeeping missions found "a persistent pattern of peacekeeping operations not intervening with force when civilians are under attack" (United Nations General Assembly 2014, 7). Because UN troops are under the control of their national governments, it can be a problem that direct confrontations with armed actors make the UN troops and their governments party to an armed conflict. There is also the question of the legal protection of peacekeepers under international humanitarian law. According to the 1994 UN Convention on Safety of United Nations and Associated Personnel, attacks against UN peacekeepers are illegal. It is not clear, however, how an international court would judge a UN mandate to use force outside of the parameters of self-defense (Rudolf 2017).

There are important critiques of UN peacebuilding activities, particularly as UN operations have expanded in scope. Roland Paris argues that, while the liberal-market democracies promoted by peace operations are not, in the long-term, a bad outcome, they are often implemented too quickly, leading to outcomes that ultimately undermine the peace (Paris 2004). Oliver Richmond and Jason Franks contend that it is the liberal Westphalian models of peacekeeping overall that undermine their overall effectiveness (2009). Séverine Autesserre (2014) highlights a number of practices that are inefficient, ineffective, or counterproductive: For example, deploying people who do not understand the language or local customs and placing interveners in management positions over local staff can result in poor outcomes. Interveners, no matter how well-intentioned, often favor thematic expertise rather than local custom and, due to the limited time frames of their missions, may opt toward quicker, top-down, technical, and often quantifiable solutions. Further, the overall inclination of peacekeepers to rely on their own expertise rather than working with local partners decreases the local population's ownership of any of these projects. For instance, who has the authority to make determinations of justice may differ from community to community. Thus a justice system that is seen to have been imposed by an outside authority may be viewed as less legitimate to the local population than would be a justice system rooted in local traditions and customs—even if the two systems were to arrive at the exact same conclusions regarding any given case. These and other issues—such as oversimplifying explanations for the causes of the conflict and collecting data on ongoing violence from other interveners or from local elites—can be counterproductive and even contribute to refueling violence.

BOX 7.1. THINK ABOUT IT . . . EVERYDAY PEACE

We should try to understand peacebuilding and state building in relation to the types of communities we ourselves would want to live in. Thus it is sometimes useful to take mental stock of our own experiences and consider how our own worldviews might influence the way we understand postconflict peacebuilding.

Consider the following questions:

1. On a scale of 1 to 10, with 10 being "most peaceful," how would you describe the community that you live in now or the one you consider "home"? What contributes to that score?
2. In your own community, what do you think contributes to peace, and what contributes to violence? Would other people in your community agree with that assessment? Why or why not?
3. Examine table 7.1, and consider how each component is present in or absent from your community. Which activities would you prioritize? Why?
4. In what ways do you feel most vulnerable? What would have to happen for that vulnerability to lessen?
5. If you can, talk to others who currently live in or have lived in your community about these questions. Are their answers the same or different from yours? Why do you think the answers are similar or different? What surprised you most about their answers?

Integrating Human Security into Postconflict Peace Operations

Determining the extent of a UN mandate and the size of the operation required to meet that mandate has been an ongoing challenge for integrating human security practice into formal postconflict peace operations. The Commission on Human Security engages this challenge in chapter 4 of *Human Security Now*, identifying multiple clusters of human security activities that should be undertaken during the postconflict period (2003, 60). These include public safety, humanitarian relief, rehabilitation and restoration, reconciliation and coexistence, and governance and empowerment. Under each activity cluster is a set of practices the report urges practitioners to take on during postconflict activities (see table 7.1). These activities are not exclusive to each other, and, at least in theory, they should all be mutually pursued (Commission on Human Security 2003). The reality of limited resources, however, means some activities are prioritized over others.

Table 7.1. Timing of and Responsibility for Core Peacebuilding Activities

Core peacekeeping activities	When does the activity need to be undertaken?	With whom does the primary responsibility lie?
Public Safety		
Control armed elements: Enforce the cease-fire, disarm combatants, and demobilize combatants.	Immediately after agreement between combatants is reached.	International actors with cooperation from violent parties.
Protect civilians: Establish law and order, fight criminal violence, clear land mines, and collect small arms.	Early, but needs institutional structure in place. International actors can provide initial protection, but not indefinitely.	International actors and then the domestic government.
Build national security institutions: Establish police and a military, and integrate or dissolve nonstate armed elements.	Early. Process is generally outlined in peace agreement.	Domestic government in cooperation with potential spoilers.
Protect external security: Combat illegal weapons and the drug trade, combat trafficking in people, and control borders.	Ongoing. Requires highly professionalized security institutions.	Domestic government with assistance from international actors and bordering states.

(continued)

Table 7.1. *Continued*

Core peacekeeping activities	When does the activity need to be undertaken?	With whom does the primary responsibility lie?
Humanitarian Relief		
Facilitate the return of conflict-affected people: Aid internally displaced persons and refugees.	Ongoing. Durable solution must lessen risk of future displacement and be agreed upon by displaced populations.	Domestic government with assistance from international actors (UNHCR).
Assure food security: Meet nutrition standards, and launch food production.	Immediate and ongoing. Food aid to address acute hunger crisis. Long-term food production requires conditions for agriculture and markets.	Domestic government with assistance from international actors (WFP, FAO).
Ensure health security: Provide access to basic health care, prevent the spread of infectious diseases, and provide trauma and mental-health care.	Immediate and ongoing. Postconflict populations have immediate medical needs. Long-term public health requires broad health infrastructure.	Domestic government with assistance from international actors (WHO).
Establish emergency safety nets for people at risk: This includes caring for women (female-headed households), children (soldiers), the elderly, Indigenous people, and missing people.	Immediate and long-term.	Domestic government with assistance from international actors.
Rehabilitation and Reconstruction		
Integrate conflict-affected people: This includes internally displaced persons, refugees, and armed combatants.	Long-term, and requires both housing and employment solutions.	Domestic government with assistance from international actors.
Rehabilitate infrastructure: Repair or construct roads, housing, power sources, and transportation systems.	Long-term.	Domestic government with assistance from international actors.
Promote social protection: This includes the provision of employment opportunities, food, health, education, and shelter.	Mostly long-term, but immediate if population is facing acute crisis.	Domestic government with assistance from international actors.

Core peacekeeping activities	When does the activity need to be undertaken?	With whom does the primary responsibility lie?
Dismantle the war economy: Fight criminal networks, reestablish a market economy, and provide microcredit.	Immediate and ongoing. Requires progress in other areas (national security institutions, rehabilitation of infrastructure, etc.).	Domestic government with assistance from international actors.
Reconciliation and Coexistence		
End impunity: Set up tribunals, and involve traditional justice processes.	Early. Process is generally outlined in peace agreement.	Domestic government and/ or international actors and/or local civil society.
Establish truth: Set up a truth commission, promote forgiveness, and restore the dignity of victims.	Early. Process is generally outlined in peace agreement.	Domestic government and/ or international actors and/or local civil society.
Announce amnesties: This includes immunity from prosecution for lesser crimes and reparation for victims.	Early and ongoing. Process is generally outlined in peace agreement.	Domestic government and/ or international actors and/or local civil society.
Promote coexistence: Encourage community based-initiatives (long-term), and rebuild social capital.	Ongoing.	Domestic government and local civil society.
Governance and Empowerment		
Establish a rule of law framework: Institute a constitution, a judicial system, and legal reform, adopt legislation, and promote human rights.	Early and ongoing. Process is generally outlined in peace agreement.	Domestic government with assistance from international actors.
Initiate political reform: This includes working through institutions and democratic processes.	Early and ongoing. Process is generally outlined in peace agreement.	Domestic government with assistance from international actors.
Strengthen civil society: Promote participation, accountability, and capacity building.	Ongoing.	Local civil society with assistance from global civil society and legislation that assists these processes.
Promote access to information: Protect an independent media and encourage transparency.	Ongoing.	Domestic government and local civil society.

Source: The above taken with minimal changes from chapter 4, Commission on Human Security 2003.

Many of the practices recommended in *Human Security Now* are identical to what once would have been considered state-building or peacebuilding practices. For example, under the *public safety* cluster, the first recommended practice is controlling armed elements, which includes enforcing cease-fires and disarming and demobilizing combatants. In addition, it recommends the building of national security institutions, such as the police and military, as well as disarming and dissolving nonstate armed groups. This fits in with the idea that the state ought to have a monopoly on the means of violence. While these are accepted practices in state building, they may not be necessary, and certainly are not sufficient, to guaranteeing human security. In fact, the state itself may be a key source for human insecurity; therefore, concentrating the means for violence in the state, without an appropriate check on its ability to apply that force, may lessen human security overall. The practice in the public safety cluster that is most closely tied to what would be considered human security is the protection of civilians. Nevertheless, even this proscribed action adopts a state-centric approach, as it's to be achieved by establishing the rule of law and fighting criminal violence, clearing land mines, and collecting small arms. Being able to do this first requires a benign state, free from internal contention—a condition often not met in a postconflict environment.

Whether human security is merely new wine for old bottles is raised within other clusters as well. In the *reconciliation and coexistence* cluster, for example, most of the suggested practices fit within what would traditionally be considered peacebuilding practice: setting up tribunals and truth commissions, as well as establishing amnesties for lesser crimes. While the cluster also includes promoting forgiveness and reparation for victims, these ideas have long been a key component of peacebuilding practice.

Ultimately, we should ask how a focus on human security changes our perspectives on state-building and peacebuilding practice. For instance, it is not unreasonable to suggest that, in order to establish durable human security, the use of violence should be limited to the state and that the state should use violence only in a way that conforms to universally accepted rights-based rule of law. The human security approach, therefore, helps identify the normative parameters around which institutional capacity can be built. This same question applies to other areas of postconflict peacebuilding, shifting our perspective from which outcomes lessen the prospects for violence to how different policy choices affect the short- and long-term human security of various groups.

Table 7.1 (above) examines the main clusters and activities that *Human Security Now* says are key to integrating human security into postconflict peacebuilding. We present it as a helpful guide for critically thinking through the questions raised in this chapter. While a full examination is too broad for the overall scope of this chapter, carefully working through each box helps conceptualize the core issues that this chapter addresses. The first column lists the main clusters and core activities identified by the Commission on Human Security (2003, 60). For each of the core activities within each cluster, we examine two questions: *When should the core activity take place?* and *With whom does the primary responsibility for implementing the approach lie?* We leave it to the reader to contemplate the overall impact each of these activities has on improving overall human security.

Working through the table, we can make several important observations regarding the integration of the human security approach into peacebuilding activities. First, international actors play an important role, but the ultimate success of their engagement will be based on local buy-in and the ability of the newly formed postconflict government, in cooperation with international actors and local civil society, to implement these policies. Second, while most peacebuilding activities need to be started immediately after an agreed-upon peace, postconflict structural conditions create obstacles. For instance, displaced populations will be unable to return if housing is unavailable or if the place they are returning to lacks basic security. Limited resources force governments and international actors to make choices about priorities. Should infrastructure spending prioritize those areas that support economic activity, such as paving a road to a factory, or should it go toward a group that was victimized during the conflict, such as building housing so that a displaced population can return to its community?

Finally, we must ask how communities emerge from a period of long-term violence.

POLICING AFTER THE TROUBLES

A key component of postconflict institution building is security-sector reform and the role of policing. Ideally, policing is the mechanism that the state uses to justly and impartially prevent and solve crimes the community has identified as problematic while respecting the rights of its citizens. Achieving that ideal, particularly within the context of postconflict peacebuilding, can be a challenge. Many conflicts are driven by sectarian, ethnic, or ideological divisions, and police forces often mirror those societal cleavages. During civil conflict there is often a melding between different security branches, with policing often being co-opted into the state's fight against insurgents. Often the government will declare a state of emergency, giving the police and other security forces extralegal authority that suspends many of the rights of its citizens. During these periods, the state's police forces may engage in serious human rights abuses or coordinate with nonstate paramilitary groups and provide a veneer of deniability for some of the most egregious violent acts that occur during conflict.

It is difficult to determine how these violations should be addressed during the transition from active conflict to the postconflict environment. On one hand, most civil conflicts are not all-consuming, and many police units and officers will have remained engaged in legitimate crime-prevention and -solving activities. One argument is that, once the conflict has been resolved, so to speak, policing should return to "normal," meaning no major institutional reforms need to be made. That said, injustices related to policing are often a root cause of the conflict. As such, not addressing inherent structural injustices within the state's policing runs the risk of reigniting the same grievances that fueled the conflict in the first place.

In addition, postconflict environments are often awash in guns, with many demobilized combatants lacking sufficient economic prospects. This can result in an increase in robberies and assaults when former combatants are not successfully integrated back into society (González Peña and Dorussen 2021). This raises the likelihood that police forces will remain mobilized in the same way but this time using the justification that the same tactics used to fight an insurgency are now necessary to combat gangs and organized crime rather than insurgents. A lack of institutional reform can also result from insufficient oversight from independent bodies. This, in turn, can result in police corruption, thus undermining the very purpose of the force itself. For this purpose, in divided societies a deliberate consideration of the institution of policing and the norms that guide it are often central to the peacebuilding process.

In Northern Ireland, policing was a key component of the Belfast Agreement, also known as the Good Friday Agreement, signed in 1998. The conflict in Northern Ireland was driven by sectarian divisions between its Catholic and Protestant populations. When Ireland gained independence from the United Kingdom in 1921, Northern Ireland's Protestant majority wished to remain united with the United Kingdom—an issue dating back to King James's colonization of Ireland in the early 1600s. Northern Ireland opted out of the Belfast Agreement, by virtue of a majority-Protestant electorate, and remained part of the UK. Many Northern Irish within the Catholic minority, however, were dissatisfied with this arrangement, fearing discrimination from the loyalist majority, and hoped for Northern Ireland to merge with the newly independent Republic of Ireland.

Following partition, Northern Ireland's Unionist government did, in fact, enact several policies that were discriminatory against the Catholic population. Policies in voting, policing, employment, and housing favored the Protestant populations, compounding grievances within the Catholic communities. In 1968, Northern Ireland's police force, the Royal Ulster Constabulary

(RUC), responded to protests against discriminatory policies with violence, further escalating the conflict. Ensuing riots helped justify the mobilization of British Armed Forces into the territory, beginning a period known as the Troubles. These were years marked by low-intensity conflict. The violence was complex, with multiple armed actors battling each other. Both sides of the conflict had nonstate paramilitary groups, most notably the Provisional Irish Republican Army (IRA) on the republican/Catholic side, and the Ulster Defence Association (UDA) on the loyalist/Protestant side. After the British state deployed its armed forces into the territory to assist the RUC (English 2003; Keefe 2019), the fighting left over three thousand dead, just over half of whom were civilian noncombatants (McKittrick et al. 2001; Conflict Archive on the Internet, n.d.).

Policing in Northern Ireland during the Troubles was highly politicized and connected to larger sectarian divisions. The RUC held strong links with the Unionist government (by the 1990s, over 90 percent of the force was drawn from Protestant communities) and was often used by Unionists as a key tool for maintaining power. The model followed in Northern Ireland was more reflective of British colonial policing practices: the RUC was based on a unitary and centralized model quite different from the community-policing models being implemented in England and Wales (Smyth 2002; Elkins 2022). In the 1970s the IRA began engaging in a series of terrorist attacks in both Northern Ireland and England, which helped justify the RUC's use of emergency powers, often in arbitrary and discriminatory ways. The tactics used by the RUC were heavily criticized by many human rights advocates as excessively draconian (Hillyard 1993; Hall and Human Rights Watch 1997), including multiple cases in which the RUC and British forces were accused of collusion with loyalist paramilitary forces (Keefe 2019). Throughout the course of the conflict, over three hundred officers were killed and thousands more people injured, creating an additional set of grievances from the loyalist communities from which the force was drawn (O'Rawe 2008).

The RUC's controversial role throughout the Troubles made policing a central component of the Belfast Agreement. The agreement, therefore, sets out the normative expectations for what policing should look like, including the expectation that the police force is "professional, effective and efficient, fair and impartial, free from partisan political control; accountable, both under the law for its actions and to the community it serves; representative of the society it polices, and operates within a coherent and cooperative criminal justice system, which conforms to human rights norms" (Kroc Institute for International Peace Studies, n.d.[b]).

Following the signing of the agreement, an Independent Commission on Policing (ICP) was convened, chaired by Chris Patten, to provide recommendations for creating a postagreement police force. Those recommendations were presented in what is known as the 1999 Patten Report. It should also be noted that building up to the Belfast Agreement, several grassroots initiatives from several sectors of Northern Ireland society, including loyalists and republicans, began to explore ways that policing could be transformed. These initiatives, while largely ignored by the government and the RUC at the time, started a dialogue about how the RUC model of policing negatively affected poorer communities throughout Northern Ireland (O'Rawe 2008).

The Patten Report extensively examines policing in Northern Ireland and proposes 175 different recommendations for reform. Because all sides in the conflict held legitimate grievances, the ICP was particularly careful to take a neutral position on the conflict, interviewing victims and participants from all sides. The first substantive recommendations of the report were related to human rights, including the establishment of independent mechanisms by which complaints against the police can be made. In addition, it addresses the imbalance between Protestants and Catholics in the force by proposing a period in which recruitment would draw an equal number from each group from the pool of qualified candidates. To further separate the RUC from its politicized past and its perceived ties to the loyalist side of the conflict, the commission recommended that the name, uniforms, and badge be changed to neutral symbols, separate from both the British or Irish states (Independent Commission on Policing for Northern Ireland 1999). Thus in 2001 the RUC became, not without controversy, the Police Service of Northern Ireland (PSNI).

Despite the Patten Report's attempts at neutrality, competing political interests within Northern Ireland sought to shape its implementation toward their own favored outcomes. Many associated with the RUC argued that any reforms were unnecessary since the conflict was now over (Smyth 2002). In fact, many former officers and their supporters have argued that their conduct during the Troubles was both legitimate and justified (Southern 2018). Sinn Féin, the political wing of the Irish republican side, wanted all recommendations from the report to be adopted; however, they did not give support to Northern Ireland's new policing structure until 2007. The demographics of the police force have changed in the intervening years, according to PSNI's workforce-composition statistics: 32 percent of its police officers now come from Catholic communities (Police Service of Northern Ireland 2021). While this is a marked increase from the days before the agreement, it still does not reflect the current balance of the two populations, as Catholic and Protestant populations are now roughly equal in number (Russell 2013).

Does Northern Ireland present a model for SSR in other divided societies? There is much to be commended for the institutional and normative transformations that have taken place in Northern Ireland. There are, however, several factors that should be taken into consideration when evaluating universal applicability. Foremost, the Belfast Agreement has held and there has not been any significant return to the previous violence. For that reason, there has not been much justification to reconstitute the police to preagreement institutional structures. There have, though, been street protests, and it should be noted that they have been handled much differently than were the violent clashes of the late 1960s. Overall, however, the police reforms have been seen as a success. Considering the framework given in the Belfast Agreement, the reforms made do match its basic principles. However, it is important to consider that police reform in and of itself is not sufficient to maintain the peace without the successful implementation of other components of a peace accord. The fact that Northern Ireland has not seen significant politically motivated violence since the signing of the accords has helped PSNI maintain its more neutral position. That said, successfully depoliticizing a police force helps take away the tools that some political actors might use to oppress political opponents and communities to begin with.

NO PEACE WITHOUT JUSTICE?
TRANSITIONAL JUSTICE AND HUMAN SECURITY

Human security is grounded in the idea that both short-term and long-term security is best guaranteed when state institutions are designed to protect human rights and carry out the just application of the rule of law. Violent conflict breaks down the rule of law, leading to massive violations of people's rights and widespread atrocities. **Transitional justice**, therefore, is the process by which a state transitions from a period of conflict into a peaceful, democratic society with a focus on redress for victims. These processes are inherently entwined with the question of how atrocities carried out by regimes and other violent actors are punished and how victims receive justice. After civil wars, victims and perpetrators must often live together in the same communities. If not remedied, long-standing resentment due to past injustices can form the narrative for future conflict.

Therefore, transitional justice is strongly linked to the question of reconciliation. **Reconciliation** is a process in which people work to overcome hatred and mistrust between groups to the extent that they are able to coexist with each other (Murithi 2008; Philpott 2012). How this actually occurs is complicated. According to Daniel Philpott, there are several important components of political reconciliation. First, reconciliation involves *the state*. The state has the capacity and the authority to carry out key acts of reconciliation, including trying and imprisoning war criminals, disbursing reparations to victims, and issuing formal apologies. While civil society and other nonstate actors play important roles in the reconciliation process, the state is seen as key. Thus, for postconflict reconciliation to succeed, the state must adopt just institutions. Second, reconciliation includes *punishment*. Punishment may be reduced or creatively applied, but an important component of any justice process is that there is an appropriate response to wrongdoing. Third, reconciliation involves the personal *participation* of victims, perpetrators, and other members of the community. This participation is seen as a key first step to healing the wounds caused by violent conflict. Fourth, a reconciliation process must address what is known as *right relationship*—that is, how the aggrieved parties reconcile enough such that they can live among one another in the day-to-day. Finally, reconciliation involves the *return to a previous condition*. Of course, this is problematic, in that preconflict states are usually built on unjust social structures. Thus reconciliation is built on an ideal of justice, and it leads us to wonder, *If these ideals were unachievable in the past, how do they become achievable in the future?*

Many cultures already have processes by which certain components of reconciliation take place. In postgenocide Rwanda, for example, a traditional form of justice called *gacaca* was used in some cases. This community-based form of justice requires the perpetrators to acknowledge their misdeeds, upon which the victims are then involved in determining how reparations should be made and how to best reintegrate the perpetrators back into the community. A similar process called *ubuntu* occurred in South Africa after the dismantling of apartheid, in which there was a strong push for victims to forgive. While these processes are aimed at helping communities find both the forgiveness and the common ground needed to move forward, some have argued that victims are often pressured to declare forgiveness and leave perpetrators with a false sense of absolution.

Accompanying these methods are more formal processes, such as **truth and reconciliation commissions (TRCs)**, convened to correctly reveal the truth of what exactly happened during a conflict or system of injustice. To get to this truth, people are given immunity or reduced sentences to testify about their role in the conflict. When the commission finishes its work, it will typically produce a report detailing its findings. The use of such commissions is widespread, and TRCs have occurred in such places as Guatemala, South Africa, Chile, Argentina, and East Timor.

Another key concern in transitional justice processes is the question of reparations for victims. For those who have been displaced or have lost property, this includes creating the conditions for which they can return to their communities and be compensated for lost property. How to compensate victims who have lost loved ones or been permanently disabled due to the conflict may be even more problematic. Restitution also raises the question of who constitutes a victim. Does someone who was displaced due to deteriorating economic conditions caused by the conflict garner the same rights to compensation as someone who was displaced due to direct violence by one of the armed actors? What about those who chose to stay in their communities, often surviving through worse conditions than the displaced who were able to flee? Even when these definitional issues can be appropriately clarified, there remains the question of who has the responsibility to compensate. Postconflict states are often strapped for resources, and the pledges for compensation may never be fulfilled. International actors may be able to provide immediate aid, but such outside assistance could leave some feeling that those responsible were never appropriately held accountable.

One important criticism of truth and reconciliation processes is that, when used, perpetrators of war crimes can remain unpunished. Some will argue that this is an unfortunate consequence for achieving peace, whereas others will counter that this ignores the basic rights of victims. Postconflict justice has always faced the challenge of determining the proper balance between amnesty, reconciliation, and criminal prosecution against those who committed the worst acts. In order for justice to be properly administered, all parties should be in general agreement that the process is fair and impartial. Not only should victims have the right to receive justice for acts committed against them, but defendants should also have the right to defend themselves and have access to legal counsel during any proceedings. However, there are a number of obstacles to establishing fair and impartial justice mechanisms. In criminal law, if an action is not specifically recognized as a crime, it cannot be prosecuted. After conflict, there simply may not be sufficiently specific domestic or international legal statutes defining the perpetrated acts of violence as criminal. This combination of weak judicial institutions and lack of political will has meant that victims of political violence have historically had very little legal recourse to justice when state institutions are unable or choose to not act. These limitations have led many human rights and legal advocates to work to create more robust international law dedicated to prosecuting war crimes and crimes against humanity.

The idea that war crimes and crimes against humanity could be punishable under international law is not new. Following the end of World War I, the acts of violence carried out by Turkey against its Armenian population sparked the question of whether the 1907 Hague Convention extended to states that carried out unconscionable acts against their own citizens (Bassiouni 2011). As discussed in previous chapters, numerous treaties were ratified throughout the twentieth century to better codify what constitutes violations of international humanitarian law; however, this expansion was not necessarily accompanied by mechanisms that can easily prosecute those crimes. If ever a prosecution were to happen, it was to happen within a domestic judicial system. In fact, one of the first actions taken by the UN General Assembly was to encourage member states to arrest war criminals who had fled and to send them back to their respective countries in order to be tried.

The lack of an enforcement mechanism fostered a belief by combatants that war crimes would ultimately go unpunished, therefore removing any checks against their committing egregious acts. This problem of impunity has led to greater efforts to give international criminal jurisdiction to outside bodies. This shift toward international institutions is reflected in the reaction to the 1999 Lomé Peace Agreement, intended to bring the brutal civil war in Sierra Leone to a close. To convince guerrilla fighters to lay down their arms, the accord offered blanket amnesty to all rebel combatants. At the time, the argument for offering said amnesty was that it was the only condition under which rebel fighters would lay down their arms.

In 1999, Sierra Leone was ranked last in the world in average years of expected disability-free life—at only 25.9 years (Mathers et al. 2000, 1688). Considering the brutality of the war, perhaps it was reasonable to bargain for peace by offering blanket amnesty. This decision, however, came under intense scrutiny from human rights organizations, and in 2000 the UN Security Council, with the support of the Sierra Leone government, voted to create the Special Court for Sierra Leone, which would have jurisdiction to try those accused of violating international humanitarian law. In the end, the court convicted members of the Civil Defense Force (CDF), the Revolutionary United Front (RUF), and the Armed Forces Revolutionary Council (AFRC), as well as former president of Liberia Charles Taylor, who had supported the RUF. Similar international tribunals have been established in Rwanda, the former Yugoslavia, and Cambodia.

To try to help close this gap between international humanitarian law and domestic courts' inability to prosecute violators, the **International Criminal Court (ICC)** was created as a permanent international body, based in The Hague, the Netherlands, with the authority to prosecute individuals (including heads of state) who are responsible for genocide, crimes against humanity, and war crimes. The ICC was established by the **Rome Statute** in 1998 and entered into force in July 2002. Currently there are 123 state parties. The creation of a permanent institution has obviated the need for ad hoc tribunals, as had been created in the former Yugoslavia, Sierra Leone, and Cambodia. In addition, a permanent court would help more clearly identify and codify prosecutable crimes. Importantly, the Rome Statute continues to give deference to the sovereign authority of a state's domestic courts and takes cases only when a state's domestic judicial systems are unable or unwilling to do so, making it a court of last resort. Additionally, only crimes that have been committed on the territory of a state party or by an individual who is a citizen of a state party are subject to the ICC's jurisdiction. There are two exceptions to this: a state that is not party to the Rome Statute can accept the jurisdiction of the ICC, or the alleged crimes can be referred to the ICC through a resolution of the UN Security Council.

While the establishment of the ICC is a tremendous leap forward in international jurisprudence, the court has faced a number of important criticisms. One criticism is its low rate of convictions. As of November 2021, there have only been four cases in which suspects were convicted by the court. In addition, many other investigations by the court did not lead to indictment and were eventually dropped. A major obstacle for prosecutors is gathering the evidence sufficient to convict. It is not enough to know that atrocities happened; conviction requires evidence that a specific individual have an order or participated in an act. Another key criticism is the fact that the court has yet to hear a non-African case. (*Note:* Several investigations and preliminary examinations have been undertaken in non-African countries that have not gone to trial. Investigations have occurred in Afghanistan, Colombia, Myanmar, Palestine, Venezuela, the Philippines, and Georgia. Preliminary examinations have occurred in Colombia, Honduras, Venezuela, Bolivia, Iraq (in which UK nationals were investigated), Ukraine, and South Korea.)

This and the fact that the ICC has issued indictments for sitting heads of state in Sudan and Kenya has led some African countries to advocate for a collective withdrawal of the African Union from the ICC. This advocacy was not shared by all AU member states: Nigeria, Senegal, Burkina Faso, Cote d'Ivoire, and others have forcibly rejected the move. In the end, the only African state to have withdrawn from the ICC was Burundi, in October 2017, after it was referred for investigation. In addition, the Philippines withdrew in March 2019 after President Rodrigo Duterte came under investigation for extrajudicial killings in his antidrug campaign.

Another issue with the ICC is the role of victims and how they perceive the court. The ICC tries to involve victims at multiple stages in the proceedings, including allowing them, through their legal representatives, to question defense witnesses, challenge evidence, and serve as witnesses. In addition, if there is a conviction, victims can take part in the reparations proceedings (Turner 2017), although there are some deficits in terms of appeals (Perez-Leon-Acevedo 2021). The ICC has also established a Trust Fund for Victims, meant to support and implement programs designed to specifically address the harm caused by the convicted (Safferling and Petrossian 2021).

Still, ICC proceedings are also notoriously slow and can take years to come to a close. Germain Katanga, for instance, spent almost seven years in detention before being found guilty for crimes against humanity. Such lengthy trials deprive victims the closure they may be seeking. Some have complained that they must continue to survive in inhumane conditions while those contributing to those conditions exist in relative comfort, awaiting trial. In fact, Bosco Ntaganda, Congolese warlord, voluntarily turned himself in, determining—probably correctly—that a prison cell in The Hague would be more comfortable and safer than the forests of Eastern Congo.

Does the existence of an international body with the authority to prosecute war crimes help lessen these crimes from occurring? If so, what impact does this have on human security? Research on this question is inconclusive, showing both positive and negative effects. Because the ICC is a court of last resort, its existence may incentivize states to improve their own judicial institutions in order to carry out prosecutions on their own and avoid ICC interference. For instance, in June 2015 the Central African Republic passed a law creating the Special Criminal Court to oversee, in cooperation with international judges and prosecutors, the prosecution of war criminals. Beth Simmons and Allison Danner (2010) suggest that many countries with atrocious human rights records are willing to join the ICC as a way to signal to their people that they will play by the rules. Such capacity building by individual states could serve as a check on ongoing and future atrocities. However, little evidence exists that would suggest the ICC itself has a deterrent effect against future atrocities. In addition, Alyssa Prorok (2017) finds that ICC involvement while a conflict is ongoing decreases the chance for peace and, in fact, prolongs the conflict.

How to appropriately approach questions of transitional justice following conflict remains a difficult question to answer. The human security approach pushes us to think about how the newly constituted state addresses the question of mass atrocity committed during warfare. While it is possible to hold some individuals accountable for the most egregious atrocities, there will remain many others who participate in atrocities at some level but remain within their communities. How communities reconcile and move beyond these traumas remains an important part of the human security approach, particularly as it relates to norm development and institution building. Recognizing the deep hurts that conflict imposes on the populations that experience it, as well as the difficulty of adequately redressing these hurts, creates the conditions in which human security needs can be addressed.

CONCLUSION

This chapter has examined the peacebuilding processes that occur post-conflict. During this period, human security threats continue to persist as people try to regain normalcy and seek justice for atrocities perpetrated during armed conflict. Human security threats persist on two levels: (1) the immediate and acute threats that arise from the actions of violent individuals and groups, whether or not they have an interest in attempting to reignite the conflict, and new violent political actors seeking to take advantage of the uncertainty of the new environment, or criminal elements and (2) the long-lasting threats that result from the damage caused by the conflict. Without adequately addressing these long-lasting threats and focusing on society's long-term durable human security, any peace will have little positive impact on these vulnerable populations.

As we discussed at the outset of this chapter, initial international efforts to address postconflict environments only dealt with human security issues as a side effect of more-straightforward national and global security goals. Changes brought about by the end of the Cold War and by pressure from human rights advocates began to bring more focused attention to postconflict peacebuilding approaches concerned with the protection of civilian populations and addressing transitional justice concerns. While there have been failures in these attempts, these processes are fairly recent in terms of international practice, and there has been a steep learning curve. Today we see greater attention paid to the role that civil society can play as well as local initiatives and more creative forms of justice. To the extent that peacebuilding efforts lay the foundation for sustainable peace, they contribute to durable human security, to which we now turn in the chapters in section III.

DISCUSSION QUESTIONS

1. How do different security perspectives affect perceptions of a peacebuilding process?
2. How do the traditional and multidimensional approaches to peacekeeping differ? What are the advantages of and drawbacks to each approach?
3. What are the obstacles to effective long-term peace if those who were responsible for committing atrocities are not held responsible for their crimes?
4. Why is it important to have local participation and support for peacebuilding efforts, including transitional justice processes? What are the implications of not having this participation and support?
5. What role should police have in a postconflict society? What reforms do you think are necessary to creating just policing?

Section III

DURABLE HUMAN SECURITY

Chapter 8

Breaking the Cycle of Insecurity

Learning Objectives

This chapter will enable readers to

1. identify human security concerns common to armed conflict and peacetime
2. connect the notions of *freedom from fear* and *freedom from want* with the issues discussed in sections II and III
3. and recognize economic insecurity as a durable human security challenge and an illustration of the cycle of security.

This chapter bridges the concepts presented in sections II and III to underscore the commonalities in human security and insecurity in armed conflict and in times of relative peace. The human security approach is often discussed in terms of "freedom from fear" and "freedom from want," with some states and organizations choosing to prioritize one or the other in keeping with national or organizational policy priorities. As we observed in chapter 1, durable human security includes protection from security concerns that are not necessarily linked to armed conflict—though they may also exist in wartime—but that threaten the daily lives and livelihoods of individuals and their communities through the effects of dysfunctional norms or institutions that create conditions for harm. Ultimately, human insecurity in armed conflict and long-term insecurity are mutually reinforcing, just as freedom from fear and freedom from want are similarly reinforcing. To achieve durable human security, security providers must strive for freedom from both fear and want. To maintain durable human security, security providers must bolster the capacity of institutions to fend off sudden threats as well as erosion by destructive norms.

When the conditions for human security exist in peacetime, the risk of violent conflict is diminished; when human security is taken into consideration in the transition from war to peace, peace is more sustainable. The reverse is also true. The first section of this chapter looks at human security in armed conflict and the notion of freedom from fear, while the second section examines durable human security and the notion of freedom from want. The third section explores economic security as an illustration of the many intertwined dimensions of durable human security; here we also consider the political, economic, and humanitarian crisis in Venezuela. The final section offers an overview of the structure of section III.

HUMAN SECURITY IN ARMED CONFLICT AND FREEDOM FROM FEAR

Threats related to human security in armed conflict are similar to threats that have traditionally been central to the state and global security approaches. Armed conflict, violence committed by nonstate armed actors, transnational terrorism, the proliferation of weapons from small arms to nuclear arsenals, and mass displacement and migration all present threats to the physical safety of individuals and communities. These same threats affect the stability and security of states and—if sufficiently widespread—the global system. The narrow view of human security emphasizes the importance of freedom from fear. Preventing violence, resolving conflicts through peaceful means, rebuilding society and promoting reconciliation after the end of armed hostilities, protecting individuals from terrorist attacks, decreasing the availability of weapons of mass destruction and the flow of small arms to conflict zones, and protecting vulnerable populations from harm contribute to freedom from fear of direct violence or imminent physical harm.

Recall the 1994 Human Development Report's definition of *human security* as protection from both sudden and chronic threats, discussed in section I (United Nations Development Programme 1994, 3). Human security in armed conflict is concerned most immediately with sudden threats and, as the chapters in section II discuss, the breakdown of norms and institutions to such an extent that direct physical violence occurs. Establishing and protecting freedom from fear can resemble efforts to protect the state, which makes the narrow view of human security appear less daunting to scholars, practitioners, and policy makers than the wider view of human security. We cannot expect to achieve human security if the state is fragile, failing, or embroiled in armed conflict. In this respect, the human security and state security approaches are synchronous: when the state is secure, it is better able to maintain institutions and promote or comply with norms that make the protection of individuals possible.

When positive societal norms and functional institutions that foster good governance are eroded and weakened, the protections from harm that individuals and communities enjoy in relative peacetime are also weakened or eliminated. In addition to the destructive power of armed conflict, competing security perspectives within the population or among decision makers contribute to the erosion of protective norms and institutions. As factions within society place their trust in different security providers, define their group differently, and perceive threats differently, the shared understandings on which stable norms and institutions rest grow less stable. For marginalized and vulnerable communities that do not enjoy the full protection of norms and institutions even in relative peacetime, insecurity worsens in armed conflict, especially if these individuals and communities are directly targeted for violence or are perceived as threats to the state or to armed factions.

Unlike efforts to protect state security, human security practice places individuals and communities at the center of all decisions and actions. The US government interned Japanese Americans during World War II as a response to the Japanese attack on the US naval base at Pearl Harbor and the fear among policy makers that individuals of Japanese descent could pose a security risk to the country. In cases like this one, human security and state security are in direct conflict, and efforts to secure the state result in erosion of human rights, freedoms, and security. When the state perceives, anticipates, or experiences threats to its stability, it can respond in ways that degrade human security. The internment of Japanese Americans also demonstrates how nativist and statist security perspectives can merge, leading policy makers to view certain groups as "others" who constitute a threat.

While the narrow view of human security is conceptually cleaner and more recognizable from the traditional security approaches, it has still encountered resistance. The perception that human security is synonymous with the doctrine of Responsibility to Protect and military intervention in states' domestic affairs has led to some criticism of the human security approach as a way to impose Western values on non-Western states. As discussed in chapter 5, UN General Assembly Resolution 66/290, in response to critiques from state policy makers, practitioners, advocates, and scholars concerned with the erosion of the principle of nonintervention and the use of military means to respond to civil and human rights concerns, articulates the synchronous nature of human security and state security, noting that human security is distinct from a responsibility to protect and does not advocate for the use of force (United Nations General Assembly 2012b, 2). Human security in armed conflict and protection of the freedom from fear must incorporate the perspectives, voices, and resources of human security actors at all levels, local and global. It is important to note that bolstering human security in conflict zones does necessarily involve military means, although exercising R2P through the UN

Security Council may use military force as a last resort in situations involving grave and widespread threats to civilian populations.

The wider approach to human security, which includes the well-being of individuals in armed conflict and in daily life outside of conflict zones, takes the cyclical nature of security into account. As we will discuss in the chapters in section III, there are connections between the enjoyment of durable human security and the overall stability of states and the international system. Better protection of overall well-being, freedoms, rights, and opportunities through efforts at the local, state, and international levels may decrease the risk of armed conflict and the human insecurity that accompanies the breakdown of norms and institutions in conflict zones.

FROM ARMED CONFLICT TO "PEACETIME": DURABLE HUMAN SECURITY AND FREEDOM FROM WANT

Durable human security relates to chronic or long-term threats to peace, security, and well-being. When a society has achieved durable human security, individuals and communities live without fear of widespread violence or armed conflict and receive equal protection of, respect for, and provision of their rights and freedoms. Durable human security encompasses the dimensions of security and insecurity that are not necessarily rooted in active armed conflict but that threaten the daily lives and livelihoods of individuals and communities—although the same violations of human rights and freedoms may exist and worsen in armed conflict.

General Assembly Resolution 66/290 observes the cyclical nature of human security in times of armed conflict and times of relative peace: "Human security recognizes the interlinkages between peace, development and human rights, and equally considers civil, political, economic, social and cultural rights" (United Nations General Assembly 2012b, 1). "Peacetime" is not always peaceful or secure for all people; this reality is at the heart of the wider view of human security. Individuals and communities experience vulnerabilities and insecurity related to socioeconomic status, political affiliation, or identity—including gender, sexuality, race, ethnicity, nationality, religion, and other salient factors. Durable human security is realized when individuals and communities enjoy freedom from fear *and* freedom from want; the concept of durable security draws from both freedoms for a broad view of human security.

Freedom from want was a crucial component of twentieth-century human rights discussions, included in US president Franklin Roosevelt's "Four Freedoms" speech, the Universal Declaration of Human Rights, and the International Covenant on Economic, Social, and Cultural Rights (as discussed in chapters 1 and 4). As noted in the 1994 Human Development Report, freedom from fear and freedom from want have both been integral aspects of human security efforts (even before the concepts gained traction), but over time state and international security practice came to favor efforts to protect freedom from fear over freedom from want (United Nations Development Programme 1994, 24). The narrow focus on freedom from fear has not been universal, of course; Japan has led efforts to secure freedom from want and improve well-being through economic development, joined by many Asian states that witnessed the effects of the 1997 Asian financial crisis and saw the importance of social safety nets (Hanlon and Christie 2016, 8–9). Of course, durable human security is about more than wealth and economic development.

Rights and protections like effective and accessible public health systems, access to adequate nutrition, opportunities for stable employment and the ability to earn a livable wage, gender equality, access to quality education, racial and ethnic equality and freedom from discrimination based on identity, and environment sustainability fall under the conceptual umbrella of freedom from want. These are the rights, freedoms, and protections that enable people to thrive, to participate actively as members of society, and to live their lives without fear of discrimination, repression, or harm. When these protections exist, so too does durable human security.

The idea of human security developed alongside a reemergence of interest in and discussion of human rights and human development within the international community, and especially at the United Nations, in the early 1990s. This was no coincidence; the establishment of human security depends in large part on the provision and fulfillment of human rights, recognition of the potential contributions of the individual to effective and sustainable economic development, and general recognition by the state and other international actors that the individual matters.

Human security requires good governance at all levels of society. When durable security exists, individuals, communities, and—by extension—states do not suffer the effects of widespread poverty, hunger, poor health, lack of access to education, gender-based violence and discrimination, the effects of environmental degradation and destruction, racial, ethnic, or sectarian violence and discrimination, or other day-to-day harms that inhibit well-being. Of course, vulnerability can always exist within a society that generally enjoys high levels of human security; our point here is that these forms of insecurity will not be systematic or widespread, and neither will they arise from entrenched norms or dysfunctional institutions.

Good governance does not imply that the international community or an entity like the United Nations must intervene militarily whenever a threat to durable human security arises, thereby eliminating the last vestiges of state sovereignty. Rather, individuals, local communities, states, and the international community should collaborate to build and safeguard the norms and institutions required to realize durable human security. In some cases, this may entail scaling up local capacity to improve gender equality or environmental protection (to name just two of the many examples). In other situations, this may involve transnational advocacy and international shaming in response to grave human rights violations. In any scenario, building and safeguarding the norms and institutions necessary to achieve durable human security becomes more difficult if factions with sharply competing security perspectives work to disrupt the process. Examining durable human security reminds us to consider the question posed in chapter 1: *Can human security exist for one person or community if obtaining that security undermines, even if indirectly, the human security of others?*

It is important to recognize that human security cannot exist without state security and that state security is jeopardized by global instability; efforts to foster durable human security must balance these considerations with the overall goal of protecting individuals from long-term threats to their well-being. The rights, opportunities, and freedoms that each individual and community prioritizes will vary across cultural contexts and experiences, which means there is no single universal prescription for achieving durable human security. Still, the ideal end state of durable human security sees individuals self-sufficient and empowered to provide for themselves, their families, and their communities; it also sees individuals secure in their persons and free from the fear of violence.

As the 1994 Human Development Report emphasizes, human security is not about "hand-outs" or paternalistic efforts to stifle individuals' ability to seize opportunities and reach goals on their own; instead, it is grounded in the recognition that insecurity generates dependence and an inability to thrive (United Nations Development Programme 1994, 24). Durable human security, then, is about "leg-ups"; but when states are unable or unwilling to guarantee the various facets of durable human security, individuals, their communities, and, ultimately, the state will face insecurity and instability.

ECONOMIC SECURITY: AN ILLUSTRATION OF THE CYCLE OF SECURITY

Economic security highlights how the many dimensions of durable human security are intertwined and mutually reinforcing. The chapters in section III each explore different dimensions of durable human security, and we want to emphasize here that these dimensions are linked, much like a spider's web: when one dimension of durable human security erodes, the structure weakens as a whole and the other parts of the web are threatened. Higher levels of economic security contribute to more-robust food and health security; the former makes it possible to access the resources necessary for the latter. The reverse is also true: economic insecurity jeopardizes access to food and health care, especially when social and institutional safety nets are weak, inequitable, or absent. Similarly, gender inequality lends itself to economic insecurity, and women experience economic inequality within the household and in society writ large (Nieuwenhuis et al. 2018). Racial and ethnic inequality and discrimination contribute to economic insecurity as well, as minority and historically excluded populations experience systematic barriers to education, employment, and health care and also suffer from income inequality and intergenerational poverty (Winship, Reeves, and Guyot 2018; Chetty et al. 2020). Economic security, like all dimensions of durable human security, is unsustainable when the norms and institutions in society perpetuate systematic inequality.

The experience of economic insecurity varies across contexts, but these diverse realities share a core definition. At the individual or household level, **economic security** is the sustained ability to access (afford) the goods and services needed to survive and thrive. This includes basic resources such as food, water, shelter, medications, and clothing, as well as essential services and opportunities like health care, education, and employment with a stable income. At the state level, economic security is the ability to keep the government, institutions, and economy operating in a sustainable way with stable growth and minimal interruption from external or internal shocks.

In wealthy states, economic insecurity most often takes the form of income inequality and poverty. In developing states, the focus of economic insecurity is extreme poverty. Poverty is about more than the lack of financial wealth; it both contributes to and stems from lack of access to education and stable employment, sufficient nutrition or food security, gender inequality and vulnerability, displacement, and lack of access to health care. Amartya Sen defines poverty as *capability deprivation*; one experiences poverty when they lack access to the resources and opportunities required to lead a life that they value. Development, then, is not just about enriching a country but entails expanding the opportunities that enable individuals to maximize their capabilities (Sen 2000). Economic security at the individual level implies that a person can reasonably expect to have access to the resources and opportunities they need to live a meaningful life today and in the future. At the state level, economic security with a human security focus seeks to protect and expand opportunities for capability development, resting on the assumption that the state's economic stability is founded at the individual and community levels. This is a challenge in wealthy states and poor states and requires a reexamination of social and economic policy and practice (Hick 2014).

Sustainable Development Goal 10 (SDG 10) focuses on reducing inequality within and between countries by 2030. The targets of SDG 10 focus on sustainable income growth for the bottom 40 percent of the world's population, empowerment and inclusion of all people, reduction of discrimination, regulation of global financial markets, improved representation of developing states within global institutions, safer migration, and more effective aid flows and remittances (United Nations Department of Economic and Social Affairs, n.d.[a]). The COVID-19 pandemic has exacerbated inequalities and economic insecurity for individuals and countries alike, rolled back progress made toward SDG 10 prior to 2020, and demonstrated the differential effects of a sudden global crisis on states and individuals.

Policies and programs intended to reduce economic inequality and poverty cannot utilize one-size-fits-all approaches. Jamila Michener and Margaret Teresa Brower (2020) observe that social and economic policies in the United States have unequal effects across racial subgroups of women, demonstrating the importance of intersectional approaches to policy making that account for systematic inequality and vulnerability. Like all dimensions of human security, economic security is intertwined with other factors; yet, when working through the three policy boxes, decision makers rarely dissect the effects of proposed policy options and ideal outcomes on subgroups of individuals or on historically excluded communities. At the international level, SDG 10 represents an effort to view economic inequality and poverty through an intersectional lens, underscoring the ties between economic insecurity and race, gender, disability, and immigration status, observing the historical inequities between states that have contributed to the economic divide between them today.

BOX 8.1. THINK ABOUT IT . . .
TRAFFICKING IN PERSONS

The "United Nations Convention against Transnational Organized Crime and the Protocols Thereto" defines *trafficking in persons* as

> the recruitment, transportation, transfer, harbouring or receipt of persons, by means of the threat or use of force or other forms of coercion, of abduction, of fraud, of deception, of the abuse of power or of a position of vulnerability or of the giving or receiving of payments or benefits to achieve the consent of a person having control over another person, for the purpose of exploitation. Exploitation shall include, at a minimum, the exploitation of the prostitution of others or other forms of sexual exploitation, forced labour or services, slavery or practices similar to slavery, servitude or the removal of organs. (United Nations Office on Drugs and Crime–Vienna 2004, 42)

Trafficking in persons is a violation of the human rights of the victims and an extreme threat to their physical security and well-being.

People of all ages and genders can become vulnerable to trafficking. Economic insecurity can be a key driver of vulnerability to trafficking. Insecurity, inequality, or lack of opportunity may lead individuals to pursue educational and job opportunities within their home country or abroad, responding to misleading advertisements or offers that place them in the hands of traffickers rather than with legitimate academic institutions or employers. Mass migration and refugee flows often involve large numbers of unaccompanied children, women traveling alone or with children, and other individuals desperately seeking safe passage out of situations of acute insecurity; people in these situations are vulnerable to exploitation and trafficking. Other threats to durable human security or conflict-related insecurity may place individuals in positions of vulnerability that render them more likely to fall victim to the many forms of trafficking in persons.

Trafficking in persons is a transnational criminal practice that exists in times of relative peace, in and around zones of armed conflict, and in wealthy and developing states alike. It is a human security threat and human rights violation that is tied to many of the forms of insecurity discussed in this book and to forms that we do not discuss here. Beyond its threat to the security of individuals, the UN Security Council Resolution 2331 (2016) also recognized that human trafficking can exacerbate armed conflict, contributing to the cycle of insecurity.

The United Nations Office on Drugs and Crime (UNODC) maintains a Global Report on Trafficking in Persons and data on individual regions, victims, and traffickers. Review the latest report (United Nations Office on Drugs and Crime–Vienna 2020), and consider the following questions:

1. How do patterns of trafficking in persons relate to threats to human security?
2. How might changes in security provision in armed conflict affect the practice of trafficking in persons?
3. What improvements in durable human security might decrease the prevalence of trafficking in persons?
4. In what ways does economic insecurity contribute to vulnerability to trafficking?
5. How might the targets within SDG 10 affect trafficking in persons? (You can read about SDG 10 at United Nations Department of Economic and Social Affairs, n.d.[c])
6. What is your country doing to address the problem of trafficking in persons? Is your national government's response focused on trafficking as a domestic (internal) problem or threat, foreign (external) problem or threat, or both? (*Note:* You may need to search beyond the UNODC for this information.)

Economic security is central to durable human security; it is what comes to mind for many people when they consider freedom from want. Although durable human security draws heavily on the notion of freedom from want, it extends beyond simply accounting for wealth and development; freedom from fear of physical violence and sudden threats to well-being are also crucial aspects of durable human security. Durable human security is weakened by chronic threats like inequality and hunger and also by a state's rapid descent into economic instability, ongoing political turmoil, and ineffective governance, as the case study of Venezuela illustrates.

Political and Economic Crisis and the Erosion of Durable Human Security in Venezuela

More than five million Venezuelans have fled the country as a compound crisis of economic collapse and democratic erosion has created severe food, health, economic, and physical insecurity (Alhadeff 2018; Bristow 2019; Bahar and Dooley 2021). The dire situation in Venezuela provides insight into the connections between economic security and durable human security. By examining instability and human insecurity in Venezuela under the Chávez and Maduro regimes, we can understand the significant effects of governance and institutions on all aspects of security. In this case study, we focus on economic insecurity, food insecurity, and erosion of human rights and democratic norms; recent history in Venezuela demonstrates that a stable and prosperous state can quickly descend into instability and insecurity quickly, with disastrous effects for the population.

Former president Hugo Chávez instituted major political, socioeconomic, and institutional changes. He was elected president in December 1998 and took office on February 2, 1999, ushering in an era of socialist policies intended to provide the poor with food and opportunities to pursue an education. This led to broad popular support for *chavismo* (or *chavism*, the left-wing political ideology rooted in the Chávez government's policies) (Bahar 2019; Peralta 2019).

The focus of his campaign was a reimagination of Venezuelan government, and the effort came at the cost of democratic checks and balances. Chávez abolished Venezuela's congress, placed the judiciary under the executive branch, gave military colleagues greater influence in the government, and eroded freedom of the press; a new constitution, drafted by a constituent assembly and approved by voters in a popular referendum in December 1999, formalized this restructuring and consolidation of power under the executive branch (Freedom House 2016). The República de Venezuela (Republic of Venezuela) became the República Bolivariana de Venezuela (Bolivarian Republic of Venezuela) in recognition of the new constitution's links to

Simón Bolívar's ideology and political philosophy, including the notion that governance in Latin America requires greater centralization of power than the more-decentralized republican approach taken in the United States.

The Bolivarian Revolution brought a slate of social reforms to Venezuela, including policies intended to make housing, education, food, and health care affordable; the poor and working classes felt that the government recognized their needs. The social programs improved human development in Venezuela, as the country's HDI value rose from 0.666 in 1995 to 0.757 in 2010 (United Nations Development Programme 2020). When Chávez took office, Venezuela was the world's third-largest oil and gas exporter, and throughout the early 2000s, revenues from these exports helped fund the expanded welfare initiatives and allowed the Chávez government to nationalize key sectors of the economy—including oil, utilities, agriculture, tourism, and transportation—and further consolidate political power under the executive and military (Reuters Staff 2012; Freedom House 2016).

Although Chávez was popular with the poor and working classes, he and his policies had political enemies, especially among business leaders and unions; after weeks of strikes and months of rumors, he was briefly ousted by a coup attempt on April 11, 2002, but reinstated two days later after mass public protests called for his return and much of the military remained loyal to him. Ties between the coup plotters and the United States aggravated tensions between the two states (Vulliamy 2002; Wilson 2002; Nugent 2019). Chávez remained in office for more than a decade after the coup attempt, with a final reelection in 2012 before his death in office on March 5, 2013. Throughout his presidency, Chávez's socialist party controlled every branch of government, eroded democratic norms, and enacted policies that depended on a continuous flow of funding from oil exports.

Nicolás Maduro succeeded Chávez as interim president and won reelection later that year. Maduro continued the policies of chavismo but faced an economic climate that made this approach to governance more precarious. Chávez had nationalized food in the early 2000s in an effort to make basic staple foods more accessible. The approach began with price caps on essential foods in grocery stores but quickly escalated to price controls on agricultural products and government expropriation of farmland from owners. Eventually the state became the main food producer, displacing the influential latifundios and removing market influence on food production and prices. Once the state controlled food production, corruption increased and production decreased, eventually forcing reliance on food imports. The Venezuelan government could afford to import food when oil revenues were high, but this practice became untenable once the price of oil declined after 2014 (Garcia and Zuniga 2019).

Analysts describe Venezuela as a petrostate, a state in which the government relies heavily on oil and gas exports, the economy centers on the oil sector and pulls workers and resources from other key sectors, political power is concentrated within a few key actors close to the head of state and corruption is rampant, and institutions do not have sufficient power to regulate economic activity or poor governance (Rendon and Mendales 2018; Cheatham and Labrador 2021). The average price of a barrel of oil steadily increased over much of Chávez's time in office, but dropped from a high of over $100 per barrel in 2014 to just over $50 at the start of 2015, hitting a low of $26 in 2016 (Cheatham, Roy, and Labrador 2021; Macrotrends, n.d.). Oil price instability continued in the years that followed, hitting extreme lows in 2020 when the COVID-19 pandemic decreased demand for oil and gas. When a state depends on oil to finance the policies and programs that keep the government legitimate in the eyes of the people, unstable oil prices trigger instability within the state.

Falling oil prices in 2014 precipitated a political and economic crisis in Venezuela: food shortages and hyperinflation ensued, the healthcare system collapsed, and social unrest increased; as the situation worsened, Maduro worked to consolidate political and economic power and make opposition to the regime more costly (Catholic Relief Services 2019). In 2014, Colectivos—armed groups tasked with protecting the Bolivarian Revolution and, by extension, supporting the Maduro government—met protests with violence. The Chávez government had banned the possession of private firearms in 2012 in response to increased crime rates but had funded and encouraged the Colectivos; Maduro's government provided arms to the vigilante groups and mobilized them in response to opposition (BBC News 2012; Markovits and Rueda 2013; United Nations Office of the High Commissioner for Human Rights 2017). Intimidation tactics did not quell the social and political unrest, and neither did they stop the economy from spiraling downward.

The opposition Democratic Unity Roundtable coalition defeated the Socialist party in the 2015 parliamentary elections in what observers viewed as retribution against chavismo and Maduro's government for the economic crisis and widespread suffering. For the first time since the Bolivarian Revolution, the opposition held a majority in the legislature (Ma 2015; Reuters 2015). By 2015 the ongoing economic crisis, particularly the high levels of inflation, had created widespread poverty. Imports of food, medicines, and medical equipment fell by roughly 70 percent between 2013 and 2016 (Bahar et al. 2019). As the economic crisis weakened the healthcare system, infant mortality increased. The combination of inflation and food shortages meant that households surviving on a minimum wage were in a precarious position, by 2017 only able to purchase about 10 percent of the food (in terms of caloric intake) that they would have been able to purchase in 2010 (Bahar et al. 2019).

The Maduro government began to replace grocery stores with government-supplied CLAP (the Spanish acronym for Local Committees for Supply and Production) boxes, using desperately needed food as political leverage (Rendon and Mendales 2018; Garcia and Zuniga 2019). Increasing the costs of political dissidence, the Colectivos again mobilized against opposition protesters in 2017, using violence with impunity (Office of the United Nations High Commissioner for Human Rights 2017). With a population increasingly frustrated by the deterioration of economic security, food security, and health security, social unrest continued, and the Maduro government's domestic legitimacy declined.

Physical security, including security from violent crime, has since further deteriorated, and the state does not hold the monopoly on the use of force. In 2014 the Venezuelan government established *zonas de paz* (peace zones) from which police and government forces withdrew in response to increased violent crime and armed attacks against police (Venezuela Investigative Unit, Insight Crime, 2017). While local residents in the *zonas de paz* are expected to keep the peace through their own vigilance, the withdrawal of police forces has paved the way for nonstate armed groups to take control and establish their own systems of order, with reported funding and support from the government itself (Hernández 2019; Salinas Rivera 2015).

Although crime statistics likely downplay the extent of physical insecurity in Venezuela, the *zonas de paz* are anything but peaceful, and high crime rates contribute to ongoing emigration from Venezuela to Colombia and other countries in the region. The state itself also presents a physical security threat, and in 2020 the United Nations accused Venezuelan state security forces of extrajudicial killings, torture, and disappearances, amounting to crimes against humanity (United Nations 2019; Staff and agencies of *The Guardian* in Geneva 2020).

Maduro claimed reelection in 2018 in a process widely viewed as illegitimate and unconstitutional, complicating the country's economic crisis with a constitutional crisis (Zambrano 2019). The opposition coalition boycotted the process, and voter turnout was under 50 percent. Maduro received 67.7 percent of the vote, an outcome rejected by opposition candidate Henri Falcón—who received 21.2 percent—and members of the National Assembly (BBC News 2018).

Because the National Assembly declared the election unconstitutional and its results null and void, Maduro's presidential term legally expired on January 10, 2019, and Venezuela had no official president. In accordance with Article 233 of the Venezuelan constitution, which specifies the line of succession, the speaker of the National Assembly, Juan Guaidó, became acting president (Zambrano 2019; BBC News 2020a). While Guaidó's authority was limited within Venezuela by Maduro's continued grasp on the presidency, much of Latin America, the United States, and the European Union recognized Guaidó as the legitimate president. Russia, China, Cuba, Turkey, Bolivia, and Nicaragua backed Maduro (Zengerle and Spetalnick 2020; BBC News 2019). In the midst of ongoing questions about government legitimacy, continued economic devastation, and increasing food insecurity, Venezuela was grossly unprepared for the COVID-19 pandemic.

The country's formerly robust healthcare system began to collapse after Chávez's death as the economic crisis took hold. Even before the economic downturn linked to falling oil prices, the state did not allocate sufficient funding to a healthcare system designed to provide free health care to all Venezuelans (a top selling point of chavismo). Further, the small percentage of GDP directed to health care (4.7 percent in 2012 and 3.4 percent in 2013) was often misused by a large, corrupt bureaucracy (Wilson 2015). Lack of funding, medical-supply shortages, and emigration of healthcare professionals led to increases in maternal and infant mortality (two reliable indicators of health security in a state), preventable deaths, and rates of previously controlled diseases. Malaria, tuberculosis, diphtheria, and other rare communicable diseases reemerged in Venezuela and spread to neighboring states as Venezuelans emigrated; the return of malaria is particularly striking, given Venezuela's success in 1961 as the first country to eradicate it (World Health Organization 2021a; Dube 2019; DeYoung 2019; Schreiber 2019).

Extreme food insecurity from 2017 onward has worsened health security as children and adults alike have suffered the effects of malnutrition, but the scale of the impact is difficult to ascertain. Maduro's government has worked to stifle the public release of information and statistics on health and food insecurity, and Human Rights Watch reports that resident physicians have been threatened with disciplinary action and expulsion from their training programs for including discussion of malnutrition in patient diagnoses (Human Rights Watch 2019). One measure of the healthcare system's decline is the increase in emigration, as lack of access to medications and health care, including prenatal care, is a key factor in some of the more than 5.3 million displaced Venezuelans' decisions to flee (Alhadeff 2018; Bristow 2019; Bahar and Dooley 2021).

The combination of diminished healthcare capacity and lack of transparency in public health foreshadowed a disastrous response to the COVID-19 pandemic. The emergence and spread of COVID-19 constituted a threat multiplier all over the world, and in Venezuela the virus compounded existing threats of food insecurity, economic insecurity, a failing healthcare system, and an authoritarian government disinclined to accept outside aid (Rendon and Sanchez 2020). As with other health indicators, information on COVID-19 cases and access to vaccines in Venezuela is suppressed by the government, but the World Health Organization has reported a total of 276,395 confirmed cases and 3,173 deaths between January 3, 2020, and July 5, 2021 (World Health Organization, n.d.[c]). In 2021, Venezuela received vaccine donations from Russia (Sputnik V vaccine), China (Vero Cell vaccine), and Cuba (Abdala vaccine), but the initial rate of vaccination was slow and the prioritization of recipients unclear, with healthcare workers and teachers—priority groups in other states—left waiting for their shots (Garcia Cano and Rueda 2021).

Throughout the pandemic, Venezuelans have continued to face harsh economic conditions, and health insecurity, food insecurity, and economic insecurity have continued to compound one another. Years of US sanctions (unsuccessful attempts to oust Maduro), hyperinflation, and further declines in oil revenue have left Maduro's government with little choice but to liberalize portions of the economy (Pons and Armas 2021; Bahar et al. 2019; Human Rights Watch 2019). Inflation in Venezuela hit a record high of 1.8 million percent in 2018 before Maduro relaxed some economic controls; but liberalization, a depreciating national currency, and fuel shortages drove the prices of consumer goods—including staple foods—higher (Pons and Armas 2020). Along with his shifting stance on liberalization, Maduro also began to accept aid from outside sources, including allied states and NGOs like the Red Cross, a change Guaidó attributed to pressure on the regime (Dube 2019; Beaumont 2019).

As other states have sought ways to strengthen social safety nets or provide economic stimulus to bolster economic security in the pandemic, Venezuela has increased taxes and fees for public utilities like trash collection, Internet access, and electricity to generate revenue for the government, placing even greater pressure on a heavily burdened population (Reuters 2020). Adding to the economic insecurity faced by business owners and consumers, cities began to levy higher taxes on local businesses in a scramble to make up for lost municipal funding that had come from the government prior to liberalization (Pons and Armas 2021). Still under heavy sanctions on oil throughout the pandemic, despite international pressure on the United States to lift them while COVID-19 has raged, Maduro has continued to blame the country's economic downturn on the United States (DeYoung 2019; Washington Office on Latin America 2020).

In January 2021, Maduro's Socialist party regained power in the National Assembly in parliamentary elections that have been widely disputed as fraudulent by the Democratic Unity coalition, outside observers, the Organization of American States, the United States, and the European Union. Voter turnout remained low, and the Democratic Unity coalition once again boycotted the elections (Cheatham and Labrador 2021; BBC News 2020b; Herrero 2020; Freden 2020). While after the 2018 elections the European Union recognized

Guaidó as the legitimate leader of Venezuela, the opposition coalition's loss to Maduro's party in 2021—despite widespread doubt regarding the validity of the process—has forced an end to EU support for Guaidó as Venezuela's rightful leader (Stott 2021).

The crises in Venezuela underscore the interdependent nature of the many dimensions of human security. Stable institutions and good governance are essential to the maintenance of durable human security. Years of democratic backsliding and corruption have compounded with economic crisis to foment political instability, economic instability and widespread poverty, extreme food insecurity, health insecurity, social unrest and violence, and emigration and displacement. Returning to human development as an indicator of durable human security, we can observe that Venezuela's HDI value reached its peak in 2015, at 0.769, and declined steadily to 0.711 in 2019 (United Nations Development Programme 2020; n.d.[b]).

Consider the notion of human security as a spider's web once again: each portion of the web is linked to the whole, and tugging on one thread causes movement in the others. When one portion of the web is damaged, the web can eventually be repaired if its fundamental threads—in society, the institutions—remain anchored and intact; when those threads are ripped away, the entire web collapses. Durable human security focuses on the threats and challenges that render people, their livelihoods, and their communities vulnerable through the effects of dysfunctional norms or institutions that create conditions for harm. The cycle of security and the vital importance of durable human security in stable states are illustrated by the role of national economic and political instability in worsening food, health, physical, and economic insecurity for individuals and communities in Venezuela, which in turn has reinforced the national-level crises.

OVERVIEW OF SECTION III CHAPTERS

Durable human security encompasses the dimensions of security that are not directly linked to active armed conflict and the considerations we discussed in the section II chapters, although those same dimensions of security are threatened in conflict zones. Durable human security is eroded in wartime and in "peacetime" when a state's institutions and norms lack the capacity to fend off sudden threats to the population's well-being or when competing security perspectives within the state's population or political and institutional decision makers erode norms and institutions in ways that disrupt the policy-making and policy-implementation processes. Pandemics, massive wildfires, economic crises, and armed conflicts are a few of the many potential threats that present sudden challenges to durable human security. When considering the erosion of norms and institutions and disruption of effective and equitable governance, factors like extreme political polarization, corrupt leadership, democratic backsliding, and racial/ethnic or socioeconomic inequality are central factors.

The chapters that follow in section III explore some, but certainly not all, of the threats to durable human security. As noted in chapter 2, the broad view of human security, with its inclusion of threats to freedom from want and insecurity in situations of relative peace, is the subject of debate. By expanding the notion of security to issues that arise outside of armed conflict, scholars and practitioners risk rendering the concept of human security too unwieldy to study and apply in policy initiatives. We contend that this risk is outweighed by the utility of understanding chronic insecurity and its links to national and global instability, especially when facing twenty-first-century threats. Widespread hunger may not trigger civil war on its own, but it can be a contributing factor to political instability (Lappé, Collins, and Rosset 1998). Gender inequality may not incite regional conflict, but research shows that states with high levels of gender inequality tend to resort to aggression first in conflict, tend to use higher levels of violence in conflict than do states with greater gender equality, and are more likely to experience civil war (Caprioli 2000; 2005; Caprioli and Boyer 2001; Hudson et al. 2012).

Durable human security may lay the foundations for long-term peace and stability, which satisfies the central aim of the narrow view of human security rooted in freedom from fear. In addition to the moral imperative to concern ourselves with big problems like chronic hunger, the effects of climate change today and in the future, pandemic disease, and gender inequality, there is analytical value in assessing the links between these problems and overall security.

The chapters in section II explore human security in armed conflict and, therefore, focus predominantly on freedom from fear and the narrow approach to human security. In contrast, each of the substantive chapters in section III considers an issue area central to the broad approach to human security and relates to both freedom from fear and freedom from want. The chapters in section III do not need to be read sequentially, although sections of chapter 12 build on some of the ideas presented in chapter 11. Since the issues highlighted in section III do not constitute the full scope of sources of insecurity that may be included in the broad view of human security, the aim of section III is not to provide an authoritative catalogue of every durable human security issue—an undertaking that would require several volumes—but, rather, to highlight illustrative problems with the goal of enabling readers to think critically about other threats to well-being in today's world.

DISCUSSION QUESTIONS

1. Consider your local community. Does your community enjoy freedom from fear and freedom from want? Are there any threats to these freedoms for the community as a whole or any subset of the community?
2. Why might states align their foreign policy priorities with either the idea of freedom from fear or freedom from want?
3. How does the wide view of human security—including both human security in conflict and durable human security—advance security provision? How does it challenge security provision?
4. Consider an acute conflict unfolding today. What obstacles to freedom from fear and freedom from want exist for the population affected by the conflict?
5. Consider SDG 10. What do you think are the main obstacles facing the achievement of this goal's targets by 2030?

Chapter 9

Health Security as Human Security

Learning Objectives

This chapter will enable readers to

1. discuss the impact of health threats on human, national, and global security
2. identify the reciprocal influence of health on human security and human security on health
3. debate the extent to which health concerns constitute security threats
4. and compare states' responses to the COVID-19 pandemic.

Infectious disease outbreaks—like the cholera epidemic and H5N1 (avian flu), Ebola, and SARS-CoV-2 (COVID-19) pandemics—make it into the headlines of global news media and national and international policy agendas alike, triggering fear in a globalized world in which a public health crisis in one state threatens to affect the citizens and stability of many others. When we think of human security as the absence of threats to an individual's well-being and ability to thrive, we see that good health is necessary for the achievement of human security. The question then becomes, *Which health issues constitute human security issues?* Clearly, protection from sudden health threats like deadly pandemic fits the definition. But are acute health crises affecting large swaths of the global population the only relevant concerns, or are noncommunicable but debilitating health issues viable human security concerns?

In this chapter we explore the interaction between overall health, health crises, and security. Of particular interest is the mutually reinforcing (and potentially mutually destructive) relationship between health and human security: health crises pose a potential threat to human security, and human security offers a promising policy orientation toward global health issues. While the parameters of which health issues are central to security have yet to be clearly defined, it is clear that health is an inextricable component of the complex web of issues that comprise human security.

HEALTH AS A HUMAN SECURITY ISSUE

The United Nations Development Programmes's 1994 Human Development Report includes threats to good health among the causes of human insecurity, noting that daily concerns like health and employment were as important as protection from war to the architects of the UN system in their early discussions at the San Francisco Conference in 1945 (United Nations Development Programme 1994, 3). Twenty-one years after the San Francisco Conference, Article 12 of the International Covenant on Economic, Social and Cultural Rights (ICESCR) asserted the "right of everyone to the enjoyment of the highest attainable standard of physical and mental health," referencing infant mortality, environmental and industrial hygiene, the "prevention, treatment and control of epidemic, endemic, occupational and other diseases," and the provision of medical care to all. In recognition of the centrality of health to the pursuit of human security, the Human Development Report observes that primary health care is a component of human development—and one that states should support through foreign assistance (United Nations Development Programme 1994, 4).

Human Security Now reiterates the need to provide basic health care at affordable costs (Commission on Human Security 2003, iv). **Health security**, therefore, is concerned with the protection of individuals from sudden or chronic health threats and with efforts to empower individuals to lead healthy lives. It is central to the definition of overall human security introduced by the Human Development Report: "safety from the constant threats of hunger, disease, crime and repression" and "protection from sudden and hurtful disruptions in the pattern of our daily lives" (United Nations Development Programme 1994, 3). Good health is especially crucial to the aspect of human security concerned with empowerment—or freedom from want.

Health concerns become durable or chronic human security issues when they arise from systemic inequality or deprivation created by societal norms surrounding individuals' health needs, the weakness or inefficiency of health care institutions, or from the structural instability imposed by active armed conflict or state collapse. A chronic disease like asthma in and of itself may impede an individual's ability to thrive: it can reduce attendance at school or work; it may limit options for locale due to environmental triggers like air pollution or allergens; it may affect the household budget if necessary prescription medications are expensive; and it may cause severe symptoms or death. Such a disease certainly constitutes an individual hardship.

Yet we would consider a chronic disease (including asthma) to be a human *security* threat only if it is the result of a widespread problem arising from a lack of institutional protections or from harmful societal norms; examples of such problems include extreme air pollution, substandard housing conditions for marginalized or impoverished groups, or lack of access to quality medical care and affordable medications for certain groups or society as a whole. Inequitable access to resources and services places historically excluded populations—especially racial and ethnic minorities, LGBTQ+ persons, and women—and low-income households in a more precarious position with respect to health security. The scale of the problem and the nature of contributing factors (societal norms or state institutions) turn an individual health issue into a human security issue, especially if the problem arises from the state's failure to protect the population (or some segment of it) from harm.

Some health security concerns arise more quickly. An **epidemic** (an unusually high incidence of disease in a community or the spread of disease to a new locality) or **pandemic** (the spread of disease across borders or on a global scale) constitutes a sudden threat to human security due to the potential for widespread effects on individuals and institutions alike. An infectious disease outbreak that spreads quickly through a population or carries devastating effects on a large scale is a sudden health threat. In addition to threatening many individuals' health in a short period of time, it carries the potential to overwhelm health care institutions, cut economic productivity, exacerbate inequality, and create social and political unrest. Such an outbreak is worsened by structural issues like lack of access to medical services, insufficient institutional capacity to treat certain health problems, or unequal distribution of expertise and resources.

Social, cultural, or religious norms that impede individuals' access to medical care can magnify the impact of chronic and sudden health concerns alike; examples include a state's or community's refusal to give international health experts access to the sick, disproportionate fatality rates among historically excluded populations, and the delay of medical care for a female family member due to gender inequality within the household. Norms and traditions surrounding care of the sick and deceased may also lead to the spread of infectious diseases through unsafe handling of bodies, as was the case during the 2014 Ebola outbreak, when transmission occurred through contact with bodily fluids containing the virus during funeral rites.

The effects of competing security perspectives within the population and among decision makers also worsen health security threats, as the inability to reach consensus within governance institutions on the best ways to mitigate health crises or a lack of trust in government-issued health recommendations among segments of the population slow progress toward mitigating the threat. For example, during the COVID-19 pandemic, political polarization within the United States contributed to politicization of public health recommendations—including stay-at-home orders, masking indoors, and taking vaccinations—and decreased the state's ability to issue, implement, and enforce policies and guidance to slow the spread of the virus. Competing security perspectives and political polarization (which often go hand in hand) make it difficult to move through the three policy boxes, stalling consensus on a definition of the threat, feasible policy options, and ideal outcomes.

As with all aspects of human security, the provision of health care, the protection of individuals from sudden or chronic health threats, and the extent to which individuals are empowered to lead healthy lives will vary with respect to factors such as state stability and resources, shifting international political relationships, and attributes related to the individual (including nationality, race, ethnicity, religion, sex, gender, age, marital status, and socioeconomic standing). While there is some overlap across states and regions, different types of health challenges confront the Global South and Global North; infectious diseases constitute serious threats to health in the South, whereas **"lifestyle" diseases** (chronic health conditions arising from a societal shift toward a sedentary lifestyle) threaten health in the North. Related to this variation in health concerns is the problem of inequality in the distribution of resources and capabilities to prevent, diagnose, and treat health problems, but this problem is not as clearly divided between the North and South, as high levels of societal inequality and related discrepancies in access to quality medical care persist across the globe (Yuk-ping and Thomas 2010, 448; Michener 2020). When infectious diseases or lifestyle diseases become pervasive, they threaten the economic and political stability of the state and potentially the region or the globe, as well as the well-being of the individual.

Health Crises as Threats to Stability

Health concerns become state security concerns when they begin to affect economic and political stability (two primary indicators of the state's well-being in the state security approach). When they are widespread throughout the population, both chronic and acute health threats create the potential for economic loss due to decreased productivity in the workforce, loss of tourism income, and the state's reallocation of resources to mitigating the problem. The scale of the problem (how widespread it is, in terms of the population affected) and the immediacy of the threat (how quickly the threat originates and spreads) determine the effects of a health threat on state, regional, or global stability. Scale and immediacy may be, but are not always, related.

Cardiovascular disease was the leading cause of death among men and women in the United States between 1999 and 2021, making it a widespread problem but not an immediate threat to the state, since it does not directly challenge the political and economic stability of the state (Centers for Disease Control and Prevention, n.d.; Ortaliza et al. 2021). The 2001 anthrax outbreak in the United States, in contrast, affected a small number of people but quickly became a state security concern. Four letters containing anthrax spores were mailed to US senators and news agencies in September and October 2001; a total of twenty-two people contracted anthrax, a total of forty-three people tested positive for exposure, ten thousand people were deemed at risk for exposure; of the twenty-two people who contracted the disease, five died (Centers for Disease Control and Prevention 2020). Anthrax had not been diagnosed in the United States since 1976, and the intentional release of the spores within threatening letters so soon after the September 11 attacks suggested a threat to the state. The US government explicitly recognized the anthrax outbreak as a national security issue because of the threat's immediacy, potential for a large-scale outbreak, and the broader political environment in which the US government and public were on alert for terrorist attacks.

A health crisis can become a matter of political stability not only because of the direct impact of the disease on economic productivity and the health of the population but also because of the way in which a state handles—or fails to address—the situation. When a state downplays the effect of disease, fails to build and maintain an effective healthcare infrastructure, is unable or unwilling to prevent the spread of infectious disease, or otherwise falls short in providing for the basic health needs of the population, there is potential for unrest, and the government risks losing its legitimacy. States' varying responses to the COVID-19 pandemic illustrate this dynamic, as this chapter's case study suggests.

When viewed through the lens of state security, health problems are prioritized on the basis of their impact on the state and its political and economic stability; this means that disproportionately more resources will be devoted to the potential threat of **bioterrorism** than to pervasive health problems like Alzheimer's disease and cardiovascular disease. Still, health is one area in which states come together regularly to cooperate in response to regional and global concerns, in addition to threats that directly affect the state's national interests. Collaborative efforts may take the form of initiatives focused on the eradication of one specific disease (like malaria or polio) or of multilateral institutions dedicated to global or regional public health (e.g., the Pan American Health Organization or the World Health Organization) (Meslin and Garba 2016; Rugemalila et al. 2007).

Health security can quickly transition from a state security concern to a global security issue. Infectious disease outbreaks are difficult if not impossible to contain in our globalized world. Disease-causing bacteria and viruses can travel across state borders in people, animals, and objects, and a total shutdown of state borders is not only politically fraught but also practically infeasible. As in the state security approach, we should consider the scale and immediacy of health threats to determine whether or not they affect global security. An acute health threat—like the 2014 Ebola outbreak, the 2015–2016 Zika virus epidemic, the ongoing burden of malaria, or the COVID-19 pandemic—poses a challenge to global stability when it is unprecedented in scope or nature (and therefore unpredictable in its scale and effects), when states lack the capacity to contain and eliminate the outbreak, when a large portion of the global population is affected, or when cross-border political or economic relations are jeopardized as a result of the outbreak.

RESPONSES TO THE COVID-19 PANDEMIC

In December 2019, reports out of Wuhan, China, of a mysterious new viral pneumonia began to worry the international medical community. On January 23, 2020, China's government placed the city of Wuhan under lockdown in an attempt to contain the novel coronavirus, SARS-CoV-2, and the disease it causes, COVID-19. A week later, on January 30, 2020, the World Health Organization (WHO) identified the novel coronavirus as a public health emergency of international concern, and on March 11, 2020, the WHO declared it a global pandemic (World Health Organization 2021b; Katella 2021).

By December 8, 2020, scientists around the world had developed over two hundred candidate vaccines, with fifty-two in clinical trials; by spring 2021, thirteen vaccines had gained approval and were in use in different countries (World Health Organization 2021b; n.d.[b]). Still, vaccines did not bring an immediate end to the pandemic. Equitable worldwide distribution of vaccine doses remained a challenge through 2021, with wealthy states claiming the largest shares of doses for their populations while collaborative efforts like the global vaccine alliance, COVAX, worked to improve access for developing countries (Gavi 2021).

When a health security threat is widespread and immediate, it can be easier for decision makers and security providers to reach consensus around problem identification and feasible policy options in an effort to reach ideal outcomes more quickly, as long as those decision makers and security providers, along with the broader population, are operating with the same or complementary security perspectives. The rapid development of vaccines demonstrates what can happen when governments, IGOs, researchers, and private enterprises work together. Countries responded in their own ways to COVID-19, and in the following we explore four approaches—two states that have been applauded for their handling of the pandemic and two that have struggled to get COVID-19 under control.

South Korea

South Korea became a model for stopping the spread of SARS-CoV-2 early in the pandemic, and its efforts saved lives and prevented the significant economic losses that other countries saw. While the country experienced multiple waves of COVID-19, South Korea's public health institutions have been able to contain the virus's spread and limit each wave's severity (Dyer 2021; Normile 2020). After experiencing an outbreak of the Middle East respiratory syndrome (MERS) in 2015, the South Korean government began planning and preparing for the next virus outbreak, including a war-gaming exercise in December 2019, just before the news of the novel coronavirus emerged from China (Martin and Yoon 2020).

Testing and communication were central to the South Korean approach; the state quickly approved domestic COVID-19 test kits, used text messaging to notify citizens of cases in their area, maintained communication between the government and the population through twice-daily press briefings, took over production of face masks when supplies of personal protective equipment (PPE) ran low, provided free treatment for patients with COVID-19, and isolated all COVID-positive people in the early stages of the pandemic (Normile 2020; Dyer 2021; Martin and Yoon 2020). In 2021, the state's approach adapted slightly as the nature of COVID-19 changed, placing limits on the size of gatherings in summer 2021 in response to rising infections due to the Delta variant's spread, and allowing patients to self-medicate at home with the assistance of daily virtual check-ins with medical staff to keep hospital beds open for the severely ill (Cha 2021).

Its flexible and robust approach to the pandemic meant that South Korea did not have to impose stay-at-home orders or require businesses to close; the key, instead, was to communicate the need for people to change their behavior to prevent the spread of the virus (Martin and Yoon 2020). The state and its institutions were not the only relevant security providers throughout the pandemic, individuals also complied with recommendations to change their behaviors and wear masks, to physically distance from others, and to wash hands frequently (Dyer 2021; Martin and Yoon 2020).

South Korea's high-tech handling of COVID-19 initially came at a cost to personal privacy: the government's ability to track and communicate the presence of cases in an area depends on the state's access to private mobile-phone data, and, initially, alerts of new cases revealed individuals' potentially identifying demographic information. Civic and religious groups sued over civil rights concerns, and the state has since anonymized cases in the contact-tracing process (Martin and Yoon 2020). The tension between individual rights and collective well-being is at the center of each state's decision-making in a pandemic, and the nature of that tension and the ways in which it is resolved—or not—hints at the relationship between individuals and the state as well as the security perspectives held by each.

Throughout the COVID-19 pandemic, the South Korean government worked to maintain transparency and build trust in public health and governance institutions, learning from the state's mishandling of MERS, in which efforts to guard information to avoid public panic led instead to misinformation and a lack of public trust (Dyer 2021). Because the state and the population viewed the threat of SARS-CoV-2 similarly, South Korea's response to the pandemic was one of the most effective in the world.

New Zealand

The government of New Zealand acted early, enacting measures to prevent the spread of SARS-CoV-2 just days after the WHO declared the virus a public health emergency of international concern. The government worked quickly to control the spread of the virus through rigorous testing, contact tracing, isolation of cases, and a requirement that everyone but essential workers quarantine at home in the early months of the pandemic in an effort to "crush the curve" (World Health Organization 2020). The government built on existing wildfire alerts to create a four-stage alert system to help the public understand current social-distancing requirements, empowering the entire population to work together to contain the virus with the support of transparent communication and decisive leadership (Government of New Zealand 2020; Jones 2020; Baker, Wilson, and Anglemyer 2020). High levels of public trust in government and social solidarity kept the state and the population united in the effort rather than at odds (Stiglitz 2020).

In February 2020, before the country had recorded any COVID-19 cases, Prime Minister Jacinda Ardern announced the closure of New Zealand's borders to anyone coming from or through China; in March the restrictions expanded to include travelers from Iran, South Korea, and northern Italy, and eventually all incoming travelers were required to self-isolate. As the virus spread globally, New Zealand closed its borders to noncitizens or nonresidents (Jones 2020). New Zealand learned from China's efforts to contain the virus quickly; while the economic costs of shutting down were high, decision makers understood that the economic and human cost of high numbers of cases would be staggering.

As a high-income country with a robust healthcare system, New Zealand was well-positioned to take a proactive approach to the pandemic. Accordingly, the public health system had the ability to enact a comprehensive testing and contact testing regimen and detect and isolate cases to reduce viral spread quickly (Robert 2020). While geographic isolation affords some protection to New Zealand, it also limits the capacity of the healthcare system to handle widespread severe illness.

Leadership was also a key factor in the nation's effective handling of the health crisis: the state's decision makers followed WHO guidance and took into account evolving evidence and insights from public health research, letting science guide their approach to the pandemic (World Health Organization 2020; Baker, Wilson, and Anglemyer 2020). Decision makers based their proactive stance on disease models that predicted COVID-19 would create an influx of patients sufficient to overwhelm the healthcare system and a disease burden that would be borne disproportionately by the Indigenous Maori and Pacific populations (Baker, Wilson, and Anglemyer 2020). Prime Minister Jacinda Ardern is widely applauded for her leadership throughout the pandemic, in particular her ability to frame the effort to eliminate COVID-19 in New Zealand as a collaborative effort by a "team of five million," and to lead effectively, decisively, and with empathy (Baker, Wilson, and Anglemyer 2020; Friedman 2020).

The United States

The United States failed to unite the population in a shared effort to stop or slow the spread of COVID-19, and the effects of the country's mistakes led to significant economic and human costs. Pew Research conducted public opinion surveys of five countries' and organizations' handling of the pandemic, finding that a median of 15 percent of respondents in the twelve countries surveyed in summer 2020 believed that the United States had handled the COVID-19 pandemic well. That number increased substantially, to 38 percent, by the summer of 2021, but the United States still received low marks from respondents in nearly every country surveyed (Devlin, Fagan, and Connaughton 2021).

Mishandling of SARS-CoV-2 by the United States is not attributable to a lack of healthcare capacity or sufficient funding to marshal resources to combat the virus but, rather, to disjointed policy making that reasserted the federal structure of the government and put state governors in charge of setting pandemic guidelines and led to competition over scarce resources like PPE and ventilators. Under then-president Donald Trump, the US government took a back seat instead of leading a unified response guided by the evolving science, while individual states were left to craft a patchwork of restrictions and responses, many of which were shaped by partisan ideology rather than public health expertise (Altman 2020).

Politicization of and misinformation surrounding the virus, vaccine, and mitigation measures led to sharp divisions within the population and among policy makers throughout the pandemic. A pervasive sense of individual freedom stalled efforts in some regions of the United States to contain the virus through measures like masking, social distancing, and vaccination. An Axios-Ipsos opinion poll in July 2021 showed that respondents in the United States were increasingly concerned about COVID-19 variants but were unwilling to change their behaviors significantly to mitigate their risk (Jackson, Newall, and Yi 2021). But COVID-19 risk was not distributed equitably across the population.

Within the United States, BIPOC (Black, Indigenous, and People of Color) communities were disproportionately affected by COVID-19 and the social, political, and economic fallout from the virus. The pandemic's disparate impact on racial and ethnic groups in the United States stems from deeply entrenched racial inequality and systemic racism that shapes health care, the education system, employment opportunities, and trust in public health institutions. BIPOC individuals were more likely to hold employment designated as essential during the pandemic, meaning they did not have the option to work remotely and thereby reduce the risk of contracting COVID-19. Paradoxically, unemployment hit Black households more sharply during the pandemic, creating or exacerbating economic insecurity (Gould and Wilson 2020). Inequitable access and implicit bias in health care means racial minorities receive lower-quality treatment, which leads to higher mortality rates and poorer health even in the absence of a pandemic (Bridges 2018; DeSimone 2021). The confluence of risk factors created disparate impacts based on race, and Black and Latino Americans are more likely than the rest of the US population to have lost a loved one to COVID-19 (Goldstein and Guskin 2020; Reja 2021).

The United States did succeed in supporting the development of highly effective COVID-19 vaccines and procuring them for the US population. The US Food and Drug Administration (FDA) granted emergency-use authorization to the Pfizer-BioNTech vaccine on December 11, 2020, and to the Moderna vaccine on December 18, 2020 (AJMC Staff 2021). After purchasing one hundred million doses of vaccine well in advance of approval, the Trump administration purchased an additional one hundred million doses of the Pfizer vaccine on December 23, 2020, bolstering the country's stockpile of vaccine (Melillo 2020). The United States also invested in large shares of vaccine from Moderna and Johnson & Johnson/Janssen in advance of each vaccine's approval.

Distribution and administration of the vaccines, however, was uneven and slow in December 2020 and January 2021. US hospitals pressured the federal government in early January 2021 for a faster vaccine rollout, and incoming president Joe Biden announced that his administration would prioritize the release of available vaccine doses once in office, setting and meeting a goal of one hundred million vaccinations in the new administration's first hundred days (AJMC Staff 2021).

Vaccination rates in the United States demonstrated continuing racial disparities, with lower vaccine uptake among BIPOC; the disparities stemmed from issues of geographic or technological access to vaccination sites, difficulty securing leave time from work to get the vaccine or manage its side effects, and lack of trust in the public health system in the United States (AJMC Staff 2021). Vaccine hesitancy became a broader issue within the US population, one linked to political ideology. Throughout 2021, misinformation and disinformation surrounding the vaccine and its effects circulated on social media and gained airtime on prominent right-wing television news networks within the United States, politicizing the vaccine in a polarized society and leading the Biden administration to search for ways to engage trusted voices to reassure vaccine-hesitant individuals (PBS 2021). By early summer 2021, US vaccination rates stalled and remained well below 50 percent of the eligible population nationwide, with much lower rates in states in the South and Midwest. These regions with low vaccination rates combined with the more highly transmissible Delta variant to fuel a resurgence of COVID-19 nationwide (Smart 2021).

The United States had the resources and capacity to respond to COVID-19 effectively with both nonpharmaceutical public health measures (like stay-at-home orders, social distancing, and masking) and mass vaccination. The US effort to combat COVID-19 was rendered less effective by sharp partisan political divisions, mistrust of science among decision makers in the Trump administration in 2020 and large segments of the population throughout the pandemic, and the related politicization of public health measures.

Brazil

Brazil faced the COVID-19 pandemic with political leaders who did not trust science—namely, President Jair Bolsonaro, whose approach to the pandemic was similar to US president Donald Trump's in the rejection of science and public health expertise. Prior to the pandemic, Bolsonaro had cut funding for Brazil's science and education ministries and universities and worked to discredit the National Institute for Space Research after the agency's satellite data alerted the world to accelerated deforestation in Brazil's Amazon region (Taylor 2021). Bolsonaro ignored the warnings from other nations, the WHO, and Brazil's own scientists as the pandemic spread to his country. He referred to COVID-19 as a "little flu," pushed unproven treatments for the virus, refused to implement public health measures at the national level to contain the virus, criticized state governors who implemented containment measures, and contributed to vaccine hesitancy by observing of those who elected to vaccinate, "If you turn into a crocodile, it's your problem" (Taylor 2021; BBC News 2021a). Political mismanagement and politicization of the virus contributed to a humanitarian disaster in Brazil (Mineo 2021).

While Brazil has a universal healthcare system with robust community health networks, state- and municipal-level agencies take guidance from the federal level; the lack of a coordinated, clear, science-based approach to the pandemic at the federal level made it difficult for state and municipal health-care agencies to respond adequately. Some state- and local-level officials loyal to the president refused to take action at all, effectively politicizing the virus and public health measures to contain it even as the death toll rose. The state's effective handling of the HIV/AIDS and Zika epidemics in the past suggest that its healthcare system could have weathered the COVID-19 pandemic more successfully had preventive measures been enacted to keep the virus from raging out of control (Mineo 2021). As the virus spread throughout the country, it strained the capacity of Brazil's hospitals, with intensive-care units operating at or near full occupancy (BBC News 2021a).

In summer 2021, mass protests broke out in response to reports of corruption involving senior officials within the health ministry who had allegedly taken bribes to purchase the Covaxin vaccine at an inflated price from its producers in India, as well as in response to Bolsonaro's failure to take action after he was alerted to the scheme. Bolsonaro attributed the allegations to the political opposition's attempts to oust him from office (BBC News 2021c). Separately, scientists studying SARS-CoV-2 variants in Brazil argued that they could not adequately assess the potential threat of new strains because the Bolsonaro administration had cut lab funding so significantly (Taylor 2021). The mishandling of the pandemic by Brazil's political leaders compounded the existing threats of economic inequality and inequitable access to hospitals and intensive care units; together these factors worsened the pandemic's effects (Mineo 2021).

The COVID-19 Syndemic

The COVID-19 pandemic not only presented a health security threat but also served as a threat multiplier, effecting other dimensions of security. It has been aptly described as a **syndemic**, a compound threat presented by the interaction of a disease and social and environmental factors (Singer et al. 2017; Horton 2020). As the different scenarios within the four states above demonstrate, the pandemic affected employment, education, mental health, poverty, food security, existing societal and global inequalities, governance and public trust in institutions, international trade, and virtually every other dimension of private and public life, but the impact of the pandemic was not equal across states, groups, or individuals (Ferreira 2021). The pandemic's effects were felt most strongly by the poor, people whose jobs and living situations involve contact with others, and those without access to quality health care (Stiglitz 2020).

We discussed the disproportionate effects of COVID-19 on BIPOC in the United States above. Similarly, in the United Kingdom, Black, Asian, and minority ethnic (BAME) migrants lost their jobs at higher rates than did White British workers, and UK-born BAME people were less likely than White British workers to have job-protection benefits like furloughs (Hu 2020). When institutions are not designed or lack the capacity to protect individuals and communities from the multidimensional threats imposed by pandemic or epidemic disease, some groups within a state's population—the historically excluded and vulnerable—will suffer disproportionately (Newman 2021).

BOX 9.1. THINK ABOUT IT . . .
WHEN HUMAN SECURITY ACTORS
CREATE INSECURITY: CHOLERA IN HAITI

We cannot neglect the role that state and nonstate actors potentially play in creating, not just mitigating, threats to health security. Chronic health problems and infectious disease outbreaks can result from environmental factors (like the spread of mosquitos that transmit malaria or Zika to new regions), shifting lifestyle trends (e.g., the sedentary workday in developed states), the evolution of viruses and bacteria over time (and especially the increased drug resistance related to the widespread overuse of antibiotics), and other natural and human-made conditions. Major health crises can also be caused by human action, and, unfortunately, sometimes these crises occur in conjunction with other human security threats and as a direct result of efforts to respond to those threats.

The cholera outbreak in Haiti that began in October 2010 is one such instance, as the infection-causing bacteria were traced to the base used by UN peacekeepers deployed to assist in the aftermath of the devastating 2010 earthquake. Latrine sewage containing human waste from a contingent of peacekeepers recently deployed from Nepal, a state in the midst of a cholera outbreak at the time, leaked into the Meille River and reintroduced cholera-causing bacteria into the water (Katz 2016b; 2016a; Gladstone 2016a).

A lack of funding to address the epidemic caused delays in the delivery of vaccines to vulnerable populations and in the reconstruction of Haiti's water and sanitation systems to prevent further spread of the bacteria (Archibold and Sengupta 2014). For years after the initial introduction of cholera onto the island, the infection continued to threaten the health security of the Haitian population—with heightened concern about the disease spreading in the aftermath of hurricanes and flooding—and contributed to concerns about the United Nations' legitimacy as an international organization.

The epidemic persisted for about a decade, sickening 820,000 people affected and killing 9,792 (United Nations 2020a). A Doctors without Borders study emphasizes that incomplete data collection and lack of access to health clinics suggest the death toll is much higher than the official account (Gladstone 2016a; 2016b). The unintended deadly consequences of the United Nations Stabilization Mission in Haiti (MINUSTAH) and the organization's official denial of the link between its peacekeepers and the outbreak until August 2016 have called into question the legitimacy of the multilateral mission in Haiti: if those who came to restore human security introduced a health crisis and did little to address the problem, then the mission's costs may outweigh the benefits.

Families of cholera victims in Haiti pressed the United Nations for restitution through the internal-claims process, external advocacy, and class-action lawsuits; but for years the organization denied fault, refused payment, and claimed diplomatic immunity when asked to appear in court (Katz 2016b). In 2016, the UN Secretary-General apologized for the organization's negligence and the role its peacekeepers had played in the epidemic and committed the UN to providing $400 million to victims, families, and their communities (Katz 2016b; Mineo 2020). Fundraising efforts have disappointed those seeking redress; by 2020, the UN had raised only $20.5 million and had spent $3.2 million out of the $400 million committed (United Nations 2020b).

While advocates pressed the UN for financial redress, attorneys brought lawsuits on behalf of victims' families to hold the UN accountable through the US court system (since the UN is headquartered in New York). A class-action lawsuit asking for financial redress for those affected by cholera was eventually dismissed by the Second Circuit Court of Appeals in New York on the grounds that the United Nations has immunity from prosecution and the case therefore lacked merit (Katz 2016b; Domonoske 2016; Moloney 2016). Similarly, *Laventure v. United Nations* came to consideration before the US Supreme Court in October 2019, but the Court refused to hear the case (Pilkington 2019). Advocates and lawyers argue that the United

Nations' failure to establish a process to provide compensation to victims' families violates human rights and that immunity does not provide a rationale for impunity (Moloney 2016).

The cholera epidemic in Haiti is a tragic example of how well-intended human security efforts can inadvertently create new, albeit unintended, human security threats. The far-reaching effects of the cholera outbreak in Haiti also illustrate the ways in which health crises present challenges to state and global security and stability. When human security actors create health crises, they face moral and political imperatives to rectify the situation, whether unilaterally or through collaboration with states and nonstate actors.

Consider the following questions:

1. Should IGOs and international security providers like the United Nations have immunity from legal consequences when their actions create harm?
2. What potential changes could improve accountability for harm done by well-intended peacekeeping operations?
3. Efforts to hold the UN accountable for the cholera outbreak in Haiti and provide compensation to victims and their families persisted even amid the COVID-19 pandemic. Why might advocates have continued their efforts even as a global public health crisis demanded resources?

RESPONSIBILITY FOR HEALTH SECURITY

From the perspective of a state or an international organization, determining whether, when, where, and how to respond to health concerns as security issues can be difficult. States may decide individually to include global health issues among their foreign policy priorities. For example, Cuba's tradition of medical internationalism melds foreign policy and community health care. The state's initiatives at home and abroad—which reach back to a deployment of medical professionals to Algeria and Guinea-Bissau in the 1960s—seek to provide community-based healthcare services, empower marginalized individuals and communities, and build up institutional capacity with the end goal of eliminating structural violence (Huish and Kirk 2007, 78–79; Huish and Spiegel 2008, 45; Yaffe 2020). Cuba's international medical policy efforts are thus in line with both the egalitarian aims of the state's revolution, the central goals of human security, and a cosmopolitan security perspective.

Japan, in its foreign policy efforts to promote global health, has explored this multifaceted issue and contributed to the immense progress made in the global battle against HIV/AIDS, tuberculosis, and malaria (Llano and Shibuya 2011; Takemi 2016, 21). Japan's human security approach centers on the principle of freedom from want and the aspects of human security most closely related to what we call durable human security; it also appears to be in line with a federalist perspective on security, making global health collaboration a central initiative for the state. A state that has adopted a human security approach will likely include health concerns among important security issues.

Yet even in the face of a devastating health crisis that presents clear challenges not only to human security but to national, regional, or global stability as well, international coordination can be difficult. We can observe at the international level a process similar to the three boxes model of policy making, wherein the representatives of each state must work to reach consensus on perception of the problem, policy options, and ideal outcomes. At the international level, states can formally discuss and coordinate their efforts through the World Health Organization, which was established in 1948 to direct and coordinate international health-policy efforts to promote physical, mental, and social well-being. The WHO functions under the auspices of the United Nations and supports states by promoting evidence-based health-policy options, providing technical advice on health issues, disseminating health research, setting norms and standards, and assessing health trends and crises (World Health Organization n.d.[a]).

The World Health Assembly, the WHO's decision-making body, consists of all WHO member states and provides a forum for discussion and coordination, much like the UN's General Assembly. It receives and considers reports and instructions from the WHO Executive Board, an elected body of thirty-four health experts. States look to the WHO for advice and assessments on health security concerns. Having a technically focused international organization can alleviate some of the challenges surrounding global collaboration in response to health threats, but it cannot guarantee that states or other human security actors respond quickly or comprehensively. The WHO's effectiveness depends on states' willingness to abide by the organization's recommendations and to support its operations, financially and logistically. If decision makers in a particular state adopt a statist or nativist security perspective rather than a federalist perspective, that state is less likely to view the WHO as an authoritative voice on health security, especially if the WHO's recommendations are out of sync with the state's current domestic and foreign policy priorities.

The Ebola outbreak in West Africa, which began in March 2014, made headlines in the global media, but the international community's response was not immediate, leaving NGOs like Médecins Sans Frontières to do much of the initial work required to train local hospital staff to treat patients and control the spread of the virus (Médecins Sans Frontières 2014). In July 2014 the WHO convened a ministerial-level meeting to bring state representatives together to determine collectively the best way to stem transmission and treat the affected populations (World Health Organization, Regional Office for Africa, 2014). Two months later, UN secretary-general Ban Ki-moon spoke to the UN Security Council and described Ebola as a security concern requiring "a level of international action unprecedented for an emergency" in the form of the United Nations Mission for Ebola Emergency Response (UNMEER) (United Nations Security Council 2014). Once the international community recognized the Ebola outbreak as a security concern and a threat not only to human security but to national and regional stability as well, the issue received priority status from international organizations and foreign states (Fidler 2004; Katz and Singer 2007). Not all health concerns will register as national or international security priorities (Ban 2003; Katz and Singer 2007), so the question of responsibility for health security is central to the discussion here.

If we accept that major health concerns (those that are life-altering or life-threatening) are human security concerns when they arise from or are exacerbated by normative or institutional factors within society, like lack of access to medical care, then we must explore the concept of responsibility for the provision of health security. Recall the table illustrating justifications for protection in a world in which human security norms are present (chapter 1, table 1.2). When states provide protection against and treatment of health security threats affecting the individual, they may do so in the interest of state preservation, because addressing health concerns is the appropriate thing to do, because it is politically expedient to address health concerns, or some combination of these motivations. When international actors cooperate to address health threats affecting individuals, they may similarly do so because it is the appropriate thing to do or because it would be too politically costly to not act. Thus we can see potential for both normative and rational political motivations driving responsibility to prevent and respond to health crises.

We cannot consider *all* health concerns to be human, national, regional, or global security threats, because casting the net of "health security" too broadly risks diverting resources and attention away from health crises that are more imminently threatening (Katz and Singer 2007). Examples of imminent health threats to the state include the 1918 influenza pandemic, the 1947 New York City smallpox outbreak, the global HIV/AIDS epidemic, the 2014 Ebola outbreak, and the COVID-19 pandemic; these health crises threatened to overwhelm resources, harm large swaths of the population, upset economic stability, and contribute to political unrest. If we apply the logic of conditional sovereignty (as discussed in chapter 5, with respect to R2P) to health security, we can formulate a process through which responsibility to address health concerns transfers from state to global entities. As chronic or acute health threats arise, it is first the responsibility of the state to assess the nature of the health issue and mobilize resources to address it. Failing successful action—whether because the state lacks adequate capacity or political will to handle the threat or because the threat is transnational in scope—the international community has a responsibility to assist the state in its efforts to mitigate the crisis. Collaboration on health issues brings together NGOs, UN or regional agencies, the WHO and other global and regional health policy organizations, and other state agencies as necessary to exchange expertise to improve global understanding of the problem and the best solution.

CONCLUSION: GOOD HEALTH AND HUMAN SECURITY

Health is a human security issue when it arises from norms, institutions, or acute crises and threatens or constrains individuals' well-being and ability to thrive. Although chronic diseases (e.g., diabetes or rheumatoid arthritis) and sudden health problems (like a heart attack or stroke) threaten an individual's overall well-being or even their survival, the inclusion of health within the range of security issues requires that we consider the scale and impact of the threat. Because assigning an issue a "security" label requires human security actors—including states and international organizations—to prioritize that issue, we must take care to not broaden the scope of human security so extensively that we dilute its meaning. Health is always a human concern, but we include health problems as human security issues when they arise from harmful societal norms or a lack of institutional protections, or when they threaten society and its institutions on a large scale. The potential for rapid transmission of an infectious disease in our globalized world means that even states and international organizations that prioritize a traditional approach to security find reasons to protect against health threats.

In September 2015 Secretary-General Ban Ki-moon unequivocally asserted that "human security depends on health security" (United Nations 2015a). There is a reciprocal relationship between health and human security: good health is at the root of an individual's ability to thrive, so progress in one begets progress in the other. Health is closely related to other aspects of durable human security, including food security, gender equality, environmental stability, poverty, and protection of human rights. If an individual's basic health needs are not met, the individual cannot realize opportunities to thrive, to pursue a fulfilling livelihood, and to contribute to the political, social, and economic advancement of society. By the same token, when other aspects of durable human security are not in place (and certainly also in times of acute armed conflict), it is difficult to ensure that the individual can lead a healthy life. Efforts to provide for human security in general pave the way for health security in particular. Health security and overall human security, then, are reciprocal influences, and policy decisions must account for the interrelated nature of health and human security more broadly.

Two key predicaments confronting states, international organizations, and other human security actors are (1) when and how to respond to health security threats should they occur and (2) where the primary responsibility for the response to health threats lies. The notion of *conditional sovereignty*, or sovereignty as the state's responsibility to protect its citizens from threats, tells us that the state bears the primary and enduring obligation to address the health needs of its people. When the state lacks the capacity to respond to a health crisis, the international community also bears a responsibility to assist the state in finding a way to address the threat. The international response to the Ebola outbreak, discussed previously, demonstrates this sense of communal responsibility (however imperfect) to assist states or regions facing a health crisis: international assistance came after NGOs and states in the affected region called for help, and delivery of financial aid and coordination between donor states and the governments of Guinea, Liberia, Sierra Leone, Nigeria, and Senegal were welcome efforts.

Still, the questions of when and how to respond and who bears primary responsibility for the response are pervasive in human security matters, and political debate can stall assistance. In addition, while the *need* to respond to a global pandemic or a regional epidemic is fairly clear (despite persistent questions of who, when, and how), other health-related concerns do not register as human security threats to all human security actors and state or international policy makers. One such dilemma is whether or not health care is a human right that states should provide for their citizens. There is global variation in the extent to which states have the political will, historical precedent, and capacity to guarantee adequate and affordable access to health care. If we accept the premise that good health is central to human security and we further accept that societal norms and institutions—including the capacity of and access to the healthcare system—either foster or degrade health security, then the question of responsibility for the provision of health care is relevant to human security policy.

Health security issues and required responses can be exceptionally clear in some cases and exceedingly murky in others, as is the case with other issues related to durable human security. Lingering questions remain surrounding the threshold with which we assess health concerns as human *security* concerns and the responsibility to act once a human security threat arises and is considered a priority, and the global community will likely resolve these questions only on a case-by-case basis for the foreseeable future.

DISCUSSION QUESTIONS

1. Is there a clear threshold beyond which a chronic disease becomes a human security threat?
2. Under what circumstances might a state have strategic (self-interested) incentives to incorporate health security into its foreign policy initiatives?
3. Does universal health care contribute to or detract from overall health security within a population? Is health care a human right?
4. Is the difference between health as a human security issue or a state or global security issue meaningful? Is the difference more or less clear regarding health concerns than other human security concerns?
5. How might the response to an epidemic differ from the response to a pandemic within each of the three approaches to security—human, national, and global?
6. Undernutrition and malnutrition are health concerns that stem from food insecurity. How do the overlapping security concerns affect human security actors' ability to respond to these threats?
7. How do the different security perspectives condition responses to a global pandemic?

Chapter 10

Gender Inequality and Security

Learning Objectives

This chapter will enable readers to

1. identify indicators of gender inequality
2. discuss the impact of gender inequality on human, national, and global security
3. understand the relationship between security perspectives and efforts to improve gender equality
4. and compare efforts to improve gender equality.

Gender inequality is a problem that plagues every society. In some places harm is more egregious and visible than in others, but gender inequality is everywhere to some extent. In chapter 4 we discussed the universality of human rights—the concept that all people are entitled to the same basic rights simply because they are human. Discrimination based on gender is pervasive, and it creates a wide range of injustices and abuses that lead to insecurity and the unequal fulfillment of rights. When gender inequality intersects with discrimination and inequality based on race, ethnicity, sexuality, religion, socioeconomic status, and other salient identities, vulnerability and insecurity are exacerbated. This chapter explores gender inequality and its connection to security, offering one way to examine how discrimination and inequality erode human security, limit the enjoyment of human rights, and threaten national and global stability and security.

In this chapter we will discuss global efforts to improve gender equality, observe the role of the nativist, statist, federalist, and cosmopolitan perspectives in shaping or impeding initiatives to advance gender equality, and highlight gender dynamics in Afghanistan and Sweden to demonstrate how various non-state and governmental actors influence gender equality–focused initiatives.

GENDER AND GENDER INEQUALITY

In informal, discussion people conflate the terms *sex* and *gender*, using them interchangeably and sometimes inappropriately in context. Strictly speaking, **sex** refers to the biological differences in human reproductive systems: a person is born with male genitalia, female genitalia, or with a combination of the two. **Gender** refers to a person's sense of being a man, woman, both, or neither, as well as the societal expectations for a person's behavior, appearance, and expression on the basis of their sex. For example, if a person is born biologically female, that person is socialized to act, speak, dress, and live within the boundaries of what society considers feminine at the time. A person who is born biologically male is similarly expected to embody and express masculine traits and behaviors. The severity of societal expectations varies across time and culture; some communities, states, or cultures condemn the subversion of gender expectations more harshly than others.

Societal expectations for how people should behave, live, and love based on their gender are **gender norms** (Goldstein 2001; Hudson et al. 2012; Sjoberg 2014). Just like all other norms, gender norms are subject to change over time. For example, during the mass mobilization of World War II, women in the United States took over jobs in factories—traditionally masculine jobs they had previously been discouraged or outright barred from taking—because so many working-age men were away at war. Observations about who can serve in the armed forces, and in what capacity, tell us a lot about a society's gender norms and expectations. More generally, what is considered feminine at one point in time may fall out of fashion in another era as society's needs or values change. Accordingly gender roles, behaviors, and expectations vary across *cultures*. The two states discussed in the vignettes in this chapter—Afghanistan and Sweden—are neither the most gender-unequal nor the most gender-equal states in the world, but people's experiences, expectations for behavior, roles, and opportunities are in sharp contrast.

Sex and gender are intricately tied together (Goldstein 2001, 2), and it is difficult to separate the concepts and their real-world implications completely. What is important to underscore, however, is that gender is a socially constructed concept: gender norms and expectations for appropriate behavior, appearance, and lifestyle are based on a consensus within society about what it means to be masculine, feminine, man, woman, or nonbinary—somewhere along the spectrum between those identities. We say *spectrum* because, although it is common to discuss sex and gender as binary concepts (where consideration extends only to the male/female or masculine/feminine dichotomy), the reality is that these distinctions are in-accurate for many people: some are born female but identify as male; some are born male but identify as female; and for some, these classifications simply do not feel comfortable at all.

Gender identity is the gender with which a person associates on the inside (one's sense of self as a man, a woman, or somewhere between or completely unrelated to the two) and is not necessarily identical to one's sex. **Gender expression** is the outward reflection of one's gender and is also not necessarily tied to one's sex; gender expression encompasses dress, mannerisms, speech, hairstyle, and other visible or audible traits a person may adopt on the out-side to reflect a sense of gender identity. Sex and gender are not truly binary concepts. (*Note:* It is important to remember that *sexuality*—the romantic or sexual preference for persons of a particular sex—is a concept that is distinct from both sex and gender. A person's sex and gender do not necessarily de-termine that person's sexuality; a female may identify as female and prefer other females, a male may identify as male and prefer females, a female may identify as male and prefer males, and so on.)

Gender inequality arises when one group is privileged over others on the basis of sex and gender. Across the globe, gender inequality almost univer-sally means that men and boys receive a larger share of resources and enjoy more freedoms, rights, and opportunities than women and girls. Such inequal-ity is most often the result of **patriarchy**, or "rule by fathers," which privi-leges masculinity (and men and boys) over all other identities and people. In a patriarchal, gender-unequal society women, girls, and LGBTQ+ persons are discriminated against because of their gender identity, gender expression, or sexuality. Gender norms create or reinforce inequality in many contexts (Enloe 2014; Hudson et al. 2012; Tickner 2001).

Discrimination and violence on the basis of sex and gender can be subtle, structural, overt, or all of these at the same time. So, how do we know gender inequality exists, and how can we compare the situations in different areas of the world? One way to measure gender inequality is the UNDP's **Gender Inequality Index (GII)**. Recognizing gender inequality as a "major barrier to human development," the UNDP introduced the GII in 2010's Human Devel-opment Report (United Nations Development Programme 2010a, 90; 2010b). The GII measures the position of women relative to men in each state, using women's reproductive health, empowerment, and economic status as indica-tors. No state has achieved gender parity—or complete equality between men and women—but the GII gives us a sense of how much a particular state needs to improve the status of women. Specifically, the index provides a mea-surement of the loss of potential human development (recall that the UNDP was the first agency to discuss human development directly), stemming from disparities between male and female economic status, empowerment, and health. To provide several examples, in 2019 Switzerland ranked first (closest in the world to achieving gender parity), Sweden ranked third, Israel ranked twenty-sixth, China ranked thirty-ninth, the United States ranked forty-sixth, Chile ranked fifty-fifth, Saudi Arabia ranked fifty-sixth, Democratic Republic of the Congo ranked 150th, and Afghanistan ranked 157th (United Nations Development Programme n.d.[a]).

Another helpful measure of gender inequality is the World Economic Forum's **Global Gender Gap Index (GGGI)**, which focuses on the economic disparities between men and women. The GGGI measures economic participation and opportunity, educational attainment, political empowerment, and health and survival in 140 states' economies. In 2021 the Global Gender Gap Report ranked Iceland closest to parity, placing Sweden fifth, Switzerland tenth, the United States thirtieth, Israel sixtieth, Chile seventieth, China 107th, Saudi Arabia 147th, and Afghanistan 156th (World Economic Forum 2021). The Democratic Republic of the Congo was not ranked. As is clear from our examples, the types of indicators used to measure gender equality determine how a particular state fares in the rankings, so it is best to use multiple measures when feasible in order to form as complete a picture as possible.

Both the GII and the GGGI compare men and women; this binary approach is common in indexes and in policy discussions, although recognition of the impact of gender norms on LGBTQ+ persons has started to emerge in recent years. Progress toward gender equality is not just a women's issue, and "gender" should never be considered synonymous with "women." Gender inequality, discrimination, and violence affect men and boys—especially those who do not fit the heterosexual masculine social ideal—and LGBTQ+ persons as well as **cisgender** women and girls (Sjoberg 2014). Indeed, our viewpoint here is that gender inequality in all its many forms negatively affects human security for all and—by extension—detracts from state and global security. Much of the focus on gender inequality in foreign and domestic policy has centered on improving conditions for women and girls. As such, the examples in this chapter focus on gender inequality's effects on women and girls with the acknowledgment that the picture is far more complex than these examples can adequately convey.

GENDER (IN)EQUALITY AND (IN)SECURITY

Gender inequality is a significant barrier to the realization of human security. It creates legal, social, economic, and political constraints on individuals and inhibits their ability to thrive; and in many places, it determines likelihood that a person will survive to old age or even past early childhood. The entrenched view that some people have less intrinsic worth than others because of their sex or gender leads to differential treatment within the home, schools, workplaces, political institutions, and daily social encounters. Girls drop out of school or attend infrequently if schools do not have facilities to allow them to manage menstruation privately (Hudson et al. 2012, 27). A family may not send a girl child to school if school fees are high, her labor is needed at home, she is married early, there is little anticipated return on the investment of education because a woman's prospects for employment are few, travel to school is dangerous, or the school itself is threatened by societal factions opposed to girls' education.

In states with lower levels of gender equality, women face obstacles to obtaining a divorce, even from an abusive spouse, or family laws prohibit a woman from maintaining custody of her children in the event of a divorce (Hudson et al. 2012, 31). Even the prosecution of violent crimes can be unequal and subjective when gender inequality exists, placing a higher burden of proof on female survivors, especially in the event of sexual violence (Westmarland and Gangoli 2011). When gender norms privilege men and marginalize or discriminate against women, it can be difficult for women and girls to pursue an education, obtain and keep paid employment, decide if and when to have children, seek out adequate health care, participate in political processes, and have a stake in household financial decisions.

Gender inequality worsens extreme dangers like natural disasters and war. In societies with higher levels of gender equality, women and men are similarly likely to survive natural disasters; as levels of inequality increase, however, women suffer violence, exploitation, and death at higher rates than men. Some reasons relate directly to the onset of disaster. For example, if girls are not taught how to swim or are not allowed to swim, they are more likely to die in the event of a flood, typhoon, or tsunami; or if social norms require women and girls to wear heavy or restrictive clothing, it is more difficult for them to flee dangers such as rising floodwaters, fires, human-made violence, or other threats.

Other threats women and girls experience at greater levels than men are less directly tied to the onset of a disaster than to the breakdown of stability that follows; women and girls in societies with lower levels of gender equality are more vulnerable to trafficking, sexual violence and exploitation, and domestic violence in times of instability (United Nations Development Programme 2010a). In armed conflict just as in natural disasters, women and girls are also more likely to carry the burden of caring for young and elderly family members, which limits the ability to flee or evacuate. Daily activities such as fetching water or cooking fuel can place women and girls in harm's way, especially when they must travel long distances through active conflict zones.

LGBTQ+ persons face gender-related vulnerabilities in humanitarian emergencies, including discrimination, violence, and difficulty accessing essential services (Knight 2016). Transgender people encounter mistrust and hostility from individuals as well as from formal state institutions and security providers, heightening their insecurity (Sjoberg 2014).

Devaluing people because of their gender makes it more likely they will suffer physical violence, poverty and deprivation, and psychological harm. Because of discriminatory gender norms that favor males over females, there are an estimated 163 million "missing" girls and women in the world; they have been lost to sex-selective abortion, female infanticide, childhood mortality, maternal mortality, suicide, and violence in many forms (Hudson et al. 2012, 28; Ray 2015). Gender inequality creates both imminent physical and chronic threats to human security, which makes it an issue that shapes the prospects for durable human security.

Initiatives that work to improve gender equality also enhance durable or long-term human security; when foreign or domestic policy initiatives attempt to change entrenched norms or understandings about the relative worth of people of different genders, opportunities expand for all individuals. Girls' education is often cited as one of the highest-yield investments in developing states (Coleman 2004; Herz and Sperling 2004; Sperling, Winthrop, and Kwauk 2016); when state governments, foreign aid, or foreign investments fund girls' education, the payoffs for families and society far outweigh the short-term costs. Education is a powerful equalizer that creates opportunities for individuals to thrive, one of the hallmarks of durable human security. When girls and women have better access to education—and when a state has higher levels of gender equality in general—birth rates and child mortality rates fall, childhood nutrition improves, communities become more stable, public health improves, the economy strengthens, and governance institutions become more democratic (Coleman 2004). In short, increased gender equality can improve durable human security.

Gender inequality becomes a human security issue when it arises from societal norms that diminish the value of individuals on the basis of gender and thereby threaten the security of those individuals. Gender inequality may be entrenched in a state's institutions because of the existence of strong gender norms that devalue individuals because of their gender; and when societal norms and state institutions perpetuate threats to well-being, human insecurity exists. Efforts to promote positive social norms that value individuals of all genders and to reform institutions like family law, political processes, employment protections, and educational systems (to name only a few) can dramatically improve the human security situation. These efforts, however, depend on consensus that gender security and equality are vital to the functioning of the community and the state.

It's Not Just about the Individual

The normative rationale for treating people of all genders equally holds that all human beings are entitled to the same rights, freedoms, and opportunities, regardless of gender. And there are clear strategic reasons for hewing to this norm. States with high levels of domestic gender equality are more stable and less inclined to aggressive foreign policy behaviors that endanger global security; states with political, social, and economic gender equality are less likely to resort to military action to settle their international disputes (Caprioli 2000, 65). Furthermore, states with higher levels of gender equality resort to lower levels of violence during international crises (Caprioli and Boyer 2001, 515). Gender inequality is not only a predictor of state behavior on the international level: states with high levels of gender inequality are also more likely to experience intrastate or civil conflict (Caprioli 2005).

Issues of gender inequality are often overlooked as central to state and global security, as "gender" translates (to many) as "women's issues" or social issues (Caprioli 2005; Hudson et al. 2012; Sjoberg 2014). If we start to untangle the complex web of gender relations and norms, we can begin to see the consequences of discrimination and violence not just for individuals but for society as a whole and the state and its foreign relations by extension. Valerie Hudson and Andrea den Boer caution that a "surplus" of men in some states has resulted from exaggerated gender inequality, characterized by excessively high **male:female sex ratios** (the number of males per one hundred females at birth in a population) resulting from son preference, sex-selective abortion, and discrimination against and abuse of girls and women. This surplus contributes to instability within the state, which in turn affects the way the state makes governance and foreign policy decisions (Hudson and den Boer 2002, 6).

Even if a state does not have a surplus of restive men, gender-based violence and inequality are still concerns relevant to security studies and policy. In their research, Hudson, Bonnie Ballif-Spanvill, Mary Caprioli, and Chad Emmett argue that gender relations are at the root of all international relations: the global financial crisis beginning in 2008 could have taken a different turn had there been more women sitting in the boardrooms of key actors; the HIV/AIDS epidemic relates back to sexual violence and exploitation, disproportionately affecting girls and women; and overpopulation and the accompanying social and economic strains could be alleviated through women's empowerment and improved reproductive freedom (Hudson et al. 2012, 1–3). If state and international policies, civil society efforts, and economic investments do more to address gender inequality, they will also begin to address some of the world's most complex—or wicked—problems.

Sweden's Feminist Foreign Policy:
Gender at the Center of International Affairs

Sweden has written gender equality into its domestic and foreign policies, demonstrating that states can (and do) make gender a pillar of statecraft. At the center of the country's stance on gender equality is the principle of fairness, the notion "that everyone, regardless of gender, has the right to work and support themselves, to balance career and family life, and to live without the fear of abuse of violence" (Sweden [government of] 2022). This principle is in-line with the central tenets of human security and the concept of durable human security. Ranked third in the 2019 GII and fifth in the 2021 GGGI, Sweden has consistently received praise for its gender equality measures at home and abroad and has been near the top of the GII since the World Economic Forum began assessing states in 2006.

A cornerstone of Sweden's international initiatives and security measures is its **feminist foreign policy**—an approach to foreign affairs that emphasizes women's participation, rights, and empowerment and gender equality. In her 2016 Statement of Government Policy, former minister for foreign affairs Margot Wallström contended that the "situation in the world calls for a feminist foreign policy that aims to strengthen women's representation and access to resources" (Wallström 2016). Having previously served as the UN secretary-general's special representative on sexual violence in armed conflict (2010–2012), Wallström was acutely aware of the very real impact of gender-based violence and discrimination, and upon her appointment as foreign minister in 2014 the Swedish government adopted a feminist foreign policy stance.

Factoring gender into foreign policy is still a novel approach and led to a diplomatic skirmish in 2015 between Sweden and Saudi Arabia (Nordberg 2015; Taylor 2015). But it places at the heart of international politics the notion that states and the international community as a whole are more secure when the entire population has full and equal access to rights and opportunities to thrive.

The Swedish government's public-facing discussion of its feminist foreign policy underscores that gender equality is a "prerequisite to achieving Sweden's broader foreign policy goals—peace, security and sustainable development" (Government Offices of Sweden, n.d.). Because the state views gender equality through the lens of national interest, its statist, federalist, and cosmopolitan perspectives on security align. Sweden's feminist foreign policy—an outwardly focused effort to promote women's rights and gender equality abroad—aligns with domestic policy designed to promote gender equality at home. The state works to ensure durable human security through higher levels of gender equality at home, and the gender inequality indexes suggest that the effort has yielded progress.

From the federalist and cosmopolitan perspectives, the state also operates in conjunction with both civil society groups and IGOs to foster global norms promoting gender equality as essential to development, peace, and stability. When decision makers within a state are able to reach an agreement on the nature of a problem or issue and the challenges it poses (in this case, how gender inequality contributes to insecurity and instability and inhibits economic development), the process of working through policy options and deciding on ideal outcomes is effective. Sweden is not immune to political gridlock, but the state's commitment to promoting gender equality after centering this focus in its foreign policy priorities has shaped its actions at home and abroad and led other states to follow suit (Vogelstein 2019; Gupta 2020).

GLOBAL EFFORTS TO IMPROVE GENDER EQUALITY

The link between gender equality and more-peaceful international politics has also driven international policy efforts. Decades-long advocacy efforts by women's rights groups, human rights organizations, the United Nations and other multilateral organizations, and states supportive of gender equality initiatives have resulted in several international agreements that hold states accountable in the face of gender-based discrimination, violence, and inequality in representation. In its earliest days, the UN declared that all people are equal and entitled to the same rights, regardless of sex (United Nations 1945). It established the Commission on the Status of Women (CSW), tasked with informing and creating policies to promote gender equality, under the Economic and Social Council (ECOSOC).

The Convention on the Elimination of All Forms of Discrimination against Women (CEDAW) was signed on December 18, 1979, and came into effect on September 3, 1981, during the UN Decade for Women (1975–1985). The binding agreement defines gender-based discrimination and establishes steps that **states parties** (states that have signed and ratified the convention) should take to end discrimination against women, including changes to the state's legal system, establishment of public institutions to prevent discrimination, and measures to prevent discriminatory actions. Several states have not signed the treaty (including Iran, Somalia, Sudan, Tonga, and the Holy See—the Vatican), and some have signed but not ratified it (including the United States and Palau). Of the 189 states parties, about 50 states have ratified CEDAW with reservations to specific articles, which limit a state's full compliance with the convention in keeping with preexisting national laws or cultural or religious constraints. CEDAW's adoption provides a legal foundation upon which gender equality advocates could work toward more extensive and inclusive protections.

The 1990s saw tremendous transnational advocacy around human rights in general and women's human rights and gender equality in particular. The end of the Cold War created more space for discussions of nontraditional security issues (as we have discussed in previous chapters), including human security, the rights and security of women and children, and gender issues (Hudson 2010, 69–72). Accordingly, during this period created a federalist security perspective began to take root. In this context, a focus on women's rights as human rights and gender equality as central to security became possible.

In addition to a shifting global political landscape, the genocidal wars in the former Yugoslavia and in Rwanda featured sexual and gender-based violence on a massive scale, creating greater global public awareness of the extreme brutality that can result from destructive gender norms. In 1995, during the Fourth World Conference on Women in Beijing, and on the heels of global press coverage of gender-based violence in war, women's human rights advocates secured another international agreement. The **Beijing Platform for Action** established women's rights as human rights, made commitments to protecting women's human rights, and called for a global shift in thinking about gender equality as a broader issue of concern for all people rather than just for one-half of the population.

Shortly thereafter, the UN's Millennium Development Goals made gender equality and women's empowerment explicit objectives to be met by 2015. MDG number 3 (MDG 3), "promote gender equality and empower women," and MDG number 5 (MDG 5), "reduce by three-quarters the maternal mortality ratio," dealt explicitly with both structural and imminent physical threats to the well-being of women and girls as part of the pursuit to end poverty, hunger, disease, and human insecurity. The Sustainable Development Goals, adopted in 2015 with a target fulfillment date of 2030, similarly address gender-based discrimination and inequality. Specifically, SDG 5—"achieve gender equality and empower all women and girls"—notes that, despite the progress made under the MDGs, women and girls still suffer violence and discrimination. Because gender norms are so deeply entrenched in culture and society, and because these norms typically privilege one group of people over all others, gender equality is an elusive objective.

At the start of the new millennium, and thanks to sustained transnational advocacy, gender became an item on the UN Security Council's agenda. The Security Council adopted **Resolution 1325** in October 2000. In chapter 6, we discussed Resolution 1325 in the context of comprehensive peace accords;

BOX 10.1. THINK ABOUT IT . . .
SUSTAINABLE DEVELOPMENT GOAL 5

SDG 5 aims to achieve gender equality and empower women and girls across the globe. In addition to ending gender-based discrimination and violence, SDG 5's targets address specific customs, practices, and entrenched norms that impede gender equality.

Three of SDG 5's targets follow:

- "Eliminate all harmful practices, such as child, early, and forced marriage and female genital mutilation."
- "Recognize and value unpaid care and domestic work through the provision of public services, infrastructure and social-protection policies, and the promotion of shared responsibility within the household and the family as nationally appropriate."
- "Ensure women's full and effective participation and equal opportunities for leadership at all levels of decision-making in political, economic, and public life."

For each of the targets, consider the following:

1. How does the custom, practice, or norm listed in each target above inhibit gender equality?
2. To what extent is each custom, practice, or norm an issue in *your* country or community?
3. What are potential sources of opposition and obstacles to change advocates and security providers might encounter while in pursuit of these specific targets?
4. How might local, national, regional, or global actors make a difference in improving gender equality?
5. SDG 5 focuses on gender equality with a specific emphasis on women and girls. What are possible advantages and disadvantages of maintaining a focus on women and girls in SDG 5 rather than in broadening consideration of gender inequality to include LGBTQ+ persons?

Source: Targets excerpted from United Nations Department of Economic and Social Affairs, n.d.(b).

it is important for us to revisit the resolution as an achievement in the push for women's involvement in international decision-making processes. The resolution was the first of the resolutions that would become the Security Council's **Women, Peace, and Security (WPS)** agenda—a set of resolutions that call, in part, for greater participation of women in conflict resolution and peacebuilding processes.

Recognizing that war disproportionately affects women and girls (for reasons including those we previously discussed as threats to durable human security) and that female voices have historically been absent from peace processes, WPS aims to improve female participation in decision-making, enhance the protection of women and girls in armed conflict, and prevent the outbreak of armed conflict. The logic behind Resolution 1325 and WPS in general is that, by making negotiations and peace processes more representative of society, peace agreements and conflict resolution will be more effective in the long run. In other words, there is a link between the human security of women and girls and the long-term stability of states. Networks of NGOs, IGOs, and civil society groups have worked to make this observation a feature of international and state policy and security practice.

Valerie Hudson and coauthors assert that the security of women serves as the basis for national and global stability: without eliminating gender inequality and gender-based violence and discrimination we cannot expect to end armed conflict or achieve national or global security. More to the point, they articulate that gender equality initiatives and efforts to improve women's security do not detract from men's security and opportunities; rather, the ability of *all* individuals to thrive is key to stability and security (Hudson et al. 2012, 200). Progress toward these goals can be made through partnerships and collaboration among a wide array of domestic and international actors. The initiatives and goals discussed here are clearly global in scope and objectives, but of course not all progress toward gender equality happens on the international level.

Gender Equality in Afghanistan: Opportunities and Obstacles

For more than two decades Western policy circles and popular discourse have been concerned with gender inequality in Afghanistan (Hirschkind and Mahmood 2002). The oppression of women under the Taliban regime became a prominent foreign policy issue in the build-up to armed intervention in Afghanistan in response to the attacks on New York City and Washington, D.C., on September 11, 2001. Systemic violations of women's human rights were cited as grounds for humanitarian intervention in Afghanistan (Kandiyoti 2008, 155). Calls for recognition of the hardships women and girls face under Taliban rule emphasize the grim reality that is life for those who happened to be born female: women could not seek employment, girls' schools were closed; universities could not educate women, women and girls had extremely limited freedom of movement, physical violence and corporal punishment were common responses to transgressions, and—perhaps the most common imagery used in Western discussions—when in public women and girls were required to be covered from head to face to toe, wearing the *burqa* (Hirschkind and Mahmood 2002, 340).

Years later, progress toward gender equality in the postconflict reconstruction phase has been slower than advocates had hoped it would be, as evidenced by the poor GII ranking Afghanistan holds (discussed at the outset of this chapter; the state ranked 157th in the UNDP's 2019 gender inequality assessment, down from 152nd in 2014). Further, the withdrawal of US and coalition forces and the Taliban's subsequent takeover of Afghanistan's government in August 2021 have created uncertainty surrounding the future of women's rights and progress toward gender equality in the state.

The issue of gender inequality in Afghanistan brings up important questions: *When a population experiences widespread gender inequality and gender-based violence and discrimination, who is responsible for bringing about positive change?* Further, *Which local, national, regional, or global actors are best positioned to foment successful long-term change?* The answers to these questions largely depend on which security perspective dominates within the state or among decision makers planning assistance or intervention. A cosmopolitan perspective is more likely to suggest efforts by grassroots women's rights and human rights networks, both within the state and transnationally. A federalist perspective focuses on global efforts between states, IGOs, and NGOs as well as the evolving international legal framework to support gender equality. In contrast, a statist perspective highlights the state's responsibility to establish fair legal frameworks and protection from harm domestically, whereas a nativist perspective emphasizes the importance of local or kinship groups in advancing or eroding gender equality.

The difficulty of addressing gender inequality in Afghanistan—in conjunction with the ultimately failed decades-long multilateral armed interventions to depose the Taliban regime and establish a secure state and functioning institutions—stems from the fact that the interventions often focused on Islamic norms and laws. Western efforts linked gender inequality to Islam, which was viewed as inherently oppressive; thus Western intervention has emphasized the importance of achieving particularly Western visions for women's rights and empowerment for Afghan women yet simultaneously has overlooked the disproportionate impact armed conflict has on women. When approaches to gender equality fail to maintain an analytical view of current conditions and how those conditions have come about and neglect the voices of affected individuals, initiatives premised on noble objectives fall short in their application.

As observes one study of US popular and political condemnation of women's oppression in Afghanistan, "A number of commentators, in discussions that preceded the war, regularly failed to connect the predicament of women in Afghanistan with the massive military and economic support that the US provided, as part of its Cold War strategy, to the most extreme of Afghan religious militant groups" (Hirschkind and Mahmood 2002, 341); in other words, the effort to stand with the women and girls of Afghanistan addressed only some of the root causes of their insecurity. The Western feminist campaign to secure Afghan women's rights also established an artificial juxtaposition of subordinated/oppressed veiled and liberated/empowered uncovered women and girls, applying a broad brush that equated voluntary observance of religious and cultural norms of modesty with the extreme political dictates of a governing regime, thus inadvertently stripping away female agency and choice where it may have been present (Hirschkind and Mahmood 2002, 352) and leading to divisions among transnational women's rights advocates over the best approach to demonstrating solidarity with Afghan women (Kandiyoti 2008, 155).

These two observations point to a potential pitfall of gender equality initiatives and those related to many other human security issues: in order to create successful and lasting change, local, national, regional, and global actors must appreciate the context in which they work, seek out support and input from beneficiaries (those whose lives are affected by the intervention or initiative), and ultimately ensure that they appreciate the *humanity* and agency of the subjects of policies and discussions. The cosmopolitan perspective looks to groups of security providers working together, united by common norms; key to the effectiveness of this collaboration is an understanding of realities on the ground. For this reason, a bottom-up approach to security provision with local voices at the heart of the effort is essential.

Collaboration between the government of the Islamic Republic of Afghanistan, Afghan civil society groups, transnational women's rights groups, and foreign government agencies over the course of two decades led the state to commit to improving the security of women and girls and expanding their opportunities to thrive. The state's revised constitution specifies legal rights and protections for women and girls, including women's participation in political, social, and cultural decision-making (United Nations Women 2020). In 2003 Afghanistan officially ratified the Convention on the Elimination of All Forms of Discrimination against Women (it had signed the convention in 1980). These changes at the state level resulted from tireless advocacy by Afghan women's rights civil society groups and support from international organizations and outside states, including the United States and the European Union. The return of the Taliban to power in 2021, however, raises numerous questions about legal protections for women as well as their participation in governance and the economy.

Afghanistan's history, governance structure, and relationship between the government and local civil society and international donors create both opportunities for and obstacles to lasting change; the influence of local governing bodies throughout much of the state means that centralized change at the level of the central government may not always diffuse effectively (Kandiyoti 2008, 175–77). The numerous positive legal changes (improvements on paper) do not necessarily affect the daily lives, security, and opportunities of women and girls in Afghanistan (Barr 2013). Further, tumultuous peace talks between the government, the Taliban, and international security providers in 2020 highlighted the reality that progress toward gender equality remains slow and vulnerable to erosion: the Afghan government's twenty-one-member delegation included four women, but the Taliban's delegation did not include any women (Amnesty International 2021; United Nations Women 2020). The withdrawal of US and NATO forces in September 2021 changed the power dynamics, removing a support system for the state and opening the door to a more-influential Taliban, which threatens progress made by and for women and girls (Amnesty International 2021).

The efforts to reduce gender inequality and to protect and expand the rights of women and girls in Afghanistan throughout the past two decades demonstrates the challenges that arise from conflicting security perspectives. Gender equality efforts in Afghanistan are rooted in both federalist and cosmopolitan perspectives that have brought together local advocates and civil society organizations, international advocates and organizations, and foreign states' decision makers; these groups share a belief in the connection between gender equality and state security, as well as the fundamental morality of women's and girls' rights as human rights. These perspectives conflict with entrenched gender norms in the country, specifically within local decision-making bodies, and—principally—the Taliban's organizing structure and perspective. To the extent that households and communities view local decision-making bodies or the Taliban as better positioned than the state to protect their security and interests, progress toward gender equality will be slow and uneven.

CONCLUSION: GENDER EQUALITY AT HOME AND ABROAD

No state can boast complete gender equality. Whether a state ranks first or last in the gender equality indexes we introduced in this chapter, there are always avenues to further reduce gender-based disparities in the provision of basic needs and opportunities and ensure freedom from violence and discrimination on the basis of sex, gender, or sexuality. Our examinations of gender equality in Afghanistan and feminist foreign policy in Sweden illustrate differing approaches and obstacles to empowering women and girls and to reducing gender-based violence and discrimination. As with any of the human security issues we discuss in this book—both in armed conflict and in "peacetime"— there is no one-size-fits-all solution to gender inequality that will work in every region, state, and locality. Instead, when devising policies and programs to empower women, LGBTQ+ persons, and other marginalized groups, civil society, states, and international organizations must consider the context-specific obstacles and influences that affect the prospects for gender equality.

The line between war and peace is almost completely blurred when we consider gender dynamics: gender inequality in "peacetime" shapes the ways in which armed conflicts are fought, and the gendered effects of armed conflict carry over into postconflict reconstruction and peace in the absence of deliberate efforts to reckon with gender inequality and insecurity. The more a state ensures equal protection of and opportunity for all people, the less likely it is to engage in aggressive foreign policy behaviors, and the more likely it is to experience social and political stability within its borders. The relationship between gender equality and peace goes the other way as well: the experience of armed conflict, state violence, intervention, and insurgency affects prospects for gender equality. Political repression, sectarian violence, displacement, and war create conditions under which progress toward gender equality rolls back. For example, amid families' concerns related to limited resources, lack of opportunities for education and employment, and threats of sexual violence and harassment, rates of child marriage among Syrian refugees living in Jordan, Iraq, and Lebanon increased for girls from 12 percent in 2011 prewar Syria to 25 percent in 2013 and 36 percent in 2018 (Save the Children 2014; Chakraborty 2019).

Gender inequality and gender-based violence and discrimination are serious impediments to an individual's ability to thrive, and foreign, domestic, and security policy must take them into account (Hudson et al. 2012). What both the academic research and the practice of international politics make absolutely clear is that gender inequality creates real barriers to the achievement of durable human security.

DISCUSSION QUESTIONS

1. How do the different measures of gender inequality vary? Is this variation problematic? Why or why not?

2. To what extent should gender concerns factor into a state's foreign policy framework?

3. To what extent should gender concerns factor into a state's domestic policy framework?

4. What are the advantages of pursuing gender equality initiatives derived from grassroots domestic actors, organizations, or movements? What are the disadvantages?

5. What are the advantages of pursuing gender equality initiatives derived from international actors, organizations, or movements? What are the disadvantages?

6. On February 24, 2022, at the onset of the Russian invasion, Ukraine's government declared martial law and required men between the ages of eighteen and sixty to remain in the country in preparation for mass mobilization against Russian forces. Military-age Ukrainian women were permitted to leave the country. Only single fathers of children under eighteen, fathers supporting several children under eighteen, or fathers of disabled children were permitted to leave the country. What assumptions about gender are at the heart of these policies? How might such policies exacerbate gender inequality?

Chapter 11

Climate Change and Environmental Security

Learning Objectives

This chapter will enable readers to

1. differentiate between *climate change* and *global warming*
2. identify the effects of global warming and climate change
3. discuss the connections between climate change and human, state, and global security
4. and identify the difficulties related to global cooperation to address climate change.

In Paris in December 2015, the international community agreed on a set of goals designed to slow or reverse the course of climate change and prevent its most catastrophic effects. As a problem that is truly global in scope, climate change affects each of the three types of security—human, national, and global—but prior international agreements had failed to generate cooperation among states. At the time of writing, the effectiveness of the Paris Agreement—and the planet—remains uncertain.

There is broad scientific consensus that climate change is human-made and poses a serious threat to the stability of ecosystems and human communities. A 2015 global public opinion poll conducted by the Pew Research Center shows that majorities in the forty countries polled viewed climate change as a serious threat. The poll also indicates that individuals in Latin America and sub-Saharan Africa are more concerned about climate change than are those in other regions and that individuals in the United States and China—the world's largest emitters of greenhouse gases—are less concerned overall. Regardless, more than three-quarters of respondents surveyed indicated that they view policy changes as essential in the fight against climate change (Carle 2015). A similar survey in 2018 finds that majorities in polled countries viewed climate change as a major threat, but substantial portions of those populations viewed climate change as only a minor threat or not a threat at all (Fagan and Huang 2019).

Recall the three boxes policy model: decision makers need to reach consensus on the nature of the problem, the range of policy options to address it, and the ideal outcome(s). Efforts to generate effective policy responses to climate change have faltered in Box 1 (perception of the problem), Box 2 (identification of policy options), and Box 3 (recognition of ideal outcomes). When there is variation in perceptions of the seriousness of a global problem like climate change, and particularly when the top contributors to that problem fail to view resolution as urgent, it will be difficult to identify comprehensive multilateral solutions to the problem and mutually agreeable outcomes.

This chapter examines climate change and the role of environmental instability in shaping security. We begin with a brief discussion of the scientific evidence for climate change before delving into the human, national, and global security implications. The next section examines international efforts to regulate greenhouse gas emissions and to set goals to prevent the worst effects of climate change. Here we also consider the work of youth climate activists. We close by looking at bottom-up efforts to address climate change and conclusions in the context of current international affairs.

GLOBAL WARMING AND CLIMATE CHANGE

In 1824 French physicist Jean-Baptiste Joseph Fourier first proposed the **greenhouse effect**, wherein gases (including water vapor and carbon dioxide [CO_2]) help to warm the Earth by trapping radiation in the atmosphere. He likened the planet's atmosphere to a glass cover over a box sitting in the sunlight: the sun's rays warm the box, and the air under the glass cover, which is in contact with the sun-warmed box, remains warm, as the glass keeps the air (and heat radiation) from escaping (American Institute of Physics 2022). Thus, as early as 1824 scientists have had an awareness of the link between gases in the atmosphere and the temperature of the Earth.

In 1896 Swedish chemist Svante Arrhenius observed that industrialization enhances the greenhouse effect of Earth's atmosphere through the burning of coal. Throughout the twentieth century engineers and scientists continued to document the effects of increased CO_2 in the atmosphere and the overall warming of the Earth, but international political recognition remained muted until the last quarter of the century (BBC News 2013).

In 1975 American geochemist Wallace Broecker published a short piece in *Science*—"Climatic Change: Are We on the Brink of a Pronounced Global Warming?" He predicted a period of "rapid warming" in the twenty-first century, with "global temperatures warmer than any in the last 1,000 years" (Broecker 1975, 460–61). Indeed, NASA data on global surface temperatures and Arctic sea ice extent indicate that 2016 broke records, with average temperatures during the first six months of the year 1.3 degrees Celsius warmer than late nineteenth-century temperatures (Lynch 2017).

Global warming refers to overall increases in the average temperatures of the Earth's oceans and atmosphere. It is caused by high concentrations of CO_2 and other greenhouse gases in the atmosphere, which trap heat and warm the Earth through the greenhouse effect. The term **climate change** is used to describe sustained changes in global or regional climate patterns that stem from overall warming. Climate change can be seen in the increased prevalence of extreme weather, like strong hurricanes or blizzards, increased frequency of droughts or polar vortexes, or changing levels of precipitation. While the terms *global warming* and *climate change* are often used interchangeably, they refer to two distinct phenomena. Of course, they're closely related: global warming causes climate change.

The Earth has experienced warming and cooling trends (or climatic changes) throughout its history, but there is scientific consensus that the current warming trend, in which average temperatures are increasing at a rate unseen in the past 1,300 years, is due to human activity—particularly the high levels of carbon dioxide and other greenhouse gas emissions present in the atmosphere since the Industrial Revolution (Intergovernmental Panel on Climate Change 2007, 5; NASA, n.d.). The Earth has experienced warming and cooling trends over time in the past, but the pace and degree of the current shift are unlike the naturally occurring cycles evident in Earth's history. In 1981, atmospheric physicists at NASA published an article in *Science* observing a 0.2-degree Celsius rise in global temperatures from the 1960s to 1980 and warning that global warming linked to atmospheric carbon dioxide could lead to drought-prone regions, melting sea ice, and climate shifts in the twenty-first century (Hansen et al. 1981). Global climate change may currently be a subject of urgent consideration—and sometimes intense political debate—but climate scientists have been pointing to the warming trend and its grave implications for decades.

A difficult question from a security standpoint emerges: *What do states and other security actors do about global warming and climate change?* States, for their part, are often inclined toward the statist security perspective where concessions and efforts to mitigate the effects of climate change are concerned, and this orientation to a truly global security problem makes cooperative solutions elusive. Climate change offers us a case study through which we can see how the various approaches to security may align in theory but conflict in practice. When viewed in terms of short- and long-term threats to individuals and communities—the vicious cycle of insecurity, and the potential for chronic human insecurity to breed national and global instability—climate change constitutes a clear security concern according to each of the three approaches. At least, in theory. In practice, especially as international **regimes** seeking to mitigate the effects of climate change lack sufficient support from key carbon-emitting states, political decision makers have placed efforts to bolster human security against climate-related threats at odds with efforts to strengthen and protect national security and the domestic economy.

THE SECURITY IMPLICATIONS OF CLIMATE CHANGE

Climate change is a threat multiplier: the effects of climate change interact with other dimensions of human security as well as national and global security to exacerbate a range of short- and long-term security issues. For this reason, any discussion of climate change is also a discussion of food security, migration, human rights, and armed conflict, as well as of a host of other acute and chronic security threats. Global warming and climate change are already contributing to sea-level rise (due to melting sea ice), shifting weather patterns, extreme weather events, wildfires, displacement, famine, and public health concerns, like the spread of mosquito-borne illness to historically cooler regions. Still, it is difficult to anticipate the exact effects climate change will have on each region of the world.

The degree of insecurity created by climate change will vary according to geography, the strength of a state's institutions and ability to adapt to and mitigate climate-related threats, and future innovation and technological advances (Salehyan 2008). Despite the fact that a high level of consensus exists among climate scientists that the warming trend throughout the past century is linked to human activity (NASA, n.d.), the fact that the effects are not uniformly visible in the near term has fueled debate among policy makers over the urgency of addressing it. As scientists and advocates have warned with increasing urgency, the time for debate has run out and the time to act decisively to stave off the worst effects of climate change is here. If states are unable or unwilling to cut their carbon emissions dramatically and adapt to the shifts brought about by climate change, then states, their populations, and the broader global community will face existential security threats in the years to come.

We classify the effects of climate change as threats primarily to durable human security. The Intergovernmental Panel on Climate Change (IPCC) has warned that the long-term effects of climatic shifts will affect individual security and well-being through changes to affected economies, loss of traditional culture and knowledge, resource scarcity, and mass migration (Adger et al. 2014). When combined with flaws in state institutions and insufficient state capacity to shelter people from, adapt to, or compensate for climate-related challenges, these effects on individuals' lives and livelihoods become human security problems.

In addition to its classification as a durable human security concern, climate change may lead to acute security threats—including armed conflict— if the chronic security issues go unaddressed or if short-term changes or extreme weather events are significant enough to trigger upheaval (Barnett and Adger 2007; Hendrix and Glaser 2007; Meier, Bond, and Bond 2007). For instance, sustained drought (due to shifting weather patterns) and famine (due to state unwillingness or lack of capacity to provide sufficient food security) may lead to unrest, displacement, armed conflict, and state instability (Adger et al. 2014; Jones, Mattiacci, and Braumoeller 2017; Notaras 2011). Climate change in and of itself may not lead directly to armed conflict; but a combination of resource scarcity, rapid mass displacement due to extreme weather events, and political, social, and economic institutions contributing to chronic insecurity may lay the groundwork for acute insecurity, unrest, and armed conflict (Evans 2010; Jones, Mattiacci, and Braumoeller 2017). The effects of climate change serve to exacerbate existing durable and acute security threats, worsening human security and—if left unchecked—state and global security.

Climate Change and Human Security

The connection between human security and climate change is already visible, especially on island nations and in low-lying areas of larger nations, drought-prone regions, and the Arctic. Extreme weather events like strong hurricanes and floods devastate communities and displace families, insufficient rainfall or drought reduces the access to and availability of food and safe drinking water in affected regions, desertification triggers migration and resource competition, sea-level rise forces people in coastal communities to abandon their homes, and melting ice in the Arctic forces Indigenous communities to adapt their livelihoods and cultural traditions or move away as the landscape changes. The effects of climate change are most immediately and harshly felt by individuals and communities who rely on natural resources to sustain their livelihoods and who have little support from the state (whether because of a lack of willingness or a lack of capacity) to compensate for chronic or abrupt scarcity or displacement (Salehyan 2008). It follows, then, that the individuals and communities that will suffer the earliest and most intense security threats linked to climate change reside within states with less capacity to adapt and are geographically vulnerable—such as states in hot, arid climates and low-lying coastal regions.

Climate change constitutes a durable human security threat, using the threshold we have discussed throughout the book, when its effects create or exacerbate other chronic security issues. For instance, climate change is linked to food insecurity when persistent drought leads to insufficient agricultural yields that in turn lead to rising food prices and lack of availability of and access to nutritious foods. Poor rainfall in Somalia has led to insufficient water supply for crops and livestock, leading to food shortages and financial instability for individuals and families. In February 2017, USAID's Famine Early Warning Systems Network (FEWS NET) estimated that 6.2 million Somalis (out of a population of roughly 10.5 million people) were in need of humanitarian assistance. Just six years prior, in 2011, famine had devastated Somalia and cost more than a quarter million lives (United Nations 2017). FEWS NET anticipated that high food-assistance needs would continue through early 2022 as a result of multiseason drought (Famine Early Warning Systems Network [2021]).

Famine in Somalia provides an example of the interaction between various forms of human insecurity: drought, political instability, armed conflict, and poverty all contribute to the context in which famine becomes widespread and threatens a large portion of the population. While poor rainfall is not the only factor contributing to famine in Somalia, drought exacerbates and combines with the political and socioeconomic factors to create human insecurity. Similarly, floods, wildfires, tropical storms, tsunamis, and other natural disasters can severely damage agriculture and alter the price and availability of certain foods, contributing to food insecurity and economic instability around the world (Food and Agriculture Organization of the United Nations 2015). When the state lacks the capacity or willingness to safeguard its population from the worst effects of climate change, human insecurity results.

Individuals living in coastal communities are at risk of displacement and unemployment if their homes gradually become unlivable due to rising tides, forcing individuals or entire communities to move inland and jeopardizing livelihoods, financial stability, and cultural traditions. The populations of the Marshall Islands, Tuvalu, Kiribati, and other island nations face the threat of displacement from rising sea levels, as do communities in low-lying coastal regions in larger states. Retreating waters also trigger migration and instability. Melting glaciers and shrinking lakes deplete the necessary freshwater reserves that are essential to the survival of communities, driving migration to urban centers or to regions with more reliable access to water. Communities in the Andean plain have been forced to migrate to the Amazon Basin as a result of dwindling freshwater reserves, and the rapid depletion of Lake Chad has displaced millions in Cameroon, Chad, Niger, and Nigeria and exacerbated the security threat posed by the insurgent group Boko Haram (Benko 2017). Displaced individuals are at greater risk of chronic insecurity as they work to start over in a new community with considerably fewer financial, social, and material resources than they once possessed.

Climate change can also pose acute, short-term, but severe human security threats. These threats come in the form of natural disasters that affect states and their populations without regard for the level of development or institutional capacity. Natural disasters present human security threats when the state lacks the capacity to remove people from harm's way to safer areas and respond with effective reconstruction and assistance after the threat has passed. This problem is not limited to developing or impoverished states, as wealthy states still find themselves underprepared to handle the human security challenges posed by natural disasters. Further, the same state may respond differently to separate events on the basis of a number of factors, including the political or cultural centrality of the location and communities affected, lessons learned from past disaster responses, and human and financial resources available for emergency management.

For example, the US Federal Emergency Management Agency (FEMA) responded differently to Hurricane Sandy in 2012 than it had to Hurricane Katrina in 2005. After the inadequate response to Katrina, a devastating category 5 storm that made landfall in the Gulf Coast states from Florida to Texas and affected an estimated half-million people and ninety thousand square miles, the US Congress passed the aptly named Post-Katrina Emergency Management Reform Act of 2006 (United States Government Accountability Office 2008). The deadly and costly results of insufficient coordination among federal agencies and between federal, state, and local agencies during and after Katrina led to the 2006 FEMA law and to changes within the agency. When Hurricane Sandy, a category 3 storm, made landfall in the Northeastern United States, FEMA had already deployed emergency-response teams to the region. Prior to the 2006 law and agency reforms, FEMA had worked under the view that emergency responders could begin operations only once an area had already been devastated; the 2006 law clarified FEMA's role and allowed for a preemptive emergency response, which was visible during and after Sandy's course (Starks 2012).

Adequate responses to human insecurity created by natural disasters require significant resources and coordination of emergency-management agencies and processes. As extreme weather events become more common, states and humanitarian-relief agencies will have to bear the cost of these efforts in order to prevent or mitigate significant human suffering. As warmer waters fuel stronger hurricanes and decreased rainfall and drought kindle more severe wildfires, these costs will continue to rise.

Climate Change and Its State and Global Security Linkages

There is a significant (and somewhat unpredictable) threshold before a climate-related issue moves from the area of human security to state security. For this reason, there may be more concern among individuals and communities before the state is driven *by national or political interests* to recognize climate change as a security threat. The push for action to reverse the course of climate change is bottom-up in some—but certainly not all—countries. The extent to which decision makers within the state view climate change as a security threat will affect the ability to work through the three policy boxes and craft effective policy to promote adaptation and resilience or to sign onto and enforce international efforts like the Paris Agreement.

Much of the rhetoric on climate change focuses on protecting resources for future generations (e.g., the children and grandchildren of today's adults), but national security policy making usually operates based on the notion of a clear and imminent threat. Hence there is a critical gap between the implications for human security and the willingness of states to act. Evidence of this gap lies in the difficulty of securing international cooperation on binding greenhouse gas emission–reduction agreements. If the state operates on a rational basis, making cost-benefit calculations prior to each action or policy decision, then the state not directly and immediately affected by climate change will hesitate to act in response to the future threat where costs of changing behavior are high and immediate and benefits of that change are diffuse and in the future. Still, even within the United States—a top carbon-emitting country and one with political factions that downplay the risks related to climate change—security professionals have begun to advocate for political recognition of the linkages between climate change and national security threats. Central to this advocacy is the notion that the deprivation, disruptions, and physical insecurity created by extreme weather events, sea-level rise, and desertification are **threat multipliers**, or phenomena that make existing security threats worse (Powers 2015; Revkin 2017).

States and international institutions like the International Monetary Fund and the World Bank have made the argument that investments in clean energy, carbon pricing, and adapting to climate change make good economic sense for states (World Bank 2013). Zambia, for instance, has been affected by climate change through droughts, floods, and a resulting increase in poverty. Recognizing the economic impact of climate change, the government has committed a significant share of its national budget to climate change adaptation, removal of unnecessary fossil fuel subsidies, and support for clean energy sources like solar and hydroelectric power (Zambia Development Agency 2017; World Bank 2013). States facing the prospect of losing large portions or the entirety of their territories to sea-level rise or unstable food supplies caused by desertification and drought will view the effects of climate change as both a human security and a national security threat, as Zambia's national budget suggests.

Climate change is, by definition, a global security concern. The melting ice in the Arctic directly affects the territorial integrity of eight countries—Canada, Denmark, Finland, Iceland, Norway, Russia, Sweden, and the United States—and threatens to create a "tipping point" for global climate change (Harvey 2016). The atmosphere does not contain borders, so the greenhouse gas emissions released by one state do not stay within that state; all share the costs of high concentrations of greenhouse gas emissions even if they did not contribute equally to the problem.

As the effects of climate change displace populations, more states will have to grapple with the decision to take in or keep out climate refugees. If inhospitable climates, drought, flooding, resource conflicts, and food insecurity create massive migration flows, the states these populations leave, those they travel through, and those in which they seek to settle will face the prospect of destabilization (Benko 2017). Climate-related threats can and will destabilize entire regions if states do not have sufficient resources and institutional capacity to mitigate the effects of extreme weather events, droughts, sea-level rise, famine, and resource conflicts. Of all of the durable and acute security threats discussed in this book, climate change is the one most directly linked to truly global instability and insecurity.

Because no single state can mitigate or solve climate change by acting alone, this particular security concern constitutes a collective action problem. In a **collective action problem**, all actors (states in this particular case) have an interest in creating a solution to a problem that affects everyone. Nevertheless, solutions often come at some cost, and this makes it difficult to convince individual actors to work toward any given solution. Since states will feel the effects of climate change differently, with states in the Global South likely to face the harshest effects earlier than wealthier states in the Global North, states will possess varying degrees of motivation or urgency to contribute to climate change mitigation and adaptation efforts.

BOX 11.1. THINK ABOUT IT . . . CLIMATE REFUGEES

The effects of climate change are visible in our world today. Drought, sea-level rise, wildfires, stronger and more frequent hurricanes and typhoons, and extreme heat disrupt daily life, displace people, and create insecurity in many regions of the world.

Rising sea levels force populations of low-lying regions to migrate inland or to larger states. Island nations like Kiribati are the first to face significant—and existential—territorial threats from sea-level rise.

If the current acceleration of sea-level rise persists, Kiribati will be fully submerged within thirty years (Taylor 2014; Goins 2018; Wadley 2013). The waters of the Gulf of Mexico have steadily encroached on Isle de Jean Charles, Louisiana, which has lost more than 90 percent of its land to rising waters since 1955 (Davenport and Robertson 2016; van Houten 2016).

Conversely, persistent or recurrent drought reduces or eliminates access to essential water resources, especially when water is mismanaged. The disappearance of Lake Poopó, once Bolivia's second-largest lake, has brought ecological disaster and economic hardship. Diversion of the lake's main tributary, the Desaguadero River, for irrigation purposes combined with drought and insufficient rainfall caused the lake to shrink dramatically and finally, in 2015, dry up altogether (NASA Earth Observatory 2016; Torres-Batlló and Marti-Cardona 2021).

Climate refugees are individuals and communities who are forced by the effects of climate change to relocate from their homes. Like refugees fleeing human-made violence and destruction, climate refugees face the challenges of loss of livelihood, physical insecurity, and loss of cultural and ancestral traditions as they seek safety and stability in a new place.

States have developed programs to help their populations in areas vulnerable to climate change adapt or resettle. For instance, in January 2016 the US Department of Housing and Urban Development directed $1 billion in grants to thirteen US states to support climate change adaptation. Isle de Jean Charles received $48 million to move the entire community—a population of about sixty people—forty miles inland to a more resilient location (State of Louisiana 2021; Beller 2016; Davenport and Robertson 2016; van Houten 2016). In 2020, Kiribati's president announced plans to work with China to raise the islands in an effort to make them more resilient to climate change (Pala 2020).

Other security providers, including NGOs and IGOs, are also working to raise awareness about the urgency of addressing climate change, assisting climate refugees, and contributing to adaption effects. The United Nations High Commissioner for Refugees has recognized climate change as a factor that exacerbates other threats and contributes to displacement and has worked to enhance protection for people displaced by natural disasters and other effects of climate change (United Nations General Assembly 2018; Gaynor 2020).

Search the Web for accounts of the changes affecting Isle de Jean Charles, Lake Poopó, and Kiribati, and consider the human security impacts of climate change on these communities.

1. How do climate refugees differ from other displaced persons?
2. What are the most pressing security issues facing climate refugees?
3. What is the state's role in providing protection for climate refugees? Does the international community have a role to play?
4. What other aspects of human security do you see in the three situations discussed here—Isle de Jean Charles, Kiribati, and Lake Poopó?

GLOBAL COOPERATION AND NATIONAL INTEREST: EFFORTS AND OBSTACLES

The states that are already experiencing the effects of climate change within their own borders are among the most vocal advocates of the need to recognize climate change as a global security threat. Many of these states formed a coalition in advance of the United Nations Climate Change Conference, the twenty-first session of the Conference of Parties, or **COP 21**, held in Paris in December 2015. The High Ambition Coalition (HAC) pushed for a warming limit of 1.5 degrees Celsius above preindustrial average global temperatures. For states like the Marshall Islands or Kiribati, warming above 1.5 degrees poses an existential threat.

At present, the world is at 1.2 degrees Celsius above preindustrial levels, and scientists are beginning to grapple with the exact ramifications of average global surface-temperature increases of 1.5 and 2 degrees. If current warming trends continue, the world will reach 1.5 degrees Celsius above preindustrial levels by 2040 (Intergovernmental Panel on Climate Change [2019]). The IPCC's Fifth Assessment Report, released in phases between September 2013 and November 2014, projects that global warming is likely to exceed the 1.5-degree mark by the end of the twenty-first century and that temperatures are likely to exceed the 2-degree mark in some scenarios.

At the time of writing, the IPCC is in the process of developing its Sixth Assessment Report, which has been released in phases since late 2021 and is scheduled to issue its final report in September 2022 (Intergovernmental Panel on Climate Change [2022]). Periodic updates between the two reporting cycles point to a bleak outlook for environmental stability without significant increases in states' commitments to fight climate change. In September 2021, UN Climate Change released a statement projecting that, based on current Nationally Determined Contributions (states' formal commitments to curb their carbon emissions), the world is on track to warm to 2.7 degrees above preindustrial levels by 2100 (Booth 2021; United Nations Climate Change 2021).

For island states, drought-prone regions, and many developing states, 2 degrees above preindustrial temperatures would likely cause mass displacement due to sea-level rise and dangerous heat, widespread food insecurity, frequent extreme weather events, irreversible coral reef die-off, and loss of territory (Silberg 2016), whereas staying below the 1.5-degree increase would reduce the likelihood of these catastrophic changes. The High Ambition Coalition is not a formal negotiating group, but it has continued to advocate for climate change mitigation after COP 21. The coalition is also broader than just the states that are immediately affected by climate change; it includes more than one hundred wealthy and developing states concerned by the alarming warming trend and its global effects. The **Paris Agreement** calls on states to limit warming to below 2 degrees Celsius and to pursue efforts to limit warming to 1.5 degrees above preindustrial levels; this agreement fell short of the HAC's goals, leaving the most vulnerable states' futures in question.

If we apply the concept of responsibility for security provision to the problem of global climate change, it is apparent that international agreements made by states would offer the most efficient path to necessary policy changes. Such an approach is most feasible when the world's decision makers, and public opinion in their respective states, adhere to a federalist security perspective. International agreements to limit states' greenhouse gas emissions and encourage the development of clean energy sources and new technologies to reduce human contributions to climate change—and implement these agreements—represent an important step toward providing security for the regions and populations most vulnerable to the effects of climate change. Absent widespread support among the world's largest economies and carbon emitters, however, international agreements fall short of generating meaningful commitments to solving the climate crisis.

Coordination to slow or reverse the course of climate change is difficult. The international community is made up of nearly two hundred states, all with different—sometimes competing—interests and varying levels of short- and long-term risk associated with climate change. Since a large share of greenhouse gas emissions come from the private sector, efforts to curb them require states to regulate economic activity; some governments are more willing to do this than others. International efforts to address climate change have sought to mitigate the collective action problem that makes states' cooperation in this area so challenging. The collective action problem in this particular case is created by (1) the shared or diffuse environmental effects of any one state's behavior, (2) the immediate economic and political costs of changing such behavior, and (3) the shared and chronologically distant benefits of taking action to combat climate change. Since some states—particularly those least negatively affected by climate change in the near future—have short-term economic or political interests best suited by *not* cooperating, international efforts have to make cooperation as politically feasible, efficient, and cheap as possible. Alternatively, or in addition, such efforts must make reneging or not joining the effort too costly.

Effective agreements to address climate change require a federalist perspective on security, one that requires states to contribute to a solution and perhaps—though not always—compromise short-term state economic gains for a future global (shared) benefit. Agreement is possible, as the international community has shown several times. Nevertheless, the substance and effectiveness of global climate agreements remain in question as the world continues to warm.

INTERNATIONAL AGREEMENTS: TOP-DOWN SOLUTIONS

When states come together to draft, sign, and ratify agreements to address shared problems, they take a top-down approach to problem-solving. The agreement reached will ideally change state-level policies and shape international-level coordination among states. Here we focus on four such agreements, three directly related to climate change and one that predates the climate change regime. Table 11.1 highlights key agreements on climate change.

A precursor to the international agreements on climate change is the **Montreal Protocol**, a treaty adopted by forty-six states in August 1987. The Montreal Protocol focuses specifically on protection of the ozone layer, and as such it lies outside of the climate change regime. As an early international effort to address a global public good (the ozone layer), the Montreal Protocol gives us an idea of what a successful environmental policy change looks like. The **ozone layer** is a portion of the Earth's stratosphere that acts as a "sunscreen" for the planet and its inhabitants, absorbing the sun's ultraviolet radiation. Its depletion leaves humans especially vulnerable to skin cancer.

The multilateral Montreal Protocol aims to reduce the production and use of ozone-depleting substances, including chlorofluorocarbons (CFCs), hydrochlorofluorocarbons (HCFCs), and hydrofluorocarbons (HFCs), noting that depletion of the ozone layer would pose dangers to human and environmental health. The Montreal Protocol entered into force in August 1989 and was eventually ratified by 197 parties (all UN member states, the European Union, Niue, the Cook Islands, and the Holy See). It was the first UN treaty

Table 11.1. Timetable of Key International Agreements Forming the Climate Regime

1992	United Nations Framework Convention on Climate Change adopted (entered into force in 1994)
1997	Kyoto Protocol signed (entered into force in 2005)
2015	Paris Agreement signed (entered into force in 2016)

to achieve universal ratification—or ratification by all states. The narrowly focused agreement has contributed to national-level policies that have effectively improved the integrity of the ozone layer by reducing or slowing the increase of concentrations of ozone-depleting substances. Since the Montreal Protocol has enjoyed success in regulating states' contributions to a global problem (ozone layer depletion), it stands to reason that agreements regulating greenhouse gases and seeking to reverse the course of climate change could work as well, given the right framing and adequate global support.

Collaboration focused on climate change as a complex set of problems is most directly traced back to the **United Nations Framework Convention on Climate Change (UNFCCC)**. The UNFCCC was adopted at the United Nations Conference on Environment and Development (or the Earth Summit) in June 1992 and entered into force on March 21, 1994. The UNFCCC, like the Montreal Protocol, has been ratified by 197 parties (all UN member states, the European Union, the Cook Islands, Niue, and Palestine). A first step toward facilitating cooperation among states to address the factors contributing to climate change, the UNFCCC's central focus is the "stabilization of greenhouse gas concentrations in the atmosphere at a level that would prevent dangerous anthropogenic interference with the climate system" (United Nations 1992, 9). As a framework convention, the UNFCCC does not place legally binding restrictions on greenhouse gas emissions or provide enforcement mechanisms. Instead, the UNFCCC functions as a framework or starting place for more specific, legally binding agreements. Efforts to reach such agreements began to take shape shortly after the UNFCCC entered into force, as states and organizations realized the need for explicit guidelines, regulations, incentives, and enforcement mechanisms.

The **Kyoto Protocol** followed the UNFCCC and committed states through legally binding emissions reduction targets. The Kyoto Protocol was signed on December 11, 1997, in Kyoto, Japan. It entered into force on February 16, 2005, and has been ratified by 192 parties (*Note:* The United States signed but did not ratify the protocol, and Canada withdrew in 2011). Building on and implementing the UNFCCC, the Kyoto Protocol tasks states, primarily developed states, with reducing their greenhouse gas emissions. State parties to the protocol share a "common but differentiated" responsibility to reduce their emissions.

The notion of *differentiated responsibility* comes from the observation, central to the Kyoto Protocol, that developed states bear the primary burden for greenhouse gas emissions reduction, as it was industrialization within these states (powered by fossil fuel consumption) that contributed most to the current concentrations of greenhouse gases in the atmosphere. The downside of holding only developed states accountable to the protocol's goals is that these states face an economic disincentive to comply, as they fear competition from states whose industries are not regulated by the protocol's emissions limits. Indeed, the United States did not ratify, Canada withdrew during the first commitment period (which ran from 2008 to 2012), and Russia, Japan, and New Zealand did not participate in the second commitment period (which ran from 2013 to 2020). As a result, the Kyoto Protocol applies to a modest portion of the world's emissions (an estimated 14 percent) and has been the subject of criticism for its inability to generate substantial policy change, curb emissions, or promote alternative approaches that may be more effective (European Council 2022; Prins and Rayner 2007). States' varying degrees of willingness to adhere to the Kyoto Protocol underscore the potential for conflict between statist and federalist security perspectives and the importance of broad support for international agreements.

The Paris Agreement is the most recent and most comprehensive follow-up to the UNFCCC and the Kyoto Protocol. As we discussed in the previous section, the Paris Agreement resulted from negotiations before and during COP 21 in November and December 2015. The global agreement, which entered into force on November 4, 2016, has 195 signatories, and 190 of those have ratified the agreement at the time of writing. Like the Kyoto Protocol, the Paris Agreement builds on the UNFCCC and places legally binding restrictions on signatories, although each state party determines its own national commitments to the effort.

Recall that the Paris Agreement aims to limit global warming below 2 degrees Celsius above preindustrial levels and to pursue efforts to stay below an increase of 1.5 degrees Celsius. The half-degree difference is significant, especially for island nations, coastal regions, drought-prone regions, coral reefs, and states whose populations are dependent on agriculture and other natural resources. Unlike the Kyoto Protocol, the Paris Agreement requires all states to set **nationally determined contributions (NDCs)**, or national goals aimed at reducing greenhouse gas emissions, pursuing clean and renewable energy sources, and mitigating the effects of climate change. The agreement requires a global stocktaking every five years in an effort to ensure transparent monitoring and reporting of progress toward NDCs.

Extending the shared obligations to developing states—especially those with large economies, like Brazil, China, India, and Mexico—addresses some of the criticism the Kyoto Protocol faced. The United States never ratified the Kyoto Protocol in large part because of policy makers' concern that economic competitors would not be held to the same environmental standards and would therefore have an edge over the developed states bound by the Kyoto Protocol's regulations. By holding all states accountable for reducing greenhouse gas emissions and limiting global warming in an effort to reduce the likelihood of catastrophic climate change, the Paris Agreement unites parties in a collective effort to address a global problem. The hard-fought agreement, however, continues to face challenges as states begin the work of implementing policy changes at home in an era of uncertain global cooperation.

THE YOUTH CLIMATE MOVEMENT:
A COSMOPOLITAN EFFORT TO SAVE THE WORLD

The youth climate movement is a prime illustration of the cosmopolitan perspective on security. Youth climate activists have worked locally and through a transnational movement to highlight and shame states' failures to adequately address the threat from global climate change. The youth climate movement—global in nature and scope—seeks to prompt state commitments to and enforcement of meaningful global climate agreements. The movement resides somewhere in between top-down and bottom-up security efforts, as youth climate activists use compelling local events and narratives to influence their home states and use international forums to attempt to urge global leaders to take the climate crisis seriously.

Greta Thunberg, speaking to *Time* in her 2019 "Person of the Year" interview, said "We can't just continue living as if there was no tomorrow, because there is a tomorrow" (Alter, Haynes, and Worland 2019). Asking for policies and behaviors that reflect the willingness to preserve "tomorrow" is the crux of the youth climate movement. These activists have organized protests and strikes, filed lawsuits, and delivered speeches to national and international decision-making assemblies, all with a central focus on the notion that world leaders and the international community have not taken the necessary steps to ensuring that the youth of today and future generations have the chance to live on a hospitable planet.

Greta Thunberg brought attention to youth climate advocacy by skipping school and sitting outside of Sweden's parliament with a sign announcing her SKOLSTREJK FÖR KLIMATET (School Strike for Climate). The logic behind the School Strike is simple and tragic: if adult politicians will not invest in children's futures, the children will not either. While Thunberg began her strike alone, it grew into the global Fridays for Future movement and the global climate strike on September 20, 2019, which attracted four million participants (Alter, Haynes, and Worland 2019). Thunberg's undistracted focus on the climate crisis and unabashed willingness to cut through diplomatic pretense to pressure and shame world leaders and the global public alike has called attention to climate science, sparked a movement, and yielded new environmental policies, including a pledge by the United Kingdom to eliminate its carbon footprint (Alter, Haynes, and Worland 2019).

Like Thunberg, youth climate activist Xiye Bastida believes that there is no hope without action, and if adults are unwilling to take action then the youth must do so (NPR/TED Staff 2020). Bastida, a New York resident who was raised in Mexico as a member of the Otomi-Toltec Indigenous community, is a leader of the Fridays for Future movement and coordinator of the Re-Earth Initiative. Bastida's childhood town, San Pedro Tultepec, was affected by drought and floods, instilling in the activist an early awareness of the effects of climate change. She has said, "For me, being eighteen years old and try-ing to save the world means being a climate activist. Before, maybe it meant studying to be a doctor or a politician or a researcher. But I can't wait to grow up and become one of those things. The planet is suffering, and we don't have the luxury of time anymore" (Bastida 2020).

Leah Namugerwa joined the Fridays for Future movement as a fourteen-year-old in 2019 after hearing about Thunberg's School Strike. Namugerwa was moved to join the youth climate movement after watching coverage of Thunberg's strikes and observing the deadly effects of climate change—landslides and drought—in her own country, Uganda. She began striking, often receiving criticism from passersby for missing school but asserting that everyone should join the fight against climate change and tweeting about climate change and actions that governments must take (Namugerwa 2019; Crowe 2019). East African countries are poised to bear the brunt of the early effects of climate destabilization through prolonged droughts, landslides, flooding, and the spread of disease. Namugerwa, like other youth climate activists, cited adult indifference as motivation to act: "I want to raise a gen-eration that cares about the environment . . . At least if the leaders can't make a difference, we can make a difference." Much of Namugerwa's advocacy focuses not on crafting new national or international policies but, rather, on simply upholding prior commitments, such as the Paris Agreement, which many of the world's states have failed to do (Crowe 2019).

Vic Barrett is an advocate for environmental justice and a plaintiff in *Juliana v. United States*. The Honduran American, who identifies as Black, Latinx, a member of the Afro-Indigenous Garifuna community, queer, and a first-generation American, was twelve years old when he and his mother lived through Hurricane Sandy and the resulting instability that followed. He has watched firsthand as the ocean has encroached on his family's home in Honduras due to sea-level rise. Barrett has worked to highlight the role of en-vironmental racism in exacerbating the effects on people of color of climate change and environmental instability. He observed, for example, that public housing in New York is mostly utilized by people of color and is also more likely to be constructed in a flood zone; when people are disenfranchised and marginalized, they are less able to advocate for themselves and their com-munities (Our Climate Voices 2016).

Barrett joined the Earth Guardians or the Juliana 21, a group of twenty-one youth plaintiffs in *Juliana v. United States*, to hold the US government accountable for its unwillingness to provide a stable future. The lawsuit alleges that the US government's contributions to climate change have "violated the youngest generation's constitutional rights to life, liberty, and property, as well as failed to protect essential public trust resources." *Juliana v. United States* was initially filed in 2015 and worked its way through the court system. On January 17, 2020, the Ninth Circuit Court of Appeals ruled that, while the plaintiffs had sufficient evidence of the government's role in causing harm due to climate change, the legislative and executive branches—not the judicial branch—should address the matter (Our Children's Trust, Youth v. Gov, n.d.).

The plaintiffs filed a petition for a rehearing in March 2020 with the support of amicus briefs from members of US Congress, but in February 2021 the Ninth Circuit upheld the March 2020 decision. In March 2021 the youth plaintiffs filed a motion to amend their complaint against the US government, and in May 2021 the US District Court of Oregon ordered the youth plaintiffs and the Department of Justice to determine a settlement. At the time of writing, settlement negotiations and a potential second amended complaint by the plaintiffs were in progress (Our Children's Trust, Youth v. Gov, n.d.). By directly challenging a state through the legal process, the plaintiffs in *Juliana v. United States* are attempting to hold a state formally accountable for harms done to today's youth and future generations, both through failure to take action to avert climate change and actions taken that have accelerated climate change and resulting harms.

Each of these youth climate activists and the many others around the world share the complaint that the world's leaders, states, and institutions have thus far failed to secure their future. This inaction by decision makers in positions of power has led to mass mobilization of the world's youth as they seek to safeguard a future for themselves and generations to come by compelling states to uphold their commitments and make new, bolder commitments that meet the urgency of the climate crisis.

SECURITY PROVISION FROM BELOW?
NEW PROSPECTS IN AN UNCERTAIN TIME

In contrast with the global youth climate movement, a trend of nationalist sentiment has swept through traditional **donor states** in Europe and the United States. Donor states contribute a large share of the financial resources necessary to sustain international agencies and coordination efforts, and an inward turn among these states presents an obstacle to global efforts to solve a number of human security problems. If donor states adopt isolationist or nationalist stances, issues like mass displacement and the Syrian refugee crisis, cases of famine and global hunger in general, and action to slow climate change are substantially more difficult to address.

Human security problems can be resolved through persistent, well-coordinated, bottom-up approaches. While the prospect of tackling climate change without the buy-in of key states is daunting, a critical mass of cities, industries, and advocacy networks may find ways to close gaps left by states. One such path involves coordinated leadership through cities. Oslo, Norway, has aggressively pursued sustainable urban development, restricting privately owned vehicles from the city center in 2019, divesting fossil fuels from pensions, and encouraging the use of zero-emissions electric bicycles and vehicles (Agence France-Presse 2015). Cities are projected to be home to two-thirds of the world's population by 2050, so efforts like Oslo's have the potential to wield significant pressure on world leaders and influence the course of climate change (Cho 2016).

Global coordination efforts are not limited to interstate coordination efforts, as demonstrated by Cities Climate Leadership Group (C40), a network of the world's largest cities devoted to addressing climate change. Founded in London in 2005, C40 is an initiative of eighty megacities, which include "six hundred million people and one quarter of the global economy," and a networking platform through which cities can exchange ideas and expertise (C40 Cities n.d.). C40 is one network within several united in the cause to bring cities to the forefront of the fight against climate change; the broader coalition also includes ICLEI–Local Governments for Sustainability, United Cities and Local Governments, and UN-Habitat. The coalition oversees the Compact of Mayors, founded in September 2014 by former UN secretary-general Ban Ki-moon and former New York City mayor Michael Bloomberg. The Compact of Mayors provided a platform for city leaders to take collective action to tackle climate change, including through public outreach and commitments to international agreements like the Paris Agreement, investments, support for research, and sustainable urban development. In June 2016 the Compact of Mayors merged with the Global Covenant of Mayors to form the Global Covenant of Mayors for Climate and Energy, now comprising 644 cities and nearly 7 percent of the global population (Global Covenant of Mayors for Climate and Energy, n.d.).

Whether or not such bottom-up efforts can succeed without effective state cooperation remains unclear, but it is notable that popular pressure for action has increased as many of the world's regions have begun to feel the effects of climate change. While the way forward on climate change is uncertain, if states are unable to coordinate top-down security provision then increased awareness of insecurity among communities and cities may trigger a different approach to international coordination led from below.

DISCUSSION QUESTIONS

1. Why might states' national interests positively or negatively influence their willingness to participate in global efforts to slow the effects of climate change? Which states are least likely to participate? Which states are most likely to participate?
2. What are the implications of climate change–related migration for national and global security?
3. Why is it difficult for states to cooperate to curb greenhouse gas emissions and pursue efforts to mitigate and adapt to climate change?
4. Does global coordination among cities offer advantages over the more traditional state-led approach? What are the potential disadvantages of this type of global bottom-up approach?

Chapter 12

Food Security

Learning Objectives

This chapter will enable readers to

1. discuss the sources and types of food insecurity
2. recognize the effects of chronic hunger, famine, and food-price instability on human, national, and global security
3. and compare situations of food insecurity in the current global context.

Food is essential to life. Without food, or with insufficient quantities of nutritious food, an individual loses the ability to work, learn, participate in social and political life, fend off disease, or flee natural disasters or human-made violence. When you think of hunger, do you think of a security threat? Do you think, instead, of a moral failing that so many people go without food in our world of plenty? It is indeed morally reprehensible that one in nine people in the world experiences chronic hunger and that almost half of all deaths in children under five years old are caused by hunger. But it is also a concern central to human security—and a problem that can contribute to national and global instability.

In this last chapter in the section on durable human security, we explore one of the most fundamental dimensions of human security: food security. In this chapter, we discuss the roots and effects of hunger, malnutrition, and undernutrition and dysfunctional distribution of resources. The discussion revisits human security concepts introduced in previous chapters in an effort to underscore the interdependent nature of human security issues in general, the chronic and acute nature of food insecurity in particular, and the need for international cooperation to address the causes and effects of food insecurity. We will also explore variation in state strength and hunger by examining famine in South Sudan and food deserts in the United States; both situations demonstrate that food insecurity is not a problem isolated within fragile or impoverished states.

HUNGER AS A HUMAN SECURITY THREAT

In its 1994 articulation of human security as a new concept, the United Nations Development Programme included hunger among the threats facing individuals and communities across the globe: "Human security is relevant to people everywhere, in rich nations and in poor. The threats to their security may differ—hunger and disease in poor nations and drugs and crime in rich nations—but these threats are real and growing" (United Nations Development Programme 1994, 15). Hunger presents a threat to durable human security, a chronic or acute problem that disrupts the daily lives and impedes the opportunities of individuals and whole communities when states lack the capacity or political will to address it.

In 1996, 185 states and the European Community met at the headquarters of the Food and Agriculture Organization in Rome to commit to the elimination of hunger and malnutrition. This global discussion yielded the Rome Declaration and Plan of Action and, therein, the following definition of food security: "Food security exists when all people, at all times, have physical and economic access to sufficient, safe and nutritious food to meet their dietary needs and food preferences for an active and healthy life" (World Food Summit 1996). When individuals and communities can afford food that meets their cultural, nutritional, and lifestyle needs, and the supply of that food is steady, we can reasonably assume that the situation is one of relative food security.

Food preferences are included in the World Food Summit's definition of food security not to suggest that individuals experience food insecurity when they lack access to their favorite foods like ice cream or a good steak. Instead, the use of the term *food preferences* points to entrenched and sometimes strict cultural or religious norms and dietary guidelines, like keeping kosher or eating halal. It also recognizes that individuals may adhere to nutritional guidelines linked to health conditions or allergies (like celiac disease or peanut allergy) or personal morality (as in the case of a vegetarian or vegan who opposes the consumption of animals or animal by-products for moral reasons). In each of these cases, it would be inappropriate and even unethical to ask an individual to accept food that does not meet their preferences, and the lack of availability of acceptable food makes it difficult for that individual to meet their nutritional requirements.

Definitions and Dimensions of Food Security

Food security depends on the fulfillment of four dimensions or pillars, including food access, availability, use, and stability (Food and Agriculture Organization of the United Nations 2006, 1). **Food access** refers to an individual's ability to purchase or otherwise acquire a sufficient amount of nutritious food to sustain their daily activities (Food and Agriculture Organization of the United Nations 2006; Sen 1981). If the price of food suddenly spikes or the individual loses their paid employment, access to food becomes more difficult. **Food availability** refers to the supply of food in the region (Food and Agriculture Organization of the United Nations 2006, 1). If an individual lives in a food desert (see the section on causes of food insecurity), if their state is the target of comprehensive sanctions, or if drought has reduced crop yields, food availability will decrease. **Food use**—or *food utilization*—refers to overall "nutritional well-being" achieved through the combination of a nutritious diet, "clean water, sanitation, and health care" (Food and Agriculture Organization of the United Nations 2006, 1). **Food stability** combines the factors of access and availability; it refers to an individual's access to food at all times, without sudden or cyclical disruptions, such as those that result from economic recession, climate change, natural disasters, armed conflict, or famine (Food and Agriculture Organization of the United Nations 2006, 1).

Hunger, undernutrition, and malnutrition are related but distinct challenges to food security. **Chronic hunger**, also referred to as *undernourishment*, is the long-term "inability to acquire enough food, defined as a level of food intake insufficient to meet dietary energy requirements" (Food and Agriculture Organization of the United Nations, International Fund for Agricultural Development, and World Food Programme 2015, 53). **Undernutrition** may result from "undernourishment, and/or poor absorption and/or poor biological use of nutrients consumed as a result of repeated infectious disease" and manifests as being underweight, too short, dangerously thin, or deficient in essential vitamins and minerals (Food and Agriculture Organization of the United Nations 2015, 53). **Malnutrition** is the result of taking in too few, too many, or the wrong nutrients such that the body does not receive the necessary balance of essential nutrients to maintain daily activities (Food and Agriculture Organization of the United Nations 2015, 53). Individuals and communities may experience periods of food insecurity without clearing the thresholds for hunger as a long-term condition, undernutrition, or malnutrition. In such cases, unemployment, poverty, food-price increases, displacement, or other factors may create a situation of **episodic food insecurity**, in which an individual's, family's, or community's access to food is limited or unpredictable but not long-term or chronic (Coleman-Jensen et al. 2016; United States Department of Agriculture, Economic Research Service, 2022b).

These conditions do not exist in a vacuum, of course. Drought, flooding, and displacement due to climate change can disrupt the supply or availability of an individuals' access to healthy foods in a region, especially when states lack the capacity to absorb shocks to the food supply (Parry et al. 2007). Armed conflict can limit or wipe out agricultural production and displace large portions of a population, laying the dangerous groundwork for **famine**, as in South Sudan (see the section on causes of food insecurity). A **famine** is a situation of extreme, usually deadly food insecurity resulting from severe lack of access to and availability of food. Indeed, parties to conflict may intentionally wield starvation as a weapon, withholding food and humanitarian relief from besieged civilians to force negotiations or surrender, as witnessed in the Syrian civil war (United Nations Security Council 2016b). Oppressive regimes may similarly use hunger and poverty as tools to try to crush political opposition and maintain control over the population (Lappé, Collins, and Rosset 1998, 122–46).

Economic instability, global food price increases, and poverty limit an individual's access to nutritious foods, a problem that affects low-income households in the United States (see the section on causes of food security in this chapter). Gender inequality can jeopardize a woman or young girl's nutrition if she is served last in a household that barely has enough to eat. Undernutrition and malnutrition rob individuals of the energy needed to engage in daily activities (like paid employment or schoolwork), thereby depriving them of opportunities and further decreasing their ability to maintain access to food (Sen 1999, 162).

If human security exists when individuals and communities are safe from chronic and acute threats to their well-being, freedoms, and physical security, then mitigating and preventing chronic hunger and episodic food insecurity must be central to any effort to promote overall human security. There is enough food in the world to feed everyone; the global quantity of food is not a direct cause of food insecurity (Clapp 2014; Lappé, Collins, and Rosset 1998, 8–14). Food-related threats become a human security issue when their root causes lie in flawed societal or political institutions and norms or in the complete breakdown of institutions, norms, and other protections in situations of acute insecurity. When food insecurity threatens a large portion of the population (as in famine or widespread chronic hunger), targets one community on the basis of identity (as in strategic starvation or famine), aligns with socioeconomic disparity (as in food deserts and insufficient social support), or results from climate change–related problems (like drought or flooding), then the state's institutions, norms, capacity to protect, or some combination of these are at work, and hunger becomes a human security issue.

The Link between Food Security and State and Global Security

When does food insecurity shift from a human security problem to a state or global security problem? In chapter 11 on climate change and environmental security, we highlighted the complex linkages between environmental security and state instability (Evans 2010; Jones, Mattiacci, and Braumoeller 2017; Notaras 2011). Food security plays a similar role, and environmental stability and food security are often interconnected.

Food insecurity can exacerbate broader insecurity within a state or region, as it has in Syria. Insufficient rainfall in Syria in the years prior to outbreak of the civil war led to low agricultural yields, displaced agricultural producers, migration from rural to urban areas, increased unemployment, and widespread discontentment with the Assad regime (Schwartzstein 2016). That chain of events, unfolding alongside the broader Arab Spring resistance movement, contributed to the outbreak of civil war in March 2011. Deteriorating national security further reduces human security, as has been the case with respect to food insecurity, among other forms of acute insecurity, in Syria's civil war: decreased food production, economic instability, currency depreciation, reduced government-funded social supports, and siege warfare created conditions in which food access and availability have been severely threatened, if not eliminated (Schwartzstein 2016; World Food Programme, n.d.).

Rising food prices also served as a contributing factor in Egypt's January 25 revolution in 2011, and food scarcity fueled protests and uprisings in Venezuela in 2017. As Francis Moore Lappé, Joseph Collins, and Peter Rosset argue, the myth that a population can be "too hungry to revolt" is just that—a myth; recent history offers many accounts in which individuals and communities mobilized against the state in response to food insecurity, poverty, and insufficient government efforts to protect the population from harm (1998, 122–28).

Beyond the context of armed conflict and unrest, a malnourished or undernourished population creates hefty economic costs realized in terms of poor school performance among children and adolescents and decreased productivity among working adults (Fan 2014). The potential for a vicious cycle exists in which weak institutions, high food prices, economic instability, conflict, and food insecurity contribute to one another and threaten individual lives and state stability (Hendrix and Brinkman 2013). If crises and situations of instability go unchecked, state insecurity creates ripple effects for regional and global security.

BOX 12.1. THINK ABOUT IT . . .
STAPLE FOODS IN DEMAND

In January 2013, British newspaper *The Guardian* published an article provocatively titled "CAN VEGANS STOMACH THE UNPALATABLE TRUTH ABOUT QUINOA?" (Blythman 2013). In it, the author cited the steep increase in the price of quinoa from 2006 onward, noting that the sudden demand for the Andean staple grain among health-conscious eaters in the Global North placed it out of reach for the Peruvians and Bolivians who have long cultivated and relied on it.

Three years later, in May 2016, the *Economist* ran another story on the effects of quinoa demand. This piece noted that quinoa consumption in Peru fell more gradually than the grain's price rose and that the average household spent only 0.5 percent of its budget on quinoa, contradicting the earlier claim that sudden price shocks caused by skyrocketing demand threatened the food security of lower-income households in the areas where quinoa is grown. The article in the *Economist* highlighted the link between higher quinoa prices and higher incomes for quinoa growers (*Economist* 2016). A study by several economists confirms this reassurance, finding that the increased price of quinoa has improved the economic well-being of quinoa-producing households and, to a lesser but still notable extent, the general welfare of the surrounding population where quinoa is grown (Bellemare, Fajardo-Gonzalez, and Gitter 2018).

Still, the overall effects of increased demand for a traditional staple food are complex. Concerns range from environmental degradation (LeVaux 2013) and the threat of falling prices (*Economist* 2016) resulting from scaled-up production of quinoa in the Andes and new regions to broader societal outcomes—including wages for agricultural workers, nutritional changes, and resource distribution, among other factors—linked to shifting quinoa prices (Bellemare, Fajardo-Gonzalez, and Gitter 2018).

Consider the following questions related to changing dietary fads and North-South economic relations:

1. How does demand for a food or product in the Global North affect the livelihoods and well-being of communities in the Global South? Can you think of other notable examples of fad foods or products, or is the case of quinoa exceptional?

2. Should states have an obligation to shield their agricultural producers from price shocks? What would be the effects of such an effort?
3. Should states have an obligation to shield their populations from food-price shocks? What would be the effects of such an effort?
4. Europe is currently the largest importer of quinoa. Noting that European producers have started to cultivate quinoa, which could increase supply and decrease the global price of the grain, should states or international organizations regulate, limit, or encourage efforts to cultivate traditional crops outside of their regions of origin?
5. How will the effects of climate change affect the supply and demand of staple crops and, accordingly, global food prices?
6. Take a look through your kitchen cabinets or pantry. Where does your food come from? Has it crossed borders and/or oceans or traveled across your own state? Or is it locally grown? What do you take into consideration when purchasing your food, and what does this suggest about your own degree of food security as an individual?

FOOD INSECURITY: CAUSES AND EXAMPLES

Food insecurity can threaten individuals and communities anywhere. Recall the four dimensions of food security: availability, access, utilization, and stability. To enjoy food security an individual must have reliable, regular access to nutritious and appropriate foods at a reasonably predictable and affordable price. Food scarcity, which affects not only availability but also access and stability, is usually not the result of insufficient quantities of food in a region; rather, it is often an issue of access limited by government policies, armed actors' strategies, entrenched social inequalities, or some combination of these factors. Amartya Sen observes that famines do not occur in wealthy, developed countries not because there is an absence of poverty but because there are safety nets in place to prevent widespread starvation and provide for basic necessities (Sen 1981, 7).

Robert Paarlberg cites the Irish Potato Famine (1845–1849), the Holodomor famine in Ukraine during the wider Soviet famine (1932–1933), and famine in China's Great Leap Forward (1959–1961) as examples of widespread, deadly, and *human-made* situations of acute hunger in nondemocratic states. Paarlberg notes that democratic governance is related to better food security because individuals in nondemocracies "lack the opportunity to take organized political action" and "serious food policy errors are often made"

(Paarlberg 2010, 3). Famines are neither natural occurrences nor accidents; they result from failed policies or the imposition of deliberate harm.

The effects of environmental degradation and climate change compound the effects of government policies: drought, desertification, flooding, deforestation, and changing weather patterns are already disrupting the stability of food sources around the world and, as chapter 11 suggests, these problems will only worsen if states fail to take action on climate change (Food and Agriculture Organization of the United Nations 2016; Lappé, Collins, and Rosset 1998, 41–57). When states lack the capacity or political will to compensate for agricultural instability and other climate-related effects on food sources, food security is jeopardized.

It is also important to note that food insecurity is not a direct result of overpopulation; the challenge of matching food production with global population growth is more complicated than economist Thomas Robert Malthus originally postulated in 1798. In *An Essay on the Principle of Population,* Malthus made the argument that food production cannot keep pace with world population growth; the central premise of his argument holds that, since food production requires "fixed assets such as land that can only be expanded slowly" but the human population grows exponentially with each generation (Paarlberg 2010, 8), widespread hunger and suffering are inevitable. Technological innovation has contradicted Malthus's argument and overall world food production has, to date, kept pace with population growth. Still, the links between overpopulation, the Earth's capacity to feed billions more humans, and food insecurity require continued study and should remain the focus of careful policy making. To continue to ensure that food production can support the nutritional needs of all people, state and global policies must address the social and economic inequalities related to poverty, high fertility rates, and distribution of resources (Lappé, Collins, and Rosset 1998, 40; Sen 1999, 205–6) and alter demand for resource-intensive foods like livestock (Smith 2014). State- and global-level policy makers and opinion shapers have considerable work to do when it comes to protecting global food security over the long term.

For hunger to pose a human *security* threat, it must be the result of shortcomings in the state's institutions, norms, or ability to protect the population. As with other threats to human security, food insecurity, even when widespread, will not threaten *everyone* in an affected region or state. Amartya Sen's observation on famines is illustrative here: "While famines involve fairly widespread acute starvation, there is no reason to think that it will affect all groups in the famine-affected nation. Indeed, it is by no means clear that there has ever occurred a famine in which all groups in a country have suffered from starvation, since different groups typically do have very different commanding powers over food, and an overall shortage brings out the contrasting powers in stark clarity" (Sen 1981, 43). The causes of food insecurity are all rooted, at least to some degree, in politics and other forms of insecurity. As a result, food insecurity will threaten some individuals and communities more than others. The question is not whether there is enough food in the world to feed everyone. Instead, we must consider why individuals are unable to access the basic nutrients they need to survive and thrive and who is responsible for protecting the right to food (Jurkovich 2020a). Improving food security and reducing or eliminating world hunger on a global scale requires a federalist or cosmopolitan security perspective among states' decision makers.

To explore the causes of food insecurity and the broad range of contexts in which hunger threatens well-being, we turn briefly to two examples: food insecurity in the United States and famine in South Sudan.

Food Insecurity in the United States

A report by the United States Department of Agriculture's (USDA) Economic Research Service estimates that, in 2015, 12.7 percent of households in the United States (15.8 million households, comprising 42.2 million people) "were food insecure at some time during the year" (Coleman-Jensen et al. 2016, 6). That rate decreased over the next few years, and in 2019 an estimated 10.5 percent of US households experienced food insecurity at some point during the year (US Department of Agriculture 2021b). These households did not necessarily experience food insecurity throughout the entire year, and food insecurity in the United States is frequently temporary or episodic rather than chronic. Of the households that experienced food insecurity, a portion "were food insecure to the extent that eating patterns of one or more household members were disrupted and their food intake reduced, at least some time during the year, because they could not afford enough food" (Coleman-Jensen et al. 2016, 6). The number of food insecure households in the United States peaked at 17.85 million households in 2011 at the height of the economic recession (Coleman-Jensen et al. 2016, 7; US Department of Agriculture 2021b). While these numbers are staggering for a wealthy country known for its excesses, the actual scale of food insecurity is likely much higher, since the USDA Economic Research Service's survey omits homeless families and individuals (Coleman-Jensen et al. 2016, 11).

As the USDA Economic Research Service's Food Access Research Atlas illustrates, food access varies across and within regions of the United States, with significant numbers of low-income individuals without access to supermarkets concentrated around cities (United States Department of Agriculture, Economic Research Service, 2022a). **Food deserts**—areas with a high population of low-income households and lack of access to available, affordable, and nutritious food sources within a set distance (usually half a mile to one mile in urban areas and ten to twenty miles in rural regions)—contribute to food insecurity, affecting both the access and the availability dimensions of food security. Food access in the United States can be measured using proximity to supermarkets, farmers' markets, or other healthy food sources, as well as family income, average neighborhood income, family vehicle access, and accessibility of public transportation (United States Department of Agriculture, Economic Research Service, 2021a). These factors can tell us about the inequality of food security in the United States, but they are also part of the bigger picture of inequality and human insecurity in a diverse nation.

Family income, availability of supermarkets, vehicle possession, and availability of public transportation are linked to other forms of social and economic inequality: food security in the United States is more common for "households with incomes near or below the federal poverty line, households with children headed by single women or single men, women and men living alone, and Black- and Hispanic-headed households" (Coleman-Jensen et al. 2016, vi). Income inequality continues to rise in the United States, and as it does, it leaves more individuals and households to survive at or below the federal poverty line, placing them at risk for food insecurity, among other hardships (Posey 2016; United States Census Bureau 2021). Income inequality, for its part, is compounded by flaws in US social norms—especially racial inequality and gender inequality (Kochhar and Fry 2014; Patten 2016)—that place individuals and communities at greater risk of insecurity because of institutionalized factors that limit their opportunities and threaten their personal safety. Although famine is rare in a state with social safety nets, like the United States, food insecurity is exacerbated when these social-support resources are unavailable, underfunded, or unattainable. Low-income individuals and families in the United States may be eligible for support through the Supplemental Nutrition Assistance Program (SNAP), an aid initiative run by the USDA's Food and Nutrition Service, if they meet the program's requirements. SNAP remains a subject of political debate within the United States, and it has come into more intense focus when policy makers have sought to reduce government spending through the budgetary process.

The COVID-19 pandemic further exacerbated household food insecurity in the United States. In April 2020, the unemployment rate in the United States reached its highest rate since the country started recording unemployment data in 1948—14.8 percent. Over a year later, in July 2021, the unemployment rate was much lower but still remained elevated, at 5.4 percent (Falk et al. 2021). The pandemic affected economic sectors differently, but temporary layoffs or furloughs and permanent job terminations reached a peak in April 2020 and gradually declined but remained elevated through 2020 and 2021, creating widespread economic insecurity (United States Bureau of Labor

Statistics 2021). Through the first year of the COVID-19 pandemic, workers in the United States fell into three categories: workers who lost their jobs, essential workers who were required to continue working in person and faced heightened health risks, and workers who were able to do their jobs remotely. Because Black workers made up a disproportionate share of essential workers and those whose jobs were cut, the pandemic exacerbated racial disparities in health, economic, and food security (Gould and Wilson 2020).

Food insecurity accompanies job loss; as households lost income, individuals and families became food insecure and began to rely on nutritional-assistance benefits and food pantries run by local charitable organizations. Additionally, supply-chain interruptions in the early weeks of the pandemic led to panic buying among those with the financial means to hoard food and essential goods like toilet paper and left individuals and households reliant on nutritional-assistance benefits with empty grocery carts (Preston 2020; Stunson 2020).

Food security, then, relates to questions of societal cohesion, public views of the state's role in providing for the well-being and economic stability of its population, and the prioritization of domestic-aid initiatives in times of economic hardship and prosperity.

Famine in South Sudan

In February 2017 the United Nations declared a famine in South Sudan and warned that one hundred thousand people faced starvation, with an additional one to five million in urgent need of food assistance (BBC News 2017; Beaubien 2017). The declaration of famine seldom comes lightly; the UN had not declared one since 2011. The Famine Early Warning Systems Network (FEWS NET) classified all regions of South Sudan in the "stressed" through "famine" levels of food insecurity for the period spanning June to September 2017, citing the impact of conflict-related displacement and active armed conflict on agricultural production, aid delivery, and economic stability (Famine Early Warning Systems Network 2017). An influx of humanitarian aid alleviated some of the direst circumstances but, in 2020 Oxfam International reported that roughly half of the population of South Sudan still faced extreme hunger (Oxfam International 2020). FEWS NET similarly observed that the food insecurity emergency in South Sudan remained one of the worst in the world and that it would likely require urgent humanitarian assistance, especially in Jonglei, Warrap, Northern Bahr el Ghazal, Upper Nile, Lakes, and Unity (Famine Early Warning Systems Network, n.d.). The severe food insecurity in South Sudan demonstrates the link between armed conflict—an acute human security threat—and food security—a durable human security issue. While we classify food security as a durable human security concern, it is important to recognize the cyclical links between durable and acute human security threats.

South Sudan became an independent state on July 9, 2011. Since its independence, the government has faced protracted conflict with armed groups across much of the state, having separated from Sudan after the Second Sudanese Civil War and struggled to rebuild infrastructure, develop economically, and improve human security following more than two decades of fighting. In December 2013, political struggles between President Salva Kiir and Riek Machar, his former deputy, led to a civil war within the new state. The South Sudanese Civil War has created high levels of food insecurity by decreasing agricultural productivity, limiting humanitarian organizations' access to vulnerable populations, disrupting trade throughout the state, and affecting individuals' ability to find paid employment to maintain household economic stability (and, thus, food security).

Armed conflict in general is a major driver of food insecurity because it creates physical insecurity that hampers food production (by threatening farmers and other food producers), destroys or renders inaccessible land that would have otherwise been used for agriculture, and displaces communities. Active hostilities also jeopardize aid delivery by shutting down routes to vulnerable populations. The presence of UN peacekeepers (through the United Nations Mission in South Sudan, or UNMISS) and humanitarian agencies likely prevented more severe food insecurity at the onset of famine, but humanitarian agencies are unable to operate in armed conflict zones when the security of their staff members is threatened. Such has been the case in South Sudan. US-based news outlet National Public Radio reported that in February 2017, when the UN declared a famine in two of the state's regions, a US humanitarian organization called Samaritan's Purse evacuated its staff amid active fighting; shortly thereafter, its remaining contingent of South Sudanese staff members was abducted (Beaubien 2017). Hostile conditions make aid delivery difficult if not impossible and increase the severity of food insecurity.

Other durable human security threats also exacerbate food insecurity. The effects of climate change and environmental instability contribute to food insecurity in entire regions as droughts and flooding render land nonarable or destroy crops. In South Sudan, extreme flooding during the rainy season devastated crops in 2019 and 2020, and the United Nations Office for the Coordination of Humanitarian Affairs forecast similarly damaging floods in its 2021 Humanitarian Response Plan (UN Office for the Coordination of Humanitarian Affairs 2021; UN News 2021b). Health crises also compound food insecurity: in 2020 and 2021 the COVID-19 pandemic complicated aid delivery to South Sudan, sapped the already limited resources of South Sudan's healthcare system, and contributed to household and national economic insecurity (UN News 2021b).

As the examples of food insecurity in the United States and South Sudan demonstrate, this particular human security threat arises in peacetime as well as in armed conflict, and both acute and durable human security issues exacerbate it. Food insecurity is not limited to the Global South; it can strike any community when the political context and institutions create a situation of limited access to enough nutritious food.

Who, then, bears the responsibility of providing for food security when it is threatened? We now turn to this question.

PROTECTION AGAINST HUNGER

The responsibility to protect individuals and communities from chronic hunger or acute food insecurity is shared, like many durable human security initiatives, among local actors, states, and the international community. States have varying degrees of social safety nets and food-assistance programs, depending on the type of government, capacity for investment in social programs, and domestic and international political priorities. State-level initiatives can go a long way toward causing chronic hunger and food insecurity but also toward ameliorating these threats if policy makers are willing to prioritize them (Bailey 2014). Since widespread, chronic food insecurity is itself an indicator of underdevelopment, states may not have the resources needed to fix the root causes of hunger.

Three agencies within the UN system are tasked with responding to hunger and food insecurity: the **Food and Agriculture Organization (FAO)**, the **World Food Programme (WFP)**, and the **International Fund for Agricultural Development (IFAD)**. The FAO was created in October 1945. Its primary functions are to serve as a discussion forum through which states can develop policy responses to hunger and disseminate technical information to improve food security in developing states. The WFP was founded in 1961 as the United Nations' food-assistance agency. While the FAO helps states work through policy options and negotiations to address food insecurity, the WFP provides humanitarian assistance directly to regions in need. The WFP's mission is to offer immediate aid and expertise with the long-term objective of a food secure world. IFAD, a financial institution focused on assisting the rural poor in developing states, formed in 1977. Its central objectives are to improve well-being and food security and reduce poverty in developing states through loans and grants to increase access to agricultural technology and related skills. The FAO, WFP, and IFAD are all headquartered in Rome, Italy.

As Jennifer Clapp and Marc Cohen observe, the UN's food agencies "have more balanced North-South representation on their governing bodies and are significant players in norm setting, data collection, technical assistance, and emergency aid" (Clapp and Cohen 2009, 6).

In addition to the UN agencies, the Bretton Woods Institutions (the World Bank and International Monetary Fund), the Group of Seven, and the Organisation for Economic Co-operation and Development have traditionally provided funding in accordance with the policy priorities and interests of donor states in the Global North, and this includes food assistance and loans or grants (Clapp and Cohen 2009, 6). States in the Global North no longer hold a monopoly on food assistance outside of the UN framework, however; China has emerged as an influential donor state since the start of its Go Global foreign policy strategy in 2005 (Zhang 2016).

Realization of global goals focused on eradicating hunger, as articulated by Millennium Development Goal 1 (eradicate extreme poverty and hunger) and Sustainable Development Goal 2 (end hunger, achieve food security and improved nutrition, and promote sustainable agriculture) requires the participation of security actors throughout the international community. It also requires deliberate, well-coordinated policies that empower communities in need, as well as accurate measurements of the scope of food insecurity. The 2015 Millennium Development Goals Report (the MDGs concluded in 2015) calculates that the "proportion of undernourished people in the developing regions has fallen by almost half since 1990, from 23.3 percent in 1900–1992 to 12.9 percent in 2014–2016" in spite of challenges posed by food-price instability, economic recession, armed conflict, political instability, and climate change–related threats (United Nations 2015b, 4, 20). This represents progress toward achieving overall food security. Still, hundreds of millions of people around the world continue to suffer from extreme food insecurity, which is why the SDGs were designed to "pick up where the MDGs left off" (United Nations 2015b, 23). SDG 2 is more comprehensive in nature than MDG 1, with targets focused on ending hunger for all people, ending malnutrition, doubling agricultural productivity, improving sustainability and resilience in agriculture, and easing trade restrictions, among other targets, to be reached by 2030 (United Nations, n.d.).

One problem with the increased level of detail in SDG 2, according to Michelle Jurkovich (2016), is that the international community does not yet have a fully reliable way to measure progress toward ending food insecurity. One reason why there is no international consensus on an appropriate way to measure food security outcomes is that there is some ambiguity about what, exactly, "hunger" is. Responding effectively to food insecurity has been a challenge for state, nonstate, and international security providers, and if we return to the three boxes policy model, we can see where difficulties arise when policy makers or security providers attempt to reach a consensus on the perception of the problem (Box 1), especially if they have competing views on responsibility to provide for security basic needs.

Recall the start of this chapter—specifically, the discussion about malnutrition, chronic hunger, and undernutrition. Should security providers focus on one type of food insecurity over the others, on all three, or only on extreme food insecurity like what we see in famines? What about food-price instability and its effects on episodic food insecurity among the poor and working classes in developed states? The responses to these questions will be conditioned by decision makers' perspectives on security provision (nativist, statist, federalist, or cosmopolitan). To protect individuals and communities from food insecurity, or any form of insecurity, decision makers and security providers must understand the nature and scope of the threat. If they cannot get past Box 1 of the three boxes, then they will be unable to reach consensus on policy options (Box 2) or the ideal outcome (Box 3).

Protection against hunger, then, requires continued collaboration not only among local, state-level, and global actors but also among those who study food security and those who implement programs to provide for it. An important message to take away from this chapter is that, although hunger is a problem in states that have fewer resources, it is not a human security threat limited to any particular region of the world. To understand the complex nature of food insecurity and work toward a solution to it, we must be willing to look at its diverse causes. Food insecurity has the potential to be globally devastating in scope; it also has the potential to be a security problem of the past if the world harnesses the right mix of technology, aid, and adjusted habits.

DISCUSSION QUESTIONS

1. Is there a fundamental difference between chronic hunger and famine? Should the policy responses differ?
2. How might local civil society actors assist with improvements to food security? What can state-level actors do? How can international organizations best serve the goal of eliminating hunger?
3. Do populations in wealthy, developed states have an obligation to change their dietary habits to maximize the efficiency of food production? Why or why not?
4. If given the task, how would you measure progress toward achieving complete global food security?
5. How might the different security perspectives shape a state's response to global hunger?

Section IV

CONCLUSIONS

Chapter 13

Human Security: An Essential Approach to Twenty-First Century Security Problems

Learning Objectives

This chapter will enable readers to

1. recognize the political and institutional requirements of human security
2. become familiar with the status of human security efforts within the UN system
3. and think critically about the importance of the human security approach in the current era.

When policy makers, practitioners, and scholars talk about security, what do they mean? Whose security matters, and how do we know what security looks like? Who or what is responsible for ensuring security? The human security approach demands a shift in thinking about these questions. In short, it requires scholars, policy makers, and security providers to embrace the individual as the subject of security theory, policy, and practice.

As we have demonstrated throughout the book, the human security approach permits a more comprehensive view of security and thus it is essential in addressing the complex security challenges that have arisen and are likely to arise in the twenty-first century. The broad view of human security accepts the importance of "protection from sudden and hurtful disruptions in the pattern of our daily lives" and "safety from the constant threats of hunger, disease, crime, and repression" (United Nations Development Programme 1994, 3)—or what we refer to as *human security in acute conflict* and *durable human security*.

Throughout the book we have taken up the question of responsibility for security provision, and in each of the prior chapters we have discussed the need to consider security challenges using the human, state, and global security approaches to ensure comprehensive policy responses, assistance efforts, and academic research. Human security does not replace the state or global security approaches; instead, human security offers a third approach to security provision that recenters analysis, policy, and practice at the level of the individual while also laying the groundwork for the kind of sustainable peace and stability that has the potential to improve state and global security. To the extent that the human security approach fills in gaps left in analysis and implementation of security policy, this third approach is not only useful but also essential to meeting the security challenges of the twenty-first century.

To round out the discussion of human security and its interaction with traditional security approaches, this chapter's first section synthesizes the requirements for establishing effective human security. The book's first chapter recalled the UNDP's 1994 Human Development Report and its first articulation of the term *human security*; in an effort to conclude our analysis, the second section of this chapter briefly assesses the current status of the human security approach at the United Nations. The third section explores the need for multiple security approaches and perspectives when dealing with complex threats facing security providers, individuals, states, and the global community in the twenty-first century, including transnational terrorism and violent extremism. The final section offers conclusions related to human security's importance as an approach to security theory, policy, and practice in a rapidly shifting global political landscape.

REQUIREMENTS OF HUMAN SECURITY

If we accept the notion that human security exists when individuals and their communities are free from chronic, long-term threats to their well-being and acute, sudden threats to their physical safety, then security provision requires protection against the effects of weapons and armed conflict as well as protection against systemic adversity and inequality and human rights violations. Human security is cyclical: positive advances in protection and empowerment in postconflict reconstruction spill over into peacetime, strengthening institutions and bolstering positive norms; erosion of human security in peacetime contributes to the conditions that create armed conflict. Acknowledging the cycle of security, we turn to a question: *What must happen in order to achieve overall human security both in conflict and postconflict settings and in the long term?* In this section we revisit the factors that contribute to high levels of human security.

In section I, we explored the historical and political conditions that led to the emergence of the human security approach, with a particular focus on the United Nations. Three changes in the international community laid the groundwork for a new approach to security provision: (1) the changing nature of war and the shift toward intrastate conflicts, (2) the UN's increased influence after the end of the Cold War and its rigid bipolar international political structure, and (3) a reaffirmation of the importance of human rights through renewed advocacy and enforcement. To observe that a new approach to human security emerged in the 1990s is not to imply that states and other security providers—or the scholars who study them—have prioritized this approach above traditional state security or even global security; as we discussed in chapter 1, states operate with their national interests at top of mind and pursue policies or actions that promote human security as a result of mixed motivations (see table 1.3). Because human security and state security are often synchronous, however, it is possible for states to pursue their security while also accounting for the human security of their citizens and foreign populations.

Achieving human security requires stability, good governance, and effective collaboration among security providers. These requirements place human security in line with the state and global security approaches in some respects and in conflict with them in others. For security providers to promote the norms and values central to human security—including the protections and freedoms included in the notions of freedom from fear and freedom from want—states and the international system must be stable. Stability is a key foundation for the institutions and norms required to pursue human security. This basic structural precursor places the human security approach neatly in line with the state and global security approaches when the state's norms and institutions align with the core tenets of human security and value the protection and empowerment of the individual.

Nevertheless, strong and stable states can—and do—still tolerate or perpetrate human rights violations, systemic discrimination and inequality, and other forms of insecurity that affect individuals and their communities without necessarily upsetting the state's ability to govern and its monopoly on the use of force. In these cases, human security and state security are directly at odds, and strengthening the state will not improve human security without significant changes in the state's governing institutions and norms.

Protection from the insecurity that accompanies acute conflict requires a stable state and an absence of widespread violence. As the chapters in section II explore, the breakdown in governance that both leads to and stems from intrastate conflict creates high levels of human insecurity. Armed conflict, mass displacement, widespread human rights violations, and protracted postconflict instability degrade not only human security but also state security—and regional or global stability if the conflict involves numerous or highly influential international actors. Because a breakdown in the state's capacity and willingness to provide a safe, secure, and equitable environment leads to acute insecurity, efforts to rebuild and restore justice after armed conflict must work to address the roots of conflict through inclusive processes that aim to promote sustainable peace for all, not just bring active hostilities to an end.

Durable human security is realized when societal norms and governance institutions prioritize the protection of human rights, human development, and individual well-being and opportunities to thrive. In contrast, flawed norms and institutions foster systemic inequality, discrimination, societal division, and deprivation; they create a lack of durable human security characterized by chronic threats to well-being. The chapters in section III discuss the linkages between durable human security issues such as economic security, food security, environmental protection, gender equality, and health security and overall state and global security and stability: by laying the foundation for empowered, self-sufficient, healthy, and engaged citizens, human security practice has the potential to support overall state and global stability. The key prerequisite for this synchronous, positive interaction is that the state must perceive its own security and stability as tied to the well-being of its people; the historical record and contemporary crises tell us that state leaders do not uniformly hold this perception.

As we noted at the outset of this chapter, the human security approach requires a shift in thinking about who is at the center of security and what security looks like; while some states, NGOs, the UN, and other security providers are working to promote a human security norm, we do not yet live in a world characterized by human security for all. How do we work toward improving human security for all? In a word, *collaboration*. Chapter 3 enumerates a list of security providers, and each of the chapters in sections II and III similarly convey the importance of a range of state and nonstate actors working to promote human security. When security providers communicate, share resources and expertise, and—most crucially—ensure the inclusion of local stakeholders, efforts to protect the safety and well-being of individuals and their communities are more successful. When efforts to provide security are out of sync with the security perspectives (nativist, statist, federalist, or cosmopolitan) of the populations toward which human security policy is directed, they are less likely to succeed in creating positive change.

As the next section discusses, human security cannot be seen as a one-dimensional solution that simply evokes states' responsibility to intervene in situations of armed violence in other states. Human security is not just a problem that exists "somewhere else." Rather, human security is a practice that practitioners, policy makers, and scholars can employ to leverage diverse insights and experiences in order to address the most pressing and complex problems arising in the twenty-first century.

THE STATUS OF HUMAN SECURITY

Where does human security stand two-plus decades into the twenty-first century? As chapter 2 discusses, the concept of human security came about amid renewed international optimism and hope for collaboration among states and nonstate actors to promote human rights and development. After September 2001, shifting foreign policy priorities of the United States (a veto-wielding permanent Security Council member, key UN donor, and influential state) and its allies threatened to sideline the human security approach in favor of more traditional security efforts to respond to the threat of transnational terrorism. The UN-authorized intervention in Libya (addressed in chapter 5) provided another blow to human security as critics viewed the operation's transition from civilian protection to use of force to topple a norm-violating regime, stoking concerns that civilian protection serves simply as a guise for intervention in states' domestic affairs. In a world marked by challenges to global collaboration, emerging threats to security at all levels, persistent inequality within and between states, and disparate views on the responsibility for security provision, human security practice faces challenges. Still, if we look at the work undertaken by the UN and its member states as well as global civil society, it is clear that the sun has not set on human security.

UN General Assembly Resolution 66/290 (referenced in chapters 3 and 5), primarily in its emphasis on the differences between human security as a general approach and the doctrine of Responsibility to Protect, signals an attempt by UN agencies to respond to the challenges facing human security providers in a world still characterized by traditional approaches to security. Rather than serving as an extension of powerful states' political interests, human security is, to the UN General Assembly, "an approach to assist Member States in identifying and addressing widespread and cross-cutting challenges to the survival, livelihood, and dignity of their people" (United Nations General Assembly 2012, 1). The key to consensus on human security is the idea of cross-cutting threats—the notion that states cannot respond effectively to novel, transnational challenges to their own security and that of their populations without accounting for the factors that improve individual well-being and physical security.

Efforts to institutionalize the human security approach throughout relevant UN agencies continue. In 2014, twenty years after the UNDP's articulation of the term *human security* in its annual Human Development Report, the UN Human Security Unit (HSU) released a strategic plan to advance human security initiatives at the UN with new clarity (United Nations Human Security Unit 2014). Building on the 2005 World Summit Outcome document and General Assembly Resolution 66/290, the strategic plan articulates the twin goals of mainstreaming human security in UN activities and extending "global awareness of human security and the usage of the human security approach" (United Nations General Assembly 2012, 13).

A year later, the HSU released its Framework for Cooperation to ensure UN system-wide application of human security principles. The framework notes that the human security approach is "people-centred, comprehensive, context-specific, and prevention-oriented" and that its application is "both timely and essential in supporting the United Nations system to further integrate and enhance its efforts to improve people's aspirations for greater peace, development and a life lived in dignity" (United Nations Human Security Unit 2015, 2, 12). In essence, this suggests a better understanding of the human security approach, its purpose, and the benefits of its application in security policy and practice is vital. We agree. Human security as a third approach to security studies and practice can conflict with traditional security priorities, but it also complements and strengthens efforts to improve state and global stability.

Progress toward the Sustainable Development Goals by 2030 and the response to global challenges like mass displacement and climate change will be the bellwethers of the success of the human security approach in the twenty-first century. In the wake of the 2008 global financial crisis and in the midst of persistent threats from transnational terrorist actors and resurgent nativist and ethnonationalist tendencies around the globe, the federalist and cosmopolitan perspectives on security face skepticism in many influential constituencies concerned by the effects of globalization and increased interdependence on their communities. When the populations of donor states fail to see the value in promoting global human security and instead pursue policies and actions motivated by local or national interest (self-interest, as discussed in chapter 1), the UN-centered human security approach is weakened. The United Kingdom's Brexit vote and the US presidential and congressional elections of 2016 pointed to a rejection of cosmopolitanism and global federalism by slim majorities of voters in both countries. States' varying degrees of willingness to cooperate with one another and heed the World Health Organization's guidance to contain and mitigate the COVID-19 pandemic similarly pointed to a trend of increasing self-interest and decreased influence of both the cosmopolitan and global federalist perspectives. Whether this is a brief moment in time or a trend toward isolationism and nationalism remains to be seen, but global cooperation is essential in the effort to realize human security for all.

Furthermore, it is imperative that discussions of human security include historically underrepresented voices and perspectives, especially those from the Global South and global civil society. Human security practiced from the bottom up, beginning with local security provision and influencing governance at higher levels, ensures that efforts to enhance safety and well-being are in line with the realities and perspectives of the population in need of assistance. General Assembly Resolution 66/290 signals awareness of the need to take Global South states' concerns into account, and the drafting process for the Sustainable Development Goals showed similar promise of inclusion. But UN agencies must take care to ensure that human security efforts empower rather than subdue, subordinate, or silence security beneficiaries.

For the UN to institutionalize the human security approach and ensure its meaningful implementation by member states, it must continue to highlight the value and strategic benefits of people-centered security policies and initiatives. We focus on the UN here because of its position at the center of human security discourse from the mid-1990s onward and its function as an institution that fosters collaboration among states and between states and nonstate actors. The same imperatives apply to other security providers seeking to promote and implement human security. With this in mind, we turn to two applications of human security to explore the opportunities and challenges facing its effective implementation.

HUMAN SECURITY AND COMPLEX QUESTIONS

We consider violent extremism and transitional justice in this section to explore both the opportunities and the challenges of utilizing human security as a practice in the twenty-first century. By focusing on these two concerns in this final chapter, we do not intend to send the message that they are the only two wicked problems confronting security scholars and practitioners in the twenty-first century. At the time of writing, the world is still grappling with the COVID-19 pandemic, issues of systemic racial, ethnic, and gender discrimination and injustice, and ongoing armed conflicts in nearly every region of the world. Russia's invasion of Ukraine has revived Cold War–era tensions and raised the specter of nuclear war—or, at the very least, a dramatic escalation of interstate war and global instability. But the world's response to Russia's invasion—including costly multilateral sanctions, private sector divestment from Russia, transfer of weapons from NATO states to Ukraine—has also demonstrated the capacity for international cooperation. There are myriad complex questions facing the world and its security providers in the current era; applying the human security principles we have explored throughout the book to questions of violent extremism and transitional justice offers a window into the utility of the human security approach.

Violent Extremism: Navigating Conflicting Approaches

Terrorism is a way for nonstate actors, generally the weaker party in any conflict with a state, to signal their commitment to an issue. Terrorist actors use violence to persuade their adversaries, rivals, and potential sympathizers (whether foreign or domestic state governments or populations) of their willingness and ability to create harm and impose costs in pursuit of a goal (Kydd and Walter 2006, 50). Terrorism is a manifestation of **violent extremism**—or the use of violence driven by ideas and ideologies that diverge from what is considered normal in society. Extremist views are linked to political, social, or religious ideology and are usually equated with fanaticism.

The use of random violence spreads fear and has the potential to generate instability—especially, but not solely, in fragile or postconflict states where governance institutions have insufficient capacity to provide security. Individual civilians, people uninvolved in any decision-making capacity related to the conflict of interest between violent extremists and their state targets, bear the brunt of the costly message sent through violent acts. Violent extremism constitutes a human security issue because of its role in violating the principle of freedom from fear of violence and creating physical harm to individuals. Further, acts of terrorism and the influence of extremist ideologies threaten to erode the rule of law in society, dimming the prospect of durable human security.

As is so often the case when discussing human security matters, the arrows also point in the other direction: a lack of human security contributes to the conditions that make individuals and communities more vulnerable to radicalization into extremist ideologies. When individuals are marginalized in society, when they directly experience or perceive harm by the state to themselves or their identity or kinship group, or when they experience deprivation of the resources and opportunities that would allow them to survive and thrive, they are more easily compelled by extremist narratives about the state, a foreign state, or the global order as a threat (Stephen 2016). The threat of domestic and transnational terrorism in the twenty-first century is a crosscutting challenge that has the potential to affect human security as well as state security and global stability.

The ways in which security providers respond to violent extremism at home or abroad can further erode or bolster security. States' efforts to counter radicalization into extremist ideologies and groups can marginalize and harm innocent individuals in the effort to preserve national security. To take one example, critics of European states' counter-radicalization programs in schools highlight the human security threats inherent in charging educators with the task of identifying students who may be vulnerable to radicalization and referring them to security or police organizations (Adebayo 2021). The **response to transnational terrorism**—or the operations of a terrorist group that involve activities or presence in more than one state—requires some degree of international coordination to address a complex threat. For instance, terrorist organizations do not legally hold territory, so how should a state respond to a terrorist attack without violating the sovereignty of the state in which the terrorist group operates? The answer to this question will vary based on the relationship between the two states, the involvement of the UN and other collective-security organizations, and the nature and magnitude of the threat. Any form of violent extremism presents a threat to both human and state security, but policy responses often pursue the latter at the expense of the former.

When we consider the policy responses to terrorist attacks or efforts to prevent future terrorist operations, these generally derive from a state security approach and the focus is less on the protection of human security than on preservation of the state's territory and institutions. Attacks may be met with policy concessions (when the state targeted by violent extremists engages in some form of compromise with the group), defensive efforts by the state to thwart future attacks (like increasing airport security or screening visitors to popular tourist sites), offensive use of force by the state to punish the group or prevent future attacks (like using drone strikes to target terror cells or engaging in military operations to take back territory held by the group), or some combination thereof.

When decision makers weigh options for combatting violent extremism from a state security approach or even a global security approach, they may not consider long-term efforts to strengthen human security, opting instead for short-term responses to prevent or respond to immediate threats and long-term efforts to improve the state's capacity. For example, a key focus of the UN Counter-Terrorism Implementation Task Force is state capacity: the UN's Global Counter-Terrorism Strategy emphasizes the need to safeguard civil aviation and ports, strengthen efforts to combat money laundering (a source of funding for terrorist activities), and secure nuclear and chemical materials to prevent access by nefarious actors (United Nations Office of Counter-Terrorism n.d.).

There is an inherent but often-obscured connection between state capacity and human security: states that do have sufficient capacity to anticipate and respond to terrorist threats may also engage in actions that undermine human security and violate human rights, including the use of torture, detention without due process, repression of civil society groups and journalists, and use of military force (which has the potential to cause civilian casualties) (Office of the United Nations High Commissioner for Human Rights 2008b). Precisely because the potential responses to the threat of terrorism conflict with the human security approach, this issue provides a useful lens on the approach's opportunities and challenges. The state security-focused response to the threat of violent extremism—whether that threat arises from domestic extremist ideologies or transnational terrorist organizations—places the state's ability to govern, guard its borders, and secure its assets at the highest priority level.

The human security approach stands to offer a comprehensive response to violent extremism and the threat of terrorist attacks, albeit over the long term, and can be used effectively in conjunction with the state security approach (Christie 2010, 174–76). State and international responses to violent extremism would look different if the focus of these responses were the human security of the target state's population (those who experience an attack or face the threat of one) as well as the population from which the terrorist group seeks to recruit new members and garner support. Such an approach might involve empowering local actors as well as states to create the foundation for durable human security and invalidating the extremists' message. Transnational terrorism presents a challenge to each of the security approaches, but this particular challenge also highlights not only the conflicts between but also the synchronous nature of the three approaches we have addressed throughout the book.

At the time of writing, the world is in a period of upheaval, much as it was when we wrote the book's first edition. Threats posed by violent extremism and ethnonationalist movements continue to challenge democratic institutions, state stability, global cooperation, and human security. These threats transcend borders, regime types, and economic strength. Addressing the threat of violent extremism through a human security approach promises a more robust and sustainable security, but the political will to invest resources in a long-term human security strategy must exist.

Transitional Justice: Fostering Durable Human Security

We noted in chapter 7 that security in both the short and long term is best guaranteed when the state and its institutions are designed and able to protect human rights and ensure the just application of the rule of law. Our focus in chapter 7 was on recovery from acute conflict and the ways armed conflict erodes rule of law and paves the way for systematic human rights violations and atrocities. These harms must be confronted if a state is to establish sustainable peace after armed conflict.

Transitional justice mechanisms enable states to transition from a period of acute conflict to a sustainable peace. They also provide the means to transition from an abusive governing regime to a democratic government. As in the aftermath of acute conflict, transitional justice during and after regime change allows a society to reckon with past wrongs and provides an opportunity to make space for the voices of those who have been harmed and the lessons learned from their lived experiences. Truth and reconciliation commissions (TRCs), criminal trials, symbolic or material reparations, public apologies, and societal discussions of memorials offer ways to engage with and redress wrongs done by a past regime, combatant groups, and individual perpetrators.

The transitional justice process supports the development or reconstruction of functioning institutions that are essential to a democratic society, but transitional justice need not only occur in the aftermath of armed conflict. It is, at its core, an effort to bring disparate factions of a society back to a place of reconciliation and peaceful coexistence.

Rising ethnonationalism, marginalization of and discrimination against minority racial and ethnic groups, and political polarization within democratic states present formidable challenges to effective governance, stable institutions, and human security. Even absent regime change or armed conflict, transitional justice mechanisms offer a potential way to ease societal divisions. For example, Colleen Murphy and Kelebogile Zvobgo (2020) argue in favor of transitional justice in the United States as a way to reckon properly with systemic racism and redress the harms done by slavery, discriminatory Jim Crow laws, and generations of systemic inequality. Some US cities and the state of California have begun the process of offering reparations for slavery and the resulting generations of systemic racism endured by Black Americans (Dixon 2020).

Efforts to redress the harms created by racist laws, institutions, norms, and practices in the United States have been met with strong opposition from significant portions of the population: a spring 2021 public opinion poll conducted by the University of Massachusetts at Amherst found that 62 percent of respondents opposed the idea of reparations for slavery, with 46 percent of respondents taking the stance that the US government "definitely should not" offer financial reparations to the descendants of enslaved people. The divisiveness of the issue becomes starker when respondents are disaggregated by race and political affiliation. Only 28 percent of White respondents supported the idea of reparations, compared with 53 percent of Asian respondents, 45 percent of Latino respondents, and 86 percent of African American respondents. Respondents' political party affiliations underscore how politically polarized racial justice efforts have become: 64 percent of Democrats supported the idea of reparations, while only 10 percent of Republicans and 29 percent of independents did (Nteta 2021). Public opinion data from the United States on the question of reparations for slavery highlight both the need for and difficulty in undertaking transitional justice efforts to help a divided society work to ensure that its institutions provide opportunities, resources, impartiality of the law, and good governance for everyone.

Prioritization of human security principles by political leaders and security providers from federal government through local government agencies is essential to such an effort. Murphy and Zvobgo acknowledge that transitional justice efforts in the United States will be difficult to apply to the US context since transitional justice mechanisms like criminal trials are better suited to atrocities involving a small number of perpetrators rather than to redress of systemic harms occurring over generations and across public and private institutions. An important element of any transitional justice effort in the United States, they note, is the perception of fairness (Murphy and Zvobgo 2020). The public opinion data on reparations underscores this point. To the extent that sustainable peace and stable governance are central goals from both a human security and state security perspective, transitional justice is an important—if difficult—step forward.

HUMAN SECURITY IN A CHANGING WORLD: THEORY AND ACTION

We now return to the question of whether or not achieving human security is possible in the twenty-first century, a time of complex threats, interconnectedness, and rapid changes. We conclude that human security is not just possible, it is essential. The human security approach enables decision makers and security providers to craft comprehensive local, state, and international policies and implement programs to assist and empower individuals and communities. Human security is not only a normative approach—although caring for our fellow humans is an inherently moral endeavor. It also carries strategic benefits, allowing states to adopt domestic and foreign policies that better provide a basis for long-term peace. As we have sought to demonstrate in each of the preceding chapters, high levels of human security improve state and global stability.

There are, of course, enduring challenges that policy makers, practitioners, and scholars should not ignore. Effective human security efforts require dialogue to bridge the gaps between scholars, states, NGOs, IGOs, and civil society. As we noted in chapter 1, these bridges can be challenging to build: prioritizing human life over the state, kinship group, or global system of states is at odds with traditional approaches to security theory and practice but is the central assumption of human security. The notion of protecting civilians and preserving life in armed conflict is well established (though not uniformly observed in practice), but the principles we discuss within durable human security demand a reimagination of security theory and practice. As we have sought to demonstrate throughout the book, the creation of functional norms and institutions that foster human security—both in armed conflict settings and in peacetime—improve security outcomes at all levels.

To navigate conflicting perspectives on who ought to provide security and for whom security ought to be provided, open and inclusive dialogue about security challenges and the ideal way forward is essential. Traditional understandings of security presume that the stable state is the sole guarantor of security: a secure state can maintain its territory and defend its borders, protect its population and institutions from external threats, manage internal threats and instability, and maintain stability in its political and economic function. According to this view, the stable state protects its population from external threats and internal instability in exchange for loyalty, taxes, and—to varying degrees as needed—military service. The social contract between state and population is the basis for the statist perspective on security, and when individuals have a high degree of trust in their state, this view predominates. The federalist perspective rests on the same core assumptions as the statist perspective but diverges in that federalists see an important role for global institutions that foster cooperation among states to tackle complex problems. The nativist and cosmopolitan perspectives see a lesser role for the state in security provision. When the state fails to provide for the security and well-being of a segment of the population or when a segment of the population feels as though they are neglected or threatened by the state, the nativist perspective will take root, and individuals will rely on members of their kinship or identity group—rather than the state—to provide for their security. Here there is an actual or perceived failure on the part of the state. The cosmopolitan perspective, in contrast, prioritizes global humanity over the moral centrality of the state; cosmopolitans view security as best provided by individuals, groups, institutions, and even states working together toward common goals and on the basis of shared norms. Here the state is not necessarily the enemy, but it is not as significant as it is in the statist or federalist perspective.

Conflicting security perspectives make the smooth design and implementation of security policy and practice more difficult. Recalling the three policy boxes, when security perspectives are at odds individuals and groups will find it difficult to agree on the perception of a problem, the range of policy options, and the ideal outcome. Dialogue across perspectives can ameliorate the challenges in policy making and implementation, presuming all stakeholders are willing to negotiate in good faith.

Furthermore, discussions about security and efforts to address global and local challenges must include the viewpoints and input of those with diverse lived experiences, especially those for whom security is provided and those who have been underrepresented in international forums, including states and civil society from the Global South. The human security approach requires security providers to talk *with* not talk down *to* the populations they aim to empower and assist. Finally, security providers must be content to embrace long-term solutions even if they do not yield immediate results. Although the signs of success in some areas of human security provision are quickly visible (like establishing a safe zone for civilians in acute conflict or getting children back to school after the end of armed conflict), fostering human security is inherently a lengthy and complex process with generational, not necessarily rapid, results.

As a third approach to security policy and practice, human security offers a comprehensive view of contemporary threats, responsibility to address insecurity, and beneficiaries of efforts to provide security. In the comprehensiveness of human security, critics have argued that the concept is vague and overly expansive or that it securitizes human rights issues and invites military responses where they are unnecessary or even counterproductive (Paris 2001; Buzan 2004; Grayson 2003; Liotta 2002; MacFarlane and Khong 2006). The complexity of the human security approach presents challenges, but in a world more defined by gray areas than stark contrasts and clear ways forward, it is essential to consider and work to protect the security and well-being of individuals and their communities.

We contend—and have sought to demonstrate throughout the book—that human security is best understood as a set of practices. Practices are most effective when they are rooted in strong norms and institutions. And for a human security norm to take shape there must be a consensus among a significant group of states, international organizations, and civil society actors that (1) individuals and their communities deserve protection from direct harm and chronic threats and (2) specific security providers are responsible for the protection and empowerment of individuals. Further, it is vital to envision a broad range of security providers that extends beyond state and multilateral armed forces, especially when contemplating ways to prevent and respond to durable human security threats; human security as an approach can and should empower local-level organizations and efforts in partnership with states and international organizations to address chronic threats to individuals and their communities.

Human security is not, we reiterate, synonymous with armed humanitarian intervention. By broadening the notion of security to include protection from acute and chronic threats, human security does not call for militarized solutions. Rather, it recognizes that chronic threats arising from dysfunctional institutions, systemic inequality, and challenging global crises ought to be addressed with an urgency similar to that which theorists and practitioners have responded to physical insecurity caused by war and armed violence. Situating human security alongside global and national security offers a promising way forward in tackling twenty-first century security challenges.

DISCUSSION QUESTIONS

1. Consider the factors that contribute to human security. Which do you consider most essential?

2. What political, institutional, structural, or logistical barriers prevent the full participation of Global South states and advocates in discussions of human security?

3. How likely is human security to be a priority among state security policy makers in the twenty-first century? If you were a security policy maker, would you prioritize human security?

4. Have evolving efforts to define and pursue human security at the United Nations yielded significant advances? Where have the efforts succeeded? Where have they fallen short?

5. How useful do you find the distinction between human, national, and global security?

Glossary

acute conflict—discord that has a substantial probability of violence

anarchic—having no overarching authority capable of punishing rule violators

battle deaths—loss of life occurring due to combat in a two-sided conflict where at least one of the belligerents is a state

Beijing Platform for Action—a manifesto adopted in September 1995 establishing women's rights as human rights, making commitments to protecting women's human rights, and calling for a global shift in thinking about gender equality as a broader issue of concern for all people rather than just for one-half of the population

Biological Weapons Convention (BWC) of 1972—an international treaty banning the development, production, stockpiling, and use of biological weapons

bioterrorism—the deliberate use of viruses, bacteria, or other disease agents to cause harm to people, animals, or plants for a political or strategic purpose

BIPOC—a term used in the United States that stands for *Black, Indigenous, and People of Color*

cease-fire—an agreement between fighting parties to stop using violence or otherwise mobilizing their forces against each other, often seen as the first step toward reaching peace

Chemical Weapons Convention (CWC) of 1993—an international treaty banning the development, production, stockpiling, and use of chemical weapons

chronic hunger—undernourishment caused by long-term lack of access to the availability of sufficient quantities of nutritious food

cisgender—the correspondence of a person's gender identity with their sex assigned at birth

civil and political rights—human rights that allow individuals to participate fully in society—including and especially in political processes—without fear of discrimination or harm, conceived to protect individuals from state repression, discrimination, and overreach, and including such rights as freedom of assembly, speech, and religion, as well as security of person and property

civil society—the sphere of voluntary action that is distinct from the state and economic spheres, which can include religious institutions, humanitarian and charity organizations, advocacy networks, and other domestic and international actors

civilian protection—the shielding of civilians from harm during armed conflict

climate change—sustained changes in global or regional climate patterns stemming from the overall warming of the Earth

climate refugees—individuals and communities forced by the effects of climate change to relocate from their homes

collective action problem—a problem affecting everyone for which actors have an interest in creating a solution but, since solutions come at some cost, for which it is difficult to convince individual actors to contribute to any given solution

collective security organizations—international organizations made up of states, tasked with the provision of security for their member states, regions, or the global system, wherein the group seeks to cooperate to protect all of their members and allies from harm

collective security system—an international structure in which predatory behavior by one state elicits a collective response by all international actors

comprehensive peace accords—agreements in which all the major parties in the conflict are involved in the negotiation process and in which the substantive issues fueling the conflict are addressed

conventions—legally binding written agreements signed, ratified, and enforced by states; international conventions are formal agreements between states

Convention on the Elimination of All Forms of Discrimination against Women (CEDAW)—signed on December 18, 1979, and going into effect on September 3, 1981, a binding agreement made during the UN Decade for Women (1976–1985) that defines gender-based discrimination and establishes steps that state parties should take to end discrimination against women, including changes to the state's legal system, establishment of public institutions to prevent discrimination, and measures to prevent discriminatory actions

COP 21—the international twenty-first Conference of Parties, held in Paris in December 2015, resulting in the Paris Agreement on climate change

cosmopolitan perspective on security—the view that security is best provided through global cooperation and acceptance of norms and governance institutions, which view leads individuals to see their security as closely aligned with the security of others around the world, regardless of differences in identity, nationality, and experiences

covenants—legally binding written agreements that states sign, ratify, and enforce; international covenants are formal agreements between states

cultural relativism—the notion that, because an individual's or society's morals, values, norms, and beliefs are rooted in their culture, history, and experiences, what is a norm for one culture cannot be expected to be a norm for another

customs (or customary law)—customs deriving from a state's adherence to specific practices over time such that they begin to take on the force of law

declarations—international agreements that do not formally possess the binding force of law but take on lawlike influence as states adhere to their provisions over time

divine right of kings—the governing principle holding that rulers are not subject to human authority but to divine—or absolute—authority

donor states—wealthy nations that contribute a large share of the financial resources necessary to sustain international agencies and coordination efforts

durable human security—the dimensions of security not necessarily related to armed conflict—though certainly possibly existing in wartime—that threaten the daily lives and livelihoods of individuals and communities, incorporating the concepts of freedom from want and freedom from fear—both essential to the realization of long-term, sustainable human security

economic security—the sustained ability to access (afford) the goods and services needed to survive and thrive, including basic resources such as food, water, shelter, medications, and clothing, as well as essential services and opportunities like health care, education, and employment with a stable income

economic, social, and cultural rights—a human's freedom to access the services and resources that allow them to thrive, including the rights to food, housing, and education

epidemic—an unusually high incidence of disease in a community or the spread of disease to a new locality

episodic food insecurity—an individual's, family's, or community's limited or unpredictable access to food

famine—the ongoing state of extreme, usually deadly food insecurity resulting from severe lack of access to and availability of food

feminist foreign policy—an approach to international affairs that emphasizes women's participation, rights, and empowerment and gender equality

first-generation rights—the earliest human rights discussed by philosophers and political actors, establishing the basis for a more participatory and less discriminatory society in which individuals do not need to fear state-perpetrated interference or harm

First Geneva Convention (1864)—an international treaty concerning the welfare of wounded combatants, establishing a right to medical care and protection for International Committee of the Red Cross members working in war zones

food access—also referred to as *food entitlement* (Sen 1981), an individual's ability to purchase or otherwise acquire a sufficient amount of nutritious food to sustain daily activities

Food and Agriculture Organization (FAO)—a discussion forum founded in 1945 through which states can develop policy responses to hunger and to disseminate technical information to improve food security in developing states

food availability—the supply of food in the region

food desert—an area with a high population of low-income households and lack of access to available, affordable, and nutritious food sources within a set distance (usually one-half to one mile in urban areas and ten to twenty miles in rural regions), contributing to food insecurity, affecting both the access and availability dimensions of food security

food stability—an individual's access to food at all times, without sudden or cyclical disruptions—such as those that result from economic recession, climate change, natural disasters, armed conflict, or famine

food use—also referred to as *food utilization*, the overall nutrition achieved through the combination of a healthy diet and access to quality health care, clean water, and sanitation

Fourth Geneva Convention (1949)—the international treaty outlining the rights of and protections for civilians in armed conflict

gender—one's personal sense of being a man, a woman, both, or neither, as well as the societal expectations for a person's behavior, appearance, and expression on the basis of their sex

gender expression—the outward reflection of one's gender that a person may adopt—and not necessarily tied to one's sex—encompassing dress, mannerisms, speech, hairstyle, and other visible or audible traits

gender identity—the gender with which a person associates on the inside (one's sense of self as a man, a woman, or somewhere between or completely unrelated to the two)—not necessarily identical to one's sex, though it may be

gender inequality—the privileging of one group over others on the basis of sex and gender

Gender Inequality Index (GII)—the UNDP's measure of the position of women relative to men in a given state on the basis of female reproductive health, empowerment, and economic status

gender norms societal expectations for how people should behave, live, and love on the basis of gender

Geneva Conventions—international treaties that outline rights and protections related to combatants, prisoners of war, and civilians caught up in armed conflict

Global Gender Gap Index (GGGI)—the World Economic Forum's measure of economic participation and opportunity, educational attainment, political empowerment, and health and survival in 140 states' economies

global security—protection of the stability of the system of states

global warming—overall increases in the average temperatures of the Earth's oceans and atmosphere, caused by high concentrations of carbon dioxide and other greenhouse gases in the atmosphere that trap heat and warm the Earth through the greenhouse effect

globalized—the state of interconnectivity of our world, that both allows people from all over the globe to exchange goods, services, and ideas and also allows security threats to cross borders quickly and easily

greenhouse effect—a process wherein gases (including water vapor and carbon dioxide) help to warm the Earth by trapping radiation in the atmosphere

Hague Convention of 1899—the multilateral treaty that proposed a framework for conflict prevention through mediation, protocols for declarations of war, and rules for humane treatment of prisoners

Hague Convention of 1907—the international agreement outlawing the use of poison gas and aerial bombing

health security—the protection of individuals from sudden or chronic health threats and also the efforts to empower individuals to lead healthy lives

human development—the advancement of the well-being of people instead of or in addition to increasing the economic wealth of a state, with particular focus given to expanding the capability and opportunities of people

Human Development Index (HDI)—a measure of growth that attempts to account for human capabilities and opportunities instead of simply measuring gross domestic product (GDP)

human rights—the rights to which all human beings are entitled, regardless of their nationality, sex, ethnicity, race, religion, language, state or territory of residence, or any other factor or status and that are universal (meaning all humans everywhere are entitled to them) and inalienable (meaning no one can deprive another human of that person's rights except through the due process of law)

human security—exists when individuals and communities from both chronic, long-term threats and from more sudden and overtly violent threats

human security approach—an effort or policy that seeks to ensure the protection of individuals and communities from harm

human security norm—a consensus among a significant group of states and international organizations that individuals and communities are entitled to protection from harm and that outside actors (including foreign states or organizations) may help to provide this protection as necessary

humanitarian assistance—the provision of aid and support without the use of force, in response to natural disasters, famine, or public health crises in another state

humanitarian intervention—the use of force within another state to protect people from harm when another government's policies and instability cause destruction and insecurity

humanitarian organizations—collectives unaffiliated with state governments (we often call them nonstate actors) that seek to protect individuals from harm, regardless of political affiliation, ethnic or racial identity, or any other characteristic and that provide aid in response to natural disasters, war and armed conflict, and public health crises

indirect violence—harm caused to civilians due to the collateral consequences of war, such as decreased access to food, clean water, or health care

intergovernmental organizations (IGOs)—organizations formed by and composed of member states, whose international-level actors help states to cooperate and coordinate efforts to address specific sets of issues

internally displaced persons (IDPs)—people uprooted from their homes due to conflict or natural disasters but remain inside their country and do not cross an international border

International Bill of Human Rights—the agreements including the Universal Declaration of Human Rights, the International Covenant on Civil and Political Rights (ICCPR), and the International Covenant on Economic, Social and Cultural Rights (ICESCR)

International Covenant on Civil and Political Rights (ICCPR) (1966) a multilateral treaty that obligates parties to protect civil and political rights

International Criminal Court (ICC)—a legal institution created as a permanent international body, based in The Hague, the Netherlands, with the authority to prosecute individuals, including heads of state, who are responsible for genocide, crimes against humanity, and war crimes

International Covenant on Economic, Social and Cultural Rights (ICESCR) (1966)—a multilateral treaty that obligates parties to protect economic, social, and cultural rights

International Fund for Agricultural Development (IFAD) founded in 1977, a financial institution focused on assisting the rural poor in developing states, whose central objectives are to improve well-being and food security and to reduce poverty in developing states through loans and grants so as to increase access to agricultural technology and related skills

international human rights law—a body of international agreements, conventions, and treaties that outline the basic rights and freedoms to which individuals are entitled

international humanitarian law—the rules of warfare that place limitations on the use of force by states and the conduct of combatants acting on behalf of states

international order—the political, economic, and normative arrangements in the international system

intrastate wars—civil wars or wars that are fought within states instead of between two or more states

jus ad bellum—the principle limiting the causes for which war is justifiable, such as self-defense or civilians persecuted by their government

jus in bello—the principle establishing the expectations for moral behavior in warfare, such as special protections for injured or surrendering combatants

jus post bellum—the principle establishing the expectation that the parties to armed conflict will rebuild and restore a just order after hostilities end

just war theory—a framework articulating when, how, and why governments may engage in warfare

just wars—hostilities undertaken with good intentions for one's own state or on behalf of others

Kyoto Protocol—an international agreement within the UN climate change framework, signed on December 11, 1997, in Kyoto, Japan, entered into force on February 16, 2005, ratified by 192 parties and committed signatories to emissions-reduction targets

"lifestyle" diseases—chronic health conditions arising from a societal shift toward a sedentary lifestyle

male:female sex ratios—the number of males per one hundred females in a population

malnutrition—a condition that results from taking in too few, too many, or the wrong nutrients such that the body does not receive the necessary balance of essential nutrients to maintain daily activities

Millennium Development Goals (MDGs)—series of global objectives adopted by the United Nations in September 2000, and meant to be achieved by 2015, that focus on eradicating poverty and promoting equality, rights, and opportunity

Montreal Protocol—a treaty adopted by forty-six states in August 1987, focusing specifically on the protection of the ozone layer

multidimensional peacekeeping—an intervention seeking to rebuild the state institutions destroyed during a conflict and that consists of a much wider array of tasks and goals than those of traditional peacekeeping operations

national security—the prioritization of the safety and stability of the political entity of the state and its territorial integrity, enabling a state to defend its borders, protect its population from outside threats, and continue its political and economic functions

nationally determined contributions (NDCs)—national goals aimed at reducing greenhouse gas emissions, pursuing clean and renewable energy sources, and mitigating the effects of climate change, as linked to the Paris Agreement

nativist perspective on security—the viewpoint that security is best provided by a group or groups below the level of the state, including sectarian, ethnic, religious, racial, or other identity groups

natural law—a foundational, unchanging morality that guides all human behavior at all times in all places

natural rights—the freedoms to which all rational human beings are entitled, a concept forming the philosophical and legal foundation for the notion of human rights

negative peace—the absence of violence

negative rights—freedoms enjoyed only when someone abstains from a specific action, requiring that the government or other entities or people not curtail an individual's choices, freedoms, beliefs, or actions

nonbinary—a gender identity that is not limited to the man/woman gender binary but falls somewhere else on the gender spectrum

nongovernmental organizations (NGOs)—nonstate entities focusing on a particular issue or set of issues and operating independently of states and IGOs

norm—a commonly accepted belief or idea that provides standards for behavior

one-sided victory—a war termination in which one side militarily defeats the other

one-sided violence—violence perpetrated against noncombatants without fear of reciprocation

ozone layer—a portion of the Earth's stratosphere that acts as a "sunscreen" for the planet and its inhabitants, absorbing the sun's ultraviolet radiation, the depletion of which leaves humans especially vulnerable to skin cancer

pandemic—the spread of disease across borders or on a global scale

Paris Agreement—the most recent and most comprehensive follow-up to the UNFCCC and the Kyoto Protocol, resulting from COP 21 negotiations, with 195 signatories, entered into force on November 4, 2016, which agreement invites states to abide by nationally determined contributions (NDCs) to lower greenhouse gas emissions and tackle climate change

patriarchy—"rule by fathers," or a system of entrenched norms and inequality that privileges masculinity (and men and boys) over all other identities and people

peacebuilding—the creation of institutional frameworks and processes that address the roots of a conflict and establish processes for reconciliation with the intention of lessening the likelihood for conflict recurrence

peacekeeping—an intervention that is typically authorized by the United Nations and involves the deployment of international military, police, and civilian personnel tasked with maintaining peace and security after a cease-fire or peace agreement

peace accord—an agreement between all or most conflict parties that outlines postconflict governance

peace enforcement—a UN operation put into place without full consent of the warring parties, with the intention of enforcing a peace

peace processes—the range of activities intended to bring about a cessation of violent conflict, including informal meetings between parties, formal negotiations, cease-fires, and formal peace treaties

peremptory norms (or *jus cogens*) authoritative standards with the binding force of law; the process through which a norm attains this status is not fully fleshed out in scholarship or international law, but among these powerful norms are bans on slavery, genocide, and international aggression

permanent five members (P5)—the permanent five members of the UN Security Council (China, France, Russia, the United Kingdom, and the United States) that have power to veto any resolution

positive peace—a condition resulting from adequate provision of social welfare, established rights, and facilitated justice

positive rights—the freedoms that are provided only when someone (usually the government, but possibly also an agency, institution, or fellow human) *does something* or takes action

principle of nonintervention—a strict interpretation of sovereignty implying that states are not to intervene in other states' affairs, including using force to stop states from violating their citizens' human rights

protection of civilians—an operational requirement for UN peacekeeping operations that is variously interpreted, with understandings ranging from protection norms found in the Geneva Conventions to the narrower goal of physically protecting civilians from harm during an ongoing peacekeeping operation

proxy war—armed conflict in which foreign states become involved in pursuit of their own national interests related to the outcome of the conflict

reconciliation—a process in which people work to overcome hatred and mistrust between groups to the extent that they are able to coexist with each other

refugees—people displaced from their homes who have crossed an international border, granted legal rights under the 1951 convention relating to the Status of Refugees

regimes—sets of international norms, rules, and expectations that facilitate cooperation among states

regional blocs—formal multilateral institutions that reduce barriers to economic and political cooperation, examples including the European Union (EU), the Association of Southeast Asian Nations (ASEAN), the African Union (AU), the Cooperation Council for the Arab States of the Gulf (or the Gulf Cooperation Council, GCC), and the Organization of American States (OAS)

Responsibility to Protect (R2P)—the doctrine holding that states are obligated to protect civilians from what are known as the four crimes: genocide, war crimes, ethnic cleansing, and crimes against humanity

Rome Statue of the International Criminal Court—the treaty framework that led to the establishment of the International Criminal Court

second-generation rights—rights that establish not only certain individual liberties but also work toward a more egalitarian society in which individuals' basic needs (food, shelter, education, and employment) are met

Second Geneva Convention (1906)—the international treaty applying to sailors in armed forces, expanding the protections of the First Geneva Convention to war at sea

security provision—the general practice of preventing or mitigating harm or of providing assistance and resources in response to situations of insecurity at the individual, state, or international level

security sector reform—the transformation of a state's security branches (i.e., armed forces, police, intelligence agencies) from fighting an active conflict to postconflict adherence to principles of the rule of law and respect for human rights

self-determination—the right of the citizens of a territory to choose for themselves what type of political system they are to live under and the expectation that the government is tasked with the protection of their rights

self-help system—a view of the international system driven by the idea that states are on their own when it comes to guaranteeing their security

self-interest—protection for oneself in its most basic form

sex—the biological differences in human reproductive systems that lead to the identification of a person as male, female, both, or neither

social contract—the agreement between individuals and a government that the latter will provide for the common security in exchange for the allegiance of its people

sovereign equality—the principle that all states are legally equal to each other

sovereignty—the idea that a state has legal jurisdiction over its territory and that other states are not to interfere in each other's internal affairs

sovereignty as responsibility—the obligation a sovereign state has to protect the human rights of its citizens

state—a centralized political entity that holds territory, has a stable population, exercises legal authority over its population, and is recognized as legitimate by its population and the other states in the world

state building—a practice that generally consists of reconstituting a core set of state institutions, a market economy, and basic rule of law provisions following a conflict

states parties—states that have signed and ratified an international agreement

statist perspective on security—sees the state as the primary provider of security but rejects or deemphasizes the universality of rights. This perspective tracks closely with the traditional or state security and global security approaches. According to this perspective, the state is the primary provider of security, and the individual expects to receive protection from the state, as established by the notion of the social contract.

strategic nonviolence—nonbelligerent resistance used to draw attention to and put pressure on an oppressive regime

structural violence—the loss of life due to indirect factors, such as poorly functioning healthcare systems, insufficient agriculture, inadequate water supplies, inequality, and other indirect physical, resource-related, or institutional threats

Sustainable Development Goals (SDGs)—a series of objectives adopted by the United Nations in 2015, with a target achievement date of 2030, that expand on and continue the work of the MDGs, with a specific focus on sustainability

syndemic—a compound threat presented by the interaction of a disease and social and environmental factors

systemic racism—(or *structural racism*) the perpetuation of racial inequality and White supremacy through the institutions, norms, and interactions that shape both government and daily life, resulting in BIPOC's unequal access to employment, education, housing, health care, political participation, and justice, among other vital resources and opportunities

terrorism—the use of violence by nonstate actors toward nonmilitary targets and noncombatant populations with the ultimate goal of sending a message to the state in which the terrorist organization is based, to the population of that state, or to foreign states and populations

third-generation rights—rights pertaining to specific groups of people

Third Geneva Convention (1949)—the international treaty protecting prisoners of war

threat multipliers—phenomena, situations, or actors that make existing security threats more dangerous

transitional justice—the process by which a state transitions from a period of conflict into a peaceful, democratic society, with a focus on redress for victims

transnational advocacy networks—a grouping of individuals and organizations connected through their pursuit of a common goal

transnational terrorism—operations of a terrorist group that involve activities or presence in more than one state

Treaty on the Prohibition of Nuclear Weapons of 2017—the international treaty banning the development, production, stockpiling, and use of nuclear weapons, not joined by any of the nuclear weapons–possessing states

truth and reconciliation commission (TRC)—a formal process with the purpose of correctly revealing the truth of what happened during a conflict or system of injustice

undernutrition—a health condition resulting from the lack of access to or availability of sufficient nutrients or the body's inability to use nutrients consumed as a result of disease

United Nations Framework Convention on Climate Change (UN-FCCC)—an international convention adopted at the Earth Summit in Rio de Janeiro in June 1992, entered into force on March 21, 1994, and ratified by 197 parties, that seeks to facilitate cooperation among states to address the factors contributing to climate change

United Nations Security Council Resolution 1325—a decision adopted on October 31, 2000, that situates women, girls, and the gendered effects of war within the scope of peace and security, and therefore on the Security Council's agenda

Universal Declaration of Human Rights (1948)—an international agreement documenting much of what we understand about human rights today, forming the basis of current definitions of *human rights* and *fundamental freedoms*

violent extremism—the use of violence driven by ideas and ideologies that diverge from what is considered normal in society, linked to political, social, or religious ideology and usually equated with fanaticism

Women, Peace, and Security (WPS)—the UN Security Council's policy agenda that comprises a set of resolutions calling, in part, for greater participation of women in conflict resolution and peacebuilding processes

World Food Programme (WFP)—an organization founded in 1961 to provide humanitarian assistance directly to regions in need, with a mission to offer immediate aid and expertise with the long-term objective of a food secure world

References

Abbas, Rushan. 2020. "International Action to Protect the Uyghur People." *Journal of International Affairs* 73 (2): 211–16. https://jia.sipa.columbia.edu/international-action-protect-uyghur-people-interview-rushan-abbas.

Acharya, Amitav. 2022. "Race and Racism in the Founding of the Modern World Order." *International Affairs* 98 (1): 23–43. https://academic.oup.com/ia/article/98/1/23/6484842.

Adamson, Fiona B. 2020. "Pushing the Boundaries: Can We 'Decolonize' Security Studies?" *Journal of Global Security Studies* 5 (1): 129–35. https://doi.org/10.1093/jogss/ogz057.

Adebayo, Gabriel O. 2021. "Counter-radicalization Policies and Policing in Education: Making a Case for Human Security in Europe." *Heliyon* 7 (2): e05721. https://doi.org/10.1016/j.heliyon.2020.e05721.

Adelman, Howard. 2001. "From Refugees to Forced Migration: The UNHCR and Human Security." *International Migration Review* 35 (1): 7–32.

Adger, W. Neil, Juan M. Pulhin, Jon Barnett, Geoffret D. Dabelko, Grete K. Hovelsrud, Marc Levy, Úrsula Oswald Spring, and Coleen H. Vogel. 2014. "Human Security." In *Climate Change 2014: Impacts, Adaptation, and Vulnerability; Part A: Global and Sectoral Aspects, Working Group II Contribution to the Fifth Assessment Report of the Intergovernmental Panel on Climate Change*, ed. Christopher B. Field, Vicente R. Barros, David Jon Dokken, Katharine J. Mach, Michael D. Mastrandrea, T. Eren Bilir, Monalisa Chatterjee, Kristie L. Ebi, Yuka Otsuki Estrada, Robert C. Genova, Betelhem Girma, Eric S. Kissel, Andrew N. Levy, Sandy MacCracken, Patricia R. Mastrandrea, and Leslie L. White, 755–92. New York: Cambridge University Press. https://www.ipcc.ch/site/assets/uploads/2018/02/WGIIAR5-PartA_FINAL.pdf.

Adler, Emanuel, and Vincent Pouliot. 2011. "International Practices." *International Theory* 3 (1): 1–36.

Agence France-Presse. 2015. "Oslo Moves to Ban Cars from City Centre within Four Years." *The Guardian*, October 19, 2015. https://www.theguardian.com/environment/2015/oct/19/oslo-moves-to-ban-cars-from-city-centre-within-four-years.

AJMC Staff. 2021. "A Timeline of COVID-19 Vaccine Developments in 2021." AJMC [*American Journal of Managed Care*] (website), June 3, 2021. https://www.ajmc.com/view/a-timeline-of-covid-19-vaccine-developments-in-2021.

Alarakhia, Safeena. 2000. *Engendering the Peace Process in West Africa: The Mano River Women's Peace Network; Guinea, Liberia, Sierra Leone*. Women's Best Practices in Africa series. Geneva: Femmes Afrique Solidarité.

Alderman, Liz. 2016. "Greek Villagers Rescued Migrants. Now They Are the Ones Suffering." *New York Times*, August 17, 2016. https://www.nytimes.com/2016/08/18/world/europe/greece-lesbos-refugees.html.

Alhadeff, Samuel. 2018. *Venezuelan Emigration, Explained*. Latin American Program, October, Wilson Center. Washington, DC: Woodrow Wilson International Center for Scholars. https://www.wilsoncenter.org/publication/venezuelan-emigration-explained.

Alter, Charlotte, Suyin Haynes, and Justin Worland. 2019. "Time 2019 Person of the Year: Greta Thunberg." *Time*, [December] 2019. https://time.com/person-of-the-year-2019-greta-thunberg/.

Altman, Drew. 2020. "Understanding the US Failure on Coronavirus—An Essay by Drew Altman." *BMJ* 370 (September): m3417. https://doi.org/10.1136/bmj.m3417.

American Institute of Physics. 2022. "The Discovery of Global Warming." April 2022. https://history.aip.org/climate/simple.htm.

Amnesty International. 2017. *Europe: A Perfect Storm; The Failure of European Policies in the Central Mediterranean*. London: Amnesty International. https://www.amnesty.org/en/documents/eur03/6655/2017/en/.

———. 2021. "Afghan Women's Rights on the Verge of Roll Back as International Forces Withdraw and Peace Talks in Stalemate." Report index no. ASA 11/4143/2021. Amnesty.org, May 24. https://www.amnesty.org/en/documents/asa11/4143/2021/en/.

Andersen-Rodgers, David R. 2015. "Back Home Again: Assessing the Impact of Provisions for Internally Displaced Persons in Comprehensive Peace Accords." *Refugee Survey Quarterly* 34 (3) (September): 24–45.

———. 2019. "Internally Displaced Persons: Norm Emergence and Strain in a Disordered World." In *The New World Disorder: Challenges and Threats in an Uncertain World*, edited by J. L. Black, Michael Johns, and Alanda D. Theriault, 229–50. Lanham, MD: Lexington Books.

Appiah, Kwame Anthony. 2019. "The Importance of Elsewhere: In Defense of Cosmopolitanism." *Foreign Affairs* 98 (2) (March/April): 20–26.

Archibold, Randal C., and Somini Sengupta. 2014. "U.N. Struggles to Stem Haiti Cholera Epidemic." *New York Times*, April 19, 2014. https://www.nytimes.com/2014/04/20/world/americas/un-struggles-to-stem-haiti-cholera-epidemic.html.

Associated Press. 2020. "China Cuts Uighur Births with IUDs, Abortion, Sterilization." AP News, June 28, 2020. https://apnews.com/article/ap-top-news-international-news-weekend-reads-china-health-269b3de1af34e17c1941a514f78d764c.

Autesserre, Séverine. 2009. "Hobbes and the Congo: Frames, Local Violence, and International Intervention." *International Organization* 63 (2) (April 15): 249–80. Available at https://www.severineautesserre.com/wp-content/uploads/2009/04 /IOSev.pdf.

———. 2014. *Peaceland: Conflict Resolution and the Everyday Politics of International Intervention.* Cambridge: Cambridge University Press.

———. 2021. *The Frontlines of Peace: An Insider's Guide to Changing the World.* Foreword by Leymah Gbowee. Oxford: Oxford University Press.

Badran, Ramzi. 2014. "Intrastate Peace Agreements and the Durability of Peace." *Conflict Management and Peace Science* 31 (2): 193–217.

Bahar, Dany. 2019. "Chavismo Is the Worst of All Sanctions: The Evidence behind the Humanitarian Catastrophe in Venezuela." Up Front. *Brookings* (blog). May 22, 2019. https://www.brookings.edu/blog/up-front/2019/05/22/chavismo-is-the-worst -of-all-sanctions-the-evidence-behind-the-humanitarian-catastrophe-in-venezuela/.

Bahar, Dany, and Meagan Dooley. 2021. "Venezuelan Refugees and Their Receiving Communities Need Funding, Not Sympathy." Up Front. *Brookings* (blog). February 26, 2021. https://www.brookings.edu/blog/up-front/2021/02/26/venezuelan -refugees-and-their-receiving-communities-need-funding-not-sympathy/.

Bahar, Dany, Sebastian Bustos, José Morales-Arilla, and Miguel Ángel Santos. 2019. "Impact of the 2017 Sanctions on Venezuela: Revisiting the Evidence." Report. *Brookings* (blog). May 14, 2019. https://www.brookings.edu/research/revisiting -the-evidence-impact-of-the-2017-sanctions-on-venezuela/.

Bailey, Robert. 2014. "Food and Human Security." In *Routledge Handbook of Human Security*, edited by Mary Martin and Taylor Owen, 188–96. New York: Routledge.

Baker, Michael G., Nick Wilson, and Andrew Anglemyer. 2020. "Successful Elimination of Covid-19 Transmission in New Zealand." *New England Journal of Medicine*, August 20, 2020. https://www.nejm.org/doi/full/10.1056/NEJMc2025203.

Baldwin, David A. 1997. "The Concept of Security." *Review of International Studies* 23 (1) (January): 5–26.

Baloch, Shah Meer. 2021. "'The Challenge for Us Now Is Drought, Not War': Livelihoods of Millions of Afghans at Risk." Global Development. *The Guardian*, September 21, 2021. https://www.theguardian.com/global-development/2021/sep/21 /drought-war-livelihoods-afghan-farmers-risk-taliban-security-forces-kandahar.

Ban, Jonathan. 2003. "Health as a Global Security Challenge." *Seton Hall Journal of Diplomacy and International Relations* 4 (2): 19–28. http://blogs.shu.edu /journalofdiplomacy/files/archives/04_ban.pdf.

Barakat, Sultan, and Sansom Milton. 2020. "Localisation across the Humanitarian-Development-Peace Nexus." *Journal of Peacebuilding and Development* 15 (2) (May 19): 147–63. https://journals.sagepub.com/doi/full/10.1177/1542316620922805.

Barnett, John, and W. Neil Adger. 2007. "Climate Change, Human Security and Violent Conflict." *Political Geography* 26 (6): 639–55. https://sta.uwi.edu/iir/nor mangirvanlibrary/sites/default/files/normangirvanlibrary/documents/Climate%20 Change%2C%20Human%20Security%20and%20Violent%20Conflict.pdf.

Barnett, Michael N., and Martha Finnemore. 2004. *Rules for the World: International Organizations in Global Politics.* Ithaca: Cornell University Press.

Barnett, Michael [N.], and Raymond Duvall. 2005. "Power in International Politics." *International Organization* 59 (1) (February 15): 39–75. https://www.cambridge .org/core/journals/international-organization/article/power-in-international-politics /F5F3C74D30A12A5C4CC9B4EFEA152967.

Barr, Heather. 2013. "Afghanistan: Failing Commitments to Protect Women's Rights." Human Rights Watch (website), July 11, 2013. https://www.hrw.org /news/2013/07/11/afghanistan-failing-commitments-protect-womens-rights#.

Bassiouni, M. Cherif. 1996. "International Crimes: *Jus Cogens* and *Obligatio Erga Omnes*." *Law and Contemporary Problems* 59 (4) (Autumn): 63–74. https://schol arship.law.duke.edu/cgi/viewcontent.cgi?article=1016&context=lcp.

———. 2011. *Crimes against Humanity: Historical Evolution and Contemporary Application*. Cambridge and New York: Cambridge University Press.

Bastida, Xiye. 2020. "If You Adults Won't Save the World, We Will." Filmed February 2020 at TED-Ed Weekend, TED World Theater, New York. Video, 8:08, posted July 2020. https://www.ted.com/talks/xiye_bastida_if_you_adults_won_t_save _the_world_we_will.

BBC News. 2012. "Venezuela Bans Private Gun Ownership." Latin America. BBC. com, June 1, 2012. https://www.bbc.com/news/world-latin-america-18288430.

———. 2013. "A Brief History of Climate Change." Science. BBC.com, September 20, 2013. http://www.bbc.com/news/science-environment-15874560.

———. 2017. "Why Are There Still Famines?" World. BBC.com, March 15, 2017. http://www.bbc.com/news/world-africa-39039255.

———. 2018. "Venezuela Election: Maduro Wins Second Term amid Claims of Vote Rigging." Latin America. BBC.com, May 21, 2018. https://www.bbc.com/news /world-latin-america-44187838.

———. 2019. "Maduro and Guaidó: Who Is Supporting Whom in Venezuela?" Latin America. BBC.com, February 5, 2019. https://www.bbc.com/news/world-latin -america-47053701.

———. 2020a. "Juan Guaidó: The Man Who Wants to Oust Maduro." Latin America. BBC.com, January 23, 2020. https://www.bbc.com/news/world-latin -america-46985389.

———. 2020b. "Venezuela: Maduro and Allies Win National Assembly Poll—Partial Results." Latin America. BBC.com, December 7, 2020. https://www.bbc.com /news/world-latin-america-55211149.

———. 2021a. "Covid: Brazil's Bolsonaro Calls Governors 'Tyrants' Over Lockdowns." Latin America. BBC.com, March 22, 2021. https://www.bbc.com/news /world-latin-america-56479614.

———. 2021b. "Who Are the Uyghurs and Why Is China Being Accused of Genocide?" World: China. BBC.com, June 21, 2021. https://www.bbc.com/news/world -asia-china-22278037.

———. 2021c. "Covid: Thousands Protest in Brazil against Bolsonaro over Pandemic Handling." Latin America. BBC.com, July 3, 2021. https://www.bbc.com/news /world-latin-america-57709301.

Beardsley, Kyle. 2011. "Peacekeeping and the Contagion of Armed Conflict." *Journal of Politics* 73 (4): 1051–64.

Beardsley, Kyle, David E. Cunningham, and Peter B. White. 2017. "Resolving Civil Wars before They Start: The UN Security Council and Conflict Prevention in Self-Determination Disputes." *British Journal of Political Science* 47 (3) (July): 675–97. https://www.cambridge.org/core/journals/british-journal-of-political-sci ence/article/resolving-civil-wars-before-they-start-the-un-security-council-and -conflict-prevention-in-selfdetermination-disputes/3AF64D5C019F97DE5F015 FECE321CB17.

Beaubien, Jason. 2017. "Why the Famine in South Sudan Keeps Getting Worse." *All Things Considered.* NPR.org, March 14, 2017. https://www.npr.org/sections /goatsandsoda/2017/03/14/520033701/why-the-famine-in-south-sudan-keeps-get ting-worse.

Beaumont, Peter. 2019. "Red Cross Aid to Venezuela to Triple as Maduro Stance Softens." New: Humanitarian Response. *The Guardian*, April 12, 2019. http:// www.theguardian.com/global-development/2019/apr/12/red-cross-aid-to-venezu ela-to-triple-as-nicolas-maduro-stance-softens.

Bellamy, Alex J. 2011. *Global Politics and the Responsibility to Protect: From Words to Deeds.* London and New York: Routledge.

———. 2012. *Massacres and Morality: Mass Atrocities in an Age of Civilian Immunity.* Oxford: Oxford University Press.

Beller, Thomas. 2016. "The Residents of This Louisiana Island Are America's First 'Climate Refugees.'" Photographs by Ben Depp. Science. *Smithsonian Magazine*, June 29, 2016. https://www.smithsonianmag.com/science-nature/residents-louisi ana-island-americas-first-climate-refugees-180959585/.

Bellemare, Marc F., Johanna Fajardo-Gonzalez, and Seth R. Gitter. 2018. "Foods and Fads: The Welfare Impacts of Rising Quinoa Prices in Peru." *World Development* 112 (December): 163–79. https://doi.org/10.1016/j.worlddev.2018.07.012.

Beltrán, William Mauricio, and Sian Creely. 2018. "Pentecostals, Gender Ideology and the Peace Plebiscite: Colombia 2016." *Religions* 9 (12): 418–37. https://www .mdpi.com/2077-1444/9/12/418/htm.

Benko, Jessica. 2017. "How a Warming Planet Drives Human Migration." The Climate Issue. *New York Times*, April 19, 2017. https://www.nytimes.com/2017/04/19 /magazine/how-a-warming-planet-drives-human-migration.html.

Black Lives Matter. "About." n.d. Accessed October 19, 2021. https://blacklivesmat ter.com/about/.

Blattman, Christopher, and Jeannie Annan. 2010. "The Consequences of Child Soldiering." *Review of Economics and Statistics* 92 (4): 882–98.

Blythman, Joanna. 2013. "Can Vegans Stomach the Unpalatable Truth about Quinoa?" Opinion: Food. *The Guardian*, January 16, 2013. https://www.theguardian .com/commentisfree/2013/jan/16/vegans-stomach-unpalatable-truth-quinoa.

Booth, William, and Tyler Page. 2021. "As Climate Pledges Fall Short, U.N. Predicts Globe Could Warm by Catastrophic 2.7 Degrees Celsius." *Washington Post*, September 17, 2021. https://www.washingtonpost.com/climate-environ ment/2021/09/17/un-climate-2030-biden/.

Boucher, David, and Paul Kelly, eds. 1994. *The Social Contract from Hobbes to Rawls.* New York: Routledge.

Boutros-Ghali, Boutros. 1992. "An Agenda for Peace: Preventive Diplomacy, Peace-making and Peace-Keeping." *International Relations* 11 (3): 201–18.

Brander, Patricia, Laure De Witte, Nazila Ghanea, Rui Gomes, Ellie Keen, Anastasia Nikitina, and Justina Pinkeviciute. 2020. "The Evolution of Human Rights." In *Compass: Manual for Human Rights Education with Young People*, 2nd ed., updated 2020, edited by Patricia Brander, Ellie Keen, Vera Juhász, and Annette Schneider, final edit and coordination by Rui Gomes, drawings by Pancho, 397–402. Hungary: Council of Europe Publishing. https://www.coe.int/en/web /compass/the-evolution-of-human-rights.

Brandt, Patrick T., T. David Mason, Mehmet Gurses, Nicolai Petrovsky, and Dagmar Radin. 2008. "When and How the Fighting Stops: Explaining the Duration and Outcome of Civil Wars." *Defence and Peace Economics* 19 (6): 415–34.

Bridges, Khiara M. 2018. "Implicit Bias and Racial Disparities in Health Care." *Human Rights Magazine* 43 (3). https://www.americanbar.org/groups/crsj/publica tions/human_rights_magazine_home/the-state-of-healthcare-in-the-united-states /racial-disparities-in-health-care/.

Bristow, Matthew. 2019. "One Risky Birth Shows How Venezuela's Diaspora Strains Its Neighbors." Business. Bloomberg.com, April 3, 2019. https://www.bloomberg .com/news/features/2019-04-03/one-risky-birth-shows-how-venezuela-s-diaspora -strains-its-neighbors.

Broecker, Wallace S. 1975. "Climatic Change: Are We on the Brink of a Pronounced Global Warming?" *Science* 189 (4201) (August 8): 460–63.

Bueno de Mesquita, Bruce, and David Lalman. 2008. *War and Reason: Domestic and International Imperatives*. New Haven, CT: Yale University Press.

Bull, Hedley. 1968. "Strategic Studies and Its Critics." *World Politics* 20 (4): 593–605.

Buzan, Barry. 2004. "A Reductionist, Idealistic Notion that Adds Little Analytical Value." *Security Dialogue* 35 (3): 369–70. https://doi.org/10.1177/096701060403500326.

Buzan, Barry, and Lene Hansen. 2009. *The Evolution of International Security Studies*. Cambridge: Cambridge University Press. Available online at https://ir101 .co.uk/wp-content/uploads/2018/10/buzan-the-evolution-of-international-security -studies-compressed.pdf.

Buzan, Barry, Ole Waever, and Jaap de Wilde. 1998. *Security: A New Framework for Analysis*. Boulder, CO: Lynne Rienner Publishers.

C40 Cities. n.d. "About C40." Accessed October 1, 2021. http://www.c40.org/about.

Caprioli, Mary. 2000. "Gendered Conflict." *Journal of Peace Research* 37 (1): 51–68.

———. 2005. "Primed for Violence: The Role of Gender Inequality in Predicting Internal Conflict." *International Studies Quarterly* 49 (2): 161–78.

Caprioli, Mary, and Mark A. Boyer. 2001. "Gender, Violence, and International Crisis." *Journal of Conflict Resolution* 45 (4): 503–18.

Caprioli, Mary, Rebecca Nielsen, and Valerie M. Hudson. 2010. "Women and Post-conflict Settings." In *Peace and Conflict 2010*, edited by J. Joseph Hewitt, Jonathan Wilkenfeld, and Ted Robert Gurr, 91–102. Boulder, CO: Paradigm.

Carle, Jill. 2015. "Climate Change Seen as Top Global Threat." Report. Pew Research Center. July 14, 2015. https://www.pewresearch.org/global/2015/07/14/climate -change-seen-as-top-global-threat/.

Carpenter, R. Charli. 2003. "'Women and Children First': Gender, Norms, and Humanitarian Evacuation in the Balkans 1991–95." *International Organization* 57 (4): 661–94.

———. 2007. "Setting the Advocacy Agenda: Theorizing Issue Emergence and Nonemergence in Transnational Advocacy Networks." *International Studies Quarterly* 51 (1): 99–120.

———. 2011. "Vetting the Advocacy Agenda: Network Centrality and the Paradox of Weapons Norms." *International Organization* 65 (1): 69–102.

Catholic Relief Services. 2019. "Venezuela Crisis: Facts and How to Help." April 3, 2019. https://www.crs.org/media-center/current-issues/venezuela-crisis-facts-and -how-help.

Cederman, Lars-Erik, and Manuel Vogt. 2017. "Dynamics and Logics of Civil War." *Journal of Conflict Resolution* 61 (9): 1992–2016.

Cederman, Lars-Erik, Nils B. Weidmann, and Kristian Skrede Gleditsch. 2011. "Horizontal Inequalities and Ethnonationalist Civil War: A Global Comparison." *American Political Science Review* 105 (3): 478–95.

Centers for Disease Control and Prevention. n.d. "About Underlying Cause of Death, 1999–2020." CDC.gov. Accessed May 12, 2022. https://wonder.cdc.gov/ucd -icd10.html.

———. 2020. "A History of Anthrax." Anthrax: What Is Anthrax? CDC.gov, last modified November 20, 2020. http://www.cdc.gov/anthrax/resources/history/.

Cha, Sangmi. 2021. "S. Korea Weighs Tighter Restrictions as COVID-19 Cases Surge." Asia Pacific. *Reuters*, July 15, 2021. https://www.reuters.com/world/asia -pacific/skorea-pm-says-further-gathering-limits-may-be-needed-covid-19-cases -rise-2021-07-16/.

Chakraborty, Roshni. 2019. "Child, Not Bride: Child Marriage among Syrian Refugees." *Harvard International Review* (Winter), August 23, 2019. https://hir.har vard.edu/child-not-bride-child-marriage-among-syrian-refugees/.

Cheatham, Amelia, Diana Roy, and Rocio Cara Labrador. 2021. "Venezuela: The Rise and Fall of a Petrostate." Backgrounder. Council on Foreign Relations (website), last modified December 29, 2021. https://www.cfr.org/backgrounder/venezuela-crisis.

Chetty, Raj, Nathaniel Hendren, Maggie R. Jones, and Sonya R. Porter. 2020. "Race and Economic Opportunity in the United States: An Intergenerational Perspective." *Quarterly Journal of Economics* (135 (2) (May): 711–83. https://academic.oup .com/qje/article/135/2/711/5687353.

Chin, Aimee. 2005. "Long-Run Labor Market Effects of Japanese American Internment during World War II on Working-Age Male Internees." *Journal of Labor Economics* 23 (3): 491–525.

Cho, Renee. 2016. "Cities: The Vanguard against Climate Change." Climate. *State of the Planet* (blog), Columbia Climate School, Columbia University, November 10, 2016. http://blogs.ei.columbia.edu/2016/11/10/cities-the-vanguard-against-cli mate-change/.

Christie, Daniel J. 1997. "Reducing Direct and Structural Violence: The Human Needs Theory." *Peace and Conflict: Journal of Peace Psychology* 3 (4): 315–32.

Christie, Ryerson. 2008. "The Human Security Dilemma." In *Environmental Change and Human Security: Recognizing and Acting on Hazard Impacts*, edited by P. H. Liotta, David A. Mouat, William G. Kepner, and Judith M. Lancaster, 253–69. Dordrecht: Springer Netherlands.

———. 2010. "Critical Voices and Human Security: To Endure, to Engage or to Critique?" *Security Dialogue* 41 (2): 169–90.

Clapp, Jennifer. 2014. "World Hunger and the Global Economy: Strong Linkages, Weak Action." *Journal of International Affairs* 67 (2) (Spring/Summer): 1–17.

Clapp, Jennifer, and Marc J. Cohen, eds. 2009. *The Global Food Crisis: Governance Challenges and Opportunities*. Waterloo, Ont.: Wilfrid Laurier University Press.

Cohen, Roberta. 2012. "From Sovereign Responsibility to R2P." In *The Routledge Handbook of the Responsibility to Protect*, edited by W. Andy Knight and Frazer Egerton, 7–21. New York: Routledge.

Coleman, Isobel. 2004. "The Payoff from Women's Rights." *Foreign Affairs* 83 (3) (May/June): 80–95.

Coleman-Jensen, Alisha, Matthew P. Rabbitt, Christian A. Gregory, and Anita Singh. 2016. *Household Food Security in the United States in 2015*. Economic research report (USDA, Economic Research Service), no. 215. Washington, DC: United States Department of Agriculture. https://www.ers.usda.gov/webdocs/publications/79761/err-215.pdf.

Commission on Human Security. 2003. *Human Security Now*. United Nations. New York: Commission on Human Security. Available online at https://reliefweb.int/sites/reliefweb.int/files/resources/91BAEEDBA50C6907C1256D19006A9353-chs-security-may03.pdf.

Commission on the Truth for El Salvador. 1993. *From Madness to Hope: The 12-Year War in El Salvador; Report of the Commission on the Truth for El Salvador*. S/25500. New York: United Nations.

Conflict Archive on the Internet. n.d. "Deaths from the Conflict in Northern Ireland by Year and Status." Table. In "Northern Ireland Violence." Accessed November 19, 2021. https://docs.google.com/spreadsheets/d/1hRidYe3-avd7gvlZWVi1YZB7QY6dKhekPS1I1kbFTnY/edit#gid=0.

Cox, Robert W. 1981. "Social Forces, States and World Orders: Beyond International Relations Theory." *Millennium: Journal of International Studies* 10 (2): 126–55.

Cranston, Maurice. 1962. *What Are Human Rights?* New York: Basic Books.

———. 1967. "Human Rights: Real and Supposed." In *Political Theory and the Rights of Man*, edited by David Daiches Raphael, 43–51. Bloomington: Indiana University Press.

———. 1983. "Are There Any Human Rights?" *Daedalus* 112 (4) (Fall): 1–17.

Crawford, Kerry F. 2017. *Wartime Sexual Violence: From Silence to Condemnation of a Weapon of War*. Georgetown University Press.

Crawford, Kerry F., James H. Lebovic, and Julia M. Macdonald. 2015. "Explaining the Variation in Gender Composition of Personnel Contributions to UN Peacekeeping Operations." *Armed Forces and Society* 41 (2): 257–81.

Crowe, Portia. 2019. "As Greta Thunberg Inspires a World Revolution, One Young Ugandan Is Bringing the Climate Fight Home." *Independent*, December 28,

2019. https://www.independent.co.uk/climate-change/news/climate-change-leah -namugerwa-greta-thunburg-activism-protest-uganda-a9261326.html.

Cunningham, David E. 2010. "Blocking Resolution: How External States Can Prolong Civil Wars." *Journal of Peace Research* 47 (2) (March): 115–27.

Davenport, Coral, and Campbell Robertson. 2016. "Resettling the First American 'Climate Refugees.'" *New York Times*, May 2, 2016. https://www.nytimes .com/2016/05/03/us/resettling-the-first-american-climate-refugees.html.

Davidson, Joe. 2012. "Uncle Sam Didn't Welcome Gay Employees." Politics. *Washington Post*, March 2, 2012. https://www.washingtonpost.com/politics/uncle-sam -didnt-welcome-gay-employees/2012/03/01/gIQAny0PmR_story.html.

DeSimone, Daniel C. 2021. "COVID-19 Infections by Race: What's Behind the Health Disparities?" Mayo Clinic, April 29, 2021. https://www.mayoclinic.org /diseases-conditions/coronavirus/expert-answers/coronavirus-infection-by-race /faq-20488802.

Devlin, Kat, Moira Fagan, and Aidan Connaughton. 2021. "Global Views of How U.S. Has Handled Pandemic Have Improved, but Few Say It's Done a Good Job." Pew Research Center (website), June 10, 2021. https://www.pewresearch.org/fact -tank/2021/06/10/global-views-of-how-u-s-has-handled-pandemic-have-improved -but-few-say-its-done-a-good-job/.

DeYoung, Karen. 2019. "Venezuela's Health System in 'Utter Collapse' as Infectious Diseases Spread, Report Says." National Security. *Washington Post*, April 4, 2019. https://www.washingtonpost.com/world/national-security/venezuelas-health -system-in-utter-collapse-as-infectious-diseases-spread-report-says/2019/04/03 /fd39a152-563e-11e9-8ef3-fbd41a2ce4d5_story.html.

Dixon, Peter. 2020. "U.S. Cities and States Are Discussing Reparations for Black Americans. Here's What's Key." *Monkey Cage* (blog), *Washington Post*, August 24, 2020. https://www.washingtonpost.com/politics/2020/08/24/us-cities-states -are-discussing-reparations-black-americans-heres-whats-key/.

Domaradzki, Spasimir, Margaryta Khvostova, and David Pupovac. 2019. "Karel Vasak's Generations of Rights and the Contemporary Human Rights Discourse." *Human Rights Review* 20 (4): 423–43. https://doi.org/10.1007/s12142-019-00565-x.

Domonoske, Camila. 2016. "U.N. Admits Role In Haiti Cholera Outbreak that Has Killed Thousands." International. *The Two-Way* (blog), NPR.org, August 18, 2016. https://www.npr.org/sections/thetwo-way/2016/08/18/490468640/u-n-admits-role -in-haiti-cholera-outbreak-that-has-killed-thousands.

Donnelly, Jack. 1982. "Human Rights as Natural Rights." *Human Rights Quarterly* 4 (3) (Summer): 391–405.

Doyle, Michael W. 2016. "The Politics of Global Humanitarianism: The Responsibility to Protect Before and After Libya." *International Politics* 53 (1): 14–31.

Dube, Ryan. 2019. "Red Cross Announces Venezuelan Aid Effort." World: Latin America. *Wall Street Journal*, March 29, 2019. https://www.wsj.com/articles/red -cross-announces-venezuelan-aid-effort-11553899904.

Dudouet, Véronique. 2021. *From the Street to the Peace Table: Nonviolent Mobilization during Intrastate Peace Processes*. Peaceworks series, no. 176. Washington, DC: United States Institute of Peace.

Dyer, Paul. 2021. "Policy and Institutional Responses to COVID-19: South Korea." Report. *Brookings* (blog), June 15, 2021. https://www.brookings.edu/research/policy-and-institutional-responses-to-covid-19-south-korea/.

Economist. 2016. "Against the Grain." Finance and Economics. Economist.com, May 21, 2016. https://www.economist.com/finance-and-economics/2016/05/21/against-the-grain.

Edwards, Adrian. 2016. "UNHCR Warns of Imminent Humanitarian Crisis in Greece." Edited by J. Clayton. UNHCR.org, March 1, 2016. https://www.unhcr.org/news/latest/2016/3/56d58c146/unhcr-warns-imminent-humanitarian-crisis-greece.html.

Elkins, Caroline. 2022. *Legacy of Violence: A History of the British Empire*. New York: Alfred A. Knopf.

English, Richard. 2003. *Armed Struggle: The History of the IRA*. London: Pan Macmillan.

Enloe, Cynthia. 2014. *Bananas, Beaches and Bases: Making Feminist Sense of International Politics*, 2nd ed. Berkeley: University of California Press.

Eriksen, Thomas Hylland. 2001. "Ethnic Identity, National Identity, and Intergroup Conflict: The Significance of Personal Experiences." In *Social Identity, Intergroup Conflict, and Conflict Resolution*, edited by Richard D. Ashmore, Lee Jussim, and David Wilder, 42–68. Oxford: Oxford University Press.

European Council. 2022. "Climate Change: What the EU Is Doing." Policies. Consilium.Europa.eu, last modified April 26, 2022. https://www.consilium.europa.eu/en/policies/climate-change/.

Evans, Alex. 2010. "Resource Scarcity, Climate Change and the Risk of Violent Conflict." World Development Report 2011, background paper, September 9, 2010. Washington, DC: World Bank. https://openknowledge.worldbank.org/bitstream/handle/10986/9191/WDR2011_0024.pdf.

Fagan, Moira, and Christine Huang. 2019. "A Look at How People around the World View Climate Change." Pew Research Center (website), April 18, 2019. https://www.pewresearch.org/fact-tank/2019/04/18/a-look-at-how-people-around-the-world-view-climate-change/.

Falk, Gene, Paul D. Romero, Isaac A. Nicchitta, and Emma C. Nyhof. 2021. "Unemployment Rates during the COVID-19 Pandemic." Congressional Research Service report no. R46554, last modified August 20, 2021. https://sgp.fas.org/crs/misc/R46554.pdf.

Famine Early Warning Systems Network. n.d. "South Sudan." East Africa. FEWS Net, accessed May 12, 2022. https://fews.net/east-africa/south-sudan.

———. 2017. "Conflict Displaces Well over 100,000 in April as Extreme Levels of Food Insecurity Persist." *South Sudan: Food Security Outlook Update* (April 2017). FEWS Net. https://fews.net/sites/default/files/documents/reports/South%20Sudan%20FSOU%2004_2017_0.pdf.

———. [2021]. "Multi-season Drought Is Expected to Drive High Food Assistance Needs through Early 2022." *Somalia: Food Security Outlook* (June 2021–January 2022). FEWS Net. https://fews.net/sites/default/files/documents/reports/somalia-food-security-outlook-202106-final.pdf.

Fan, Shenggen. 2014. "Ending World Hunger and Undernutrition by 2025." *IFPRI Blog*, International Food Policy Research Institute, June 2, 2014. http://www.ifpri.org/blog/ending-world-hunger-and-undernutrition-2025.

Fayyad, Abdallah. 2020. "Welcome to the New Civil Rights Era." Opinion. *Boston Globe*, July 10, 2020. https://www.bostonglobe.com/2020/07/10/opinion/welcome-new-civil-rights-era/.

Fearon, James D. 1995. "Rationalist Explanations for War." *International Organization* 49 (3) (Summer): 379–414.

Ferreira, Francisco H. G. 2021. "Inequality in the Time of COVID-19." *Finance and Development* (June): 20–23. International Monetary Fund. https://www.imf.org/external/pubs/ft/fandd/2021/06/pdf/inequality-and-covid-19-ferreira.pdf.

Fidler, David P. 2004. "Germs, Norms and Power: Global Health's Political Revolution." *Law, Social Justice and Global Development* 1. https://www2.warwick.ac.uk/fac/soc/law/elj/lgd/2004_1/fidler/.

Finnemore, Martha. 1996. "Constructing Norms of Humanitarian Intervention." In *The Culture of National Security: Norms and Identity in World Politics*, edited by Peter J. Katzenstein, 153–85. New York: Columbia University Press.

Finnemore, Martha, and Kathryn Sikkink. 1998. "International Norm Dynamics and Political Change." *International Organization* 52 (4) (Autumn): 887–917.

Firchow, Pamina, and Roger Mac Ginty. 2017. "Measuring Peace: Comparability, Commensurability, and Complementarity Using Bottom-Up Indicators." *International Studies Review* 19 (1) (March): 6–27.

Flores, Thomas Edward, and Irfan Nooruddin. 2009. "Democracy Under the Gun: Understanding Postconflict Economic Recovery." *Journal of Conflict Resolution* 53 (1): 3–29.

Fontan, Victoria. 2012. *Decolonizing Peace*. Lake Oswego, OR: World Dignity University Press.

Food and Agriculture Organization of the United Nations. 2006. "Food Security." *Policy Brief* 2 (June). http://www.fao.org/forestry/13128-0e6f36f27e0091055bec28ebe830f46b3.pdf.

———. 2015. *The Impact of Natural Hazards and Disasters on Agriculture, and Food Security and Nutrition*. [Rome]: FAO. http://www.fao.org/3/a-i5128e.pdf.

———. 2016. *The State of Food and Agriculture, 2016: Climate Change, Agriculture and Food Security*. Rome: FAO. https://www.fao.org/3/i6030e/i6030e.pdf.

Food and Agriculture Organization of the United Nations, International Fund for Agricultural Development, and World Food Programme. 2015. *The State of Food Insecurity in the World: Meeting of the 2015 International Hunger Targets; Taking Stock of Uneven Progress*. Rome: FAO. http://www.fao.org/3/i4646e/i4646e.pdf.

Fortna, Virginia Page. 2008. *Does Peacekeeping Work? Shaping Belligerents' Choices after Civil Wars*. Princeton: Princeton University Press.

Freden, Bradley A. 2020. "OAS Resolution Condemns the Fraudulent Elections in Venezuela." News and Events. US Mission to the Organization of American States, USOAS.USMission.gov, December 9, 2020. https://usoas.usmission.gov/oas-resolution-condemns-the-fraudulent-elections-in-venezuela/.

Freedom House. 2016. "Freedom in the World 2016: Venezuela; Freedom in the World 1999." Archived at http://archive.ph/VQJLE.

Friedman, Uri. 2020. "New Zealand's Prime Minister May Be the Most Effective Leader on the Planet." Politics. *The Atlantic*, April 19, 2020. https://www.theatlantic.com/politics/archive/2020/04/jacinda-ardern-new-zealand-leadership-coronavirus/610237/.

Gaglias, Alexis. 2016. "The Hidden Heroes of Greece's Refugee Crisis." The Worldpost. *HuffPost*, last modified June 6, 2016. https://www.huffpost.com/entry/volunteers-with-greek-refugees_n_574f54b3e4b0eb20fa0cb52c.

Galtung, Johan. 1969. "Violence, Peace, and Peace Research." *Journal of Peace Research* 6 (3): 167–91.

———. 1996. *Peace by Peaceful Means: Peace and Conflict, Development and Civilization*. Oslo: PRIO.

Garcia Cano, Regina, and Jorge Rueda. 2021. "Despite Ally Donations, Few Venezuelans Get COVID-19 Vaccine." APNews.com, July 2, 2021. https://apnews.com/article/caribbean-europe-venezuela-coronavirus-vaccine-health-a13a9f95174cab7162c43cd106e506c2.

Garcia, Cardiff, and Mariana Zuniga. 2019. "Why Are Venezuelans Starving?" *The Indicator from Planet Money* (blog), NPR.org, March 20, 2019. https://www.npr.org/transcripts/705259623.

Gavi. 2021. "COVAX and World Bank to Accelerate Vaccine Access for Developing Countries." Gavi.org, July 26, 2021. https://www.gavi.org/news/media-room/covax-and-world-bank-accelerate-vaccine-access-developing-countries.

Gaynor, Tim. 2020. "'Climate Change Is the Defining Crisis of Our Time and It Particularly Impacts the Displaced.'" UN Refugee Agency, UNHCR.org, November 30, 2020. https://www.unhcr.org/news/latest/2020/11/5fbf73384/climate-change-defining-crisis-time-particularly-impacts-displaced.html.

Gbowee, Leymah. 2011. *Mighty Be Our Powers: How Sisterhood, Prayer, and Sex Changed a Nation at War; A Memoir*. With Carol Mithers. New York: Beast Books.

Ghobarah, Hazem Adam, Paul Huth, and Bruce Russett. 2003. "Civil Wars Kill and Maim People—Long after the Shooting Stops." *American Political Science Review* 97 (2) (May): 189–202.

Gifkins, Jess. 2016. "R2P in the UN Security Council: Darfur, Libya and Beyond." *Cooperation and Conflict* 51 (2): 148–65.

Gladstone, Rick. 2016a. "Cholera Deaths in Haiti Could Far Exceed Official Count." *New York Times*, March 18, 2016. https://www.nytimes.com/2016/03/19/world/americas/cholera-deaths-in-haiti-could-far-exceed-official-count.html.

———. 2016b. "Lawmakers Urge John Kerry to Press UN for Haiti Cholera Response." *New York Times*, June 29, 2016. https://www.nytimes.com/2016/06/30/world/americas/haiti-cholera-john-kerry-congress.html.

Global Centre for the Responsibility to Protect. 2019. "R2P References in United Nations Human Rights Council Resolutions." Globalr2p.org, October 2019. Text available at https://www.globalr2p.org/wp-content/uploads/2019/10/HRC-Resolutions-R2P-19-October-2019.pdf.

Global Covenant of Mayors for Climate and Energy. n.d. "Who We Are." GlobalCov enantofMayors.org, accessed May 12, 2022. https://www.globalcovenantofmayors .org/who-we-are/.

Goins, Samantha. 2018. "Sea-Level Rise and Climate Migration: The Story of Kiribati." *Vibrant Environment* (blog), Environmental Law Institute, July 16, 2018. https://www.eli.org/vibrant-environment-blog/sea-level-rise-and-climate-migra tion-story-kiribati.

Goldstein, Amy, and Emily Guskin. 2020. "Almost One-Third of Black Americans Know Someone Who Died of Covid-19, Survey Shows." Health. *Washington Post*, June 26, 2020. https://www.washingtonpost.com/health/almost-one-third-of-black -americans-know-someone-who-died-of-covid-19-survey-shows/2020/06/25/3ec1 d4b2-b563-11ea-aca5-ebb63d27e1ff_story.html.

Goldstein, Joshua S. 2001. *War and Gender: How Gender Shapes the War System and Vice Versa*. New York: Cambridge University Press.

González Peña, Andrea, and Han Dorussen. 2021. "The Reintegration of Ex-combatants and Post-conflict Violence: An Analysis of Municipal Crime Levels in Colombia." *Conflict Management and Peace Science* 38 (3): 316–37.

Gould, Elise, and Valerie Wilson. 2020. "Black Workers Face Two of the Most Lethal Preexisting Conditions for Coronavirus—Racism and Economic Inequality." Report. Economic Policy Institute, EPI.org, June 1, 2020. https://files.epi.org/pdf /193246.pdf.

Government Offices of Sweden. n.d. "Feminist Foreign Policy." Accessed July 15, 2021. https://www.government.se/government-policy/feminist-foreign-policy/.

Government of New Zealand. 2020. "New Zealand COVID-19 Alert Levels." United against COVID-19, Govt.nz, March 21, 2020. https://web.archive.org/web /20200321030901/https://covid19.govt.nz/assets/COVID_Alert-levels_v2.pdf.

Grayson, Kyle. 2003. "Securitization and the Boomerang Debate: A Rejoinder to Liotta and Smith-Windsor." *Security Dialogue* 34 (3) (September): 337–43.

Gupta, Alisha Haridasani. 2020. "What Do Sweden and Mexico Have in Common? A Feminist Foreign Policy." In Her Words. *New York Times*, July 21, 2020. https:// www.nytimes.com/2020/07/21/us/sweden-feminist-foreign-policy.html.

Gurr, Ted Robert. 2000. *Peoples versus States: Minorities at Risk in the New Century*. Washington, DC: United States Institute of Peace Press.

Hall, Julia A., and Human Rights Watch. 1997. *To Serve without Favor: Policing, Human Rights, and Accountability in Northern Ireland*. New York: Human Rights Watch. https://www.hrw.org/reports/1997/uk1/.

Hanlon, Robert J., and Kenneth Christie. 2016. *Freedom from Fear, Freedom from Want: An Introduction to Human Security*. North York and Ontario: University of Toronto Press.

Hansen, J., A. Lacis, D. Johnson, P. Lee, D. Rind, and G. Russell. 1981. "Climate Impact of Increasing Atmospheric Carbon Dioxide." *Science* 213 (4511): 957–66.

Hansen, Lene. 2000. "The Little Mermaid's Silent Security Dilemma and the Absence of Gender in the Copenhagen School." *Millennium: Journal of International Studies* 29 (2): 285–306.

Harris-Short, Sonia. 2003. "International Human Rights Law: Imperialist, Inept and Ineffective? Cultural Relativism and the UN Convention on the Rights of the Child." *Human Rights Quarterly* 25 (1) (February): 130–81.

Harvey, Fiona. 2016. "Arctic Ice Melt Could Trigger Uncontrollable Climate Change at Global Level." Polar Regions. *The Guardian*, November 25, 2016. https://www .theguardian.com/environment/2016/nov/25/arctic-ice-melt-trigger-uncontrollable -climate-change-global-level.

Hathaway, Oona A., and Scott J. Shapiro. 2018. *The Internationalists: How a Radical Plan to Outlaw War Remade the World*. New York: Simon and Schuster.

Hehir, Aidan. 2012. *The Responsibility to Protect: Rhetoric, Reality and the Future of Humanitarian Intervention*. New York: Palgrave Macmillan.

———. 2016. "Assessing the Influence of the Responsibility to Protect on the UN Security Council during the Arab Spring." *Cooperation and Conflict* 51 (2): 166–83.

Henderson, Stacey. 2017. "The Arms Trade Treaty: Responsibility to Protect in Action?" *Global Responsibility to Protect* 9 (2): 147–72.

Hendrix, Cullen S., and Henk-Jan Brinkman. 2013. "Food Insecurity and Conflict Dynamics: Causal Linkages and Complex Feedbacks." *Stability: International Journal of Security and Development* 2 (2): 1–18. https://www.stabilityjournal.org /articles/10.5334/sta.bm/.

Hendrix, Cullen S., and Sarah M. Glaser. 2007. "Trends and Triggers: Climate, Climate Change and Civil Conflict in Sub-Saharan Africa." *Political Geography* 26 (6) (August): 695–715. https://www.sciencedirect.com/science/article/abs/pii /S0962629807000844.

Hernández, Rafael. 2019. "La guerra silente de las zonas de paz." Noticias. *Vice Argentina*, April 1, 2019. https://www.vice.com/es/article/xwbb4n/la-guerra-silente -de-las-zonas-de-paz.

Herrero, Ana Vanessa. 2020. "Maduro Consolidates Power in Venezuela, Dominating Election Boycotted by Opposition." The Americas. *Washington Post*, December 7, 2020. https://www.washingtonpost.com/world/the_americas/venezuela-election -national-assembly-maduro-guaido/2020/12/06/8a9fee74-35d2-11eb-8d38-6aea 1adb3839_story.html.

Herz, Barbara, and Gene B. Sperling. 2004. *What Works in Girls' Education: Evidence and Policies from the Developing World*. New York: Council on Foreign Relations.

Hick, Rod. 2014. "Poverty as Capability Deprivation: Conceptualising and Measuring Poverty in Contemporary Europe." *European Journal of Sociology/Archives Européennes de Sociologie/Europäisches Archiv Für Soziologie* 55 (3) (December): 295–323.

High-Level Panel of Eminent Persons on the Post-2015 Development Agenda. 2013. *A New Global Partnership: Eradicate Poverty and Transform Economies through Sustainable Development*. Report. United Nations. New York: United Nations. https://sustainabledevelopment.un.org/content/documents/8932013-05%20-%20 HLP%20Report%20-%20A%20New%20Global%20Partnership.pdf.

Hillyard, Paddy. 1993. *Suspect Community: People's Experience of the Prevention of Terrorism Acts in Britain*. London: Pluto Press in association with Liberty.

Hirschkind, Charles, and Saba Mahmood. 2002. "Feminism, the Taliban, and Politics of Counter-insurgency." *Anthropological Quarterly* 75 (2) (Spring): 339–54.

Hoffmann, Stanley. 1981. *Duties beyond Borders: On the Limits and Possibilities of Ethical International Politics*. Syracuse, NY: Syracuse University Press.

Horton, Richard. 2020. "Offline: COVID-19 Is Not a Pandemic." *Lancet* 396 (10255) (September 26): 874. https://www.thelancet.com/journals/lancet/article/PIIS0140 -6736(20)32000-6/fulltext.

Howard, Lise Morjé. 2008. *UN Peacekeeping in Civil Wars*. Cambridge: Cambridge University Press.

Howe, Paul. 2019. "The Triple Nexus: A Potential Approach to Supporting the Achievement of the Sustainable Development Goals?" *World Development* 124 (December): 104629.

Hu, Yang. 2020. "Intersecting Ethnic and Native-Migrant Inequalities in the Economic Impact of the COVID-19 Pandemic in the UK." *Research in Social Stratification and Mobility* 68 (August). https://www.sciencedirect.com/science/article /pii/S0276562420300640.

Hudson, Natalie Florea. 2010. *Gender, Human Security and the United Nations: Security Language as a Political Framework for Women*. New York: Routledge.

Hudson, Valerie M., and Andrea den Boer. 2002. "A Surplus of Men, a Deficit of Peace: Security and Sex Ratios in Asia's Largest States." *International Security* 26 (4) (Spring): 5–38.

Hudson, Valerie M., Bonnie Ballif-Spanvill, Mary Caprioli, and Chad F. Emmett. 2012. *Sex and World Peace*. New York: Columbia University Press.

Huish, Robert, and Jerry Spiegel. 2008. "Integrating Health and Human Security into Foreign Policy: Cuba's Surprising Success." *International Journal of Cuban Studies* 1 (1) (June): 42–53. https://ucl.scienceopen.com/document_file/e7dda8f3 -f112-4d9b-83b2-0111f38402a7/ScienceOpen/41945989.pdf.

Huish, Robert, and John M. Kirk. 2007. "Cuban Medical Internationalism and the Development of the Latin American School of Medicine." *Latin American Perspectives* 34 (6): 77–92.

Hultman, Lisa, Jacob Kathman, and Megan Shannon. 2013. "United Nations Peacekeeping and Civilian Protection in Civil War." *American Journal of Political Science* 57 (4) (October): 875–91.

Human Rights Watch. 2019. "Venezuela: UN Should Lead Full-Scale Emergency Response." News. HRW.org, April 4, 2019. https://www.hrw.org/news/2019/04/04 /venezuela-un-should-lead-full-scale-emergency-response.

———. 2021. "'Break Their Lineage, Break Their Roots': China's Crimes against Humanity Targeting Uyghurs and Other Turkic Muslims." Report. HRW.org, April 19, 2021. https://www.hrw.org/report/2021/04/19/break-their-lineage-break-their -roots/chinas-crimes-against-humanity-targeting.

———. 2022. "Ukraine: Apparent War Crimes in Russian-Controlled Areas." News. HRW.org, April 3, 2022. https://www.hrw.org/news/2022/04/03/ukraine-apparent -war-crimes-russia-controlled-areas.

Human Security Center, Human Security Report Project, Simon Fraser University. 2011. *Human Security Report 2009/2010: The Causes of Peace and the Shrinking Costs of War*. Vancouver, BC: Oxford University Press.

Independent Commission on Policing for Northern Ireland. 1999. *A New Beginning: Policing in Northern Ireland; The Report on the Independent Commission on Policing for Northern Ireland*. Colegate, Norwich: The Crown. Available online at https://cain.ulster.ac.uk/issues/police/patten/patten99.pdf.

Intergovernmental Panel on Climate Change. 2007. "Summary for Policymakers." In *Climate Change 2007: The Physical Science Basis; Working Group I Contribution to the Fourth Assessment Report of the Intergovernmental Panel on Climate Change*, edited by Solomon, Susan, Dahe Qin, Martin Manning, Melinda Marquis, Kristen Averyt, Melinda M. B. Tignor, and Henry LeRoy Miller Jr., and Zhenlin Chen, 1–18. Cambridge: Cambridge University Press. https://www.ipcc.ch/site/assets/uploads/2018/05/ar4_wg1_full_report-1.pdf.

———. [2019]. "Frequently Asked Questions: FAQ 1.1: Why Are We Talking about 1.5°C?" and "Frequently Asked Questions: FAQ 1.2: How Close Are We to 1.5°C?" In *Global Warming of 1.5°C: An IPCC Special Report on the Impacts of Global Warming of 1.5°C Above Pre-industrial Levels and Related Global Greenhouse Gas Emission Pathways, in the Context of Strengthening the Global Response to the Threat of Climate Change, Sustainable Development, and Efforts to Eradicate Poverty*, ed. Valérie Masson-Delmotte, Panmao Zhai, Hans-Otto Pörtner, Debra Roberts, Jim Skea, Priyadarshi R. Shukla, Anna Pirani, Wilfram Moufouma-Okia, Clotilde Péan, Roz Pidcock, Sarah Connors, J. B. Robin Matthews, Yang Chen, Xiao Zhou, Melissa I. Gomis, Elisabeth Lonnoy, Tom Maycock, Melinda Tignor, and Tim Waterfield, 5–9. [Geneva]: IPCC. https://www.ipcc.ch/site/assets/uploads/sites/2/2019/05/SR15_FAQ_High_Res.pdf.

———. [2022]. "Sixth Assessment Report." https://www.ipcc.ch/assessment-report/ar6/.

International Commission on Intervention and State Sovereignty. 2001. *The Responsibility to Protect: Report of the International Commission on Intervention and State Sovereignty*. December 2001. Ottawa: International Development Research Centre. https://idl-bnc-idrc.dspacedirect.org/bitstream/handle/10625/18432/IDL-18432.pdf.

International Criminal Court. 2011. *Rome Statute of the International Criminal Court*. Updated from the original statute, signed in Rome, July 17, 1998. Updated text available at https://www.icc-cpi.int/sites/default/files/RS-Eng.pdf.

Jackson, Chris, Mallory Newall, and Jinhee Yi. 2021. "Americans Growing More Concerned about COVID-19, yet Unwilling to Take Additional Safety Precautions or Change Behavior." Ipsos (website), July 20, 2021 Updated text available at https://www.ipsos.com/en-us/news-polls/axios-ipsos-coronavirus-index.

Jackson, Jean E. 2007. "Rights to Indigenous Culture in Colombia." In *The Practice of Human Rights: Tracking Law between the Global and the Local*, edited by Mark Goodale and Sally Engle Merry, 204–41. Cambridge: Cambridge University Press.

Jensen, Steven L. B. 2016. *The Making of International Human Rights: The 1960s, Decolonization, and the Reconstruction of Global Values.* Cambridge: Cambridge University Press.

Jervis, Robert. 2017. *Perception and Misperception in International Politics.* Princeton, NJ: Princeton University Press.

Jones, Anna. 2020. "How Did New Zealand Become Covid-19 Free?" Asia. BBC News, BBC.com, July 10, 2020. https://www.bbc.com/news/world-asia-53274085.

Jones, Benjamin T., Eleanora Mattiacci, and Bear F. Braumoeller. 2017. "Food Scarcity and State Vulnerability: Unpacking the Link between Climate Variability and Violent Unrest." *Journal of Peace Research* 54 (3): 335–50.

Joshi, Madhav, Jason Michael Quinn, and Patrick M. Regan. 2015. "Annualized Implementation Data on Comprehensive Intrastate Peace Accords, 1989–2012." *Journal of Peace Research* 52 (4): 551–62.

Joshi, Madhav, and John Darby. 2013. "Introducing the Peace Accords Matrix (PAM): A Database of Comprehensive Peace Agreements and Their Implementation, 1989–2007." *Peacebuilding* 1 (2): 256–74.

Jurkovich, Michelle. 2016. "Venezuela Has Solved Its Hunger Problem? Don't Believe the U.N.'s Numbers." *Monkey Cage* (blog), *Washington Post*, September 21, 2016. https://www.washingtonpost.com/news/monkey-cage/wp/2016/09/21/venezuela-has-solved-its-hunger-problem-dont-believe-the-u-n-s-numbers/.

———. 2020a. *Feeding the Hungry: Advocacy and Blame in the Global Fight against Hunger.* Ithaca, NY: Cornell University Press.

———. 2020b. "What Isn't a Norm? Redefining the Conceptual Boundaries of 'Norms' in the Human Rights Literature." *International Studies Review* 22 (3) (September): 693–71.

Kaldor, Mary. 2005. "Old Wars, Cold Wars, New Wars, and the War on Terror." *International Politics* 42: 491–98.

———. 2007. *Human Security: Reflections on Globalization and Intervention.* Cambridge: Polity.

Kalyvas, Stathis N. 2001. "'New' and 'Old' Civil Wars: A Valid Distinction?" *World Politics* 54 (1) (October): 99–118.

Kandiyoti, Deniz. 2008. "The Politics of Gender and Reconstruction in Afghanistan: Old Dilemmas or New Challenges?" In *Gendered Peace: Women's Struggles for Post-war Justice and Reconciliation*, edited by Donna Pankhurst, 155–85. New York: Routledge.

Kang, Seonjou, and James Meernik. 2005. "Civil War Destruction and the Prospects for Economic Growth." *Journal of Politics* 67 (1) (February): 88–109.

Karim, Sabrina, and Kyle Beardsley. 2017. *Equal Opportunity Peacekeeping: Women, Peace, and Security in Post-conflict States.* Oxford Studies in Gender and International Relations. New York: Oxford University Press.

Katella, Kathy. 2021. "Our Pandemic Year—A COVID-19 Timeline." Family Health. Yale Medicine (website), March 9, 2021. https://www.yalemedicine.org/news/covid-timeline.

Katz, Jonathan M. 2016a. "The Killer Hiding in the CDC Map." Foreigners. *Slate*, April 24, 2016. https://slate.com/news-and-politics/2016/04/what-caused-haitis -cholera-epidemic-the-cdcs-museum-knows-but-wont-say.html.

———. 2016b. "U.N. Admits Role in Cholera Epidemic in Haiti." *New York Times*, August 17, 2016. https://www.nytimes.com/2016/08/18/world/americas/united -nations-haiti-cholera.html.

Katz, Rebecca, and Daniel A. Singer. 2007. "Health and Security in Foreign Policy." *Bulletin of the World Health Organization* 85 (3) (March): 233–34. https://www .ncbi.nlm.nih.gov/pmc/articles/PMC2636232/.

Keck, Margaret E., and Kathryn Sikkink. 1998. *Activists Beyond Borders*. Ithaca, NY: Cornell University Press.

Keefe, Patrick Radden. 2019. *Say Nothing: A True Story of Murder and Memory in Northern Ireland*. New York: Doubleday.

Kendi, Ibram X. 2019. *How to Be an Antiracist*. New York: One World.

Keohane, Robert O., and Joseph S. Nye Jr. 1973. "Power and Interdependence." *Survival* 15 (4): 158–65.

King, Gary, and Christopher J. L. Murray. 2001. "Rethinking Human Security." *Political Science Quarterly* 116 (4) (Winter): 585–610.

Knight, Kyle. 2016. "LGBT People in Emergencies—Risks and Service Gaps." Human Rights Watch, HRW.org, May 20, 2016. https://www.hrw.org/news/2016/05/20 /lgbt-people-emergencies-risks-and-service-gaps.

Kochhar, Rakesh, and Richard Fry. 2014. "Wealth Inequality Has Widened along Racial, Ethnic Lines since End of Great Recession." Pew Research Center, December 12, 2014. http://www.pewresearch.org/fact-tank/2014/12/12/racial-wealth-gaps -great-recession/.

Kreutz, Joakim. 2010. "How and When Armed Conflicts End: Introducing the UCDP Conflict Termination Dataset." *Journal of Peace Research* 47 (2): 243–50. https:// www.researchgate.net/publication/227574647_How_and_when_armed_conflicts _end_Introducing_the_UCDP_Conflict_Termination_dataset.

Kroc Institute for International Peace Studies. n.d.(a). "Peace Accords Matrix." University of Notre Dame, ND.edu, accessed May 9, 2022. https://peaceaccords .nd.edu.

———. n.d.(b). "Police Reform: Northern Ireland Good Friday Agreement." Peace Accords Matrix, University of Notre Dame, ND.edu, accessed May 24, 2022. https://peaceaccords.nd.edu/provision/police-reform-northern-ireland-good-friday -agreement.

Kuperman, Alan J. 2013. "A Model Humanitarian Intervention? Reassessing NATO's Libya Campaign." *International Security* 38 (1) (Summer): 105–36.

Kydd, Andrew H., and Barbara F. Walter. 2006. "The Strategies of Terrorism." *International Security* 31 (1) (Summer): 49–80.

Lacina, Bethany, and Nils Petter Gleditsch. 2005. "Monitoring Trends in Global Combat: A New Dataset of Battle Deaths." *European Journal of Population/Revue européenne de Démographie* 21 (2): 145–66.

Lai, Brian, and Clayton Thyne. 2007. "The Effect of Civil War on Education, 1980– 97." *Journal of Peace Research* 44 (3) (May): 277–92.

Lappé, Francis Moore, Joseph Collins, and Peter Rosset. 1998. *World Hunger: Twelve Myths*. With Luis Esparza. New York: Grove Press.

Lederach, John Paul. 1997. *Building Peace: Sustainable Reconciliation in Divided Societies*. Washington, DC: United States Institute of Peace Press.

LeVaux, Ari. 2013. "It's OK to Eat Quinoa." Food. *Slate*, January 25, 2013. https:// slate.com/human-interest/2013/01/quinoa-bad-for-bolivian-and-peruvian-farmers -ignore-the-media-hand-wringing.html.

Liotta, Peter H. 2002. "Boomerang Effect: The Convergence of National and Human Security." *Security Dialogue* 33 (4): 473–88.

Llano, Rayden, and Kenji Shibuya. 2011. "Japan's Evolving Role in Global Health." Commentary. National Bureau of Asian Research, NBR.org, June 9, 2011. https:// www.nbr.org/publication/japans-evolving-role-in-global-health/.

Lund, Michael S. 1996. *Preventing Violent Conflict: A Strategy for Preventive Diplomacy*. Washington, DC: United States Institute of Peace.

Lynch, Patrick. 2017. "2016 Climate Trends Continue to Break Records." Climate. NASA.gov, last modified August 6, 2016. https://www.nasa.gov/feature/god dard/2016/climate-trends-continue-to-break-records.

Ma, Alexandra. 2015. "Will a Venezuelan Opposition Party's Election Victory Bring Real Change?" The Worldpost. *HuffPost*, December 19, 2015. https://www.huffpost .com/entry/venezuela-elections-david-smilde_n_56745723e4b0b958f6567bd8.

Mac Ginty, Roger. 2014. "Everyday Peace: Bottom-Up and Local Agency in Conflict-Affected Societies." *Security Dialogue* 45 (6) (December): 548–64.

Mac Ginty, Roger, and Oliver P. Richmond. 2013. "The Local Turn in Peace Building: A Critical Agenda for Peace." *Third World Quarterly* 34 (5): 763–83.

MacFarlane, S. Neil, and Yuen Foong Khong. 2006. *Human Security and the UN: A Critical History*. Bloomington: Indiana University Press.

MacKenzie, Megan. 2015. *Beyond the Band of Brothers: The US Military and the Myth that Women Can't Fight*. Cambridge: Cambridge University Press.

Macrotrends. n.d. "WTI Crude Oil Prices—10 Year Daily Chart." Macrotrends.net, accessed June 30, 2021. https://www.macrotrends.net/2516/wti-crude-oil-prices -10-year-daily-chart.

Maizland, Lindsay. 2021. "China's Repression of Uyghurs in Xinjiang." Backgrounder. Council on Foreign Relations, CFR.org, March 1, 2021. https://www.cfr .org/backgrounder/chinas-repression-uyghurs-xinjiang.

Mallavarapu, Siddharth. 2015. "Colonialism and the Responsibility to Protect." In *Theorising the Responsibility to Protect*, edited by Ramesh Chandra Thakur and William Maley, 305–22. Cambridge and New York: Cambridge University Press.

Malsin, Jared. 2021. "Mass Graves Stir Anger as Libya Seeks an Elusive Peace." World. *Wall Street Journal*, October 22, 2021. https://www.wsj.com/articles/mass -graves-stir-anger-as-libya-seeks-an-elusive-peace-11634905670 (pay wall).

Markovits, Martin, and Manuel Rueda. 2013. "Venezuela Election Is a High Stakes Affair for Local Vigilante Groups." ABC News, March 27, 2013. https://abcnews .go.com/ABC_Univision/ABC_Univision/venezuela-election-high-stakes-affair -local-vigilante-groups/story?id=18822407.

Marks, Thomas A. 2004. "Ideology of Insurgency: New Ethnic Focus or Old Cold War Distortions?" *Small Wars and Insurgencies* 15 (1): 107–28.

Martin, Mary, and Taylor Owen. 2010. "The Second Generation of Human Security: Lessons from the UN and EU Experience." *International Affairs* 86 (1) (January): 211–24. Available for download from https://doi.org/10.1111/j.1468 -2346.2010.00876.x.

Martin, Timothy W., and Dasl Yoon. 2020. "How South Korea Successfully Managed Coronavirus." *Wall Street Journal*, September 25, 2020. https://www.wsj.com/arti cles/lessons-from-south-korea-on-how-to-manage-covid-11601044329 (pay wall).

Mason, T. David, and Sara McLaughlin Mitchell, eds. 2016. *What Do We Know about Civil Wars?* Lanham, MD: Rowman & Littlefield.

Mathers, Colin D., Ritu Sadana, Joshua A. Salomon, Christopher J. L. Murray, and Alan D. Lopez. 2001. "Healthy Life Expectancy in 191 Countries, 1999." *Lancet* 357 (9269): 1685–91.

McKittrick, David, Seamus Kelters, Brian Feeney, Chris Thornton, and David McVea. 2001. *Lost Lives: The Stories of the Men, Women and Children Who Died as a Result of the Northern Ireland Troubles*. Edinburgh: Random House.

McSweeney, William. 1999. *Security, Identity and Interests: A Sociology of International Relations*. Cambridge: Cambridge University Press.

Médecins Sans Frontières. 2014. "Ebola: International Response Slow and Uneven." News and Stories. DoctorsWithoutBorders.org, December 1, 2014. https://www .doctorswithoutborders.org/latest/ebola-international-response-slow-and-uneven.

———. 2017. "G7 Fails to Provide Humane Response to Global Displacement Crisis." News and Stories. DoctorsWithoutBorders.org, May 27, 2017. https:// www.doctorswithoutborders.org/latest/g7-fails-provide-humane-response-global -displacement-crisis.

———. 2018. "'No One Was Left': Death and Violence against the Rohingya in Rakhine State, Myanmar." Report. MSF.org, March 9, 2018. https://www.msf.org /myanmarbangladesh-'no-one-was-left'-death-and-violence-against-rohingya.

Meier, Patrick, Doug Bond, and Joe Bond. 2007. "Environmental Influences on Pastoral Conflict in the Horn of Africa." *Political Geography* 26 (6) (August): 716–35. https://www.sciencedirect.com/science/article/abs/pii/S0962629807000820.

Melillo, Gianna. 2020. "What We're Reading: US Buys More Pfizer Vaccine; Walmart Sued Over Opioid Crisis; 2020's Deadly Toll." *American Journal of Managed Care*, AJMC.com, December 23, 2020. https://www.ajmc.com/view /what-we-re-reading-us-buys-more-pfizer-vaccine-walmart-sued-over-opioid-cri sis-2020-s-deadly-toll.

Meslin, Eric M., and Ibrahim Garba. 2016. "International Collaboration for Global Public Health." In *Public Health Ethics: Cases Spanning the Globe*, edited by Drue H. Barrett, Leonard W. Ortmann, Angus Dawson, Carla Saenz, Andreas Reis, and Gail Bolan, 241–84. Public Health Ethics Analysis vol. 3, series edited by Michael J. Selgelid. Switzerland: Springer International Publishing. https://link.springer .com/content/pdf/10.1007%2F978-3-319-23847-0.pdf.

Michener, Jamila. 2020. "Race, Politics, and the Affordable Care Act." *Journal of Health Politics, Policy and Law* 45 (4): 547–66.

Michener, Jamila, and Margaret Teresa Brower. 2020. "What's Policy Got to Do with It? Race, Gender and Economic Inequality in the United States." *Daedalus, the Journal of the American Academy of Arts and Sciences* 149 (1) (Winter): 100–18. https://www.amacad.org/sites/default/files/publication/downloads/Daedalus_Wi20_7_Michener%20Brower.pdf.

Mineo, Liz. 2020. "Forcing the UN to Do Right by Haitian Cholera Victims." National and World Affairs. *Harvard Gazette* (blog), October 6, 2020. https://news.harvard.edu/gazette/story/2020/10/a-decade-of-seeking-justice-for-haitian-cholera-victims/.

———. 2021. "Why the COVID-19 Outbreak in Brazil Has Become a Humanitarian Crisis." National and World Affairs. *Harvard Gazette* (blog), April 28, 2021. https://news.harvard.edu/gazette/story/2021/04/harvard-public-health-expert-discusses-brazils-covid-19-crisis/.

Moloney, Anastasia. 2016. "U.S. Judge Upholds U.N. Immunity in Haiti Cholera Case." Healthcare and Pharma. Reuters.com, August 19, 2016. https://www.reuters.com/article/us-haiti-cholera-idUSKCN10U1H6.

Murithi, Tim. 2008. *Ethics of Peacebuilding*. Edinburgh: Edinburgh University Press.

Murphy, Colleen, and Kelebogile Zvobgo. 2020. "Not a Moment but a Movement: The Case for Transitional Justice in the U.S." Global, Justice and Law, National. *Ms.*, December 16, 2020. https://msmagazine.com/2020/12/16/movement-transitional-justice-united-states/.

Nagata, Donna K., Jackie H. J. Kim, and Teresa U. Nguyen. 2015. "Processing Cultural Trauma: Intergenerational Effects of the Japanese American Incarceration." *Journal of Social Issues* 71 (2) (June): 356–70.

Nakaya, Sumie. 2003. "Women and Gender Equality in Peace Processes: From Women at the Negotiating Table to Postwar Structural Reforms in Guatemala and Somalia." *Global Governance* 9 (4) (October–December): 459–76.

Namugerwa, Leah. 2019. "School Strike for Climate: A Day in the Life of Ugandan Student Striker Leah Namugerwa." EarthDay.org, June 6, 2019. https://www.earthday.org/school-strike-for-climate-a-day-in-the-life-of-fridays-for-future-uganda-student-striker-leah-namugerwa/.

NASA. n.d. "Scientific Consensus: Earth's Climate Is Warming." Global Climate Change: Vital Signs of the Planet. NASA.gov, accessed May 25, 2022. https://climate.nasa.gov/scientific-consensus/.

NASA Earth Observatory. 2016. "Bolivia's Lake Poopó Disappears." Earth Observatory. NASA.gov, January 23, 2016. https://earthobservatory.nasa.gov/images/87363/bolivias-lake-poopo-disappears.

Ndongo, Oumar. 2020. "Women's Wartime Struggle for Peace and Security in the Mano River Union." In *Preventive Diplomacy, Security, and Human Rights in West Africa*, edited by Okon Akiba, 153–74. Cham, Switz.: Palgrave Macmillan.

Newman, Edward. 2010. "Critical Human Security Studies." *Review of International Studies* 36 (1): 77–94.

———. 2016. "Human Security: Reconciling Critical Aspirations with Political 'Realities.'" *British Journal of Criminology* 56 (6): 1165–83. https://doi.org/10.1093/bjc/azw016.

————. 2021. "COVID-19: A Human Security Analysis." *Global Society*, 1–24. https://doi.org/10.1080/13600826.2021.2010034.

Nianias, Helen. 2016. "Refugees in Lesbos: Are There Too Many NGOs on the Island?" Europe. *The Guardian*, January 5, 2016. https://www.theguardian.com /global-development-professionals-network/2016/jan/05/refugees-in-lesbos-are -there-too-many-ngos-on-the-island.

Nieuwenhuis, Rense, Teresa Munzi, Jörg Neugschwender, Heba Omar, and Flaviana Palmisano. 2018. *Gender Inequality and Poverty Are Intrinsically Linked: A Contribution to the Continued Monitoring of Selected Sustainable Development Goals.* New York: UN Women.

Nordberg, Jenny. 2015. "Who's Afraid of a Feminist Foreign Policy?" News Desk. *New Yorker*, April 15, 2015. https://www.newyorker.com/news/news-desk/swe dens-feminist-foreign-minister.

Normile, Dennis. 2020. "Coronavirus Cases Have Dropped Sharply in South Korea. What's the Secret to Its Success?" News: ScienceInsider. *Science*, March 17, 2020. https://www.sciencemag.org/news/2020/03/coronavirus-cases-have-dropped -sharply-south-korea-whats-secret-its-success.

Notaras, Mark. 2011. "Food Insecurity and the Conflict Trap." Peace and Security. *OurWorld*, United Nations University, August 31, 2011. https://ourworld.unu.edu /en/food-insecurity-and-the-conflict-trap.

NPR/TED Staff. 2020. "Xiye Bastida: How Are Young People Making the Choice to Fight Climate Change?" *TED Radio Hour*, NPR.org, May 22, 2020. https://www .npr.org/2020/05/22/860168455/xiye-bastida-how-are-young-people-making-the -choice-to-fight-climate-change.

Nteta, Tatishe. 2021. "UMass Amherst/WCVB Poll Finds Nearly Half of Americans Say the Federal Government Definitely Should Not Pay Reparations to the Descendants of Slaves." UMass.edu, April 29, 2021. https://www.umass.edu/news/article /umass-amherstwcvb-poll-finds-nearly-half.

Nugent, Ciara. 2019. "Why Venezuela Revives Historical Tensions Over U.S. Intervention in Latin America." *Time*, January 25, 2019. https://time.com/5512005 /venezuela-us-intervention-history-latin-america/.

O'Rawe, Mary. 2008. "Policing Change: To Reform or Not to Transform?" In *Northern Ireland after the Troubles*, edited by Colin Coulter and Michael Murray, 110–32. A Society in Transition series. Manchester: Manchester University Press.

Ortaliza, Jared, Kendal Orgera, Krutika Amin, and Cynthia Cox. 2021. "COVID-19 Continues to Be a Leading Cause of Death in the U.S. in June 2021." *Peterson-KFF Health System Tracker* (blog), July 1, 2021. https://www.healthsystemtracker.org /brief/covid-19-continues-to-be-a-leading-cause-of-death-in-the-u-s-in-june-2021/.

Our Children's Trust, Youth v. Gov. n.d. "Legal Actions: Juliana v. United States." OurChildrensTrust.org, accessed October 1, 2021. https://www.ourchildrenstrust .org/juliana-v-us.

Our Climate Voices. 2016. "Vic Barrett: White Plains, New York." OurClimate Voices.org, June 20, 2016. https://www.ourclimatevoices.org/2019/vicbarrett.

Oxfam International. 2020. "Hunger Crisis in South Sudan." Oxfam.org, February 20, 2020. https://www.oxfam.org/en/what-we-do/emergencies/hunger-crisis-south -sudan.

Paarlberg, Robert. 2010. *Food Politics: What Everyone Needs to Know*. Oxford: Oxford University Press.

Paffenholz, Thania. 2014. "Civil Society and Peace Negotiations: Beyond the Inclusion–Exclusion Dichotomy." *Negotiation Journal* 30 (1): 69–91.

———. 2021. "Perpetual Peacebuilding: A New Paradigm to Move Beyond the Linearity of Liberal Peacebuilding." *Journal of Intervention and Statebuilding* 15 (3): 367–85.

Pala, Christopher. 2020. "Kiribati's President's Plans to Raise Islands in Fight against Sea-Level Rise." World. *The Guardian*, August 10, 2020. http://www.theguard ian.com/world/2020/aug/10/kiribatis-presidents-plans-to-raise-islands-in-fight -against-sea-level-rise.

Paris, Roland. 2001. "Human Security: Paradigm Shift or Hot Air?" *International Security* 26 (2): 87–102.

———. 2004. *At War's End: Building Peace after Civil Conflict*. Cambridge: Cambridge University Press.

Parry, Martin L., Osvaldo F. Canziani, Jean P. Palutikof, Paul J. van der Linden, and Clair E. Hanson, eds. 2007. *Climate Change 2007: Impacts, Adaptation and Vulnerability; Working Group II Contribution to the Gourth Assessment Report of the Intergovernmental Panel on Climate Change*. Cambridge: Cambridge University Press. https://www.ipcc.ch/site/assets/uploads/2018/03/ar4_wg2_full_report.pdf.

Patten, Eileen. 2016. "Racial, Gender Wage Gaps Persist in U.S. despite Some Progress." Fact Tank. Pew Research, July 1, 2016. http://www.pewresearch.org/fact -tank/2016/07/01/racial-gender-wage-gaps-persist-in-u-s-despite-some-progress/.

PBS NewsHour. 2021. "U.S. Surgeon General on Delta Variant, Vaccine Hesitancy and COVID Long Haulers." PBS.org, July 2, 2021. https://www.pbs.org/news hour/show/u-s-surgeon-general-on-delta-variant-vaccine-hesitancy-and-covid -long-haulers.

Peralta, Eyder. 2019. "'Chavismo' Fades as Venezuela's Poor Suffer." With Lulu Garcia-Navarro. *Weekend Sunday Edition*, NPR.org, February 17, 2019. https:// www.npr.org/2019/02/17/695536858/chavismo-fades-as-venezuela-s-poor-suffer.

Perez-Leon-Acevedo, Juan-Pablo. 2021. "Victims and Appeals at the International Criminal Court (ICC): Evaluation under International Human Rights Standards." *International Journal of Human Rights* 25 (9): 1598–1624. https://www.tandfon line.com/doi/full/10.1080/13642987.2020.1859483.

Pettersson, Thérése, Shawn Davies, Amber Deniz, Garoun Engström, Nanar Hawach, Stina Högbladh, and Margareta Sollenberg Magnus Öberg. 2021. "Organized Violence, 1989–2020, with a Special Emphasis on Syria." *Journal of Peace Research* 58 (4): 809–25. https://doi.org/10.1177/00223433211026126.

Philpott, Daniel. 2012. *Just and Unjust Peace: An Ethic of Political Reconciliation*. New York: Oxford University Press.

Pilkington, Ed. 2019. "Haitians Urge Judges to Find UN Culpable for Cholera Outbreak that Killed Thousands." World. *The Guardian*, October 1, 2019. http://www
.theguardian.com/world/2019/oct/01/haiti-cholera-2010-un-us-supreme-court.

Pinaud, Margaux. 2021. "Home-Grown Peace: Civil Society Roles in Ceasefire Monitoring." *International Peacekeeping* 28 (3): 470–95.

Police Service of Northern Ireland. 2021. "Workforce Composition Statistics." PSNI. Police.uk. https://www.psni.police.uk/inside-psni/Statistics/workforce-composition-statistics/.

Pons, Corina, and Mayela Armas. 2020. "Venezuela's Timid Gains in Taming Inflation Fade as Food Prices Soar." Emerging Markets. Reuters.com, May 11, 2020. https://www.reuters.com/article/us-venezuela-economy-idUSKBN22N26A.

———. 2021. "In Venezuela's Survival Economy, Local Taxes Become Latest Challenge for Business." Business News. Reuters.com, March 29, 2021. https://www
.reuters.com/article/us-venezuela-taxes-idUSKBN2BL250.

Posey, Kirby G. 2016. "Household Income: 2015." United States Census Bureau, US Department of Commerce. https://www.census.gov/library/publications/2016/acs
/acsbr15-02.html.

Powers, Jon. 2015. "Climate Change Is the 'Mother of All Risks' to National Security." *Time*, November 6, 2015. http://time.com/4101903/climate-change-national
-security/.

Preston, Stephanie. 2020. "COVID-19: Why Hoarding Supplies Is Human Nature, According to a Behavioral Neuroscientist." World Economic Forum, April 2, 2020. https://www.weforum.org/agenda/2020/04/evolution-coronavirus-covid19-panic
-buying-supplies-food-essentials/.

Prins, Gwyn, and Steve Rayner. 2007. "Time to Ditch Kyoto." *Nature* 449 (October): 973–75.

Prorok, Alyssa K. 2017. "The (in) Compatibility of Peace and Justice? The International Criminal Court and Civil Conflict Termination." *International Organization* 71 (2): 213–43.

Pruitt-Young, Sharon. 2021. "Slavery Didn't End on Juneteenth: What You Should Know about This Important Day." NPR.org, June 17, 2021. https://www.npr
.org/2021/06/17/1007315228/juneteenth-what-is-origin-observation.

Quinn, J. Michael, T. David Mason, and Mehmet Gurses. 2007. "Sustaining the Peace: Determinants of Civil War Recurrence." *International Interactions* 33 (2): 167–93.

Ramsbotham, Oliver, Tom Woodhouse, and Hugh Miall. 2016. *Contemporary Conflict Resolution*. 4th ed. London: Polity.

Rawls, John. 1971. *A Theory of Justice*. Cambridge: Harvard University Press.

Ray, Debraj. 2015. "Where Are All the Women?" World Economic Forum, October 19, 2015. https://www.weforum.org/agenda/2015/10/where-are-all-the-women/.

Reja, Mishal. 2021. "A Hidden Pandemic: Grief in the African American Community." Health. ABC News, February 2, 2021. https://abcnews.go.com/Health
/hidden-pandemic-grief-african-american-community/story?id=75613917.

Rendon, Moises, and Jacob Mendales. 2018. "The Maduro Diet: Food v. Freedom in Venezuela." Center for Strategic and International Studies, CSIS.org, July 9, 2018. https://www.csis.org/analysis/maduro-diet-food-v-freedom-venezuela.

Rendon, Moises, and Lucan Sanchez. 2020. "Covid-19 in Venezuela: How the Pandemic Deepened a Humanitarian Crisis." Center for Strategic and International Studies, CSIS.org, September 23, 2020. https://www.csis.org/analysis/covid-19-venezuela-how-pandemic-deepened-humanitarian-crisis.

Reuters Staff. 2012. "Factbox: Venezuela's Nationalizations under Chavez." Media and Telecoms. Reuters.com, October 8, 2012. https://www.reuters.com/article/us-venezuela-election-nationalizations-idUSBRE89701X20121008.

Reuters. 2015. "Venezuela's Opposition Wins Resounding Election Victory." The Worldpost. *HuffPost*, last modified December 8, 2015. https://www.huffpost.com/entry/venezuela-election-opposition-victory_n_56659501e4b079b2818f1dea.

———. 2020. "Cash-Strapped Venezuela Hikes Public Service Fees amid Coronavirus Outbreak." Business News. Reuters.com, March 19, 2020. https://www.reuters.com/article/us-health-coronavirus-venezuela-economy-idUSKBN2162EG.

Reveron, Derek S., and Kathleen A. Mahoney-Norris. 2011. *Human Security in a Borderless World*. Boulder, CO: Westview Press.

Revkin, Andrew. 2017. "Trump's Defense Secretary Cites Climate Change as National Security Challenge." ProPublica, March 14, 2017. https://www.propublica.org/article/trumps-defense-secretary-cites-climate-change-national-security-challenge.

Richmond, Oliver P., and Jason Franks. 2009. *Liberal Peace Transitions: Between Statebuilding and Peacebuilding*. Edinburgh: Edinburgh University Press.

Robert, Alexis. 2020. "Lessons from New Zealand's COVID-19 Outbreak Response." *Lancet Public Health* 5 (11): e569–70. https://doi.org/10.1016/S2468-2667(20)30237-1.

Roberts, Sean R. 2020. "How the Uyghurs Became a 'Terrorist Threat.'" In *The War on the Uyghurs: China's Internal Campaign against a Muslim Minority*, 63–95. Princeton: Princeton University Press.

Royal Embassy of Saudi Arabia, Information Office. 2015. "Statement by Saudi Ambassador Al-Jubeir on Military Operations in Yemen." Published by PR Newswire, March 25, 2015. http://www.prnewswire.com/news-releases/statement-by-saudi-ambassador-al-jubeir-on-military-operations-in-yemen-300056316.html.

Rudolf, Peter. 2017. "UN Peace Operations and the Use of Military Force." *Survival* 59 (3): 161–82.

Rugemalila, Joas B., Olumide A. T. Ogundahunsi, Timothy T. Stedman, and Wen L. Kilama. 2007. "Multilateral Initiative on Malaria: Justification, Evolution, Achievements, Challenges, Opportunities, and Future Plans." *American Journal of Tropical Medicine and Hygiene* 77 (6): 296–302. https://www.ncbi.nlm.nih.gov/books/NBK1691/.

Russell, Raymond. 2013. *Census 2011: Key Statistics at Northern Ireland and LGD Level*. Research paper NIAR 005-13. Northern Ireland Assembly, Research and Information Service, February 20, 2013. http://www.niassembly.gov.uk/globalassets/documents/raise/publications/2013/general/russell3013.pdf.

Safferling, Christoph, and Gurgen Petrossian. 2021. "Reparation for Victims." In *Victims Before the International Criminal Court*, 231–322. Erlangen, Ger.: Springer.

Salehyan, Idean. 2008. "From Climate Change to Conflict? No Consensus Yet." *Journal of Peace Research* 45 (3): 315–26.

Salinas Rivera, Alexander. 2015. *Venezuela: The Sunset of Rule of Law*. ICJ Mission Report 2015. Geneva: International Commission of Jurists. https://www.icj.org/wp-content/uploads/2015/10/Venezuela-Sunset-of-Rule-of-Law-Publications-Reports-2015-ENG.pdf.

Sandbu, Martin. 2015. "Critics Question Success of UN's Millennium Development Goals." Special report. *Financial Times*, September 14, 2015. https://www.ft.com/content/51d1c0aa-5085-11e5-8642-453585f2cfcd.

Save the Children. 2014. *Too Young to Wed: The Growing Problem of Child Marriage among Syrian Girls in Jordan*. London: Save the Children.

Schreiber, Melody. 2019. "Researchers Are Surprised by the Magnitude of Venezuela's Health Crisis." *Goats and Soda* (blog), NPR.org, April 5, 2019. https://www.npr.org/sections/goatsandsoda/2019/04/05/709969632/researchers-are-surprised-by-the-magnitude-of-venezuelas-health-crisis.

Schwartzstein, Peter. 2016. "Inside the Syrian Dust Bowl." *Foreign Policy* (blog), September 5, 2016. https://foreignpolicy.com/2016/09/05/inside-the-syrian-dust-bowl-icarda-assad-food-security-war/.

Second Continental Congress. "Declaration of Independence." 1776. Philadelphia, July 4, 1776. Held in the United States National Archives, Washington, DC. Transcription available at https://www.archives.gov/founding-docs/declaration-transcript.

Semelin, Jacques. 2011. "Introduction: From Help to Rescue." In *Resisting Genocide: The Multiple Forms of Rescue*, edited by Jacques Semelin, Claire Andrieu, and Sarah Gensburger, 1–14. New York: Columbia University Press.

Sen, Amartya. 1981. *Poverty and Famines: An Essay on Entitlement and Deprivation*. Oxford: Oxford University Press.

———. 1999. *Development as Freedom*. New York: Anchor Books.

———. 2000. *Development as Freedom*. Reprint edition. New York: Anchor.

Sharp, Gene. 1998. "Nonviolent Action in Acute Interethnic Conflicts." In *The Handbook of Interethnic Coexistence*, edited by Eugene Weiner, 371–81. New York: Continuum Publishing.

Shemyakina, Olga. 2011. "The Effect of Armed Conflict on Accumulation of Schooling: Results from Tajikistan." *Journal of Development Economics* 95 (2): 186–200.

Silberg, Bob. 2016. "Why a Half-Degree Temperature Rise Is a Big Deal." Global Climate Change: Vital Signs of the Planet. NASA.gov, June 29, 2016. https://climate.nasa.gov/news/2458/why-a-half-degree-temperature-rise-is-a-big-deal/.

Simmons, Beth A., and Allison Danner. 2010. "Credible Commitments and the International Criminal Court." *International Organization* 64 (2): 225–56.

Singer, Merrill, Nicola Bulled, Bayla Ostrach, and Emily Mendenhall. 2017. "Syndemics and the Biosocial Conception of Health." *Lancet* 389 (10072): 941–50. https://doi.org/10.1016/S0140-6736(17)30003-X.

SIPRI. 2021. "World Military Spending Rises to Almost \$2 Trillion in 2020." Press release. Stockholm Institute for Peace Research (website), April 26, 2021. https://sipri.org/media/press-release/2021/world-military-spending-rises-almost-2-trillion-2020.

Sjoberg, Laura. 2014. *Gender, War, and Conflict*. Cambridge: Polity.

Smart, Charlie. 2021. "Where People Are Most Vulnerable to the Delta Variant." *New York Times*, July 29, 2021. https://www.nytimes.com/interactive/2021/07/29/us /delta-variant-risk-map.html.

Smit, Anneke. 2012. *The Property Rights of Refugees and Internally Displaced Persons: Beyond Restitution*. New York: Routledge.

Smith, Heather, and Tari Ajadi. 2020. "Canada's Feminist Foreign Policy and Human Security Compared." *International Journal* 75 (3): 367–82. https://journals.sage pub.com/doi/full/10.1177/0020702020954547.

Smith, Pete. 2014. "Malthus Is Still Wrong: We Can Feed a World of 9–10 Billion, but Only by Reducing Food Demand." *Proceedings of the Nutrition Society* 74 (3): 187–90. https://www.cambridge.org/core/journals/proceedings-of-the-nutrition-so ciety/article/malthus-is-still-wrong-we-can-feed-a-world-of-910-billion-but-only -by-reducing-food-demand/E9C057BDFE4EA2E178D90719D9A23E84.

Smyth, Jim. 2002. "Community Policing and the Reform of the Royal Ulster Constabulary." *Policing: An International Journal of Police Strategies and Management* 25 (1): 110–24.

Southern, Neil. 2018. *Policing and Combating Terrorism in Northern Ireland: The Royal Ulster Constabulary GC*. Sheffield: Palgrave MacMillan.

Spagat, Michael, Andrew Mack, Tara Cooper, and Joakim Kreutz. 2009. "Estimating War Deaths: An Arena of Contestation." *Journal of Conflict Resolution* 53 (6): 934–50. https://doi.org/10.1177/0022002709346253.

Sperling, Gene B., Rebecca Winthrop, and Christina Kwauk. 2016. *What Works in Girls' Education: Evidence for the World's Best Investment*. Washington, DC: The Brookings Institution.

Staff and agencies of *The Guardian* in Geneva. 2020. "Venezuela: UN Accuses Maduro Government of Crimes against Humanity." Americas: Venezuela. *The Guardian*, September 16, 2020. http://www.theguardian.com/world/2020/sep/16 /venezuela-un-report-crimes-against-humanity-maduro-government.

Starks, Tim. 2012. "Katrina's Lessons Seen in Response to Sandy." *Congressional Quarterly* (blog), December 9, 2012. http://public.cq.com/docs/weeklyreport /weeklyreport-000004197197.html.

State of Louisiana. 2021. "Isle de Jean Charles." https://isledejeancharles.la.gov/.

Stephan, Maria J., and Erica Chenoweth. 2008. "Why Civil Resistance Works: The Strategic Logic of Nonviolent Conflict." *International Security* 33 (1): 7–44.

Stephen, Ekpenyong Nkereuwem. 2016. "Youth Radicalization and the Future of Terrorism in Nigeria." *Canadian Social Science* 12 (10): 42–50. Available for download from https://doi.org/10.3968/8873.

Stiglitz, Joseph. 2020. "Conquering the Great Divide." *Finance and Development* (September). https://www.imf.org/external/pubs/ft/fandd/2020/09/COVID19-and -global-inequality-joseph-stiglitz.htm.

Stott, Michael. 2021. "EU Drops Recognition of Juan Guaidó as Venezuela's Interim President." *Financial Times*, January 6, 2021. https://www.ft.com/content /aa372f3a-a1ac-41da-848a-46355fc3ec4f.

Strasheim, Julia. 2019. "No 'End of the Peace Process': Federalism and Ethnic Violence in Nepal." *Cooperation and Conflict* 54 (1): 83–98. https://journals.sagepub.com/doi/10.1177/0010836717750199.

Stunson, Mike. 2020. "WIC Shoppers Struggle to Find Groceries during COVID-19." News. *Sacramento Bee*, March 24, 2020. https://www.sacbee.com/news/coronavirus/article241456946.html.

Sweden [government of]. 2022. "Equal Power and Influence for Women and Men—That's What Sweden Is Aiming For." Gender Equality. Sweden.se, last modified February 15, 2022. https://sweden.se/society/gender-equality-in-sweden/.

Takemi, Keizo. 2016. "Japan's Global Health Strategy: Connecting Development and Security." *Asia-Pacific Review* 23 (1): 21–31.

Taylor, Adam. 2015. "How Saudi Arabia Turned Sweden's Human Rights Criticisms into an Attack on Islam." World. *Washington Post*, March 24, 2015. https://www.washingtonpost.com/news/worldviews/wp/2015/03/24/how-saudi-arabia-turned-swedens-human-rights-criticisms-into-an-attack-on-islam/.

Taylor, Colin. 2014. "Flooding Threatens to Completely Submerge Kiribati in the Next 30 Years." American Security Project, June 10, 2014. https://www.americansecurityproject.org/flooding-threatens-to-completely-submerge-kiribati-in-the-next-30-years/.

Taylor, Luke. 2021. "'We Are Being Ignored': Brazil's Researchers Blame Anti-science Government for Devastating COVID Surge." News In Focus. *Nature* 593 (7857) (May 6): 15–16. https://doi.org/10.1038/d41586-021-01031-w.

Tickner, J. Ann. 2001. *Gendering World Politics: Issues and Approaches in the Post–Cold War Era*. New York: Columbia University Press.

Torres-Batlló, Juan, and Belen Marti-Cardona. 2021. "Lake Poopó: Why Bolivia's Second Largest Lake Disappeared—and How to Bring It Back." *The Conversation*, January 11, 2021. http://theconversation.com/lake-poopo-why-bolivias-second-largest-lake-disappeared-and-how-to-bring-it-back-152776.

Tran, Mark. 2012. "Mark Malloch-Brown: Developing the MDGs Was a Bit like Nuclear Fusion." Global Development. *The Guardian*, November 16, 2012. https://www.theguardian.com/global-development/2012/nov/16/mark-malloch-brown-mdgs-nuclear.

Tull, Denis M. 2018. "The Limits and Unintended Consequences of UN Peace Enforcement: The Force Intervention Brigade in the DR Congo." *International Peacekeeping* 25 (2): 167–90.

Turner, Jenia Iontcheva. 2017. "Defense Perspectives on Fairness and Efficiency at the International Criminal Court." In *Oxford Handbook on International Criminal Law*, edited by Kevin Jon Heller, 39–66 . Oxford: Oxford University Press.

United Nations. n.d. "Millennium Development Goals and Beyond." UN.org, accessed May 17, 2022. https://www.un.org/millenniumgoals/bkgd.shtml.

———. 1945. "Charter of the United Nations and Statute of the International Court of Justice." San Francisco, June 26, 1945. https://treaties.un.org/doc/publication/ctc/uncharter.pdf.

———. 1969. "Vienna Convention on the Law of Treaties, 1969." Vienna, May 31, 1969. https://legal.un.org/ilc/texts/instruments/english/conventions/1_1_1969.pdf.

———. 1992. "United Nations Framework Convention on Climate Change." New York, May 9, 1992. http://unfccc.int/files/essential_background/convention/back ground/application/pdf/convention_text_with_annexes_english_for_posting.pdf.

———. 2015a. "'Human Security Depends on Health Security,' Ban Says, Calling on Nations to Be Proactive." UN News, September 26, 2015. https://news.un.org/en /story/2015/09/509912-human-security-depends-health-security-ban-says-calling -nations-be-proactive.

———. 2015b. *The Millennium Development Goals Report, 2015.* New York: United Nations. https://www.un.org/millenniumgoals/2015_MDG_Report/pdf/MDG%20 2015%20rev%20(July%201).pdf.

———. 2017. "Urgent Scale-Up in Funding Needed to Stave Off Famine in Soma-lia, UN Warns." UN News, February 2, 2017. http://www.un.org/apps/news/story .asp?NewsID=56094#.WPEChFLMyi4.

———. 2019. "UN Human Rights Chief 'Hopeful' Venezuelan Authorities Are Ready to Address Violations, Calls for Dialogue." Human Rights. UN News, July 4, 2019. https://news.un.org/en/story/2019/07/1041902.

———. 2020a. "Haiti Cholera Outbreak 'Stopped in Its Tracks.'" Health. UN News, January 24, 2020. https://news.un.org/en/story/2020/01/1056021.

———. 2020b. "UN Committed to a 'Brighter Future' for Haiti, as Independent Rights Experts Call for More Action on Behalf of Cholera Victims." Human Rights. UN News, April 30, 2020. https://news.un.org/en/story/2020/04/1062962.

———. 2021a. "Rights Experts Concerned about Alleged Detention, Forced Labour of Uyghurs in China." Human Rights. UN News, March 29, 2021. https://news .un.org/en/story/2021/03/1088612.

———. 2021b. "South Sudanese 'One Step Away from Famine,' as UN Launches Hu-manitarian Response Plan." Humanitarian Aid. UN News, March 16, 2021. https:// news.un.org/en/story/2021/03/1087492.

United Nations Climate Change. 2021. "Full NDC Synthesis Report: Some Progress, but Still a Big Concern." Press release. UNFCCC.int, September 17, 2021. https:// unfccc.int/news/full-ndc-synthesis-report-some-progress-but-still-a-big-concern.

United Nations Conference on Sustainable Development. 2012. *The Future We Want.* Outcome document of the United Nations Conference on Sustainable Develop-ment, Rio de Janeiro, Brazil, June 20–22, 2012. New York: United Nations. https:// sustainabledevelopment.un.org/content/documents/733FutureWeWant.pdf.

United Nations Department of Economic and Social Affairs. n.d.(a) "Do You Know All 17 SDGs?" Sustainable Development. SDGS.UN.org, accessed May 9, 2022. https://sdgs.un.org/goals.

———. n.d.(b). "Sustainable Development: Goals; 5—Achieve Gender Equality and Empower All Women and Girls." SDGS.UN.org, accessed May 25, 2022. https:// sdgs.un.org/goals/goal5.

———. n.d.(c). "Sustainable Development: Goals; 10—Reduce Inequality Within and Among Countries." SDGS.UN.org, accessed July 9, 2021. https://sdgs.un.org /goals/goal10.

United Nations Development Programme. n.d.(a) "Gender Inequality Index (GII)." Human Development Reports. HDR.UNDP.org, accessed July 12, 2021. http://hdr .undp.org/en/content/gender-inequality-index-gii.

———. n.d.(b) "Venezuela (Bolivarian Republic Of)." Human Development Reports. HDR.UNDP.org, accessed July 5, 2021. http://hdr.undp.org/en/countries /profiles/VEN.

———. 1994. *Human Development Report, 1994*. New York: Oxford University Press. https://digitallibrary.un.org/record/240220?ln=en.

———. 2010a. "Gender and Disasters." Bureau for Crisis Prevention and Recovery, October 2010. Available for download at https://www.undp.org/content/dam/undp /library/crisis%20prevention/disaster/7Disaster%20Risk%20Reduction%20-%20 Gender.pdf.

———. 2010b. *Human Development Report, 2010: The Real Wealth of Nations; Pathways to Human Development*. 20th anniversary edition. New York: United Nations. https://hdr.undp.org/sites/default/files/reports/270/hdr_2010_en_com plete_reprint.pdf.

———. 2015. *The Millennium Development Goals Report, 2015*. Edited by Catherine Way. New York: United Nations. https://www.un.org/millenniumgoals/2015_MDG _Report/pdf/MDG%202015%20rev%20(July%201).pdf.

———. 2020. "The Next Frontier: Human Development and the Anthropocene: Venezuela (Bolivarian Republic Of)." *Human Development Report, 2020*. HDR.UNDP .org. http://www.hdr.undp.org/sites/all/themes/hdr_theme/country-notes/VEN.pdf.

United Nations General Assembly. 1948. Universal Declaration of Human Rights. Paris, December 10, 1948. Text available at https://www.un.org/en/about-us/uni versal-declaration-of-human-rights.

———. 2000. Resolution 55/2. *United Nations Millennium Declaration*, A/RES/55/2. September 18, 2000. https://documents-dds-ny.un.org/doc/UNDOC/GEN /N00/559/51/PDF/N0055951.pdf?OpenElement.

———. 2005. Resolution 60/1. *2005 World Summit Outcome*, A/RES/60/01. September 16, 2005. https://www.un.org/en/development/desa/population/migration /generalassembly/docs/globalcompact/A_RES_60_1.pdf.

———. 2009. Resolution 63/677. *Implementing the Responsibility to Protect: Report of the Secretary General*, A/63/677. January 12, 2009. https://www.un.org/ruleof law/files/SG_reportA_63_677_en.pdf.

———. 2012. Resolution 66/290. *Follow-Up to Paragraph 143 on Human Security of the 2005 World Summit Outcome*, A/RES/66/290. September 10, 2012. https://documents-dds-ny.un.org/doc/UNDOC/GEN/N11/476/22/PDF/N1147622 .pdf?OpenElement.

———. 2013. *Open Working Group of the General Assembly on Sustainable Development Goals*, A/67/L.48/Rev.1. January 15, 2013. https://www.un.org/ga/search /view_doc.asp?symbol=A/67/L.48/Rev.1&Lang=E.

———. 2014. *Evaluation of the Implementation and Results of Protection of Civilians Mandates in United Nations Peacekeeping Operations: Report of the Office of Internal Oversight Services*, A/68/787. March 7, 2014. Available for download at https://digitallibrary.un.org/record/767929?ln=en.

————. 2015. *Advisory Group of Experts on the Review of the Peacebuilding Architecture addressed to the President of the General Assembly and the President of the Security Council.* Follow-up to the outcome of the Millennium Summit, A/69/968 -S/2015/490. June 30, 2015. Available for download at https://digitallibrary.un.org /record/798480/files/A_69_968_S_2015_490-EN.pdf.

————. 2018. *Report of the United Nations High Commissioner for Refugees: Part II, Global Compact on Refugees,* A/73/12 (Part II). Reissued for technical reasons September 13, 2018, New York. https://www.unhcr.org/en-us/excom /unhcrannual/5ba3a5d44/report-united-nations-high-commissioner-refugees-part -ii-global-compact.html.

————. 2021. Resolution 75/277. *The Responsibility to Protect and the Prevention of Genocide, War Crimes, Ethnic Cleansing and Crimes against Humanity,* A/ RES/75/277. May 18, 2021. https://www.globalr2p.org/resources/2021-unga-r2p -resolution/.

United Nations General Assembly, Security Council. 2000. *Report of the Panel on United Nations Peace Operations,* A/55/305-S/2000/809. August 21, 2000. https:// peacekeeping.un.org/sites/default/files/a_55_305_e_brahimi_report.pdf.

————. 2017. *Report of the Peacebuilding Commission,* A/71/768-S/2017/76. January 27, 2017. https://www.un.org/ga/search/view_doc.asp?symbol=A/71/768.

United Nations High Commissioner for Refugees. 2015. "Lesvos Island—Greece: Factsheet." UNHCR factsheet. UNHCR.org, November 12, 2015. Downloadable at https://data2.unhcr.org/en/documents/details/46447.

United Nations Human Security Unit. 2014. *Human Security Unit: Strategic Plan, 2014–2017.* New York: United Nations. https://www.unocha.org/sites/dms/HSU /HSU%20Strategic%20Plan%202014-2017%20Web%20Version.pdf.

————. 2015. "Framework for Cooperation for the System-Wide Application of Human Security." September 2015. https://www.un.org/humansecurity/wp-content /uploads/2017/10/Framework-for-Cooperation-for-the-System-wide-Application -of-Human-Security.pdf.

United Nations Millennium Development Goal Gap Task Force. 2015. *Millennium Development Goal 8: Taking Stock of the Global Partnership for Development.* Report 2015. New York: United Nations. Available for download at https://digi tallibrary.un.org/record/802820/.

United Nations Office for the Coordination of Humanitarian Affairs. 2021. *Humanitarian Response Plan: South Sudan.* New York: United Nations. https://www .humanitarianresponse.info/sites/www.humanitarianresponse.info/files/documents /files/south_sudan_2021_humanitarian_response_plan_print.pdf.

United Nations Office of Counter-Terrorism. n.d. "UN Global Counter-terrorism Strategy." UN.org, accessed November 12, 2021. https://www.un.org/counterter rorism/un-global-counter-terrorism-strategy.

United Nations Office of the High Commissioner for Human Rights. 2008a. *Frequently Asked Questions on Economic, Social and Cultural Rights.* Fact sheet no. 33. Geneva: United Nations. https://www.ohchr.org/sites/default/files/Documents /Publications/FactSheet33en.pdf.

————. 2008b. *Human Rights, Terrorism, and Counter-terrorism*. Geneva: United Nations.

————. 2017. *Human Rights Violations and Abuses in the Context of Protests in the Bolivarian Republic of Venezuela from 1 April to 31 July 2017*. August 2017. Geneva: United Nations. https://www.ohchr.org/Documents/Countries/VE /HCReportVenezuela_1April-31July2017_EN.pdf.

United Nations Office on Drugs and Crime–Vienna. 2004. *United Nations Convention against Transnational Organized Crime and the Protocols Thereto*. New York: United Nations. https://www.unodc.org/documents/middleeastandnorthafrica /organised-crime/UNITED_NATIONS_CONVENTION_AGAINST_TRANSNA TIONAL_ORGANIZED_CRIME_AND_THE_PROTOCOLS_THERETO.pdf.

————. 2020. *Global Report on Trafficking Persons, 2020*. New York: United Nations. https://www.unodc.org/documents/data-and-analysis/tip/2021/GLOTiP _2020_15jan_web.pdf.

United Nations Peacebuilding Support Office. 2011. "From Rhetoric to Practice: Operationalizing National Ownership in Post-conflict Peacebuilding." Workshop report, June 2011. https://www.un.org/peacebuilding/sites/www.un.org.peacebuild ing/files/documents/national_ownership_report.pdf.

United Nations Refugee Agency. n.d. "Syria Emergency." UNHCR.org, accessed May 18, 2022. https://www.unhcr.org/en-us/syria-emergency.html.

United Nations Security Council. 1994. "Final Report of the United Nations Commis- sion of Experts Established Pursuant to Security Council Resolution 780 (1992)," S/1994/674. May 27, 1994. https://digitallibrary.un.org/record/231536?ln=en.

————. 1999a. "Report of the Secretary-General to the Security Council on the Pro- tection of Civilians in Armed Conflict," S/1999/957. September 8, 1999. Available for download at https://digitallibrary.un.org/record/279462?ln=en.

————. 1999b. Resolution 1270 (1999). [*On establishment of the UN Mission in Sierra Leone (UNAMSIL)*], S/RES/1270. October 22, 1999. https://documents -dds-ny.un.org/doc/UNDOC/GEN/N99/315/02/PDF/N9931502.pdf?OpenElement.

————. 2000. Resolution 1325 (2000). [*On women and peace and security*], S/RES/1325. October 31, 2000. https://peacemaker.un.org/sites/peacemaker.un.org/files/SC _ResolutionWomenPeaceSecurity_SRES1325%282000%29%28english_0.pdf.

————. 2007. *Report of the Secretary-General on the Protection of Civilians in Armed Conflict*, S/2007/643. October 28, 2007. http://www.securitycouncilreport .org/atf/cf/%7B65BFCF9B-6D27-4E9C-8CD3-CF6E4FF96FF9%7D/Civil ians%20S2007643.pdf.

————. 2011. Resolution 1973 (2011). [*On Libya*], S/RES/1973. March 17, 2011. https://documents-dds-ny.un.org/doc/UNDOC/GEN/N11/268/39/PDF/N1126839 .pdf?OpenElement.

————. 2013. Resolution 2098 (2013). [*On extension of the mandate of the UN Organi- zation Stabilization Mission in the Democratic Republic of the Congo (MONUSCO) until 31 Mar. 2014*], S/RES/2098. March 28, 2013. http://unscr.com/en/resolutions /doc/2098.

————. 2014. "With Spread of Ebola Outpacing Response, Security Council Adopts Resolution 2177 (2014) Urging Immediate Action, End to Isolation of Affected

States." Meetings Coverage. UN.org, September 18, 2014. http://www.un.org/press/en/2014/sc11566.doc.htm.

———. 2016a. Resolution 2331 (2016). [*On trafficking of persons in armed conflicts*], S/RES/2331. December 20, 2016. http://www.un.org/en/ga/search/view_doc.asp?symbol=S/RES/2331(2016).

———. 2016b. "Starvation by Siege Now 'Systematic' in Syria, Assistant Secretary-General Tells Security Council, amid Warnings that Tactic Could Be War Crime." Meetings Coverage. UN.org, January 15, 2016. https://www.un.org/press/en/2016/sc12203.doc.htm.

United Nations Trust Fund for Human Security. 2016. *Human Security Handbook: An Integrated Approach for the Realization of the Sustainable Development Goals and the Priority Areas of the International Community and the United Nations System.* January 2016. New York: United Nations. https://www.un.org/humansecurity/wp-content/uploads/2017/10/h2.pdf.

United Nations Women. 1995. "Fourth World Conference on Women." UN.org, September 1995. https://www.un.org/womenwatch/daw/beijing/platform/.

———. 2020. "Safeguard Women's Rights and Participation in Peacebuilding Now, Says Afghan Activist Zarqa Yaftali to the UN Security Council." UNWomen.org, November 5, 2020. Archived at https://reliefweb.int/report/afghanistan/safeguard-women-s-rights-and-participation-peacebuilding-now-says-afghan-activist.

United States Bureau of Labor Statistics. 2021. "Temporary Layoffs Remain High Following Unprecedented Surge in Early 2020." *TED: The Economics Daily*, BLS.gov, February 10, 2021. https://www.bls.gov/opub/ted/2021/temporary-layoffs-remain-high-following-unprecedented-surge-in-early-2020.htm?view_full.

United States Census Bureau. 2021. "Real Household Income at Selected Percentiles: 1967 to 2014." Census.gov, last modified October 8, 2021. https://www.census.gov/library/visualizations/2015/demo/real-household-income-at-selected-percentiles--1967-to-2014.html.

United States Department of Agriculture, Economic Research Service. 2021a. "Documentation." ERS.USDA.gov, last modified May 24, 2021. https://www.ers.usda.gov/data-products/food-access-research-atlas/documentation/.

———. 2021b. "Food Security and Nutrition Assistance." ERS.USDA.gov, last modified November 8, 2021. https://www.ers.usda.gov/data-products/ag-and-food-statistics-charting-the-essentials/food-security-and-nutrition-assistance/.

———. 2022a. "Food Access Research Atlas." ERS.USDA.gov, last modified March 14, 2022. https://www.ers.usda.gov/data-products/food-access-research-atlas/.

———. 2022b. "Frequency of Food Insecurity." ERS.USDA.gov, last modified April 22, 2022. https://www.ers.usda.gov/topics/food-nutrition-assistance/food-security-in-the-us/frequency-of-food-insecurity/.

United States Government Accountability Office. 2008. "Actions Taken to Implement the Post-Katrina Emergency Management Reform Act of 2006." GAO-09-59R. November 21, 2008. https://www.gao.gov/assets/gao-09-59r.pdf.

United States Senate. 1950. *Employment of Homosexuals and Other Sex Perverts in Government: Interim Report Submitted to the Committee on Expenditures in the Executive Departments by Its Subcommittee on Investigations Pursuant to S.*

Res. 280 (81st Congress); A Resolution Authorizing the Committee on Expenditures in the Executive Departments to Carry Out Certain Duties. Senate document, 81st Congress, 2nd session, no. 241. December 15, 1950. Washington, DC: United States Government Printing Office. Archived at https://www.washington post.com/r/2010-2019/WashingtonPost/2012/03/02/National-Enterprise/Graphics /DOMASenRptNov1950.pdf.

van Houten, Carolyn. 2016. "The First Official Climate Refugees in the U.S. Race against Time." *National Geographic*, May 25, 2016. https://www.national geographic.com/science/article/160525-isle-de-jean-charles-louisiana-sinking-cli mate-change-refugees.

Venezuela Investigative Unit. 2015. "Despite Rampant Crime, Venezuela's 'Peace Zones' Remain." Brief: Megabandas. *InSight Crime* (blog). January 28, 2015. https://insightcrime.org/news/brief/despite-security-failures-venezuela-peace -zones-remain/.

Verveer, Melanne, and Anjali Dayal. 2018. "Women Are the Key to Peace." *Foreign Policy* (blog), November 8, 2018. https://foreignpolicy.com/2018/11/08/women -are-the-key-to-peace/.

Vogelstein, Rachel. 2019. "Sweden's Feminist Foreign Policy, Long May It Reign." Argument. *Foreign Policy* (blog), January 30, 2019. https://foreignpolicy .com/2019/01/30/sweden-feminist-foreignpolicy/.

Vulliamy, Ed. 2002. "Venezuela Coup Linked to Bush Team." World News. *The Guardian*, April 21, 2002. http://www.theguardian.com/world/2002/apr/21/usa .venezuela.

Wadley, Davina. 2013. "Kiribati: Climate Change and Inequity." *Refugees International* (blog), June 4, 2013. https://www.refugeesinternational.org/reports/2013/6/4 /kiribati-climate-change-and-inequity.

Wallström, Margot. 2016. "Statement of Government Policy in the Parliamentary Debate on Foreign Affairs 2016." Ministry for Foreign Affairs, Government Offices of Sweden, February 24, 2016. http://www.government.se/speeches/2016/02/state ment-of-government-policy-in-the-parliamentary-debate-on-foreign-affairs-2016/.

Walt, Stephen M. 1991. "The Renaissance of Security Studies." *International Studies Quarterly* 35 (2): 211–39.

Walter, Barbara F. 2002. *Committing to Peace: The Successful Settlement of Civil Wars*. Princeton: Princeton University Press.

Wanis-St. John, Anthony, and Darren Kew. 2008. "Civil Society and Peace Negotiations: Confronting Exclusion." *International Negotiation* 13 (1): 11–36.

Washington Office on Latin America. 2020. "New Report Documents How U.S. Sanctions Have Directly Aggravated Venezuela's Economic Crisis." Press release. WOLA.org, October 29, 2020. https://www.wola.org/2020/10/new-report-us -sanctions-aggravated-venezuelas-economic-crisis/.

Weber, Max. 1946. "Politics as a Vocation." In *From Max Weber: Essays in Sociology*, edited by H. H. Gerth and C. Wright Mills, 77–128. Oxford: Oxford University Press.

Weinstein, Jeremy M. 2006. *Inside Rebellion: The Politics of Insurgent Violence*. Cambridge University Press.

Weisman, Steven R. 2004. "Irate over 'Stingy' Remark, U.S. Adds $20 Million to Disaster Aid." *New York Times*, December 29, 2004. http://www.nytimes.com /2004/12/29/world/worldspecial4/irate-over-stingy-remark-us-adds-20-million-to -disaster-aid.html.

Welsh, Jennifer M. 2021. "The Security Council's Role in Fulfilling the Responsibility to Protect." *Ethics and International Affairs* 35 (2): 227–43.

Westmarland, Nicole, and Geetanjali Gangoli, eds. 2011. *International Approaches to Rape*. Portland, OR: The Policy Press.

Wibben, Annick T. R. 2016. "The Promise and Dangers of Human Security." In *Ethical Security Studies: A New Research Agenda*, edited by Jonna Nyman and Anthony Burke, 102–15. New York: Routledge.

Wilson, Peter. 2015. "The Collapse of Chávezcare." Dispatch. *Foreign Policy* (blog), April 27, 2015. https://foreignpolicy.com/2015/04/27/chavez-maduro-healthcare -venezuela-cuba/.

Wilson, Scott. 2002. "Chavez Raises Idea of U.S. Role in Coup." *Washington Post*, May 5, 2002. https://www.washingtonpost.com/archive/politics/2002/05/05 /chavez-raises-idea-of-us-role-in-coup/8cb634fd-75db-4cc1-9c83-b217e469d6c8/.

Winship, Scott, Richard V. Reeves, and Katherine Guyot. 2018. "The Inheritance of Black Poverty: It's All about the Men." Report. *Brookings* (blog), March 22, 2018. https://www.brookings.edu/research/the-inheritance-of-black-poverty-its -all-about-the-men/.

Wolfers, Arnold. 1952. "'National Security' as an Ambiguous Symbol." *Political Science Quarterly* 67 (4): 481–502.

World Bank. 2013. "World Bank, IMF Leaders Make Economic Case for Climate Action." WorldBank.org, October 9, 2013. http://www.worldbank.org/en/news/fea ture/2013/10/08/world-bank-imf-leaders-make-economic-case-for-climate-action.

World Economic Forum. 2021. *Global Gender Gap Report 2021*. Insight Report, March 2021. Geneva: World Economic Forum. https://www3.weforum.org/docs /WEF_GGGR_2021.pdf.

World Food Programme. n.d. "Syrian Arab Republic." WFP.org, accessed August 5, 2021. http://www1.wfp.org/countries/syrian-arab-republic.

World Food Summit. 1996. "Rome Declaration on World Food Security." Rome, November 13, 1996. http://www.fao.org/docrep/003/w3613e/w3613e00.htm.

World Health Organization. n.d.(a) "About WHO: What We Do." WHO.int, accessed May 17, 2022. http://www.who.int/about/what-we-do/en/.

———. n.d.(b) "Timeline: WHO's COVID-19 Response." WHO.int, accessed May 17, 2022. https://www.who.int/emergencies/diseases/novel-coronavirus-2019 /interactive-timeline.

———. n.d.(c) "Venezuela (Bolivarian Republic of)." WHO Coronavirus Disease (COVID-19) Dashboard with Vaccination Data. WHO.int, accessed July 5, 2021. https://covid19.who.int/region/amro/country/ve.

———. 2020. "New Zealand Takes Early and Hard Action to Tackle COVID-19." WHO.int, July 15, 2020. https://www.who.int/westernpacific/news-room/feature -stories/item/new-zealand-takes-early-and-hard-action-to-tackle-covid-19.

————. 2021a. "Countries and Territories Certified Malaria-Free by WHO." WHO. int, last modified June 30. https://www.who.int/teams/global-malaria-programme /elimination/countries-and-territories-certified-malaria-free-by-who.

————. 2021b. "Listings of WHO's Response to COVID-19." WHO.int, last modified January 29, 2021. https://www.who.int/news/item/29-06-2020-covidtimeline.

World Health Organization, Regional Office for Africa. 2014. "Special Ministerial Meeting on Ebola Virus Disease in West Africa Accra, Ghana, 2–3 July 2014." Afro.WHO.int. https://www.afro.who.int/news/special-ministerial-meeting-ebola -virus-disease-west-africa-accra-ghana-2-3-july-2014.

Wucherpfennig, Julian, Philipp Hunziker, and Lars-Erik Cederman. 2016. "Who Inherits the State? Colonial Rule and Postcolonial Conflict." *American Journal of Political Science* 60 (4) (October): 882–98.

Yaffe, Helen. 2020. "The World Rediscovers Cuban Medical Internationalism." [*London School of Economics*] *Latin America and Caribbean* (blog), April 8, 2020. https://blogs.lse.ac.uk/latamcaribbean/2020/04/08/the-world-rediscovers-cuban -medical-internationalism/.

Younis, Mona. 2004. "Former President of Ireland, Mary Robinson, a Human Rights Voice that Will Not Be Silenced." 2004 annual meeting of the American Sociological Association, Public Sociologies, San Francisco. *Footnotes* (February). https:// www.asanet.org/sites/default/files/savvy/footnotes/feb04/indexone.html.

Yuk-ping, Catherine Lo, and Nicholas Thomas. 2010. "How Is Health a Security Issue? Politics, Responses and Issues." *Health Policy and Planning* 25 (6) (November): 447–53. https://academic.oup.com/heapol/article/25/6/447/584995.

Zambia Development Agency. 2017. "2017 Budget Aims to Restore Economic Growth." ZDA.org, November 14, 2016. Archived at https://fr-fr.facebook.com /PromoteZambia/posts/1338980282827566:0.

Zambrano, Diego A. 2019. "Guaidó, Not Maduro, Is the De Jure President of Venezuela." *Legal Aggregate*, Stanford Law School blog, February 1, 2019. https://law .stanford.edu/2019/02/01/guaido-not-maduro-is-the-de-jure-president-of-venezuela/.

Zampano, Giada, Liam Moloney, and Jovi Juan. 2015. "Migrant Crisis: A History of Displacement." *Wall Street Journal*, September 22, 2015. http://graphics.wsj.com /migrant-crisis-a-history-of-displacement/.

Zelizer, Craig, and Valerie Oliphant. 2013. "Introduction to Integrated Peacebuilding." In *Integrated Peacebuilding: Innovative Approaches to Transforming Conflict*, edited by Craig Zelizer, 3–30. Boulder, CO: Westview Press.

Zengerle, Patricia, and Matt Spetalnick. 2020. "U.S. to Keep Backing Venezuela's Guaido after December Election, Envoy Says." World News. Reuters.com, August 4, 2020. https://www.reuters.com/article/uk-venezuela-usa-idUKKCN25029E.

Zhang, Junyi. 2016. "Chinese Foreign Assistance, Explained." Order from Chaos. Brookings.edu, July 19, 2016. https://www.brookings.edu/blog/order-from-chaos /2016/07/19/chinese-foreign-assistance-explained/.

Zieliński, Tadeusz. 2021. "On Theory and Practice of No-Fly Zones in Humanitarian Intervention." *Studies in Conflict and Terrorism* (July): 1–18.

Zvobgo, Kelebogile, and Meredith Loken. 2020. "Why Race Matters in International Relations." *Foreign Policy* (blog), June 19, 2020. https://foreignpolicy.com /2020/06/19/why-race-matters-international-relations-ir/.

Index

About the Authors

David Andersen-Rodgers is professor of political science at California State University, Sacramento. His teaching and research have focused on human security, conflict-induced displacement, foreign policy decision-making, and small-arms proliferation.

Kerry F. Crawford is associate professor of political science at James Madison University in Harrisonburg, Virginia. She is author of several books, including *Wartime Sexual Violence: From Silence to a Condemnation of a Weapon of War* (2017), *Human Security: Theory and Action* (with David Andersen-Rodgers, 2018, Rowman & Littlefield), and *The PhD Parenthood Trap: Caught between Work and Family in Academia* (with Leah C. Windsor, 2021). She teaches and researches subjects related to human security, conflict-related sexual violence, United Nations peacekeeping, public opinion on civilian casualties, and gender and bias in the academic profession.